Silk Stockings AND BALLOT BOXES

Silk Stockings & Ballot Boxes

WOMEN & POLITICS IN NEW ORLEANS, 1920-1963

PAMELA TYLER

The University of Georgia Press
❑
Athens & London

Paperback edition, 2009
© 1996 by the University of Georgia Press
Athens, Georgia 30602
www.ugapress.org
All rights reserved
Designed by Richard Hendel
Set in Minion and Eagle types by Tseng Information Systems, Inc.
Printed digitally in the United States of America

The Library of Congress has cataloged the hardcover edition of this book as follows:
Library of Congress Cataloging-in-Publication Data

Tyler, Pamela.
Silk stockings & ballot boxes : women and politics in New Orleans, 1920-1963
Variant Title: Silk stockings and ballot boxes
323 p. [8] p. of plates : ill. ; 25 cm.
ISBN 0-8203-1790-X (alk. paper)
Includes bibliographical references (p. [253]-302) and index.
1. Women in politics—Louisiana—New Orleans—History—20th century. 2. New Orleans (La.)—Politics and government. 3. Louisiana—Politics and government—1865-1950. 4. Louisiana—Politics and government—1951- I. Title.
HQ1236.5.U6 T95   1996
305.42'09763 20   95-11197

Paperback ISBN-13: 978-0-8203-3455-4
ISBN-10: 0-8203-3455-3

British Library Cataloging-in-Publication Data available

TO MAMA AND DADDY,

with love

CONTENTS

Acknowledgments, ix

List of Abbreviations, xi

Introduction, 1

❑

CHAPTER 1: Woman Suffrage: Before and After, 9

❑

CHAPTER 2: Class, Gender, and the Kingfish, 32

❑

CHAPTER 3: "Women of Brains and Standing": The New Orleans League of Women Voters Undone and Reborn, 78

❑

CHAPTER 4: The Pleasures of Partisan Politics: The Independent Women's Organization, 122

❑

CHAPTER 5: "The City Fathers Need a Mother": Martha Gilmore Robinson's 1954 Campaign for City Council in New Orleans, 169

❑

CHAPTER 6: In Two Worlds: Rosa Freeman Keller, Race and Reform, 203

❑

Conclusion, 238

Notes, 253

Index, 303

ACKNOWLEDGMENTS

It is the most pleasant task of this entire process of authorship to take time and space to thank those individuals who deserve far more than these few lines can adequately convey. I begin by thanking someone who is no longer living, but who lives vividly in my daily thoughts. I was infinitely fortunate in having a loving, patient, and charming grandmother who, from my earliest memories, captivated me by telling long and richly detailed stories of "one time, when. . . ." It is undoubtedly from Ethel McGarrah Wellons that I received my earliest doses of history and from her role as custodian of family anecdotes and kinship connections that I came to appreciate, first, my own family's past, and, later, the past in general. I could not let this opportunity pass without acknowledging her profound influence on a grateful grandchild.

The generosity of mentors and colleagues astounds me when I reflect upon it. I thank Richard B. Allen for the pleasure of his company, for the ongoing tutorial in jazz, and for his embodiment of the best of the oral historian's technique. I thank John Boles for awakening me to the existence of something called "southern history" and teaching a class so special that I actually walked faster to get there. I thank Larry Powell, Sylvia Frey, and Pat Maney, who saw this project in its first incarnation as a dissertation and helped me in so many ways to shape it into something better. I thank Jacquelyn Dowd Hall and the late William Ivy Hair for their valuable insights and suggestions concerning this manuscript.

For Clarence Mohr I have very special thanks; he made the transition from mentor to friend so smoothly that I never noticed it, but merely woke up one day to find that we were having long and animated conversations about my research and his research and the state of the world in general. Whether wearing the hat of mentor or friend, he has always been inspiring and generous, pointing me toward opportunities and prodding me when I needed prodding.

I thank members of the Carolina Research Seminar in the Research Triangle of North Carolina, a community of wonderfully articulate and original scholars whose insights I always found stimulating. I thank the community of southern women historians, a vibrant and capable group, whose ideas I have received with keen interest at conferences and whose company I have enjoyed under any and all circumstances.

From North Carolina State University, I received welcome financial support in the form of a travel grant, a summer stipend, and a semester of leave, for all of which I am grateful. To Noreen Miller, history department secretary, a special thank-you for help on many occasions.

I thank the many archivists and librarians who made my work so much easier by being knowledgable and pleasant, among them Bill Meneray, Robert Scherer, Mary LeBlanc, Helen Burks, Kevin Fontenot, and Courtney Page of Tulane University's Howard-Tilton Memorial Library. Marie Wendell of the Earl K. Long Library at the University of New Orleans was always gracious and efficient. In particular, Wayne Everard and Irene Wainwright, archivists at the New Orleans Public Library's Louisiana Collection, seemed to take a positive delight in tracking down obscure sources and showed patience and persistence beyond belief in helping me with photographs; in short, they were simply indispensable.

Sincere thanks go to the people at the University of Georgia Press, most notably to Karen Orchard for her patience and encouragement. Thanks also to Kelly Caudle and Grace Buonocore for applying their talents on my behalf.

I think of this book in many ways as a valentine to New Orleans, a city that has captivated me since the day I first arrived there, more than fifteen years ago. I thank the numerous citizens of New Orleans who consented to be interviewed for this project, for sharing their memories and impressions, and for being gracious to this nonnative who was groping to understand the folkways and mores of life in their Crescent City. In particular I am grateful to Pani Kolb, Blondie Labouisse, Mary Morrison, Cynthia Ware, and James H. Gillis for sharing useful insights about New Orleans women and politics.

I take special pleasure in thanking the circle of friends who enjoyed my political anecdotes (cheerfully tolerating third, fourth, fifth tellings of them) and who shared anecdotes of their own as the evenings stretched later and later — Rocco Marinaccio, Dan Purrington, Gay Gomez, Garry Boulard, Dan and Duey White, and Nancy Anderson. Susan Krantz I thank most of all, for a bushel basketful of reasons.

While the flaws that are to be found in this book are the result of my own inadequacies and/or stubbornness, much that is good in it is owing to the kindness and helpfulness of all those named above. What a pleasure it is to acknowledge the debt.

ABBREVIATIONS

AAUW	American Association of University Women
CAPS	Committee for Action on the Peabody Survey
CCDA	Crescent City Democratic Association
GNOCC	Greater New Orleans Citizens' Council
HEL	Honest Election League
HUAC	House Un-American Activities Committee
IWO	Independent Women's Organization
LWV	League of Women Voters
NAWSA	National American Woman Suffrage Association
NOLWV	New Orleans League of Women Voters
NORD	New Orleans Recreation Department
OPPVL	Orleans Parish Progressive Voters League
RDO	Regular Democratic Organization
SCHW	Southern Conference for Human Welfare
SOS	Save Our Schools
WCU	Woman Citizens' Union
WSP	Woman Suffrage Party

Well-to-do professional and society people [were] sometimes referred to as "the silk stockings." . . . We used to call the opposite of the silk stockings, the blue-collar working men and women, "the mullets," for those wonderful little fish that follow their leader in droves.
—*Lindy Boggs,* Washington through a Purple Veil

INTRODUCTION

Tucked behind a brick wall that shuts out the sounds of passing tourists stands a lovingly restored small house, its shuttered windows, upper and lower galleries, and pastel facade revealing the unmistakable influence of the West Indies. Banana leaves rustle; a fountain burbles soothingly. Seated here in her home in the French Quarter of New Orleans, a well-known activist was reflecting on the local women with whom she had worked in an array of community organizations since the 1930s. Together they had successfully pressed for substantive changes in state and local government, public schools, race relations, zoning, preservation, and more. Over the decades, their efforts for change had yielded an ample harvest in New Orleans. Yet the septuagenarian speaker offered a paradoxical evaluation. "We were *conservative*," she said thoughtfully. She paused as if considering the roster of individuals with whom she had collaborated. "I would say we were *all* pretty conservative."[1]

This book examines the activities of organized upper- and middle-class women in New Orleans in the twentieth century, with emphasis on their behavior in the political arena. The definition of political activity, for the purpose of this study, encompasses exercising or seeking power in the governmental or public affairs of a state or city, an intentionally broad view that allows scrutiny of women's lobbying efforts and their work in voluntary associations, as well as their voting records and their candidacies.[2]

The year 1920 stands as a watershed in U.S. history, marking the enfranchisement of American women. Upon the ratification of the Nineteenth Amendment, jubilant suffragist leader Carrie Chapman Catt proclaimed that women were "no longer petitioners, . . . not wards of the nation, . . . but free and equal citizens."[3] The heroic, seventy-two-year battle for woman suffrage has been chronicled at length by capable historians, in groundbreaking early works by Eleanor Flexner, A. Elizabeth Taylor, and Aileen Kraditor, and more recently in research by Ellen Carol DuBois, Andrew and Anne Firor Scott, Marjorie Spruill Wheeler, and Elna Green.[4]

The political actions of post-1920 women, however, have attracted relatively little attention from scholars. What were the actual effects of women voting, for example, and can an observer safely assume that "getting the vote" was the equivalent of "putting women into politics"? Alas, even the most cursory examination of the political terrain at the end of the twentieth century forces one to conclude emphatically that such an equation is absurd. Politics remains overwhelmingly male to this day, despite the entry of some women into some positions of power and policy making.

What, then, did happen after women became voters? Did passage of the Nineteenth Amendment elevate women to full citizenship and remove the barriers to women's integration into political life? Again, merely to pose the question is to provoke a knowing smile on the face of one's listener or reader. For women in 1920, there lay ahead the struggle for jury service, for admission to the inner circles of party decision making, for the right to represent the party as nominees for office, and for the power to shape platforms and policies. Obtaining the vote did not confer a new role upon women but only the opportunity to define a new role for themselves.[5]

For example, should women serve on juries? When politicians still feared the impact of the much-dreaded "women's bloc," twenty states responded by giving women this right. But from 1922 until 1935, only one additional state did so, as fear of women's voting clout evaporated. Even states allowing service let women refuse solely on the basis of sex or made them take the initiative by requesting that their names be placed on jury lists. Not until 1975 did a Supreme Court ruling settle once and for all the question of whether women, by right of being fully enfranchised citizens of the Republic, belonged, as a consequence, in the jury pool. For most of this century, jury service did not come automatically with suffrage for women, and neither did respect, candidacies, or policy-making roles in politics.[6]

Political scientist Virginia Sapiro warns against trying to gauge women's full political participation by weighing their participation in electoral politics only. "Voting is not necessarily indicative of anything other than paying ritual fealty to the political system of which one is a member," she writes, noting that political scientists currently debate whether voting is even a rational act.[7]

Political communication is one nonvoting way in which women have influenced politics, most commonly by talking to people in an attempt to influence their ideas about politics, contacting public officials, writing letters to editors, and participating in protests or demonstrations. Women have also engaged in electoral activity by attempting to influence others' votes by conversing with them, attending rallies or meetings, wearing buttons or sporting bumper stickers, and giving and raising money. Another frequent female way of influencing politics is through community participation, working with others to solve a community problem.[8]

Brief reflection on the foregoing ideas leads one to the conclusion that "politics" can surely be practiced with or without the vote. Women have traditionally wielded indirect political influence by their skillful lobbying for causes and their appeals to authorities for action. Indeed, Suzanne Lebsock goes so far as to label the period from 1880 to 1920 "a great age for women in politics," even though during these four decades, most women were voteless![9] Lebsock concludes that women during that era exercised a profound influence on politics, especially in such areas as education, health, welfare, safety, and morality, and constituted the core of the Progressive Movement. Working in the separatist tradition of women's voluntary associations, middle- and upper-class women of the Progressive Era accomplished an astonishing amount of beneficial community work, won community respect, and rendered themselves forces that politicians had to heed, all without the vote. In New Orleans, no less than in any other American city, this pattern held true.

The political influence that voteless women wielded before 1920 was of course indirect; their alleged power was predicated on their remaining in their "appropriate" sphere. What happened when women as enfranchised voters had the opportunity to exercise direct political influence? This book addresses that question, on a microcosmic level, taking the arena of women's influence on politics in New Orleans as its focus. Possessing the ballot, New Orleans women could choose between continuing to act collectively and unobtrusively via "women's clubs" on the one hand and integrating themselves into the larger political process on the other.

In assessing the impact of the franchise on women's political clout, one must employ a dual yardstick, capable of measuring political influence that was both direct and indirect in its operation. This study examines the issue of how women's votes changed the political process and indeed whether woman suffrage made a difference in politics, parties, and elections in the turbulent world of New Orleans political life. It also focuses on women's traditional reliance on voluntary associations and lobbying as means to exert political influence indirectly.[10]

Close study of New Orleans after 1920 reveals that southern women faced a number of postsuffrage alternatives, all of which had far-reaching cultural and psychological implications. In deciding whether to embrace partisanship or shrink from it, whether to segregate themselves as a "women's bloc" or to seek influence within male-dominated political institutions, whether to abandon older women's groups reflecting the "separate spheres" tradition or to preserve those groups as foundation stones for a new and more participatory political edifice, New Orleans women were struggling with underlying issues of cultural allegiance and female identity at both the individual and the collective level. In the end they would resolve that struggle as previous generations of southern reformers had done, by melding elements of tradition and modernity into a formula for change that looked toward the future without turning a blind eye on the past.

To explore these issues is to delineate the path women followed from private life to public roles. In New Orleans and throughout the South, the post-1920 political initiatives of newly enfranchised women have remained largely invisible to students of rank-and-file feminism. Given the upper-class status of many female activists and their reluctance to repudiate the external forms of a deeply ingrained patriarchal ethos, it was perhaps all but inevitable that their activities would be ignored or misread by posterity. In the following pages, the reader will encounter narratives of the lives of New Orleans women, not one of whom overtly embraced the concept of "women's rights" or knowingly participated in a women's movement. Yet, while never rhetorically questioning male dominance in public life, by their very actions they eroded it. Without particularly supportive fathers or husbands, these women created larger roles for themselves and other women, independent roles, permanent public roles. They found issues that engaged their attention, and they moved resolutely into the arena of politics in order to make their views known, focusing renewed attention on the kind of state and local issues that had originally inspired women to seek a greater voice in public affairs. In the process, they enlarged women's roles and enhanced possibilities by their examples. By charting their own courses, setting goals regardless of societal, familial, or spousal consent, they created a different adult role for women in New Orleans.

Looking at southern women of privilege, that is, educated and economically secure women, means realizing the limiting effects of racial hierarchy and class stratification. The women under scrutiny here formed very tight bonds among themselves, but their sense of sisterhood did not, in most cases, overcome the formidable barriers erected by race and class. Yet all of the women whose stories are recounted here challenged some aspect of the status quo in New Orleans. By definition, then, they were *not* conservatives. But were they liberals? Since "liberalism" is at least as much abused and misunderstood a concept as "feminism," one hesitates to enter this particular ideological thicket, but certainly, in the sense of nineteenth-century usage, they were. Like liberals of a previous age, they embraced greater individual freedom, greater individual participation in government, and constitutional, political, and administrative reforms to secure these objectives. The speaker of the introduction categorized herself and her colleagues as "pretty conservative" to emphasize that, by the standards of the late twentieth century, when she offered her assessment, they were neither radical, liberal, nor feminist.[11]

For the last century and more, New Orleans middle- and upper-class women have joined women's associations just as have women all over the United States. Tocqueville long ago commented on the American enthusiasm for voluntarism, and, although the ingredients usually associated with the formation of the women's club movement (urbanization, industrialization, growth of a middle class, more education and leisure time for women) came fairly late to New Orleans, as to most of the South, for all of the twentieth century there has been a plethora of associations in which women "joiners" could expend their time and talents. Some of the most fascinating of these bodies have been political organizations, and it is their history, as well as the stories of the women who led them, that is told here.

The leaders of these women's groups knew one another well; many enjoyed friendships that, in some cases, extended back to college or even childhood days. The women leaders shared ties to the planter-business elite that had long dominated New Orleans and Louisiana politics; they were well educated, married, and economically secure. Because their socialization encouraged it, they made the choice to devote themselves to marriage, motherhood, and domestic life rather than taking employment outside the home. But these women never became completely domesticated or privatized; they always looked beyond the home. Their activities represent a bridge linking the pre-1920 progressive women reformers with the female activists who emerged during the rebirth of feminism in the 1960s.[12]

A group of history students once inquired about this research on women's clubs, wondering aloud *what kind* of women's clubs. "Garden clubs?" they asked. "Book clubs? Bridge clubs?" There was something pathetic and telling about the circumscribed nature of their first responses. Like those college students, most of society has not yet developed a habit of evaluating seriously the contributions of "volunteers," the nonsalaried women workers who for decades have made a difference by devoting themselves to better schools and parks, museums and music, child and animal welfare, historical preservation, hospitals, and good government. Why does society adopt a dismissive attitude when considering a women's club project? Why do some people pretend to think of women's clubs as groups to be found posing behind the silver teapot or nibbling idly at luncheons at which nothing is ever accomplished and catty repartee rules the day? How, one wonders, did "society ladies" become a stereotype that evokes the harpies in Truman Capote's later fiction ("Le Cote Basque," for example) or the cinematic horrors of Clare Booth Luce's *The Women*? The images are embedded in a popular culture that often allows a few negative representations of fictional women to crowd out what should be indelible memories of mothers, grandmothers, and other prefeminist women for whom volunteer work and club projects assumed a profound personal and political meaning over the years. Now, as demographic and economic forces render the woman who is not a part of the paid labor force an increasing rarity, and as the scarcity of Scout leaders, grade mothers, and "volunteers" of every stripe creates unexpected and unhappy consequences, perhaps the times are more propitious for serious examinations of the activities of club women, those perennially disparaged and patronized "volunteers."

The women of this study left a lasting mark on New Orleans. Their work changed the community, but their work also changed them. I am indebted to Arlene Kaplan Daniels for the concept of the "invisible career," which she applies to women civic leaders from the volunteer world.[13] Many of the most active of these New Orleans women created invisible careers for themselves in the course of living lives of service to others. Just as business and professional careers demand time, devotion, commitment, and skill, so too do invisible careers in civic leadership. A club career did not merely fill leisure time; for many women leaders, it eliminated leisure time altogether.[14] While putting their abilities and time at the service of the community, unpaid New

Orleans women of the educated, affluent sector earned rewards that, though not bankable, were nonetheless valuable. They gained prestige, experience, a sense of virtue, feelings of efficacy, public recognition, outlets for talents, mental and emotional stimulation, and the rewards that come from working with others toward a desired goal—what Daniels calls "psychic income."[15]

Why write about women's political activities in New Orleans, as opposed to any other southern city? Although there is an impressive and expanding literature on the urban South, many of these recent works omit analysis of the contributions of women to city life. More than a decade ago, Anne Firor Scott pointed out the dearth of scholarly research on southern women's organized activities and in particular cited the vacuum existing on women's associations in the important southern cities of Atlanta, Richmond, and New Orleans.[16] Since that time, works by Darlene Roth, Jacqueline Rouse, Elsa Barkley Brown, and others have placed the women of Atlanta and Richmond under the historical scrutiny they deserve. But the experience of New Orleans women has remained unexamined, a trackless land waiting for an explorer to map it out. Moreover, there is considerable satisfaction in "doing" local history and keeping one's focus on one significant community.

New Orleans suffers from a lingering reputation of being hidebound, tradition ridden, so steeped in its own decadence and lethargy that it will not rouse itself even though purposeful strides and an open attitude toward nonnatives long ago allowed Atlanta, Houston, and Miami to eclipse the once mighty Crescent City.[17] The chapters that follow show that, although complacency over the status quo and reluctance to seek change cannot accurately be charged to the women of New Orleans, on the issue of disdain for outsiders, which observers have accused members of the New Orleans establishment of harboring, local middle- and upper-class women deserve a mixed report. Pride in birth, ancestry, and traditions ran strong among them. Reflecting on New Orleans society earlier in this century, one woman said, "I hate to sound like the typical old lady saying how much nicer it was, but it was— New Orleans was really a cultured, small southern city where everybody . . . knew everybody, where there was a closeness. . . . The New Orleans that I knew . . . was a little closed corporation. Delightful people."[18] One cannot say with certainty how widely this attitude was shared among local women; moreover, many of them welcomed the opportunity to work with newcomers for needed changes.

New Orleans, the setting for this book, technically possesses a climate that is *sub*tropical, but in its extraordinary heat and humidity that distinction is often lost on people, who feel that it approximates their *idea* of the tropics. Did the steambath climate rot the politics? One hesitates to be so flippant, but the temptation is great. The brilliant writer A. J. Liebling noted the similarities between life in New Orleans and life in Hellenic, Arab, and Mediterranean countries and claimed that politics in the Crescent City were "of an intensity and complexity" matched, in his experience, "only in the Republic of Lebanon."[19] At any rate, the politics of New Orleans and Louisiana are and have long been colorful, intense, deceptive, and corrupt on the grand scale.

Even the most casual observers know something of the elements that make up the Crescent City culture: the tawdry nightlife on Bourbon Street, ghostly gleaming sepulchres in ancient cemeteries, periodic visitations by devastating hurricanes, banana trees, crepe myrtles and oleanders, a social elite fascinated with the ritual of tossing plastic beads to hordes of screaming strangers, a firm commitment to eating well among both the hoi polloi and the elite, wrought-iron balconies and the smell of coffee roasting, a reputation for casual race relations and a tolerance for sexual unorthodoxy—and the whole bizarre gumbo scented by more than a whiff of decadence, accompanied by strains of jazz. New Orleans, the Odd, the Exotic, forms the backdrop for this story of women and politics.

The women ... in point of manners and character have a very marked superiority over the men.

—*Visitor to New Orleans in 1808*

CHAPTER ONE

WOMAN SUFFRAGE

BEFORE AND AFTER

New Orleanians speak of their city as "the city that care forgot," a fond reference to the local mystique, woven of a lush semitropical climate, a fascinating pastiche of cultural influences, and a pronounced tolerance for the sensory pleasures offered by restaurants, festivals, and the wide-open nightlife, epitomized for casual observers by the annual frenzy of Mardi Gras. To cynics and wits, however, New Orleans is "the city that forgot to care." Their thoughts rest not on oysters, Sazeracs, jasmine, and jazz but on less savory aspects of the old Mississippi River port.

Problems have beset New Orleans ever since Bienville established the city in 1718 "on one of the most beautiful crescents in the river."[1] Some ills, namely, the persistent flooding and the occasional hurricanes and outbreaks of yellow fever, devolved from his questionable choice of location. But other problems had little to do with Mother Nature and much to do with human nature.

Throughout nearly three centuries of existence, New Orleans has presented a record of chronic political rascality. From the very outset, venal and incompetent administrators plagued this centerpiece of Louisiana, beginning with French colonial governors and their aides. Some historians trace the chronic corruption to the prevailing French attitude that a political office was a piece of property that the officeholder should use for profit.[2] The colony's early political development differed significantly from that of other American states: alone among the states, Louisiana sheltered a population accustomed to autocratic French and Spanish colonial governors and devoid of experience with democratic forms of government. Until the mid-nineteenth century, only men of property were entitled to suffrage; government by gentlemen was the norm for a citizenry that was, in general, politically passive.

The years after Reconstruction witnessed a decline in ethical conduct among officeholders. By the late nineteenth century, Louisiana "had become a byword for political corruption and general lawlessness."[3] Ballot box stuffing, use of false-bottomed boxes, tampering with registration rolls, falsifying returns, and overt physical intimidation of voters were common practices. In an 1894 election, a local Democratic official, asked by a northern observer to estimate the number of votes that would be cast, replied placidly, "Just as many as we need." A close student of the low level at which southern politics was played under the "Redeemers" of the late nineteenth century stated flatly that "the brazenness with which the Louisianians fabricated returns still shocks one accustomed to tales of election chicanery in this period."[4]

In the Louisiana State Lottery, there was dishonesty of another sort. Licensed by the state legislature, the lottery collected some twenty-eight million dollars a year but distributed less than fifteen million dollars in prizes. After paying a flat fee of only forty thousand dollars annually to the state, it kept all the rest. With this gigantic slush fund, "it debauched legislators, muzzled the press, made and unmade public officials . . . and exercised a power greater than that of the State government itself." New Orleans was the lottery's "epicenter" and flamboyant Orleanian Major E. A. Burke, who robbed the state of nearly two million dollars and absconded to Honduras in 1889, the lottery's key man in state government. In addition to blatant election fraud, the venality of the lottery, and the antics of duelist-gambler-embezzler Burke, turn-of-the-century New Orleans experienced rampant police corruption. Furthermore, despite a climate and topography that virtually ensured serious street flooding and the contamination of the water supply, the South's largest city lacked any municipal drainage, sewerage, or water purification system. Ineffective law enforcement, great poverty, and general neglect characterized urban life in New Orleans at the dawn of the twentieth century.[5]

It was a political machine that brought long-needed improvements to New Orleans. The Regular Democratic Organization (also called the RDO, Old Regulars, Choctaws, the Ring) dominated New Orleans political life from its creation in the late nineteenth century until a few years after the death of its gifted leader, Martin Behrman, in 1926. With tight organization in each of the city's seventeen wards, the Old Regulars consistently occupied each of the seventeen aldermanic posts. When, in 1912, reform elements succeeded in bringing the commission form of government to the city as a progressive move, the Old Regulars merely reasserted their grip and dominated that body as well, effectively thwarting the reformers' intent. At their zenith, the Old Regulars determined the candidates for every electoral post and, with a machine's efficiency, routinely put them into office. Martin Behrman, their impressive chieftain, served as New Orleans mayor for eighteen years between 1904 and 1926.[6]

For three decades, the Old Regulars ran New Orleans, delivering city services adequately and sparing the city any instances of major embezzlement or malfeasance. While the entire population gained from their implementing the city's first municipal drainage, sewerage, and water purification systems, the commercial classes in particular benefited from modernization of the port, construction of the Public Belt Railroad, and improvements in the levee system. This record of achievement was chiefly due to the wisdom of Mayor Behrman, of whom it was often said that he was "better than his crowd." The even-tempered, hardworking mayor enjoyed popularity with all classes and unfailingly looked after the interests of New Orleans in Baton Rouge. A scholar who chronicled the history of the Regular Democratic Organization alleged tepidly that the "morality of the Machine was as good as the general moral tone of business and of the society in which it existed," and John M. Parker, the quintessential silk stocking reformer, respected Behrman and "never questioned his personal dedication or honesty."[7]

The poor people of New Orleans received concrete assistance and a caring attitude from Old Regular precinct captains, who efficiently distributed material aid.[8] Each captain knew the voters of his precinct, their habits, vices, needs, and interests. Precinct captains often ran barber shops, corner groceries, or bars and thus had ample personal contact with their neighbors; each was quick to dispense charity for those who needed assistance, to fix scrapes with the law, and to secure jobs for the faithful. The 262 precinct organizations formed the structure upon which the Old Regular machine was built, and patronage jobs gave the machine its power, energizing the people to become fervent Old Regular partisans. The unfailing intensity with which the Old Regulars fought the advocates of civil service laws provides evidence of the importance machine leaders attached to having a large pool of unprotected jobs at their disposal.

Each Old Regular ward boss usually held a municipal job that was sufficiently untaxing to allow him to devote ample time to duties for the machine. The precinct leader's premier task was to see that every prospective Old Regular voter in his area had registered and paid his poll tax, for, above all else, the machine existed to perpetuate itself, which it could do only by winning elections. Indeed, so familiar was the average Old Regular precinct captain with the voters of his precinct that on election day, he knew exactly who had not yet voted and could send for them to come and vote. In the minds of the reformist opposition, the machine was nothing but an organization of self-serving office seekers, "a corrupt, dictatorial, wasteful and undemocratic octopus."[9]

Producing loyalty sufficient to carry his precinct for the machine was the cardinal task to which every precinct leader applied himself. Although carrying one's precinct for the Old Regulars was the only yardstick of success for a precinct captain, some elementary arithmetic will demonstrate that the task was less than herculean. In an average New Orleans precinct of 400 registered voters, the precinct leader controlled, at a minimum, 100 votes through various ties of longstanding loyalty. Even in the unlikely event of a 100 percent voter turnout, to be assured of carrying his precinct for the Old Regular ticket, the captain had only to win, by any means, 101 other votes. Judicious distribution of temporary jobs, circus tickets, food baskets, coal, and racetrack passes inevitably sufficed. A favor done for one individual resulted in a ripple effect, for that person's family members were expected to feel gratitude and to vote accordingly. Precinct leaders routinely received election day money from ward bosses and spent these funds to gain maximum effect. Captains preferred to spend their money on individuals who had at least three or four votes in their immediate family; "bachelors and old maids were . . . greatly despised."[10] Adept at getting out their vote, machine leaders traditionally relished a low voter turnout, a situation that enabled them to win by capturing only a handful of the votes outside their solid core of loyalists.

The precinct captains' work stands in contrast to that of the Old Regulars' opposition. Without the leverage of past favors, without patronage, the opposition's task of persuading more than half the voters in an average precinct to desert the Regular Democratic Organization, a source of largesse in most precincts, and to vote not for tangible benefits but for a nebulous ideal called "good government" seemed formidable indeed.

The machine controlled the voter registration office and commonly padded the rolls with the names of dead people, imaginary people, and people who had moved away. A common Old Regular enterprise involved paying the poll taxes of groups of indigents, designating them "disabled," and, by virtue of a law that allowed disabled voters to receive assistance in voting, sending Old Regular hirelings into the booths with the so-called "disabled" voters to "vote" them in droves, all under the complacent eyes of Old Regular election commissioners. Mayor Behrman consistently opposed the opposition's periodic efforts to remove illiterate voters from the polls and thus eliminate a significant portion of the machine's base.[11]

On election day, the thoroughly politicized local police proved loyal allies of the Old Regulars, often physically intimidating opposition voters and detaining opposition leaders on spurious charges. The routine, but unheeded, pleas of the opposition that policemen be banned from the polls gave testimony to the partisan role played by the police. In addition, police officers commonly called on all the small shop owners before the election to urge that they vote "right."

If the foregoing tactics proved too subtle to deliver a majority in a precinct, the capable Old Regulars could resort to ballot box stuffing, nonstandard arithmetic, and more. Such irregularities were rarely contested in court, since virtually all officials concerned in election cases were allied with the machine. In short, by the 1920s the Old Regulars' city machine, "one of the most prehensile in the nation," seemed well equipped to perpetuate itself in power in New Orleans ad infinitum.[12]

The New Orleans machine's power extended even to the choice of governors. Alone, New Orleans voters could not elect a candidate, but the vote they cast represented one-quarter of the state's total vote. Because Catholic south Louisiana and Protestant north Louisiana customarily failed to agree, the city of New Orleans often held the crucial vote and could, by careful alliance with one faction or the other, throw the election to a chosen candidate. In the gubernatorial races between 1900 and 1924, the Old Regulars backed the winning candidate every time but twice. Mayor Martin Behrman boasted that his control of the election machinery in his city was such that, with only overnight notice, he could deliver twenty-five thousand votes in Orleans Parish to any candidate.[13]

In the 1920s, the New Orleans delegation to the legislature in Baton Rouge consisted of nine of the thirty-nine senators and twenty of the one hundred members of the House. Most owed their seats to the Old Regulars' activities on their behalf. Discipline among these legislators was strict; the Orleans delegation voted as directed by the inner core of the RDO, the "Caucus," made up of the seventeen Old Regular ward leaders and Mayor Behrman.

Because of its unanimity, the Orleans delegation in Baton Rouge was formidable. At the bidding of the Caucus, it routinely voted with the state's planter-business elite, catering to private utilities at the expense of New Orleans ratepayers, opposing employer liability laws, and balking at homestead taxation exemptions. In short, the RDO carefully respected the conservative wishes of the urban business classes in legislative matters, even when those wishes hurt their working-class loyalists. The conclusion seems unavoidable that, in return for the right to make money, much of the commercial elite acquiesced in Old Regular control of politics and patronage in New Orleans, and, conversely, the Old Regulars accepted control of the thousands of city jobs and their payrolls as a quid pro quo for surrendering policy making to the elite. A pronounced social gulf separated the business elite and the rank and file of Old Regulars, but both groups acted to perpetuate the RDO hegemony—the lower classes enthusiastically, the business interests cynically.[14]

This, then, was the early-twentieth-century political status quo in New Orleans, a city firmly in the grip of a popular but corrupt political machine. The narrative now turns to the response of one particular group to that situation, namely, the city's middle- and upper-class women, who, though voteless when the century dawned, were not without recourse to alter conditions in New Orleans. Indeed, "a strong argument can be made that women's greatest political power occurred through indirect activity."[15] In the voteless decades before 1920, women's voluntary associations grew in numbers and in influence throughout the nineteenth century, until, by the 1890s, they were displaying "a strong tendency ... to move toward community activism," a development that saw women involved in all manner of community concerns, from schools and hospitals to juvenile courts, libraries, and playgrounds.[16]

Although not voters, women in New Orleans nevertheless improved their city and affected the distribution of power and resources in their community; they made their influence felt in many avenues of city life. In most cases, local women controlled few financial resources of their own, but Josephine Louise Newcomb (1816–1901) was an exception. A wealthy widow left childless and grieving by the death of her delicate, precocious daughter, Newcomb used her fortune to establish the Sophie Newcomb College of Tulane University, the country's first coordinate college for women affiliated with a men's college but maintaining its own faculty, buildings, and policies.[17] Opened in 1887,

Newcomb College rapidly assumed a role of prominence as *the* institution of higher education for the daughters of the New Orleans elite.

As the years passed, Newcomb alumnae filtered out into the city in an ever widening stream; many came to exercise significant influence on the civic affairs of New Orleans, gradually moving women's sphere into the public arena. Graduates left Newcomb College with a sound liberal arts education, but perhaps more important, they left with the vivid experience of having known capable women in responsible positions. In 1909, for example, fully two-thirds of the Newcomb faculty members were women. In the disciplines of Latin, Greek, biology, chemistry, and mathematics, all the instructors were female.[18] Immersed in the total experience of a single-sex college, Newcomb students drew confidence, vigor, self-esteem, and identity from their years of sorority and community. Ultimately, these qualities acted as a powerful acid to dissolve their traditional women's reluctance to become involved in civic affairs, and particularly in the "male" world of politics. The institution's first president confessed that he observed in Newcomb students "a responsiveness to ideals, a growing persistency of purpose, and an initiative which [he] had not at first suspected."[19] Thus, Josephine Louise Newcomb's legacy was ultimately worth far more than the $3.6 million that she gave to the college memorializing her daughter.

Sophie Newcomb College came too late for an early generation of New Orleans women who nonetheless managed to leave their imprint on some of the city's institutions. Sophie Bell Wright (1866–1912), a small, frail woman encased in a steel brace and walking only with crutches, initially earned her city's esteem by founding, guiding, and expanding a free night school for poor working boys, funded by profits from her day school for young ladies. Like many women of the Progressive Era, she worked through women's clubs— the Women's Christian Temperance Union, the United Daughters of the Confederacy, the State Congress of Mothers, the Prison Reform Association, the King's Daughters—to press government to improve human welfare and to act when government would not. She raised funds to build an annex for crippled children at a New Orleans hospital, lobbied successfully for a bill raising educational standards for nurses, and worked to secure public baths and playgrounds. Her indirect political influence was considerable and evidently satisfactory to her, for she remained resolutely opposed to woman suffrage until her early death at age forty-six.[20]

Eleanor McMain (1866–1934) built a solid reputation for social service when, after study at Jane Addams's Hull House, she became director of the New Orleans settlement Kingsley House, a post she held for thirty years. She worked with progressive associations, among them the Day Nursery Association, the New Orleans Playground Committee, the Tenement House Association, and the Anti-Tuberculosis League, and understood well the exercise of indirect political influence. In 1906 and 1908 she lent her support to a successful campaign for adoption of laws regulating the labor of women and children and again in 1910 for a compulsory school attendance law. She believed in turning a spotlight of public scrutiny onto bad conditions, thus publicizing them and building pressure on politicians to act.[21]

Because the Tulane Medical School refused to accept women applicants, Sara Tew Mayo (1869-1930) had to leave New Orleans to gain admission to a medical college. After receiving her M.D. from the Women's Medical College of Pennsylvania, she began medical practice in New Orleans in 1898, only to be rebuffed by the medical society and the local hospitals. Marginalized as many early female doctors were, Mayo ran a free clinic at Eleanor McMain's Kingsley House and served as staff physician at St. Anna's Asylum for destitute women; finally, in cooperation with six other women physicians, she opened the city's first hospital for women and children. Although it required years, her agitation for the admission of women to the Orleans Parish Medical Society finally bore fruit in 1913. Perhaps because of the stinging rejections she had experienced at the hands of male physicians, Mayo was a staunch advocate of woman suffrage.[22]

Sophie Bell Wright, Eleanor McMain, and Sara Tew Mayo all won the *Times-Picayune* Loving Cup, a prestigious community honor awarded annually and indicative of the highest regard for a local individual's civic contributions. That Wright, McMain, and Mayo all won public recognition for their good works among the city's poor and powerless demonstrates their political ability and success at working with donors, commissions, the legislature, and the mayor to gain support and funds for various worthy projects.

Although their sex kept them voteless and bound in "feminine" roles, they did not face the handicap of race that confronted black women with similar civic-minded inclinations. The Phillis Wheatley Club, numbering more than one hundred middle-class African-American women as members, established the Phillis Wheatley Sanitarium in 1896 for "the hospitalization of Negroes in Louisiana and the training of Negro nurses," starting humbly with one room and seven beds.[23] From this small beginning the facility grew into Flint-Goodridge Hospital, a four-story, 150-bed facility, which was for much of the twentieth century the only private hospital in New Orleans serving the African-American population.[24] Because the female founders experienced serious difficulty in raising funds, New Orleans University assumed their debt and took over the facility after only one year. The fact remains, however, that black women of New Orleans were in the forefront of efforts to improve health care for their race. Although in pursuit of a worthy community project, they won no large donations, no attention from the mayor or legislature. Their lack of success in influencing the distribution of resources indicates that such indirect political influence as black women could command represented too little clout to overcome the dual handicaps presented by race and sex at the turn of the century.

In the late nineteenth century, white women of New Orleans awakened to some of the disabilities that sex placed on them. A German woman, dying at St. Anna's Asylum, an institution for destitute women and children, revealed that she had one thousand dollars in savings and on her deathbed made a will leaving that sum to St. Anna's. Members of the board of control, all female, witnessed the document, only to learn with bitter regret that the will was invalid: as women, they could not legally witness a will. As one woman recalled, "The bequest went to the State—and the women went to thinking and agitating."[25]

That woman, Caroline Thomas Merrick (1825–1908), herself felt the sting of sexism five years later when, as a member of the New Orleans Educational Society, which admitted male and female members, she produced a committee report but had to hand it over to a man for its reading at the meeting. The sting intensified when she found that she would be permitted no part in the annual election of officers, though she had paid the same five-dollar dues as the men and had been a working member of an important committee. Offended by the double standard, Merrick ceased to attend meetings and noted, in a comment that practically shouts the extent of her wifely economic dependence, "I requested my husband to discontinue paying my dues."[26]

Although frequently rebuffed for venturing "out of their sphere," southern middle- and upper-class women of both races increasingly construed their socially sanctioned responsibility for the morality, welfare, and health of their families as requiring them to leave their homes to reach the community around them. Anne Firor Scott has described the explosion of organizational activity among women who sought not to eliminate their "sphere" but to expand it. First church groups, prayer circles, tract societies, then women's clubs and reform associations steadily led women to an acquaintance with the worst of society's ills. Evils such as child labor, tuberculosis, slums and overcrowding, industrial exploitation of women, prostitution, lack of adequate municipal services, barbaric conditions in prisons and asylums, and more required government action rather than altruistic female philanthropy, and women soon realized it. Many, though not all, of the female reformers of the Progressive Era embraced woman suffrage as the reform that they needed most of all, for only the vote would arm them with direct political influence. Only the vote would really win politicians' respect.[27]

Caroline Merrick became an early convert to the cause of woman suffrage and, in 1892, organized nine New Orleans women into the first suffrage association in Louisiana, the Portia Club. In 1895, that group underwent a schism out of which was formed the Era Club (for "Equal Rights Association"), a body that, as Merrick phrased it, "soon outgrew its mother." The Portias and the Era Club cooperated to form the Louisiana Woman Suffrage Association and appear to have worked amicably to foster support for suffrage, though the Era Club rapidly eclipsed its more conservative ancestor in prestige, membership, and achievements.[28]

The successes of the Era Club were largely due to the leadership of two dynamic women, sisters Jean and Kate Gordon. Throughout their lives both women championed numerous progressive causes and enjoyed remarkable triumphs. Among their victories were struggles for the prevention of cruelty to animals, for the treatment and control of tuberculosis, for the use of rubber tires on ambulances, for the admission of women to Tulane Medical School, for the creation of a juvenile court system and an institution to shelter orphaned and retarded girls, and for bills to regulate the labor and working conditions of children and women.[29]

Both were aristocratic, articulate, often humorous, sometimes acerbic. On one occasion, Jean (1865–1931), venting her frustration at the industrialists who thronged the legislature to oppose regulatory legislation for mills and canneries, remarked, "One, not knowing any better, would have been convinced that the most healthful, remunerative, educational place in the entire world in which to develop children was a mill or oyster cannery. One fairly tingled to spend the rest of life shucking oysters or peeling shrimp."[30] Her sister Kate (1861–1932) commented wryly to a friend of her own reputation as a crusader for a tuberculosis hospital and of Jean's fame as founder and superintendent of a home for retarded girls. "In the community I am now known as Tuberculosis Gordon and Jean as Feeble-minded Gordon. Take your choice."[31] These comments, of course, were directed to friendly audiences. When dealing with the power structure of their city and state, the Gordons demonstrated typical southern courtesy and forbearance, "gentle gracious manners," and "a sweet, sunny smile which [took] off the rugged edge of some plain truth so gently and sweetly told."[32] They understood instinctively the importance of the image of the southern lady.

While still in their thirties, the Gordons showed a natural inclination for politics. The 1898 constitutional convention, though impervious to appeals for woman suffrage, had offered women "a mere crumb" in the form of the right for property-owning, taxpaying women to vote on issues of taxation.[33] The following year, reform elements in New Orleans, prodded by the Women's League for Sewerage and Drainage, of which Kate Gordon was president, proposed to end the city's nightmarish relationship with nature by taking steps to curb the frequent yellow fever epidemics and street flooding attributable to primitive sewerage disposal and poor drainage. To this end, they backed passage of a two-mill property tax increase to fund creation of a modern sewerage and water board. The issue would be decided by the city's property owners, and for the first time, the voices of the females among them would be heard.[34]

Having the right to vote was not the same as exercising it. Custom had long conditioned most women to regard politics as utterly inappropriate for them, and most men did little to disabuse them of that view. Anticipating that many women would be "reluctant to face the rigors of the polling place," the Gordon sisters conducted an intensive canvass of women property owners in order to obtain their proxies so that they might cast their ballots for the timid.[35] Since each proxy required a witness, and bitter experience had taught New Orleans women that they were deemed unfit for that role by the law, Kate Gordon recruited the family's African-American coachman "Sam" to witness the proxies she collected around the city. Gordon reported that she obtained three hundred proxies while "three hundred very conservative women had an opportunity to compare their legal standing with Sam's."[36]

The successful outcome of the election was a victory for progressive reformers in the city and a personal triumph for Jean and Kate Gordon. The local press accorded them "all the glory," avowing that "they probably did as much work for the special tax as all the men in this city put together." In appreciation, the mayor presented Kate Gordon with a gold-handled umbrella, and a businessmen's league gave her a medal.[37] The proxy episode certainly provided fuel for the Gordons' future suffrage activities.

Without a vote in any issue save taxation and unable to participate in selecting their legislative representatives, New Orleans women resorted to indirect political influence in the early twentieth century in order to effect needed reforms. To achieve passage of a child labor statute, Jean Gordon investigated the conditions of working children, presented a report to the state legislature, enlisted the backing of the lieutenant governor, won coverage of "her" issue in the press, and relentlessly urged people to contact their lawmakers about the issue. Unable to ignore such steady and growing pressure for action, the legislature passed a child labor act in 1906 and provided that women could serve as factory inspectors. Jean Gordon was appointed first female factory inspector in New Orleans and served as such for five years, on her own insistence without pay. Her noblesse oblige instincts led her to conclude that such posts should be the exclusive province of upper-class women, who could serve without remuneration and would presumably prove invulnerable to the temptations of bribery. Her efforts on behalf of child laborers, and her long years of work for "feeble-minded" girls, won her the title "the Jane Addams of the South."[38]

Clearly there was much good that women could do without the vote. But, raging at women's impotence after having witnessed the defeat of one child labor bill, a bitter Jean Gordon reacted to the consequences of her sex's voteless condition.

> We have learned that the interests of women and children will never be a vital issue until made so by women for women. . . . And we also learned (what we had suspected) that the much-boasted influence of the wife over the husband in matters political was one of the many theories which melt before the sun of experience. The wife of every representative present was heartily in sympathy with the child labor bill, but, when the roll was called, the husbands answered "no" and those wives realized how weak a weapon was influence and in that moment were sown the seeds of a belief in the potency of the ballot beyond that of "woman's influence."[39]

Not surprisingly, both Gordons became suffragists, but it was Kate who assumed leadership of the suffrage fight in Louisiana, with staunch support from the Era Club membership. She headed the Louisiana state suffrage association for a decade (1904–1913) and assumed national prominence in the women's movement, addressing the annual convention of the National American Woman Suffrage Association (NAWSA) in 1900 and serving as its corresponding secretary from 1901 until 1909. Her efforts weighed heavily in the decision to hold the group's 1903 convention in New Orleans, a move that boosted suffrage in the South.[40]

As Marjorie Spruill Wheeler has noted, southern suffragists stood apart from the mainstream of southern ideas on women's rights, but on racial matters, particularly the question of black suffrage, "radical they were not." While simple justice demanded that women should vote, some southern women also recognized the expedient aspect of favoring ballots for white women of the South as a countervailing weight against black votes, a means by which "the negro as a disturbing element in politics [would] disappear." Southern men who ridiculed or ignored an argument from justice on the nature of women's rights might listen when scolded for "putting the ballot into the hands of . . .

black men, thus making them the political superiors of . . . white women," and might embrace woman suffrage when it was depicted as the bulwark of white supremacy.[41]

As her comment about the episode of "Sam" the coachman witnessing "ladies'" proxies perhaps foreshadowed, Kate Gordon ranked as the most outspokenly Negrophobic of the prominent southern suffragists, routinely using phrases such as "fool niggers," "cornfield darkies," and "coon nature" in her speeches. Her approach to woman suffrage emphasized the necessity of a *state* constitutional amendment to enfranchise women as the way to safeguard the sacred principle that only the states could set voter qualifications. A federal amendment to the U.S. Constitution, the favored avenue to suffrage of the majority of NAWSA members, was anathema to Gordon, representing to her federal "meddling" in a states' rights issue, which could conceivably lead to federal action to undo recent measures disfranchising African Americans.

The disfranchisement of black voters by the 1898 Louisiana constitution pleased Kate Gordon, but, ironically, she would have gone further in disfranchising efforts than the lawmakers. Gordon was no champion of uneducated white womanhood, or manhood for that matter. She deplored both the "understanding" clause, which, as executed by compliant registrars, allowed illiterate whites to vote while barring illiterate blacks from the privilege, and the "grandfather" clause, a transparent loophole for illiterate whites that offered voting rights to anyone whose grandfather had voted before 1867.[42] Rather than relying on the discriminatory application of voting requirements to ensure white supremacy in the South, Gordon at one time favored a suffrage measure that would have subjected both male and female voters to strict education and property requirements, thus boosting the number of educated, propertied voters without increasing the number of illiterates at the polls. At another point, she wanted to campaign for enfranchisement of white women only, but she reluctantly abandoned this approach when southern lawmakers balked at its glaring unconstitutionality.

Kate Gordon never wavered in her advocacy of a state suffrage amendment as the only acceptable path for enfranchising women, and this stance put her out of step and often at loggerheads with NAWSA. Over time, all prominent southern suffragists except the Gordons and their ally Laura Clay of Kentucky backed a federal amendment as the surest route to suffrage. Devoutly longing for votes for women, Kate Gordon nonetheless supported the concept of state sovereignty so staunchly that, in a sad turn of events, she actually worked to defeat the passage of the federal woman suffrage amendment in 1920.[43]

In 1913–14, disagreement over the state-versus-federal issue created a permanent fissure in the New Orleans suffrage movement. After resigning her NAWSA office in 1913 to protest the association's growing preference for a federal amendment, Kate Gordon had formed the Southern States Woman Suffrage Convention (SSWSC) to push for passage and ratification of state suffrage amendments in the South and had urged NAWSA to stay out of the South. Resenting Gordon's increasingly imperious ways and disagreeing with her exclusive emphasis on states' rights, federal amendment suffragists in New Orleans formed the Woman Suffrage Party (WSP) of Louisiana to work in consonance with NAWSA. In an action that drew criticism from the local press, Gordon's Era Club began expelling any member who affiliated with the WSP instead of the SSWSC.[44]

In 1914, a newly reorganized Era Club emerged, purged of federal amendment supporters, with Kate Gordon in the presidency. True to their club's name, the women pursued a spectrum of women's rights issues, among them campaigns to persuade Tulane Medical School to admit women, to pressure the mayor and members of the legislature, who could each name one recipient of a scholarship to Tulane University, to share those scholarships with Newcomb College by naming women, and to prod the city to name women to city boards.[45]

Perhaps the most touching project undertaken by the women of the Era Club was their effort to gain recognition for their organization's key role in securing the passage of crucial funds for creating the Sewerage and Water Board at the turn of the century, which effectively took New Orleans into the modern age in terms of water quality, sewerage disposal, and flood control. Members had noted the city administration's commemoration of various men via plaques on municipal buildings and keenly felt the absence of any public token of recognition of *their* role in civic betterment. They kept up a steady but fruitless campaign to win this recognition "in order that the future [would] know the services rendered by women," as they explained in a letter to Mayor Behrman.[46]

These efforts were of secondary importance, however; the raison d'être for the Era Club was states' rights woman suffrage. Kate Gordon's strength of personality sufficed to keep the reconstituted Era Club out of the federal amendment camp, but it required her constant attention to prevent defections as chances of passage of a federal amendment increased. In 1916, she engineered a vote in which the organization, still trying to maintain its increasingly strained relationship with NAWSA, declared itself unwilling to raise money for the national suffrage association solely for use in backing a federal amendment. The membership reiterated its commitment to a state suffrage amendment as the only acceptable path to the vote.[47]

Gordon was overjoyed when the 1916 Democratic convention adopted a platform declaring its support for "extension of the franchise to the women of the country, *State by State,* on the same terms as to the men,"[48] but she was unhappy with NAWSA president Carrie Chapman Catt's "Winning Plan" for achieving suffrage, also unveiled that year. Catt rightly believed that a federal amendment was within reach and, while not flatly rejecting work on state amendments, favored campaigns for state suffrage amendments only where success was judged highly likely. Such a course would build momentum for a federal measure via the cumulative effect of adding states one by one to the suffrage column. To this end, she instructed southern suffragists not to launch any campaigns for state suffrage amendments without NAWSA approval. Clearly, Catt feared failure in the South.[49]

Predictably, the states' rights–obsessed Kate Gordon reacted with outrage to Catt's dictum, denouncing her tactics as "a form of kaiserism." Woodrow Wilson's 1918 shift, first to endorse, then to appeal personally for passage of the federal suffrage amendment, astonished Gordon, who had evidently assumed that the president's southern background would endow him with hypersensitivity to infringements upon states' rights and who reported that she had consequently "lost a great deal of respect" for him.[50]

It was a triumphant Kate Gordon who saw a chance to prove the strategists of NAWSA and the president himself wrong when, in April 1918, the governor of Louisiana, Ruffin G. Pleasant, called for adoption of a state suffrage amendment and personally requested Gordon to write a memorial framing the issue to the legislature. Ignoring Catt's concerns that a suffrage defeat at the state level would diminish the momentum NAWSA had built up for the federal amendment, Gordon, utterly confident of victory, pressed forward with lobbying and publicity efforts. Temperamentally unable to patch over old differences with the New Orleans federal amendment supporters who had split from the Era Club a few years earlier, the imperious "Miss Kate" coldly rebuffed their sincere overtures regarding cooperation on the state suffrage campaign. Thus there was no mutuality of effort with the Woman Suffrage Party. Separately, the two factions of women began to work for a common goal, suffrage via an amendment to Louisiana's constitution.

Although Gordon deeply distrusted the federal amendment contingent of suffragists for what she saw as their willingness to achieve suffrage by a means that would, in her view, threaten white supremacy and lead to masses of enfranchised African Americans, matters of style as well as of substance separated them. The straitlaced Gordon deplored the smoking, the cocktail drinking, and the generally worldly facade of the New Orleans NAWSA faction, commenting once on the shock to "staid country members [of the legislature]" engendered by a lobbyist from the NAWSA group. "Mrs. Philip Werlein drew out her cigarette in the dining room of the Istrouma Hotel," she reported with distaste, "and proceeded to blow the smoke through her nose."[51] A month later, she again remarked on the "unladylike" behavior of some suffrage advocates. "I cannot believe that hobnobbing with the liquor representatives, drinking cocktails morning and night, and smoking cigarettes were vote getters. The comments upon them were anything but complimentary."[52] Her consciousness of the traditional role of "southern lady" dictated acceptable behavior for suffrage advocates; clearly she found the "fast set" of federal amendment advocates wanting in the requisite gentility.

Pressure from suffragists of both federal and state amendment persuasions won endorsements for the state suffrage measure from both of Louisiana's U.S. senators, all Louisiana congressmen except one, and the state's Democratic national committeeman. In September 1918 the state legislature passed the suffrage amendment, and on November 5 the measure faced the voters of the state. Gordon was understandably crushed when the measure failed narrowly at the polls. Outside New Orleans, the suffrage amendment won ratification, but it lost among the city's voters by a margin of nine thousand votes. This development occurred largely because Martin Behrman, the powerful mayor of New Orleans, fearing the possible reform consequences of enfranchising thousands of women voters, withheld his support and instructed the Caucus of Old Regular ward leaders ("his henchmen," as Gordon called them) to turn out their vote against the amendment.[53]

On the heels of this defeat, while the rest of the city was celebrating the news of the armistice in France, to Gordon's dismay the Era Club met to consider supporting the federal measure, which was now gaining popularity in Congress. The force of Gordon's dominant personality prevailed, however; she prevented this betrayal of her ideals, and the group eventually voted unanimously to renounce heresy and hold fast to the states' rights doctrine their leader championed so zealously.[54]

To upbraid Mayor Behrman for his betrayal of the state's suffragists, Gordon and her members organized a protest rally at the historic Liberty Place Monument. The choice of the Liberty Place Monument was highly symbolic. In September 1874, members of the New Orleans White League, bent on overthrowing Republican rule, had clashed in armed combat with three thousand black militiamen and five hundred metropolitan police, temporarily routing them and thumbing their noses at the Reconstruction regime. For three giddy days, white conservatives held the government. This ended when President Grant forthwith dispatched six regiments of federal troops to crush the insurrection.[55] The area of Canal Street where the fighting had occurred became sacred soil to white conservatives in the city, and for generations, certain families considered it a point of great honor to have an ancestor who had participated in the "Battle of Liberty Place."[56] Gordon addressed an assembly of prosuffrage men and women at this site, thereby evoking the efforts of a previous generation of New Orleanians to assert states' rights in the face of federal "excesses." The resolution adopted at the rally praised the men of the White League for their defense of state sovereignty and deplored "the political condition" in the city that made it possible "for one man to impose his will upon the voters of the community and defy the will of the state."[57]

With the defeat of the state suffrage amendment in Louisiana, events on the woman suffrage front rapidly passed beyond Kate Gordon's ability to control. The Nineteenth Amendment to the U.S. Constitution moved successfully through both houses of Congress and began a steady march toward ratification in one state after another. In a sad irony, Kate Gordon turned all her energies to blocking its ratification in a succession of southern states, harping on the concepts of state sovereignty and white supremacy and reaching new rhetorical lows. "By a federal amendment negro women would be placed on the same par with white women," she warned, "and . . . while white men would be willing to club negro men away from the polls, they would not use the club upon black women."[58]

Although Gordon still favored votes for women by state action, in her zeal to block a federal amendment she often shared a platform with outright antisuffragists. The distinctions between a states' rights suffragist and an antisuffragist must have been largely lost on the public. She wrote to Laura Clay that she feared she was "grouped with the Anti's," and indeed she was. Her states' rights faction ultimately teamed with the antisuffragists to defeat the Anthony Amendment in Mississippi and in Louisiana. As all eyes turned to Tennessee, she and Anne Pleasant, wife of Louisiana's governor, traveled to Nashville to continue the battle. There Pleasant confronted the mother of young prosuffrage legislator Harry Burn in a blatant attempt to persuade her to influence him to change his vote. Wrote Mrs. Burn of the aggressive Pleasant, "[She] was very insulting to me in my home, and I had a hard time to get her out of my home."[59]

In August 1920, seventy-two years after the first public advocacy of votes for women at Seneca Falls, woman suffrage became a reality when the lawmakers of the Volunteer State ratified the Nineteenth Amendment. As a defeated Kate Gordon wearily made her way home from Tennessee, her sister Jean issued a bitter statement to the *New Orleans Times-Picayune:* "Tennessee has disgraced the South. I can only say that I am glad that it is not Louisiana which has brought this ignominy upon us. I am in the position of the woman that has worked for suffrage all her life, and now that it has come about I do not want it."[60]

The specific circumstances under which New Orleans women got the vote must weigh heavily in any evaluation of the use to which they put the ballot in their first decade of suffrage. Many of the most prominent men and women in Louisiana public life had arrayed themselves against passage of the Nineteenth Amendment. The Louisiana state legislature spurned the Anthony Amendment, bolstered in their resolve by former governor Ruffin Pleasant, his wife Anne, and Governor John M. Parker, among other notables.

Technically, Governor Parker professed a "hands-off" attitude toward the amendment, but his neutrality seemed a betrayal to suffragists in light of his high-profile past in the Progressive Party. Parker had attended the 1912 Progressive convention, where party leaders crafted a reformist platform that endorsed woman suffrage. Subsequently he spoke favorably of it and in 1916 included woman suffrage in his platform when he ran unsuccessfully for governor. Thus his announcement in 1920 that he had "no official connection" with the cause of woman suffrage left many suffragists utterly chagrined and certainly gave aid and comfort to the antisuffragist opposition.[61]

The highly conservative southern antisuffragists tended to have associations with "the world the slaveholders made," with the antebellum planter class, with the redeemers and conservative Democrats of the 1870s, and with the disfranchisers of 1898. An elite group, long accustomed to exercising influence, the antisuffragists associated woman suffrage with those who carried the values of urban, middle-class Louisiana, and they basically saw woman suffrage as "an attack on their own political and economic hegemony." Interestingly, their social and economic background closely resembles that of the states' rights suffragists, such as Kate Gordon.[62]

Kate Gordon's often high-handed leadership style had alienated many suffragists, and her doctrinaire ideology built around states' rights factionalized the movement in her hometown so badly that one daily newspaper was moved to deplore the situation in print. Although a male editor had praised her years earlier, during the drainage tax struggle, for her "sweet, sunny smile," Gordon's sweetness and sunniness failed her as the years progressed, particularly in her dealings with other suffragists. Wrote a Woman Suffrage Party member after the Era Club split, "If Miss Kate could be silenced or eliminated in some way, the cause of suffrage in La. would certainly benefit.... In plain words, she is a d——d nuisance."[63]

Kate Gordon, the woman who arguably had the most public persona of any female New Orleanian of her era, had devoted great energy to championing a state suffrage amendment, then to inveighing against a federal suffrage amendment, not because of the effect it would have on women but because of the effect she maintained it would have on southern blacks. Over the years of the suffrage crusade, Gordon, the most prominent suffragist in New Orleans, preached totally contradictory messages, almost certainly confusing many local women about the suffrage question.

Given this turbulent prelude to enfranchisement, it is not surprising that after 1920 many New Orleans women approached the ballot with uncertainty or turned away altogether. The persistence of antisuffragist attitudes served to inhibit female voter registration and participation in Louisiana and throughout the country. A 1923 study found that women nonvoters in Chicago cited "objections of husband to women voting" or "disbelief in women's voting" as the chief cause of their not registering. In 1924, women were only 28 percent of the registered voters in Louisiana, whereas in Rhode Island, for example, their totals were 50 percent higher. Strong antisuffrage sentiment, the legislature's 1920 vote against the federal suffrage amendment, and the particularly traditional cultural norms of the Bayou State all combined to keep Louisiana women of the 1920s away from politics to a very considerable degree.[64]

The Orleans Parish registrar of voters announced that a period of open registration for women voters would extend from September 15 through October 2, 1920, to enable women to participate in the national elections of 1920. His announcement tells us much about the lingering view of women as fundamentally different from men, as he promised a graduate nurse and a corps of nurses' aides on duty at the women's registration site, presumably to minister to those women overcome by the daring nature of their venture into the male world of politics.[65]

In 1920, out of a total population in Orleans Parish of 387,219, there were 22,299 white women and 1,797 black women who registered to vote. The corresponding figures for white men and black men were 56,134 and 802. Thus, in the first year of woman suffrage, women in New Orleans composed approximately 25 percent of those registered to vote. Obviously, if all women eligible to register had done so, the percentage of women in the electorate would have been around 50 percent, or roughly the same as the percentage of women in the population. In 1920, only half of the women eligible to register actually did so.

Table 1 shows the voter registration figures for Orleans Parish for the years 1920 to 1944. The white women's vote dropped by more than 8,000 in 1922, with white women accounting for only 21.6 percent of all registered voters that year. White women's registration climbed to 25,524 in 1924, nearly double the absolute number of white women who had been registered only two years earlier. In 1926, the total of registered white women increased by almost 5,000,

TABLE 1. *Registered Voters, Orleans Parish, 1920–1944*

Year	Total	White Men	%	White Women	%	Black Men	%	Black Women	%
1920	81,032	56,134	69.3	22,299	27.5	802	1.0	1,797	2.2
1922	64,781	50,335	77.7	13,987	21.6	380	0.5	79	0.1
1924	90,019	63,747	70.8	25,524	28.3	596	0.6	152	0.1
1926	102,716	71,064	69.2	30,745	29.9	751	0.7	156	0.1
1928	100,256	68,772	68.6	29,436	29.4	1,505	1.5	298	0.3
1930	117,347	77,588	66.1	37,631	32.1	1,811	1.5	317	0.3
1932	123,619	78,526	63.5	43,966	35.6	1,040	0.8	87	0.07
1934	126,614	78,648	62.1	47,966	37.9	1,022	0.8	91	0.07
1936	161,398	90,057	55.8	70,303	43.5	922	0.5	116	0.07
1938	164,641	91,493	55.5	72,125	43.8	908	0.5	115	0.06
1940	159,919	86,255	53.9	73,055	45.6	543	0.3	66	0.04
1942	160,600	86,354	53.7	73,587	45.8	531	0.3	128	0.07
1944	166,400	87,438	52.5	78,110	46.9	631	0.4	221	0.1

Source: Report of the Secretary of State to His Excellency the Governor of Louisiana (Baton Rouge: Ramires-Jones Printing Co., 1921, 1923, 1925, 1927, 1929, 1931, 1933, 1935, 1937, 1939, 1941, 1943, 1945).

to 30,745, but it then dipped a bit in 1928. After an initial surge to the polls in 1920, when 1,797 black women registered, the numbers of black women who registered declined steeply and then began to inch upward feebly. The total had reached only 298 by 1928. White women outnumbered black women as registered voters by a ratio of approximately 11:1 in 1920, but white men in the same year outnumbered black men as registered voters by an enormous 56:1 ratio.

In New Orleans, women registered in slightly higher numbers than the state average in the early years of suffrage. In 1928, however, the percentage of women in the Orleans Parish electorate, 29.7 percent, slipped slightly below the state average of 30.5 percent. In that same year, 1928, women, taken as a percentage of registered voters statewide, accounted for 45.2 percent in Rhode Island and 47.2 percent in Vermont. Even Chicago, with its many enclaves of ethnicity (important because in the 1920s researchers had found a positive correlation between Italian, Irish, and German ancestry and opposition to woman suffrage among women) had an electorate that was 43.2 percent female in 1928.[66]

However, what about female voter *turnout*? Unfortunately, it is impossible to know with numerical certainty the impact of women's ballots, since only

Illinois counted men's and women's ballots separately and kept records by sex from 1913 to 1921. There, wards with the lowest percentage of foreign-born residents and the highest property values recorded the highest turnout among women voters. In "the best residential districts," women's political clubs were found to be effective in getting women to vote.[67]

Meanwhile, made superfluous by the ratification of suffrage, the National American Woman Suffrage Association evolved into the League of Women Voters in 1920. In New Orleans, the Woman Suffrage Party, composed of federal amendment backers, dissolved itself in December, its members forming the nucleus of the first New Orleans League of Women Voters. Elizabeth Thomas Werlein (1887–1946), the widow of prominent businessman and civic leader Philip Werlein, became the group's first president.[68]

Nationally, only 2 percent of NAWSA's membership enrolled themselves as league members; though no figures are available for New Orleans, it appears that the chapter was a small one. The League of Women Voters steered a consciously nonpartisan course, stressing voter education and citizenship training for women. Aid was necessary to overcome decades of steady cultural pressure that had taught women that they were *by nature* unsuited to politics, a "naturally" masculine endeavor. Marguerite Wells, president of the National League of Women Voters, commented in 1929 that women were acquiring "voting habits" gradually and that this was "precisely what [was] to be expected."[69] But individuals acquire habits at varying paces, and the League of Women Voters in New Orleans had not yet instilled the "voting habit" into the city's female population when the decade ended. New Orleans white and black women never totaled more than 29 percent of the registered voters of the city during the 1920s.

Given what is known of the often bitter dissension among women suffragists about tactics, strategy, and ideology in the years leading up to 1920, it is surprising that anyone ever expected the nation's women to vote as a "bloc." Yet belief in "the women's bloc," which historian Nancy Cott dismisses as "an interpretive fiction . . . requiring a willing suspension of disbelief," persisted.[70] Because popular culture celebrated women as morally superior "angels of the house," many were the comments about women cleaning up politics with their purifying ballots. Women themselves had contributed to this view, Jane Addams frequently speaking of "municipal housekeeping" as lying well within the scope of a woman's abilities, for example.

It is true that historians are only now beginning to probe the signal role that women played in progressivism, and as they do, more and more is known about women's efforts to reform the ills of society. Yet women are composed of more variables than sex. Their class background, race, age, geographic locale, religion, marital status, and ethnicity could all potentially prove stronger factors in their decision making than membership in the female half of the human race. Would the wives and daughters of New Orleans saloon keepers and brewers, for example, align themselves with a "women's bloc" on the issue of prohibition? Would local women oyster shuckers join a "women's bloc" in support of protective legislation limiting women's hours, or might they see a mandatory limit on their hours as an unwanted brake on their ability to earn? Would Catholic women in the Archdiocese of New Orleans applaud or deplore Margaret Sanger's battles with the legal system as she worked to legalize birth control information and devices for married women in the 1920s? Merely being female did not confer membership in a "women's bloc," as 1920s politicians at first feared. A wise Carrie Chapman Catt had warned suffragist speakers in 1915 against promising "what women [would] do with the vote."[71]

During the suffrage campaign, suffragists said little about whether electing women to office was a priority. Catt had warned that male politicians would want to bar women from party councils at which candidates were chosen and platforms made. In the 1920s the proverbial smoke-filled room was still a central fact of political life, the antithesis of the home, and an unlikely citadel for women to breach. It is interesting that less than a year after its formation, the New Orleans League of Women Voters passed a resolution reflecting upon the unfriendly and exclusionary attitude of local politicians toward women.

> Whereas the evident reluctance of men politicians to receive the newly enfranchised women voters into their innermost councils has resulted in depriving both parties of the judgment and counsel of women . . . and Whereas few women have as yet ventured into the political arena and aspired to public office, Be it resolved that the League of Women Voters . . . urges women to fit themselves for office . . . to register and pay their poll taxes . . . and also demands that the men at the head of party organizations allow their women to have a voice in choosing candidates and in formulating principles of action.[72]

Although sincere and even impassioned, the league resolution had little impact on the political status quo.

Elizabeth Werlein resigned her League of Women Voters presidency in less than a year, beginning a decade of declining fortunes for the group. Sketchy records show little continuity and high turnover in offices during the 1920s and reveal a striking paucity of communication with the national headquarters of the League of Women Voters in comparison with chapters in other states.[73] Although she became a registered voter, Kate Gordon never affiliated with the League of Women Voters and never sought public office herself. She remained a civic activist until her death in 1932, working steadfastly for antituberculosis programs and managing the Milne Home for Girls after her sister Jean's death.

New Orleans elected no women to its city governing bodies in the 1920s, nor did any woman serve as one of the seventeen powerful ward leaders for the Regular Democratic Organization. Alone among the forty-eight states, Louisiana had no woman serving in its legislature in the 1920s. At decade's end, the voter registration percentages for New Orleans women lagged behind those for the state of Louisiana and behind those for women in other states. Thus, one concludes a survey of the political health of New Orleans women in the 1920s by pronouncing them anemic and in need of a tonic. The next decade would bring such a tonic in the person of Huey P. Long.

Why does not the highest legislative body of government investigate charges against United States Senator Huey Pierce Long? Does the Senate . . . intend to close its eyes. . . . Has it forgotten that national character is the touchstone of national greatness?
—Hilda Phelps Hammond

CHAPTER TWO

❑

CLASS, GENDER, AND

❑

THE KINGFISH

Although at one level this chapter is about a women's organization, it is most clearly the story of one woman's single-minded battle, a near obsession with a man who, in her reckoning, represented pure evil. Her motives were mixed; her immediate effect was negligible; yet, in the long run, her actions led other women, privileged like herself, to venture beyond their accepted familial and social worlds and into the realm of politics.

The contrasts between the pair of antagonists are noteworthy. He lived his life in the arena of public affairs, she, before her crusade, almost entirely in the private sphere of home, family, and friends. He was brilliant, crude, pugnacious, flamboyant; she was also brilliant but genteel, steadier in temperament, bred to be tasteful at all costs. Both relished argument for the sake of argument; both dominated conversations. His formative experiences included selling cooking oil and patent medicine door to door in rural northern Louisiana in 1910; hers numbered riding in a horse-drawn carriage to New Orleans's French Opera House to make her bow before the smiling circle of her parents and their friends, a privileged debutante and queen of a Mardi Gras ball that same year. He relished off-color stories with the boys in the smoking car, enjoyed a drink a good deal too much, and generally displayed the attributes of a successful drummer, Willy Loman incarnate years before Arthur Miller conceived of him. She counted among her skills caring properly for the family sterling, arranging flowers, and conversing fluently in French. Hers was the charmed life afforded by a combination of old money and unassailable social position. In the normal flow of life, their paths would never have crossed. But the normal flow of life had ceased in the Louisiana of the early 1930s, and the paths of Huey P. Long and Hilda Phelps Hammond did cross, with memorable consequences.

Huey Long in 1932 was a freshman member of the U.S. Senate, having served one turbulent term as his state's governor. Despite such a short time in office, his accomplishments for Louisianians outshone those of his predecessors. Modern highways replaced dirt roads; steel bridges spanned rivers and bayous; Louisiana youngsters carried free textbooks, issued by the state. State revenues were ample, thanks to a long-overdue severance tax on oil and gas, imposed over the outraged howls of Standard Oil. Showering benefits on a people parched for them, Huey Long banished forever the tradition of Bourbon governments that promised little and did less.

There was a dark side to Huey Long and what, in the days of Hitlerism and Stalinism, came to be called Longism. By scattering state sinecures among the woefully underpaid state lawmakers and exacting loyalty as a requirement for keeping the lucrative state posts, Long, in the depth of the depression, bought majorities in both houses of the legislature. Installing a puppet governor, the aptly named O. K. Allen, to do his bidding in Baton Rouge while he worked in Washington, Long continued to dominate his state, commanding the dutiful Allen to call special legislative sessions, timed to coincide with his hurried trips home. Dozens of laws were rammed through in such sessions, without debate and often without a full reading; it was enough to know that "the Kingfish" wanted them. His monumental influence extended beyond the legislature and into the state judiciary, where "Long judges" routinely upheld the legality of his actions.

Severance tax revenues gave Long a huge budget in lean times. With it he created a vast patronage system, enabling him to bind the economically stricken people to him. At its peak in 1935, the Long machine controlled approximately 25,000 jobs, which, in the standard calculation of the day, meant

125,000 guaranteed, deliverable votes, as certain as sunrise. The small electorate of registered voters was only about 300,000, in a state population of more than 2 million.[1]

In those pre–civil service days, job security depended on only one thing—loyalty to Huey Long. Stories abound concerning his fabled capacity for retaliation. A broad streak of vengefulness ran through Long, leading him to heap personal abuse on his adversaries to an unprecedented extent. So extreme were his statements of vilification that one observer commented that Long "would not have been allowed to live a week if the code duello had still been in force."[2] Long's wrath was not appeased by simply punishing an individual offender. He often broke the luckless opponent's family and occasionally his or her friends as well. Such a fate befell Hilda Phelps Hammond in the 1930s.

Hilda Phelps was born in New Orleans in 1890, daughter of the associate publisher of the local *Times-Democrat* and his wife, a former Carnival queen who reigned as Comus's consort in 1884. Hers was the pleasant childhood afforded by social position. School meant classes with the Misses Una and Jennie Prentiss, who taught, among more scholarly pursuits, the manners expected of ladies. Among their iron commandments were "Do not raise your voices" and "Never cross your knees." It was during these early years of indoctrination that young Hilda "became distinctly conscious of two worlds within the one—the world of petticoats and the world of trousers." Later, at Sophie Newcomb College in New Orleans, she reached a conclusion reached by countless young women over time: "All that a girl had to do was to grow up to be charming, marry and live happily ever."[3]

Hilda shone at Newcomb. Like 80 percent of her classmates, she lived at home, but she spent long and happy days and evenings on the Washington Avenue campus, immersed in extracurricular activities when not attending class. She participated in a sorority, delighted in public speaking, won the Agonistic Award, given annually to the college's best debater, and, in her final year, was her classmates' choice as 1909 senior class president.[4] After her graduation, she was formally presented to society in 1910. Her parents no doubt waited for the expected ritual of courtship and marriage to ensue, but in this they were disappointed. Whether by design or lack of opportunity, their only daughter did not become engaged. The passing years found her busily involved in various acceptable civic projects, chief among them her leadership of the state Woman's Committee of the Council of National Defense during World War I, in which position she, like the other forty-seven state chairwomen, worked to mobilize the women of her state in industry, food administration, health, savings, and other areas critical to the war effort.[5]

Was her unmarried state a matter of choice? Did she, like many educated women of the Progressive Era, prefer a single life? When the great mobilization of 1917 thrust Pennsylvanian Arthur B. Hammond into uniform and shuffled him west to New Orleans preparatory to sending him to France, eight years had passed since Hilda Phelps's graduation from Newcomb College. The time and the man were right; they met and began a wartime romance that culminated in a stylish wedding in Trinity Episcopal Church. The twenty-seven-year-old postdebutante was thus launched into her life as the spouse of a young Yankee lawyer. The armistice found the Hammonds still in New Orleans, parents of a ten-day-old son.

After demobilization, they chose to make New Orleans their permanent home rather than return to Hammond's home in the North. In 1922 the New Orleans Dock Board engaged Arthur Hammond as attorney. After the disastrous Mississippi River flood of 1927, the local levee board retained him to represent it in some lawsuits brought by ruined property owners who had suffered dreadful losses. Thus, with a handsome salary of four hundred dollars a month from the dock board, supplemented by a retainer fee from the levee board, the Hammonds seemed secure and prosperous; three more children were born to them in the 1920s.[6]

The idyll ended when Huey Long, then governor, secured a majority of dock board members loyal to him and had them dismiss several executive employees. According to Hilda Phelps Hammond, her husband offered his resignation as attorney "if the holding of that retainership involved alignment . . . with Huey Long," but he was asked to remain. Meanwhile he concluded his work with the suit-beset levee board in December 1929. In March 1930, lightning struck. Long fired Hammond, citing a law that forbade "double dipping" by state employees. The state attorney general ruled that Hammond's particular employment situation was not illegal, but Long boasted, "*I* ruled it *was* illegal and kicked him out of both of them."[7] By absolutely no coincidence, Arthur Hammond's dismissal followed close on the heels of the *New Orleans Times-Picayune*'s vigorous editorial opposition in March 1930 to a highway bond issue that Long wanted adopted. Esmond Phelps, attorney for the *Picayune*, son of its former publisher and a major stockholder in the paper, had volunteered his services to lead the 1929 impeachment effort against Huey Long, earning Long's lasting enmity. He was the brother of Hilda Phelps Hammond. Long biographer T. Harry Williams notes that Long "had chosen the Hammond episode to display his power nakedly, to show . . . what he could do if he wanted to."[8]

This was not Hilda Phelps Hammond's first experience with a financial reversal. She vividly recalled her embarrassment as a child when, following her grandfather's death, the family home was lost and they were forced to move. She remembered her aristocratic grandmother's remark as their possessions were loaded by movers: "There's nothing so humiliating as showing one's bedding to the world." Hilda Phelps Hammond's public reaction to her 1930 reversal of fortune was stoic. "My husband and I accepted the dismissal with a sense of pride. A good client had been lost at a time when [that] was not to be laughed off by any lawyer, but . . . to us the dismissal was a badge of honor," she later wrote.[9]

Honor was not negotiable with merchants, however, and a period of genuine economic retrenchment began for the Hammonds. The neighborhood grocer "carried them" on credit for long stretches of time, and the children resigned themselves to wearing hand-me-down clothing. Unable to maintain an automobile, the family walked or took the streetcar. Few clients wanted an attorney whose name allegedly appeared in the Kingfish's storied "S.O.B. book"; few would risk a court date before a Long judge represented by a lawyer who was anathema to Long. Although Arthur Hammond continued to venture forth to an office daily, it was with a growing sense of futility and despair. No clients came. "What's the use?" his children heard him lamenting to his wife one morning. "I might as well be selling shoes."[10] Three years after Hammond was fired, a group loyal to Long asserted with satisfaction, "Unless Esmond Phelps has secured some other sinecure for him, it is safe to say he has never earned one hundred dollars a month since his dismissal."[11]

Hilda Phelps Hammond did what she could to supplement their meager finances. Even though she was not an accomplished cook, she began writing a weekly recipe article for the *Times-Picayune*.[12] Avoiding the test kitchen, she pirated recipes from friends and concentrated on embellishing them with historical anecdotes. New Orleans culinary classics such as café brûlot and daube glacé earned her ten dollars each. In a city where birth and family connections were paramount, Hilda Phelps Hammond, a former debutante and Carnival queen, and Arthur Hammond, a member of the city's exclusive Boston Club, fared better than they might have without money anywhere else. Yet, as members of the elite reduced to a no-frills existence and faced with the imperative of keeping up appearances, they must have suffered innumerable indignities to their pride. There can be no doubt that Long's actions stung them. Nor can there be doubt that Hammond and her husband despised Huey Long as the very epitome of an upstart, a crude parvenu who had bypassed the old gentry with his hated but effective political machine and whose actions had brought keen financial distress to them.

Meanwhile, Long's political career was running smoothly. In 1932 he chose John Overton of Alexandria to challenge Edwin Broussard for the latter's U.S.

Senate post. With Long's prestige and support behind him, Overton handily defeated the incumbent and appeared bound for Capitol Hill, where his arrival would elevate Long to Louisiana's senior senator. However, in the days following the primary, protests of voting irregularities surfaced. A week after his defeat, Broussard asked a Senate subcommittee to investigate the election for fraud, citing forced contributions to Overton from state and city workers, promises of political jobs and threats of discharge from the same, and illegalities at the polls. He charged that virtually all arms of state government were politicized to back Long's candidates, including the highway and conservation commissions, the state board of health, Charity Hospital, the insane asylums, the New Orleans Dock Board and Levee Board, the tax commission, and the state penitentiary.[13] When a preliminary inquiry by the subcommittee in October 1932 convinced its members that an investigation was warranted, the stage was set for events that led eventually to the birth of a women's political movement in New Orleans.

On the morning of February 3, 1933, the Senate subcommittee on campaign expenditures convened in a small room in the Canal Street Customs House to consider charges that Senator-elect John Overton had used foul tactics to win the recent race.[14] That afternoon, Hilda Phelps Hammond went to tea at the Prytania Street home of her friend Kitty Monroe Westfeldt, where the hostess regaled the several women present with accounts of the hearings she had attended that morning. Wife of an affluent coffee importer and daughter of a chief justice of the Louisiana Supreme Court, Westfeldt was indisputably a member of the New Orleans elite. She and her husband were listed in the New Orleans Social Register; both her husband and her father belonged to the city's exclusive Boston Club. Very likely, she had attended the hearings hoping to see Huey Long, the hated political boss, get his comeuppance at the hands of the "gentlemen" of the Senate. After listening to Westfeldt's tale, Hammond resolved that she would attend the subcommittee's next session. It turned out to be a momentous decision.

Overflow crowds packed the tiny hearing chamber each day, with state jobholders turned out en masse, lounging in the corridors and stairwells. Huey Long, acting as legal counsel for his protégé Overton, totally dominated the proceedings. He freely interrupted the chairman, fired questions, interpreted for the committee, and mugged irrepressibly to the home crowd, so that the senators, quite unaccustomed to such behavior, appeared to have lost control of their investigation. As the hearings wore on, Long's mischievous disrespect soured into bullying and disruptive rudeness. He yawned audibly, laughed contemptuously, sang "My Blue Heaven" under his breath in a show of studied indifference to the proceedings, and finally, losing his temper completely, engaged in a shouting match with the committee's counsel, General Samuel Tilden Ansell, drawing roars of approval from the partisan crowd. The *New Orleans States* ventured that "no police court in history ever saw such sustained defiance and disorder as this investigative committee of the U.S. Senate—not without somebody going behind bars for contempt."[15]

Tempers flared when Ansell attempted to ascertain Overton's campaign spending by questioning Seymour Weiss, manager of the Roosevelt Hotel, Long's favorite haunt and unofficial headquarters in New Orleans. Weiss, financial head of Overton's campaign, spurned each question, growling "None of your business" in answer to inquiries from the senators, who nonetheless chose not to cite him for contempt. Eventually other testimony brought out the fact that Weiss had followed a policy of all cash and no records in the disbursement of funds during the Overton campaign.

Evidence of irregularities at the polls tumbled forth as Ansell probed the so-called dummy-candidate device. In that prevoting machine era, voters marked paper ballots and deposited them in locked ballot boxes; official election commissioners counted the ballots when the polls closed. The individuals entrusted with this crucial task were selected by lot from names of friends and supporters submitted by candidates running for local office. Those individuals chosen then monitored the polling places all day and remained after the polls closed to count votes. By odds, the results of a random drawing yielded commissioners aligned with each candidate on a more or less even basis, which in theory made for an honest and accurate count, since neither candidate's backers would dominate the precincts.

Testimony revealed that the Long machine, in order to ensure the election of John Overton, took aggressive steps to subvert the system. By inducing carefully chosen "dummy candidates," ringers who had no intention of completing the race, to file their candidacies, the Long organization filled the pot with names of pro-Long (thus pro-Overton) commissioners. When, as planned, the "dummy candidates" withdrew their candidacies at the last minute, the names of their potential commissioners remained, a stocked pond, a vast batch from which would be drawn an overwhelming majority of election commissioners loyal to Huey Long.[16]

Although anti-Long feeling had been high in New Orleans, the dummy-candidate device nullified it. In 105 of the 262 precincts in the city, or 40 percent of the total, Senator Broussard had not one commissioner; in 125 other precincts, or 47 percent, he was represented by only one commissioner of the five. Of the total of 1,310 commissioners serving, 1,100 were Overton's men. Broussard had a majority of commissioners in only one precinct in the entire city.[17] A parade of witnesses told of irregularities perpetrated and countenanced in the New Orleans precincts in which Long-Overton commissioners dominated. They allegedly had allowed ineligible voters to vote, while turning away on technicalities eligible citizens known to be anti-Long and dissuading others by blatant strong-arm tactics. The transcript of the Senate hearings reveals dozens of allegations of illegal acts, all aimed at the same goal—securing a large vote for Overton.

The two weeks of Senate hearings in New Orleans coincided with Carnival, a forty-day period of frenzied reveling preceding Lent and culminating in Mardi Gras, "Fat Tuesday." Carnival, then as now, had a public face, extravagant parades with pomp and glitter, horses, plumes, satins and trinkets, staged by the local elite to the delight of the masses, and a private face, lavish balls of rigid protocol, featuring the season's debutantes and staged for the elite alone. While the city's three dailies awarded front-page coverage to every heated Senate hearing session, printed all testimony verbatim, and offered photographs of the principals, page one also served up column after column of Carnival queens and Mardi Gras floats for eager readers. Ironically, although Huey Long and his closest associates held the state politically in the palm of their hand, socially, they could get no closer to the sanctum sanctorum of Mardi Gras, the ultraexclusive balls of Rex and Comus, than the front page of the local newspaper. In contrast, the impecunious Arthur Hammond, one-time employee of the state whom Long had dismissed in pique, not only held membership in one of the two most prestigious Mardi Gras krewes but ultimately served as captain, a signal honor among the city's small social elite. In early 1930, Governor Long was still smarting over being snubbed by all of the old-line Carnival krewes, after making it very plain, in 1929 and again in 1930, that he wanted an invitation to participate in one of their major balls. Significantly, he was the only governor since Reconstruction to have been omitted.[18]

On the opening day of the Senate hearings, fourteen women attended, and their numbers grew daily, eventually swelling to more than sixty. Among them were the city's leading clubwomen, affluent and educated, anti-Long to a woman. Their presence clearly irked Senator Long, whose ire reveals something of the class animosity that characterized the Longs and the anti-Longs. In extremely volatile proceedings notable for their utter lack of decorum, in which spectators often nearly came to blows in the expression of partisan feelings and frequently had to be restrained, Long's only specific protests were directed at the society matrons. Seemingly unperturbed by fisticuffs and shouts, he demanded instead that the chairman "suppress these catcalls" after the women had laughed scornfully at some of his remarks. His reaction also seems to indicate his feeling that disdain from women was more difficult to endure than any reaction from men. Women had entered a male arena in which Huey Long felt they did not belong. Their laughter threatened him with its subversive potential.[19]

When the senators adjourned to return to Washington, their lawyer declared with conviction that the evidence yet to be heard was sufficient in quantity to necessitate another session. "The evidence . . . points to the hideous fact that Louisiana is in the grip of political racketeers headed by Senator Long. Mr. Overton's election was accomplished by them. . . . By force and fraud they control all election machinery . . . they put their henchmen in as election commissioners to control the precincts and these commissioners by force and fraud dominate polling places, voters and balloting."[20]

As a child, Hilda Phelps had often heard her father say, "You cannot fool with Uncle Sam. . . . Uncle Sam tolerates no foolishness."[21] As an adult, her conception of government had changed little; indications are that she fully expected the U.S. Senate, after examining documentation demonstrating that Overton might have obtained his seat by fraudulent means, to refuse to allow him to take his oath on Inauguration Day. Such an expectation, of course, ignored party affiliation, majority and minority status, and the venerable Senate tradition of logrolling, or quid pro quo, all pragmatic factors that might reasonably influence a Senate decision. To Hammond, who viewed life as a series of moral absolutes, the matter was simplicity itself. In this case, an election had been conducted illegally; therefore, to preserve their honor, the senators had to deny the beneficiary of that illegal election a seat among their ranks.

Thus, March 4, 1933, found Hammond seated beside a radio with three other women, straining to hear not the stirring words of Franklin Roosevelt but news of Overton's fate. After what seemed an interminable wait, a broadcaster's voice told the tale—Overton had taken his oath along with the others and was indeed a U.S. senator.[22] The next day, a Sunday, twenty-nine women of uptown New Orleans met at Kitty Westfeldt's home, 2340 Prytania Street, a former plantation house of antebellum vintage and the oldest home in the city's exclusive Garden District. In later years women would laughingly call it "the cradle of democracy" in self-conscious but proud reference to their fledgling political activities there.[23] Probably every woman there could have echoed Hammond, who later wrote of herself at that time: "Imbedded in the convictions that ruled my life was the understanding that the political world was a world for men. . . . Imbued with the tradition that the world of politics was a man's world, it never entered my head that I ought to do more than drop a vote in the ballot box. I was married, a mother of young children— for me there was but one world, the home."[24]

The twenty-nine agreed vaguely on the need to "do something" to nullify Overton's victory. They were profoundly disturbed by what they saw as a hideous miscarriage of justice. In common with countless other women reformers, they were seeking to cleanse foulness, a foulness the more alarming to them because it festered in the highest reaches of national government. They lacked knowledge of practical politics but possessed a touching faith in government. Their consensus was that the senators simply lacked sufficient information about the Louisiana situation. They hoped to remedy everything by providing information. Convinced that a forceful restating of the case against Overton would move the Senate to act, they elected, with no sense of irony, to write letters to acquaint the senators with the results of the Senate investigation. In addition, they decided to write to women friends in other states and ask them to join the letter writing, thus pressuring their senators to reconsider the Overton matter. One of the women drew a parallel between the activity they proposed and the Committees of Correspondence of early America. They chose Hammond as chairman and christened themselves simply the Women's Committee of Louisiana. Significantly, the group firmly rejected a suggestion that they be guided by men; Hammond wrote acerbically that she "had no intention of becoming chairman of a ladies' auxiliary."[25]

Hammond assigned tasks to the members. A typical week's duty included writing letters to two senators, writing to two people in other states, and obtaining two new members for the Women's Committee. Utilizing Christmas card lists, personal address books, and connections of alumnae networks, the women began to write, getting out the word all over the country about Huey Long and his brutal chokehold over Louisiana politics. A potpourri of petitions began pouring in to the Senate, some seeking Overton's ouster, others charging Long in energetic language with graft, election fraud, and general unfitness for office. By mid-April 1933, only six weeks after the New Orleans women began their efforts, Long requested that the Senate invoke some sort of gag rule to stop the torrent of petitions, which vilified him and his protégé. So faithful was Hammond to her self-imposed task of writing all the senators weekly that they came to call her epistles the "Monday messages."[26]

In their correspondence to the senators, the women consistently adopted a self-effacing tone, underlining their status as "mere" women with their rhetoric of humility. Phrases such as "I am conscious that I do not understand political ways" and "I am no lawyer" were common. Usually there followed a quite lucid summary of conditions in Louisiana that served to belie their claims of inferiority but was rendered inoffensive by the women's carefully nonthreatening tone. Typical is a letter from New Orleanian Martha Gilmore Robinson to Senator Thomas Connally.

> I am going to write to you just to let you know how women of my type, women who have never taken any part in politics but have always occupied themselves with their homes and children, feel about the political corruption of Lousiana. I have four sons and if I can help it, they are not going to inherit the conditions that exist here today.... It is not surprising that you people of other states do not want to be given the task of "washing our dirty linen." We are responsible for ... not being on our jobs as citizens, and it is up to us to clean our own house. This we are organizing to do, and though we expect a long, uphill fight we are determined to get our house in order.... But there is a phase of our corruption that has seeped beyond the borders of our state and of our control. Two men from this state, elected by a domination so corrupt as to be almost unbelievable, sit in the Senate. You are a member of the special committee appointed by that body to see that the methods by which its members are sent to it are clean and above reproach — that is why I write to you.[27]

Disclaiming any knowledge of or involvement in politics heretofore, Robinson characterized her motive for writing the three-page letter as a wish to shield her sons from corrupt conditions in Louisiana. (Interestingly, she fails to mention her *daughter's* welfare, indicating some ambivalence, perhaps, over whether women really "belonged" in politics.) Also typical of the women's letters is a rather Victorian tone in which words such as *honor* and *courage* were employed without apology. Because the members of the Women's Committee honestly saw events in terms of moral absolutes, they adopted an exalted moral tone. Wrote one matron to a U.S. senator, with no idea of hyperbole, "Our courage is equal to our fear, and we women are determined not to stop until an intolerable situation is remedied."[28]

Voters for little more than a decade and understandably unsophisticated about politics, some Women's Committee members realized their limitations keenly. "I wish that I knew all the workings of the government," wrote one. "I am so basely ignorant." Lack of detailed knowledge of governmental affairs did not stop her, however, though she confessed that the whole household laughed at her.[29]

In that spring of 1933, when Congress was dealing with the avalanche of New Deal legislation that constituted the storied Hundred Days session, economic recovery measures held top priority; a matter such as election irregularities in a Louisiana primary seemed fated for oblivion. At this juncture, the Women's Committee decided to send Hilda Phelps Hammond to Washington to lobby the senators personally. As the women collected the seventy-five dollars for Hammond's railroad ticket and ten-day stay, some voiced whispers of disapproval about her plans. Hammond noted caustically that her typical critic was likely to be "some woman who packed her bags every summer and went to the mountains, or to the seashore, leaving her husband behind for a solid two months."[30] This barb was a direct hit, squarely summing up the hot-weather behavior of affluent New Orleans women of that era, who customarily summered, sans husbands, on the gulf coast of Mississippi or in the North Carolina mountains. It galled Hammond to hear criticism from her wealthy friends for behavior that she viewed as a crusade and saw in stark contrast to their pleasant holidays. Nevertheless, the fact that she was traveling alone, leaving behind her husband and four young children, shocked many. Wearing a borrowed fur jacket against the nip of a chilly April, Hammond journeyed to Washington for the first time in her life. Self-assured though she seemed, it caused her, a well-bred and fairly sheltered woman, some inner turmoil to negotiate the nation's capital alone, to inquire directions and ask names, to eat alone in her hotel dining room and move about the city unescorted.[31]

Doggedly, she met individually with each senator on the investigating committee: Sam G. Bratton (D-N. Mex.), Robert D. Carey (R-Wyo.), Thomas Connally (D-Tex.), Marvel M. Logan (D-Ky.), and John G. Townsend (R-Del.). In addition, she buttonholed other lawmakers to plead her case. Everywhere, she found a profound reluctance to resume the election probe. Republicans cited the Democratic majority and claimed to be overruled at every turn, and Democrats raised the familiar standard of states' rights and demurred that a Louisiana election was Louisiana's business. Yet, when she left the capital, Hammond had somehow wrung from the committee members grudging promises that they would indeed return in the autumn to complete their inquiry in New Orleans.[32]

The explanation for the senators' acquiescence to the women's demand that the probe be resumed lies not solely nor even chiefly with Hammond's persuasive powers. Huey Long's help in campaigning for the national Democratic ticket in 1932 had been so great that no Democrat, from the White House on down, wanted to act in any way to oppose such a clearly popular individual. Thus, the Democratic members of the investigating committee had flatly refused to be part of a probe into the Louisiana election situation in February 1933. Consequently, only Republicans had participated. Shortly into the Hundred Days, however, the Roosevelt administration reassessed Huey

Long. Roosevelt had ceased to believe that Long was just another rustic buffoon spouting populist promises for public consumption. Although Long had supported Roosevelt energetically in 1932, his scorn for the fledgling New Deal's circumspection had rapidly rendered him a radical thorn in the more moderate FDR's side. Arthur Schlesinger reported that Roosevelt had initially tried to "bring [Huey] round," but "sometime in the spring [of 1933], Roosevelt decided to write Long off." Thus it is likely that the resumption of the investigation resulted from the Roosevelt administration's displeasure with Long as well as from charges of fraud brought by sincere Louisiana women.[33]

To note simply that Huey Long was a "prominent" senator fails to do him justice. He was "the favored radio diversion . . . the most talked-of member of the House or Senate; more questions were asked about him by visitors than about any other representative of the people."[34] Unfettered by any effort to be "statesmanlike," he was always quotable, ready with a facetious sally or a scathing denunciation, usually in highly personal terms. By June 1933, Long had broken fully with FDR and was blasting the president for his failure to adopt drastic wealth redistribution measures, garnering national press attention daily. The fact that most of the stories were generously tinged with ridicule did not deter Long; to this freshman senator with an eye for the main chance, bad publicity was infinitely preferable to being ignored.

In late summer of 1933, Long's penchant for headline making proved embarrassing and provided an opening wedge for the Women's Committee's national campaign against him. Newspapers reported his inebriated conduct at the exclusive Sands Point Beach Club on Long Island, where he was a member's guest, and his hasty, bloody-faced retreat from the men's room after an unspecified but ungentlemanly incident there. His weekend spree was reported nationally, as was the fact that promoters at Coney Island's Luna Park had offered him one thousand dollars nightly to appear there as a freak attraction. Once in New Orleans, snarling and surly, Long, his thirst for publicity temporarily quenched, ducked reporters and sent his bodyguards to assault the local paparazzi. Newspapers were soon reporting that Long had written to Al Capone, languishing in federal prison on a tax evasion rap, offering to arrange the gangster's release if he would confess that he had arranged the attack at Sands Point on behalf of "the moneyed interests."[35]

Nothing reveals the class gulf between Huey Long and the staunch anti-Long element quite so well as the Sands Point incident. Well accustomed to drinking in homes and private clubs themselves (both during and after Prohibition), the upper-class "better element" dripped contempt for the upstart Long, obviously unable to conduct himself appropriately. News reports had mentioned details of his spree, depicting him drunkenly snatching asparagus off people's dinner plates and affronting men's dancing partners by his brash attempts to cut in. It was as if Willy Loman had been turned loose in an Edith Wharton novel. No doubt elite New Orleanians felt a thrill of disgust at the stories, reminding themselves that, political strongman or not, this petty dictator could *never* breach their social strongholds.

The description of Long offered by one denizen of southern aristocratic womanhood is representative of what the upper-class women of New Orleans felt about their opponent: "Huey Long was a strange man. I saw him make speeches on the floor of the Senate and I would be so embarrassed by his behavior. He was always scratching himself and getting wax out of his ears and picking his nose and picking his teeth. He was just *vulgar*."[36]

By sheer chance, Long's much publicized incident at Sands Point coincided with Hilda Phelps Hammond's first appeal to American women that appeared in many national papers. Condemning Long's attacks on Roosevelt, she warned that "this state menace ha[d] now become a national menace" and urged the women of America to stand with Louisiana women "in concerted effort to insist that the United States Senate . . . rigorously judge the character and conduct of this man."[37] Queried about Hammond's appeal to the women of the nation, Long sneeringly characterized it as a movement of "ousted politicians hiding behind the skirts of women." A group of women supporters of Long, led by a female employee of the state board of health, adopted a resolution attacking Hammond and her group, declaring in memorable prose, "Venomous and rebuked public characters, unable to make any impression from the show of their own faces, have cowardly skulked behind the petticoats of their womenfolk."[38]

In truth, significant links did exist between some of the women and various ousted state politicians. The executive board of the Women's Committee clearly reveals the class orientation of the group. Table 2 lists them by name and shows that nine of the ten executive board members were listed in the city's Social Register of 1927; eight were related to members of the exclusive Boston Club. Two sisters in the group were daughters of a former chief justice of the Louisiana Supreme Court; one woman was the wife of a prominent New Orleans attorney; one belonged to a local coffee-importing family. The only Jewish woman in the group was extremely active in civic matters and had served as president of the National Council of Jewish Women. Other prominent Women's Committee members were Mrs. James Craik Morris, the wife of the Episcopal bishop for the region; Mary Railly, a Newcomb College graduate who headed child welfare in New Orleans, July (Mrs. Arthur) Waters, daughter of a former Louisiana congressman, and Martha G. (Mrs. R. G.) Robinson, also a Louisiana congressman's daughter. Like the board mem-

TABLE 2. *Upper-Class Affiliations of Executive Board of Women's Committee of Louisiana, 1933*

Name	Social Register, 1927	Male Relative in Boston Club
Coleman, Nita Hunter	yes	yes
Dunbar, Ethelynn	yes	yes
Fletcher, Carrie	no	?
Friend, Ida Weiss	yes	no
Hammond, Hilda Phelps	yes	yes
Labouisse, Alice Monroe	yes	yes
Labouisse, Catherine	yes	yes
Legendre, Olive Martindale	yes	yes
Lyons, Anna Monroe	yes	yes
Westfeldt, Martha Gasquet	yes	yes

Source: New Orleans Social Register, 1912, 1927; Stuart Omer Landry, *History of the Boston Club, Organized in 1841* (New Orleans: Pelican, 1938).

bers, all were listed in the city's Social Register, and all had male relatives in the Boston Club. Thus, the makeup of the Women's Committee was solidly of the city's "establishment." The members were eminently respectable, with families deeply rooted in Louisiana; their outlook was conservative but not reactionary. They were the social elite of the city, an elite who had in times past been accustomed to having their voices, or, more correctly, the voices of their fathers and husbands, listened to in matters of state government.[39]

These women and their families "suffered from the events of their time not through a shrinkage in their means but through the changed pattern in the distribution of deference and power."[40] The pattern of the past had conditioned these women to their fathers, husbands, and male friends having influence in state and local affairs, being respectfully sought out for advice, advice that was received deferentially. Yet it was perfectly obvious to all that Huey Long governed Louisiana without their input and that, given his public works program, he could continue to be elected without their support. Long made no effort to cultivate the elite; his contempt for them was manifest, as was theirs for him.

Martha Gasquet (Mrs. George) Westfeldt, a prominent New Orleanian and Women's Committee member, composed a parody entitled "Alice in Hueyland, As Seen by the Dodo." Although none too clever, it nevertheless mocked Long energetically and enjoyed considerable circulation among her social circle. Reflecting the fact that the anti-Long element had begun calling Long "the Crawfish," in mockery of his self-styled title of Kingfish, Westfeldt concocted a recipe for crawfish bisque that poked fun at Long's Sands Point debacle and at his egging in Louisiana: "1 large LONG crawfish / 1 tablespoon OVERTON butter / 8 years or more of Thyme. Place craw-fish in hot soup where it will feel quite at ease in its naturally overstuffed and overheated condition. Some recipes call for rotten eggs to be thrown in at the last minute."[41] This example of ridicule reflects the contempt for Long that was widespread among the elite.

The torrent of letters to U.S. senators and others from the Women's Committee proved a genuine irritation for Long by autumn of 1933. In his autobiography, he denounced the letter writers roundly, noting that "the womenfolk of those defeated by [him] in politics and of those dismissed from State service" were spreading "clap trap" and "propaganda."[42] The women responded with phone calls to New Orleans department stores, threatening to cancel their charge accounts unless displays of *Every Man a King* were dismantled and stores ceased to sell the book. This tactic failed, but sales lagged badly; Long's book went through only one printing.[43]

Having begun by demanding investigation of John Overton's election, Hammond within six months shifted the focus of her committee's efforts. In September 1933 she called for Huey Long's political hide. This change in emphasis discomfited the U.S. senators, one of whom wrote to a Women's Committee member to suggest bluntly that "the people of Louisiana ought not to expect their mistakes in the choice of representatives to be corrected or revised by action of the Senate." Voicing the anti-Long view of elections in her state, Hammond countered, "Does Senator Robinson understand that there is no choice of representatives in Louisiana, that . . . the Long machine controls with a whip hand the election machinery of this state?"[44]

From this point on, the Women's Committee was more anti-Long than anti-Overton in rhetoric and energies. The change in emphasis was possibly a strategic blunder, since no one asserted that Long had risen to the Senate by fraudulent election, whereas investigators had actually amassed evidence demonstrating that Overton's election was tainted. Hammond's demands that the Senate judge Huey Long's character and conduct indicate that the encouraging national response to her committee's anti-Long efforts had led the women to believe the U.S. Senate might conceivably review allegations of Long's moral turpitude, unfitness for office, and political bossism. In this hope they were mistaken.

Although the Senate investigating committee had pledged to resume inquiry into Overton's election in October 1933, its only paid investigator, John

Holland (an attorney who had worked for the Senate on the Teapot Dome case a decade earlier), remained idle in Washington, forbidden by the committee to travel to Louisiana to gather evidence. Spurred by this state of affairs, and emboldened by the overwhelmingly negative national reaction to Long's Sands Point contretemps, Hammond in exasperation at last abandoned the meek tone of petitioner and fired a hot telegram off to the five committee members, chastising them for foot-dragging.

> If you actually intend to hold hearings in Louisiana in October, it is apparent that you also intend that no preparations and no further gatherings of evidence shall be made for such hearings.... Your attitude is consistent with only one reasonable theory, namely that you are attempting to save Sen. Long and Sen. Overton.... We beg to say that the conduct of your committee up to date necessarily raises the inference that the practical and political purpose is to thwart the investigation and whitewash the fraud whereby Sen. Long and Sen. Overton secured the latter's election. Sen. Long has openly boasted that the word has gone out to lay off him. We prefer to disbelieve Sen. Long's statement but the attitude of your committee must seem to confirm its truth.[45]

From Senator Marvel Logan (D-Ky.) came an icy response. "I attribute your telegram of September 10 to inexperience or ignorance or both. Therefore I hope that the committee will not proceed against you for contempt but do not offend again."[46] Spurred to impudence by Logan's unmistakable threat, Hammond dispatched a scorching wire.

> We regret, Senator, that we must offend again. We are glad to say that we are inexperienced in the field of practical politics, but we are not ignorant of the inactivity of your committee, and we must repeat that we can take no other view than that such inactivity is in violation of the duty imposed upon each of you by the Senate resolution authorizing and directing the investigation.... Women of Louisiana cannot be frightened off from statements of truth by any such telegrams as yours.[47]

Subsequent to this sulfurous exchange, welcome publicity at last came Hammond's way without the asking. Washington columnist Lowell Mellett, soon to become a prominent New Dealer, ridiculed Logan's "chivalry."[48] Nationally, people began to voice doubt about the integrity of the Senate investigation and to speculate about a "whitewash." Hammond's sarcastic tongue had nettled Senator Logan. Clearly indignant, he huffed, "There was no excuse or justification for her sending such a telegram. I can forgive her because she is ... probably greatly exercised about local conditions, but ...

I am glad that I do not belong to that class that tries to get even with anyone. . . . I am only sorry for people that have no greater control over their emotions."[49] But, in short order, Logan was to see an entire city of people who failed to meet his standards for emotional control. The Senate subcommittee, with both Republican and Democratic members in attendance, at last journeyed to New Orleans and resumed hearings on November 13, 1933, amid an atmosphere little short of frenzy.

Much had happened in Louisiana politics since the committee's February visit. For the first time since his narrow escape from an impeachment conviction in 1929, Long's grip on his state seemed shaken. The urban press in Louisiana was spewing anti-Long headlines; the Women's Committee was bombarding the Senate subcommittee with demands that all its members resign; Hammond had completed a tour of the East, meeting with women leaders in six states and arousing their wrath against the Senate's "dilatory attitude." Long, pelted with rotten eggs and fruit in Alexandria and confronted by Monroe spectators who shouted uncharacteristically hostile questions, now traveled fully surrounded by bodyguards and refused to answer any queries unless they were received in writing before he began to speak. A midnight group in Shreveport had demolished two forty-foot signs on the new bridge that labeled the structure with Long's name.[50]

In this volatile atmosphere, the Women's Committee had reason to feel optimistic. The nation at large seemed to be coming to share its view of Huey Long as one unfit to serve in the U.S. Senate. A week before the Senate hearings resumed, in November 1933, the *New York Times* opined that Long was threatened with "loss of the political czardom of Louisiana" and faced "the most desperate fight of his career." "The most omnious sign is that Huey Long is being laughed at." Featuring a photograph of Hilda Phelps Hammond, the article specifically credited the Women's Committee of Louisiana with starting the laughter and adding to it at Long's expense.[51]

Laughter was only one of many sounds heard when the senators convened in the Scottish Rite Cathedral on Carondelet Street in New Orleans, the change of venue made necessary by throngs of spectators desiring to attend the hearings. Although the committee no doubt heartily desired inconspicuous sessions, national attention by this time was focused on New Orleans, owing in great measure to Hilda Phelps Hammond's singular exertions to force continuation of the inquiry. Droves of reporters and scores of local society matrons competed with "the payroll boys" for space in the chamber. Tempers had grown so short and nerves so taut that it required very little provocation to set off courtroom explosions. The committee chairman often gaveled in vain as partisans on both sides vented their feelings almost at will. (In his memoirs, he recalled pounding so hard on one occasion that the gavel's head flew off and splashed into a pitcher of water, soaking him.) Even read half a century later by a researcher in the dispassionate setting of a library, the transcripts of those hearings have an unmistakable and sustained tone of violence and raw emotion. A *New York Times* editorial reported that "such frenzy, yelling, howling, cheering, pounding of desks and stamping of feet [had] seldom been heard" and mused about "more passionate energy and vociferation than [were] conceivable in [the North's] colder and primmer climate." The writer speculated that perhaps New Orleanians existed on "a steady diet of pelican stuffed with firecrackers," and another ventured knowingly, "Maybe it's the gin."[52]

New Orleans artist Angela Gregory, an alumna of Newcomb College, was among the Women's Committee contingent who attended the hearings; she went not merely to observe but to sketch the proceedings for the group's records. She recalled with obvious distaste that Huey Long's bodyguards quite conspicuously carried weapons into the hearing chambers: "Talk about terrorism! And Huey just put on a show. He had these men [Senate subcommittee members] under his fingers—he's gotten them where he wanted them before they walked in. Huey was running up and down the place. We were so nervous we couldn't even think about making sketches!"[53]

Early events foreshadowed bizarre things to come. The Honest Election League, an all-male group with a women's auxiliary, had previously energetically urged resumption of the inquiry. Now, it announced its withdrawal from the effort, charging that it did not believe the committee intended to conduct a thorough probe. This development was followed by a similar move by former senator Edwin Broussard, whom Overton had defeated. His attorney announced that his client too had lost all confidence in the committee's integrity and was likewise withdrawing from the case.[54]

Events during the hearings revealed that Hilda Phelps Hammond had lost whatever awe she had had of the U.S. Senate. On several occasions, clearly exasperated at the senators' bland courtesy to Long's associates or frustrated at their naïveté about political conditions in Louisiana, she rose from her seat in the gallery to address the committee directly—behavior that the committee tolerated. No other woman is recorded as having spoken out even once, let alone repeatedly as Hammond did. In one exchange, her criticism provoked Senator Logan to reprimand her, saying, "Mrs. Hammond, you have no right to attempt to run the affairs of this committee." She coolly countered his reprimand by calling the inquiry a farce.[55]

A few days later, a witness tried to convince the committee of the degree of intimidation at work in Louisiana, alleging that potential witnesses were muzzled by literal fear of reprisals from the Long machine. One incredulous senator observed that the Constitution guaranteed each state a republican form of government and suggested that if in fact things were really so bad, the state legislature should ask the United States government to intervene and restore a republican form of government. Again Hammond rose from her spectator's seat. Sarcasm tinged her voice as she addressed his remarks. "I want to ask you if you, by any chance, are laboring under the delusion that the State Legislature of Louisiana is NOT in the vicious grip of Longism?"[56]

In the third and final week of hearings, Huey Long himself arrived from Washington and simply took the session by the throat. Although the committee had been scrupulous in requiring witnesses to answer questions and had barred rambling statements of partisan feeling, they gave Long generous leeway. After more than an hour, which he used to fling accusations at his enemies and to take liberties with the proceedings generally, Hammond's patience was exhausted. She voiced the hearty exasperation of the anti-Longs when she rose to demand in disgust, "I ask you, is the United States Senate afraid of Huey Long?" Her barbed question was reported in a national magazine, which noted that "the gibe caused Elbert Thomas of Utah [acting chairman that day] to put on his hat and depart amidst cheers and jeers."[57]

Long's newspaper, the *American Progress,* reported to the Long loyalists across the nation their leader's view of the proceedings and routinely ridiculed Hammond, "the self-styled social leader." Read one headline, "Her Husband Fired from Two Payrolls by Governor Long's Administration, Now She Resorts to Vulgar Display and Contemptible Conduct toward the Senate Committee." The social chasm that separated the Long and anti-Long camps gaped open wide in the *Progress*'s reports of the hearings. It primly scolded "misguided friends from the so-called social circles [who] behaved after the fashion of bar-room hangers-on and brought the Senate committee hearings down to the level of a back-alley dog fight."[58]

Hammond's conduct was quite literally "contemptible," if by that Long's newspaper meant to imply that she was showing contempt for the Senate committee. Yet she was not escorted out by the sergeant at arms, much less cited for contempt. Of course, her repeated interruptions were only in keeping with the general lack of decorum to which the Long partisans contributed with their frequent menacing outbursts, catcalls, and hoots. She was a transgressive woman in a "male" setting (a Senate hearing room), adopting behavior from the "male" model and going unpunished for it.

During the hearings, when asked about Hammond under oath, Huey Long snorted, "I never spoke to that woman and I never will!"[59] Long's biographer T. Harry Williams called Hammond "redoubtable," but there is little doubt that in private Long called her more than that. Ordinarily, when public figures annoyed Long, he resorted to ridicule. History books are the richer for his references to President Roosevelt and Harold Ickes as "Prince Franklin, Knight of the Nourmahal" and "the cinch bug of Chicago" and a cast of Louisiana characters whom he christened "Turkey Head" Walmsley, "Whistle Britches" Rightor, and "Feather Duster" Ransdell.

No sobriquet that Long coined for Hilda Phelps Hammond ever made it into print during his life. However, in a book written shortly after Long's death, a partisan biographer alleged that, on radio, Huey hurled "such epithets as 'tar-brush' and 'nigger-baby'" at the Phelps family and thus at Hilda Phelps Hammond.[60] (For her brother Esmond he employed the racist nickname "Shinola.") Long was noted for making such reckless charges against members of his opposition, alleging that they were tainted by Negro blood, and such a thrust would certainly have been in character for him.

That she was a woman may have given Long pause; he could have alienated some of his followers by attacking a female and proving himself lacking in courtesy, although contemporary sources indicate that he was indeed lacking. (By his own admission, he had his wife, with whom he chose to spend very little time, flown to the 1932 Democratic convention in Chicago so that he could "show these damned skirts [that he knew] how to treat a lady."[61]) His reticence on Hammond seems to indicate a true white-hot anger at her that could never be masked with levity, a resentment that may have been rooted in class animosity, just as her attitude toward him rested in part on class prejudice. Perhaps as stinging a goad as class was gender; he must have seen as intolerable the situation of being scorned and scolded publicly by a woman. At any rate, Long's complete failure to joke publicly about Hammond or the Women's Committee seems highly significant.

Meanwhile, the senators in charge of the investigation of Overton's election seemed dismayed to learn that so many Louisianians wished to come forward with tales of fraud. Said one, "It is not lack of testimony, it is too many witnesses," noting that if all were allowed to testify, it could have taken "10 years to get through."[62] After three weeks of verbal pyrotechnics, the senators departed to prepare their report for the full Senate. National editorial opinion agreed with Hammond that the committee had "dallied over its work" and was "not eager to give Long any disquieting trouble."[63]

When Congress convened on January 3, 1934, Hilda Phelps Hammond was on hand to file with Vice President John Nance Garner a formal petition asking that the Senate oust Huey Long. After detailing Long's alleged shortcomings at length, the Women's Committee petition slyly reminded the Senate of its vast importance and powers and then urged it to protect its sterling honor "by casting from its midst a man whose name ha[d] become a synonym for corruption."[64]

A second petition from the Women's Committee asked that charges against Long made by former Louisiana governor John Parker be transferred from the Judiciary Committee (where Long, a member of that committee, had them buried) to the Privileges and Elections Committee for investigation. In a carefully orchestrated attack, Hammond and four Women's Committee members who had joined her in Washington diligently visited every senator on the Judiciary Committee to press for the change of venue. On January 10, jurisdiction over the charges against Long went to the Privileges and Elections Committee, a clear victory for the Women's Committee and a small defeat for Huey Long.[65]

On January 16, 1934, the Senate received the report of the Campaign Expenditures Committee (the Connally Report), which had examined the Louisiana situation. The report roundly condemned much of Louisiana political practice: "The dummy candidate system is a vicious and abhorrent political practice. It ought not to be countenanced in any free government. . . . Fairness and impartiality on the part of election officials are absolutely essential to a free and honest ballot. The dummy candidate system is an invitation to corruption."[66]

The Connally Report concluded that fraud had indeed been perpetrated in New Orleans. However, it professed inability to judge its extent or to reckon the election's outcome without fraud. Although Overton had never condemned the system and was the beneficiary of gains won by fraudulent practice, the committee found "no probative evidence . . . that Senator Overton personally participated in or instigated any fraud." The report reached its peroration with a blast at the political status quo in the Pelican State.

> Some witnesses testified to the stuffing of ballot boxes. Others testified to open voting by the commissioners; others testified to the casting of votes by those who were not entitled to vote; others testified that assaults were made on watchers . . . others testified to the failure to properly count the votes. . . . Some persons were reluctant to testify because they claimed to fear reprisals against themselves or relatives. The situation in Louisiana as it relates to elections cannot be defended. The political organizations there play the political game according to the standard that the result is the important thing and the means of obtaining it are secondary considerations. . . . The Long organization absolutely dominated the politics of the State. It further appears that Senator Huey P. Long and his lieutenants completely controlled the affairs and policies of that organization and that

he directed the Overton campaign. Long dominates and controls not only the Governor of Louisiana and his policies, but also directs and controls all, or practically all, of the State departments and their employees.[67]

After such a strong indictment, the Connally Report's conclusion was a disappointing anticlimax. Although Connally commented that the hearings in Louisiana had made him feel as if he were "wallowing in mud," and although he admitted frankly that "the tremendous record [the committee] collected showed the tremendous corruption of the Long machine," he and his committee declined to make any recommendation to the full Senate. The committee submitted its report and several thousand pages of testimony "for any other purpose which the judgment of the Senate may suggest." The report urged neither Overton's exoneration nor his expulsion. Said Connally, "I had gone to Louisiana to pass on the election of Overton, not on Huey Long or his mob's misconduct."[68] While Overton interpreted the Connally Report as an exoneration, the Women's Committee argued that a receiver of stolen goods (Overton) should not be allowed to keep the booty (a U.S. Senate seat) even though someone else (the Long organization) had committed the theft.

Long's weekly *American Progress* professed to see the Connally Report as "a complete vindication" for Overton and seized the opportunity to sneer at Hammond and the Women's Committee. "The latest feat of fit-throwing by the enemies of Senator Huey P. Long has ended with the fit-throwers flat on their backs from exhaustion and the audience completely unimpressed by their antics." It clucked a collective tongue at the "most insulting behavior from the very woman whose Great Egyptian Hair-Tearing Act had brought [the Senate investigators] to Louisiana."[69]

The stinging caricatures by Long's talented cartoonist Trist Wood continued unabated, jeering at the Women's Committee. Mocking letters and threats came Hammond's way. She found rotten vegetables thrown on her doorstep and a black crepe ribbon tied to the doorknob of the Women's Committee headquarters. Of her cohorts in the Women's Committee, Hammond wrote that "no Greeks ever held the pass at Thermopylae more valiantly than these women stood their ground."[70]

Although the Honest Election League, former senator Broussard, and now the Senate investigating committee itself had thrown in the towel, the Women's Committee fought on alone. Hammond explained its members' stubbornness by speaking in terms of morality. "They knew that something was wrong with the government that they loved and they were in this battle to the end."[71] Out of their modest budget, the women retained General Samuel

Ansell and former Senate investigator John Holland to represent them in their next dealings with the Senate.[72]

With their attorneys they prepared a lengthy petition demanding Overton's ouster, and at considerable expense, they had copies printed and bound for all ninety-six senators. The document reminded the senators of four facts: (1) the constitutional right of petition; (2) the constitutional right of each house of Congress to judge election returns and qualifications of its members; (3) the existing record of fraud detailed in the Connally Report; and (4) the Women's Committee's belief that the use of fraudulent methods to secure election of a candidate was sufficient cause to declare that candidate not entitled to his seat.[73] Their goal was to see the matter reported out of committee and considered by the full Senate, where they hoped that Republicans might be joined by some disaffected Democrats in a vote. Since, however, out of the entire Senate, Hammond could find no senator willing to sponsor her petition, her hope was a thin one.

Like all the others calling for the expulsion of Overton or Long, or both, this petition went to Senator Walter George's Committee on Privileges and Elections. At the hands of George, Hammond and the Louisiana women suffered a setback, arranged and slyly executed by this courtly Georgia Democrat. On the first day of hearings before his committee, the chairman reminded Hammond and her attorney that these proceedings were unique, since never in the Senate's history had a petition from mere citizens, not introduced by a sponsoring Senate member, led to hearings to consider a Senator's expulsion.[74]

Sensing an ally in George, Overton rose to urge that any further inquiry be abandoned. Observing that others who had preferred charges had subsequently retired from the struggle, Overton said, "Finally all that is left before the Committee today are the charges made by Mrs. Hammond."[75] He felt no need to explain why charges brought by a body of two thousand eminently respectable women from his state and largely confirmed by a Senate investigation should be ignored, but events revealed that Senator George needed no explanation.

Having ascertained that the Women's Committee had witnesses who would appear when called, George said that his committee would hear Long and Overton first and then would fix a date for a hearing at which the Louisiana witnesses would be heard. Instead, at the end of the month, the George Committee heard one witness and then recommended that the full Senate vote to drop further consideration of charges against Overton and Long, which, by voice vote, the Senate gladly did.[76] The inning was ended abruptly without the Women's Committee ever coming to bat.

The explanation for this odd turn of events lay with the one witness whom Senator George had chosen to call—Anne (Mrs. Ruffin G.) Pleasant of Shreveport, Louisiana, elderly wife of a former state governor, bitterly anti-Long but not associated with the Women's Committee. Appearing without counsel to read a statement that she had written herself, she made a rambling, ludicrous, sometimes incoherent attack on Long. Senator George then took the unusual step of allowing Huey Long, who was not a committee member himself, to cross-examine Mrs. Pleasant at length. A rather brutal performance followed, with Long browbeating and discrediting an obviously sincere but unsophisticated woman. For example: "You were treated for a mental disease, were you not?" "Is it not a fact that you undertook to have your husband arrested?"[77]

Senator George gave a leisurely hearing to this rather pathetic woman, realizing full well that her poor performance would inevitably tar the Women's Committee and predispose his committee to end its hearings. Senators could assume that Mrs. Pleasant's testimony was representative of what the Women's Committee would present only if they ignored a great deal: the carefully prepared petitions from Hammond and her attorney, the streams of letters, the reasoned arguments that Hammond had mounted in the offices of senator after senator. After first telling Hammond and her attorney that he would fix a date for their witnesses and then allowing Mrs. Pleasant's disjointed and unimpressive testimony, Senator George had disingenuously informed the Senate that they had presented none. This ploy left the senators with the impression that Mrs. Pleasant's allegations were in fact representative of the Women's Committee charges.

Senator George evidently found the hostile petitions against Long to be distasteful and lacking in privilege; consequently, he simply determined to derail the Women's Committee. Later events showed that the men of the Senate found Huey Long quite distasteful themselves, but the brotherhood of the world's most exclusive club prevailed. Long benefited from George's refusal to allow a fellow senator to be chastised in such a way by critics, particularly women critics, who were not of that esteemed body.

Having been euchred out of her chance to present a case against Overton, Hammond still refused to concede. In the waning hours of the Seventy-third Congress, she determined to deliver personally to John Nance Garner yet another Women's Committee petition demanding Senate action, delivery of which would require referral to an appropriate committee for consideration. Planting herself squarely in the Senate reception room, Hammond refused to budge until she could see the vice president. Delivery of her calling cards sent senators scuttling out rear exits. In good time, she intercepted Mr. Garner, who assured her avuncularly that her petition would go into that day's *Congressional Record*. Thus, the Women's Committee had served notice on the departing senators that, adjourn though they might, this unpleasant issue would again await their attention when they reassembled in January 1935. The petition warned, "In conclusion, Senators, let us say that you may discharge committees at will, but you cannot kill this issue. The women of Louisiana assure you that the fraud and corruption of Mr. Long and Mr. Overton will be a live question as long as these senators sit in the Senate of the United States."[78]

Buoying Hammond up was a telegram that came from her membership, commending her on her efforts in Washington. "We are as one with you.... The women's committee dedicates itself anew to the task . . . to prove that women united on a moral issue are a force that cannot be denied."[79] Echoing their dedication was the letter that Hammond sent to every senator as the session concluded. "The Senators must realize that the women of Louisiana have no intention of giving up this fight. National decency and national honor are at stake."[80]

Again and again, one notices the exalted rhetoric of the Women's Committee communications. Such terms as *decency, honor, morality, patriotism, character, law, duty,* and *shame* reveal the women's conviction that disinterested thinking and selfless action were essential to good government.

Bluntly charging that the Senate was "patently afraid to investigate charges concerning Long," Hammond's petition, filed as the Senate adjourned in June 1934, noted pointedly that only three days before adjournment, Senator George had requested an appropriation for the purpose of briefing the huge record so that his committee members could review the Connally Committee's voluminous evidence in condensed form. But, only three days later, the request was dropped. In a scathing statement to the press, Hammond scored the Senate for cowardice.

> Obviously fearing Mr. Long's opposition, the committee . . . suddenly and miraculously would have the Senate believe that it knows what is in the record and abandons its own resolution seeking the paltry sum of two thousand dollars to brief the record—a paltry sum indeed, compared with the quarter of a million dollars expended by the Senate in the investigation of the Republican machine in Pennsylvania in the Vare case. Why the about-face? Is the Senate still mindful of Mr. Long's threat when he said, "Never touch a porcupine unless you expect to get some feathers in you." "Lay off the man whom you want to lay off of you." "Another safe rule to

follow is to just let the other man alone and he is not going to bother you."

Or, has the Senate become alarmingly conscious of Mr. Long's sound trucks?[81]

It would be easy to dismiss Hilda Phelps Hammond as an obsessed or comic figure, sending the busy senators into hiding when she haunted their doors with yet another petition caviling about "honor" and "decency." It would also be wrong. In the passage quoted above, Hammond had actually struck at the heart of the matter, stating that which virtually everyone knew yet few dared articulate.

Huey Long was not respected by his colleagues, but he was most certainly feared. A loose cannon capable of blasting away at any conceivable target, Long seemed to divine each adversary's weakness with uncanny accuracy and then to batter away at it. Unrestrained by old-style chivalry, unimpressed by the pomposity that often passed for oratory, Long spoke in unvarnished cadences that could deflate pomposity, mock the mighty, and reveal the ridiculous in a matter of seconds. Crowds never failed to fill the galleries when he spoke in the Senate, which he did often. Because he seemed incapable of being embarrassed or chastened, not one of his fellow senators wanted to chance a clash with him. To attack Senate majority leader Joseph Robinson (D-Ark.), he read aloud a list of corporations represented by Robinson's law firm, a stunt that genuinely frightened the senators. He became "a terror to his less gifted colleagues. He pulled skeletons out of closets and swung them high in the air for all to see. He mimicked the speech and walk of those he didn't like, goading the hapless ones while the galleries howled. Most of the Senators knew they were no match for Huey. The rules were out the window."[82]

Clear testimony to Long's persuasive powers even in another politician's bailiwick had come in 1932. When no woman had ever been elected to the Senate in her own right, Long made a one-week foray into the neighboring state of Arkansas to campaign for Hattie Carraway. When she defeated six men overwhelmingly to win a Senate seat, savvy observers awarded most of the credit for her amazing upset to Long's thirty-nine fiery speeches on her behalf.[83]

Long used state-of-the-art technology to deliver his populist messages. He was one of the earliest politicians in the nation to use radio and loudspeaker trucks, and no one used them to better effect. After his triumphal sweep through Arkansas, senators in other rural states worried about the possibility of a Long foray into their territories to campaign against their reelection. He was fully aware of his phenomenal ability to sway voters, as he revealed when he shouted to U.S. senator Pat Harrison, "If you break the unit rule, you sonofabitch, I'll go into Mississippi and break you!"[84]

Given these facts, there can be no doubt that Hammond hit a nerve every time she scolded the U.S. Senate for being afraid of Huey Long. Senator Carter Glass of Virginia had told some of the Women's Committee members who visited him, "You're perfectly right, you're absolutely right . . . but you're not going to win."[85] Many people who had resigned themselves to the fact that opposing Long was hazardous doubtless wished not to be reminded of their less-than-courageous stand by this small, genteel woman with the one-track mind.

With Congress out of session, the Women's Committee members went to work to raise money. Since the summer of 1933, they had maintained a modest headquarters in two small rooms on St. Peter Street, in what was then a down-at-the-heels area of the French Quarter in New Orleans. They paid for office overhead and Hammond's travels with contributions they solicited from city businessmen. Time and again, the women encountered the same response from wealthy New Orleanians: they gave handsome sums but stipulated anxiously that their contributions must not become known. They voiced concerns that if their anti-Long feelings became known, their property assessments could be raised overnight, their clients might lose faith in them, or the thoroughly politicized dock board could refuse them space on the wharves. The commercial elite of New Orleans, most of whom were relatives or friends of the Women's Committee members, found themselves in a previously unthinkable situation: their sacred right to make money was imperiled by Huey Long, whose comprehensive control of Louisiana institutions constituted an ominous threat to them.[86]

In need of funds, the women arranged "Sacrifice Week." All along, they themselves had withheld stray dollars from household budgets, but now, in June 1934, they called for sacrifices on a large scale. The very nature of their "sacrifices" underlines their elite status. From their studio in the French Quarter, they held an heirloom sale of cherished possessions that they donated to help the cause. Paisley shawls, laces, earrings, china, rare books, paintings, Newcomb pottery, Oriental rugs, mahogany furniture, and countless other treasures were their "offerings on the altar of decency in government," as Hammond phrased it. Not all the offerings were grand. Having no heirloom to give, one woman, like Jo in *Little Women,* sent a package that contained a mass of her red-gold hair. Another gave a beautiful Persian cat, which the women quickly adopted as headquarters mascot. Seeking a name for the docile creature, they considered christening her for "a nice mild senator who sits down when Huey Long talks," but objected one woman crisply, "She'd have to have ninety-five names to fulfill that requirement."[87]

The heirloom sale proved a great public relations success, winning major publicity for the women's fight. Previously cynical editors praised this "picturesque tribute to a political cause," "the significant and affecting sacrifices," the "heroism" involved. The *Albany (N.Y.) News* asserted, "All the country wishes them success in their effort." The *Chicago Tribune* noted that their example must have touched the "heart and conscience of every American." "These women of Louisiana are upholding the heroic tradition of pioneer womanhood." The *Memphis Commercial Appeal* marveled at the sight of "Southern women . . . stripping their homes of almost priceless antiques and personal belongings of great personal value" and warned, "Those against whom they are crusading had best look to cover. . . . There is a great deal more for Huey Long to fear from that spirit than there is from . . . male political factions opposed to him."[88] The *Houston Post* paid perhaps the highest tribute, crediting Hammond's group with "providing the organization and the sustained effort behind which all opposition" was centering.

> The women's fight is establishing a historical precedent. . . . [Their] determined fight on the Long type of politics in Louisiana . . . is unique in the annals of this country. . . . Since Mrs. Hammond entered the fray, the opposition has been solidified and the grip of the Kingfish . . . weakened. . . . The fight proves that in politics too the female of the species may be more deadly than the male.[89]

Long and his cronies were moved to jeer rather than to salute. His *American Progress* printed a mock classified ad, allegedly from Hammond, offering for sale "one heirloom shop in fashionable section of New Orleans. Hot and cold running hate available at all times."[90]

Deadly or not, the women had suffered setbacks at the hands of the U.S. Senate. Intent on having their grievance redressed by the Senate, an elite body, they utterly ignored the Louisiana electorate, a tacit admission that the bulk of voters in fact felt satisfaction with Long and his protégé Overton. The Women's Committee significantly did not mount voter registration campaigns designed to increase the electorate, evidently assuming that most Louisianians, whether registered or not, supported Long. It gave very little energy to attempts to sway public opinion in Louisiana. Hammond spoke to Louisiana audiences only a few times during the fevered years of the anti-Long crusade. Instead, the Women's Committee members redoubled their letter writing to friends in other states, urging them to pressure their senators to force inquiry into the Louisiana political situation. Because publicity in other sections of the country was imperative to the Women's Committee, Hammond traveled extensively in the North and East, accepting invitations to address women's organizations, always carrying the message that Long was a national problem.

"Democrats and Republicans who think they can use him will learn that they will have to reckon with him as a national menace. What has happened in Louisiana can happen to the country," she warned. When her listeners argued that Long was only a joke in Washington, she countered, "That's what happened in Louisiana. They thought he was a joke, and he got stronger and stronger. You've got to fight Huey Long. You can't laugh him down. He has an excellent chance of becoming dictator of the United States." In New York, she reiterated, "This is a national, not a state matter. It is a fight for decency in government and politics.... When a man is so powerful that he can stop investigations of fraud by the United States Senate, that man is a menace to the whole United States."[91]

Hilda Hammond understood that publicity was the lifeblood of the Women's Committee. To influence members of the U.S. Senate to act against Long, it was essential that the press nationally should keep up a drumbeat of anti-Long stories. Toward this end, Hammond contacted publishers, editors, and reporters in the hope that they would allow her to tell her version of the political situation in Louisiana. She wrote or spoke to Eugene Meyer, Walter Lippmann, Malcolm Cowley, Hodding Carter, Barry Bingham, and Drew Pearson's brother, as well as droves of lesser-known journalists, in her quest for publicity for her cause. Keen disappointment resulted when the March of Time edited out clips of Women's Committee members in its 1935 newsreel focusing on Long. But the film's director explained to Hammond that "the opposition, which was 'news' at the time, ha[d] not developed 'newswise' since then."[92]

Hammond received favorable response from a handful of organizations and from many, many individuals in all parts of the country. Moved to action by the Senate's inaction, the Harvard Liberal Club wrote to undergraduate political organizations at more than one hundred American colleges, characterizing Long as "a ruthless political demon" and urging his ouster from the Senate.[93] Hammond regularly received a great volume of mail and consistently accepted numerous speaking engagements.

A New York artist designed a mock medal that honored the unknown man who had assaulted Long in the infamous men's room incident in August 1933. The medal depicted a grotesque caricature of Long being struck in the face by a fist coming up out of a washbowl. When, to everyone's surprise, it turned into a runaway best-seller at ten cents apiece, the artist gave the proceeds to the Women's Committee.⁹⁴ *Collier's* magazine arranged a dinner at a New York hotel at which Kingfish medals were sold to raise money for the Women's Committee and Hilda Phelps Hammond gave the after-dinner speech. Her usual appeal for national support closed her remarks: "The women of Louisiana turn to the women of America and say: 'This is your problem also, for Huey Pierce Long is now a Senator of these United States. We appeal to you now. Stand by us. Join us.'"⁹⁵ Long dismissed the affair by reminding the Senate that *Collier's*, after all, belonged to the hated house of Morgan.

In late 1934, the Women's Committee produced its strongest rhetorical salvo of the battle, a twenty-four-page pamphlet entitled "Is the Senate Afraid of Huey Long?" This brochure, which Hammond researched and wrote, presented facts from past cases that stood as precedents. The U.S. Senate had refused to seat Senators-elect William Lorimer of Illinois in 1912, Frank L. Smith of Illinois in 1928, and William S. Vare of Pennsylvania in 1929, refusing in each case to accept their election credentials after discovering evidence of corruption in the electoral process.⁹⁶

Hammond's pamphlet attacked the states' rights argument advanced by many who held that the federal government ought never to intervene in elections, which were matters best regulated by the several states. Hammond thundered, "Democrats took the aggressive and forced these men out of the Senate. The Senate did not say to the people of Pennsylvania, nor to the people of Illinois . . . — 'THAT IS YOUR BUSINESS.' Why is Mr. Huey Long the exception?"⁹⁷

Hammond quoted respected Senators William Borah of Idaho and Walter George of Georgia inveighing in the past in strong language against tainting their august body of lawmakers with unfairly elected members. Said Borah, "If they have proven it [fraud] in part only . . . of course I would NOT VOTE to seat him." Said George, "If the actual facts DISCLOSE FRAUD . . . then the Senate has the RIGHT to say . . . 'we will EXERCISE OUR POWER to prevent your coming into THIS BODY.'"⁹⁸

Hammond's pamphlet included critical editorial comment from leading newspapers, among them the *Chicago Tribune,* the *Philadelphia Inquirer,* the *Dallas News,* the *Los Angeles Times,* and the *Houston Post.* The *Tribune* editor had jibed, "The committee avoided all the conclusions it could avoid, leaving the inference that the corruption was attributable to high water in the river or something festering in the bayous."⁹⁹ At the end of every page appeared Hammond's by-now famous question, set in bold capitals: "IS THE SENATE AFRAID OF HUEY LONG?"

Like any public figure, Hilda Phelps Hammond paid a price for recognition and public notoriety. Long's personal newspaper, the *American Progress,* delighted in mocking her in front-page cartoons that reminded readers of the class gulf between Long and Hammond and reiterated the idea that her husband's dismissal was her motive for attacking Long. One cartoon, "Hilda in Eruption," depicted the petite, attractive Hammond as a skinny hag, screaming "Murder! Fire! Down with Huey! Curses on them Senators!" Another pictured circus freaks in cages, with one cage labeled "Hilda—a cross between a lemon and a fog horn. Eats Senators alive." A bit of doggerel accompanying it jeered, "Rub-a-dub-dub! I want a swill tub, Screamed Hilda the Picayune damsel, Give my hubby two jobs, We've got to be snobs, Send for Holland and dear General Ansell." A mock handwriting analysis presented her signature as a shaky X and opined, "It is a fanatical hieroglyphic of an outraged woman driven into frenzy. . . . The thickness of the two strokes forming the cross leads me to believe that two things must have caused her present frenzied condition, maybe she lost two jobs."[100]

The Long forces always tried to establish linkage between Arthur B. Hammond's dismissal from his dock board post and his wife's implacable opposition to Long. Long's biographer T. Harry Williams took up this version and repeated it, asserting that "the immediate result [of Long's firing Hammond] was to create for himself an unrelenting enemy. Hammond's redoubtable wife, Hilda Phelps, swore vengeance on the man who had humiliated her husband."[101]

However, since Hammond lost his post in March 1930, and since his wife did not form the Women's Committee until March 1933, one may reasonably reject Williams's claim that Hilda Phelps Hammond was motivated only, or even primarily, by a thirst for revenge. Hammond spoke often of her "tremendous hatred for corrupt government, and particularly for the effect of that . . . government on the morale of the people and the morals of [the] young." She employed the time-honored imagery of politics as domestic science before women's audiences, urging, "We should all come forward and help the men clean house." To a member of the Senate investigating committee, she explained herself this way: "I am resisting the most vicious political machine that has ever gripped a state—Longism. It may be that you do not realize that I am fighting for an ideal in Government. . . . I should like you to feel that I am not an individual in this—I represent a cause."[102]

Another factor explaining Hammond's long campaign has to do with how she saw her sex. Like many an educated woman of her generation, Hilda Phelps Hammond (1890–1951) believed in the moral superiority of women and subscribed to the doctrine that a body of high-minded women in pursuit of a just goal would not be bested by any opponent. "Women are a force when they unite upon a moral issue," she wrote.[103] A characteristic passage in

Hammond's book, written a year after Long's death, reveals how she viewed women's role in the anti-Long struggle.

> A time has come for American women to act. If suffrage for women is to be more than a meaningless duplication of the efforts of men in politics, the American woman must make a telling contribution to the political life of this country. She must lead when men falter; she must tend the lamp of decency in national government when the spark flickers; she must lift up the torch of honor and justice when men in high places let it fall; she must ceaselessly kindle the light of truth which is the birthright of this nation.[104]

Hammond enjoyed her celebrity as spokeswoman for the Women's Committee. Her contemporaries had always viewed her as brilliant, a natural leader; she had served as president of the class of 1909 at Newcomb College and was hailed thirty-five years after her death by a former Women's Committee member, herself highly educated and sophisticated, as "the smartest woman" she ever knew, "much smarter than her brother."[105] Encumbered with a husband who could not earn a living for his family and who seemed inordinately occupied with social considerations, and herself endowed with a nimble mind, sharpened by an unusually good education, Hammond at times chafed against her prescribed domestic role. Her daughter said of her, "She didn't cook, she didn't sew, she didn't garden." She liked to think, speak, and write; she liked to lead. Finding herself praised in the nation's urban press must have yielded satisfaction that assuaged to some extent the frustration caused by her precarious financial situation. A local paper reported that she was "conferring daily with prominent women leaders from all over the East," and she had of course become a familiar fixture in the U.S. capital since April 1933, making seven journeys there in a year and a half and meeting with most senators as well as President Roosevelt.[106]

Hammond understood the uses of publicity, but unlike her adversary Huey Long, she resented public mention that did not present her cause in a serious light. (It is simply impossible to imagine Hammond engaging in Long's dunk-or-crumble debate over pot liquor and corn bread, for example.) The first article run by a national chain of newspapers came in September 1933, and, while she welcomed the exposure, she regretted the tone of the article.[107] Titled "Women Seek Scalp of Huey Long," it pictured a cartoon of an angry hag chasing Long with a broom. Patronizing jokes and facetious comments about "women on the war-path" were all too common, of course; it is to Hammond's credit that she succeeded in having her group's cause taken at all seriously by the media.

Another sort of ridicule awaited her. Frances Parkinson Keyes, a transplanted northerner who eventually came to outdo New Orleanians in her rather ostentatious practice of local customs, painted an unmistakable portrait of Hammond in her best-selling novel *Crescent Carnival,* published in 1942. Her character Josephine Cutler was the leader of the women's movement in Louisiana, admirable and earnest, filled with genuine ability and a phenomenal energy. "But some of her friends could not help wishing that she would occasionally relax and enjoy herself, and permit them to do the same, when they were in her company. She was growing grimmer and grimmer; she was becoming more and more exclusively the zealot."[108] Being critical was "a lifetime habit" with Josephine Cutler, a fictional Hilda Phelps Hammond whom everyone in uptown New Orleans recognized. She was carping, insensitive, obsessed, unwomanly, and unattractive.[109]

Despite Hammond's speeches, the women's letters, and strong editorial encouragement from much of the nation's press, the Senate steadfastly declined to act. All the rhetoric, pamphlets, and correspondence left ninety-six senators unmoved. What best explains their studied indifference? Long's sheer unpredictability, rhetorical style, and propensity for freewheeling accusations must count heavily in any assessment of Senate inaction, but, as in virtually every other aspect of southern history, any answer neglecting the role of black southerners would be incomplete.

More than sixty years after the passage of the Fifteenth Amendment, voting in the South remained a white prerogative. Anything that threatened to activate the constitutionally guaranteed but unattained franchise for blacks attracted immediate, vigorous opposition from the southern congressional delegation and southern citizens. A case in point is Kate Gordon's stand on woman suffrage. She opposed the Nineteenth Amendment because by allowing the federal, rather than the state, government to guarantee votes for women, it raised the specter of blacks taking their place at the polls some day.

Another example of the link between blacks voting and states' rights in southern reasoning was the concerted southern opposition to poll tax reform, wherein the southern bloc was so effective that it thwarted national sentiment for poll tax repeal for decades. Virginia Foster Durr, who for more than ten years led the National Committee to Abolish the Poll Tax, noted, "The Southern Congressmen were just terrified of the race issue. They immediately translated the fight against the poll tax into the race issue."[110] Their logic held that as long as election procedures were left to the individual states, southern blacks would never cast ballots. But once allow the federal government to look too closely into voting behaviors, requiring some and forbidding others, and Negro voting would follow just as surely as the cotton boll follows the blossom. Convinced of this certainty, white southerners nowhere defended the concept of states' rights so energetically as in the area of voting.

When Hilda Phelps Hammond besieged the U.S. Senate with impassioned entreaties to investigate a Louisiana election, she was asking southern senators to abandon their long-standing obsession with race and to risk the sanctity of states' rights. She was asking them to pass judgment on the qualifications of voters in a sovereign state *and* to allow senators from the remainder of the country to judge southern elections. In his comments during the 1933 Senate hearings in New Orleans, Kentucky's Senator Marvel Logan hinted at a Pandora's box effect to follow: "We are going to have trouble, we people from the South, over that, just as certain as the world. What are you going to do in Texas when they come in and say, because you don't let the Negroes vote, or in Alabama or Mississippi, or some of these other States, that you cannot take your seat. Whenever the control of the Senate passes over to some of the eastern, northern or western Senators, that is the thing we have hanging over us."[111]

He no doubt spoke for the majority of white southerners when he said, "It would be a sad day for Louisiana ... whenever it develops that the Senate ... or the President ... or anyone else can come into the affairs of the State.... It is a sovereign state." Hammond observed in disgust, "Every Senator ... fairly wallowed in the doctrine of states' rights whenever Huey Long was mentioned."[112]

Precedents did exist for examining an election, finding fraud, and denying a senator-elect his seat. But in Hammond's oft-cited Lorimer, Smith, and Vare cases, none of the states in question was below the Mason-Dixon line. No precedent existed for a Democratic-controlled Senate to turn its scrutiny on an election in Dixie.

Furthermore, precedents existed wherein the Senate had condemned the excessive use of money and the accompanying appearance of bribes and payoffs to voters (Smith and Vare). In the case of Overton, the investigators never established the amount of money spent on his campaign because Seymour Weiss, the financial manager, allegedly had kept no records and had conducted all transactions in cash. Moreover, in cases of refusal to seat a senator-elect, a member of the Senate or the vice president had objected to his taking the oath while questions about his election remained unanswered, but in the case of Overton, Hammond had been unable to find even one member of the Senate willing to ask Overton to stand aside while the investigation continued.[113]

Hammond's unflattering question echoed through the nation: "I ask you, is the United States Senate afraid of Huey Long?" In the eyes of senators, other factors offset Long's personal, ethical, and rhetorical excesses: namely, Long's well-known penchant for attacking his opponents, the mounting strength of his Share Our Wealth movement, which was exhibiting appeal far outside Louisiana, and the ever present southern concern with preventing blacks from voting. With sufficient pressure from a variety of sources, Hammond might have had more success with the Senate, though it is doubtful that they would have moved against Long without legions of support. But she failed to win endorsement from any organizations of national stature. In particular, the cool detachment of such women's organizations as the Daughters of the American Revolution and the League of Women Voters incensed her.

> Indeed, there seemed to be no national organization of women which had room on its program for decency in government.... The patriotic organizations were, of course, too busy caring for the tombs and parlors of dead American statesmen to concern themselves with whether America had any living statesmen or not, while the national organizations whose names sounded promising turned out to be "nonpolitical" — a strange term which made it impossible for them to take even a squint at government.[114]

Through the summer of 1935, the Women's Committee continued its by-now standard activities. An endless routine of appeals and speeches by Hammond, petitions, fund-raising, and letter writing featured the same message: Huey Long is a menace to republican liberties, a menace of national consequence. Then came the shocking denouement of September 1935: Long's life snuffed out; his alleged assassin brutally murdered by Long's bodyguards; events pertaining to the killings muffled in rumor and confusion.

Hammond chose the occasion of Long's murder to excoriate the U.S. Senate for its refusal to act on the Women's Committee requests. Noting that the Senate had to accept "a share of the responsibility" for the tragedy, she scolded: "For three years Louisiana citizens, dreading and abhorring violence and seeking a just and peaceful remedy for the shocking conditions in this state, have informed the Senate that the ballot box in Louisiana has been destroyed; that the republican form of government ... had perished.... Yet the Senate turned deaf ears to their pleas to be heard and shirked its constitutional duty."[115]

In the months that followed Huey Long's death, most of Louisiana wanted only a return to normalcy, a retreat from the heated political invective that had so long characterized Louisiana politics. The bitter warfare between Long's Louisiana and the Roosevelt administration ceased with "the second Louisiana purchase," a sub-rosa agreement between Long's inheritors and the national government whereby Louisiana supported Roosevelt both in Congress and at the 1936 Democratic National Convention and in return the Justice Department dropped criminal tax proceedings against Long cronies and permitted federal monies to flow into the state.

In a more striking rapprochement, the anti-Longs in large measure buried the hatchet once the most visible symbol of Longism was gone. Long's most important successors, Governor Richard Leche and Mayor Robert Maestri of New Orleans, were not as brazen or provocative in wielding power as Huey had been. Dick Leche, a jovial, heavyset man, was sunny of disposition and easy to like; on most occasions, big Bob Maestri was silent and inoffensive. Hammond experienced this new live-and-let-live attitude with distaste. New Orleans businessmen were unanimous in their negative attitude toward her continuing campaign against Longism: "Let us have peace," they said.[116]

Leche's retention of Long's vast powers did not arouse the anti-Longs to righteous indignation because Leche's policies "hewed closer to conservatism than any had dared predict possible for a successor of the Kingfish."[117] Leche boosted business, lured industries to locate in his state through corporate tax breaks, and pursued a vigorous antiunionism. These policies warmed conservative anti-Long hearts among the business-planter elite. Many anti-Longs who had found Huey Long anathema in the past, and who would in the future be revolted by revelations of the extensive graft practiced by his successors in office, were not overly discomfited by Long's inheritor Leche. The graft was not particularly visible, nor was it excessive; the snarl was gone from the face of government: much of the New Orleans elite seemed at ease with Dick Leche in control in Baton Rouge.

It has been argued that "reaction to the Leche administration [was] a fairer test of the sincerity of the anti-Longs' position than . . . their attitudes toward Huey or the Scandals."[118] Judged by this litmus test of reaction to Long's successors, Hilda Phelps Hammond proves pure. Her opposition was to Longism, not merely to Long. She was not placated by a genial governor who laughed often and wielded his power clandestinely; the fact that his administration provided a sunny climate for business interests did not satisfy her. In a radio address during the 1936 gubernatorial campaign, Hammond scored those business leaders who backed Leche "because 'Dick Leche [was] a nice guy'": "There isn't a single, solitary person within the sound of my voice who does not know that a vote for Leche is a vote . . . to continue a corrupt grafting government, which has operated through intimidation, reprisals and special privileges. . . . If that is what you want, Mr. Businessman, say so and vote so—and God knows you will get it."[119]

She stoutly denied that her motives in her crusade against Longism were based on personal hatred for Huey Long, maintaining that his corrupt government and its vitiating effects on the morale and morals of young Louisianians lay at the root of her implacable opposition. She did not conceal her contempt for business leaders who sought to make peace in 1936 by working with Long's successors. She scorned those who in the past "feared to risk a dime out of their cash registers by openly, frankly and honestly fighting the conditions for which Huey Long stood" and spoke sardonically of "practical" men of commerce. "I have an intense hatred for that philosophy of government which teaches our boys and girls that those things which are dishonest in everyday life are entirely proper and honest in political life, where instead of dishonest they are are sugar-coated under the head of *practical*." [120]

This outspokenness against the Leche administration put Hammond at odds with the very group for which she had once served as champion, the anti-Long elite. Knowing that Huey Long lay dead was reform enough for many of them. Probably they felt that Long's successors were simply not clever enough to wield his power as he had, and events proved them correct. Long had looked to a future without him and had predicted prison for his cronies, saying, "If those fellows ever try to use the powers I've given them without me there to hold 'em down, they'll all land in the penitentiary." [121] The fact that the storm of opposition had subsided in Louisiana did not go unremarked. "Mayor [T. Semmes] Walmsley and a little group of society women, led by Mrs. Hilda Phelps Hammond, are about all there is left of the once powerful opposition," noted a columnist in the *New York Times Magazine* in 1936. [122]

The experience of becoming a voice crying in the wilderness was a trying one for Hammond. For most anti-Longs, the years of struggle were an aberration; it was time to get back to business. For Hammond, the crusade should not falter or flag; the cause was just. Four months after Long's death, reporters interviewed her at the railroad station just before she entrained for Washington, where she said she would battle "the ghost of Longism." [123]

Publicity for the Women's Committee grew increasingly hard to obtain. Hammond's single-mindedness annoyed more people than it moved; her ceaseless hectoring found few listeners after Long's death. A contemporary of Hammond's summed up the effect of the struggle on Hammond: "I think she was a brilliant woman, but she was completely disillusioned by the whole thing. She was like Joan of Arc. She was convinced she was right, and I think she was. She was so disillusioned over the whole thing. In the end, it broke her." [124]

Deprived of its most visible target, Huey Long himself, the Women's Committee gradually unraveled despite Hammond's energies. The group's values remained the same; its members still opposed corruption, lawlessness, and vulgarity, but when corruption, lawlessness, and vulgarity were not personified in one superb devil image, they lost much of their ability to motivate. The Women's Committee ceased to press its demand for John Overton's expulsion from the U.S. Senate. There are no press references to Women's Committee activities after 1937. Overton held his seat in the U.S. Senate until his death in 1948, when young Russell B. Long, Huey's son, won election to succeed him. The irony of that development cannot have been lost on a disillusioned Hammond. By then, however, she had reverted to the passive political behavior of her young womanhood, just dropping a ballot into the ballot box at election time.

The atrophying of the Women's Committee, once a body of more than two thousand women, indicates that the factor motivating most members must have been intensely negative feelings toward Huey Long himself. Although they certainly opposed his antidemocratic methods, his contempt for law, his frequent resort to force, they also hated *the man* himself: his crudities, his vulgarity, his calculated effrontery. When the living symbol of Longism died, much of the animus fueling the Women's Committee evaporated. Although truly alarmed at the antidemocratic tendencies of Longism, some Women's Committee members must also have absorbed some of their fathers' and husbands' relief at the return of a conservative business climate in Louisiana under Long's successors.

In many ways, the Women's Committee *was* Hilda Phelps Hammond. Without consulting her membership or even her executive board, she issued statements to the press at will in the name of the committee. As sole spokeswoman for the group, she traveled extensively. Her dominant personality allowed her to guide all discussions within the group and to achieve adoption of her plans. Jessie Daniel Ames, leader of the Association of Southern Women to Prevent Lynching, illustrated the same situation. Her biographer says of her: "In the final analysis, the association would remain, as it had begun, circumscribed by the abilities and perceptions of its leader."[125]

In the conversations that she reported in her memoir of the women's anti-Long movement, Hammond displayed a most abrasive manner. Again and again, she recounted bitter and insulting comments she alleged she made to senators when they proved unenthusiastic about ousting Huey Long from their midst. She often appears, in her own words, as humorless and self-righteous.[126]

The women in Hammond's group shared two motivations with her, namely, moral outrage over Long's dictatorial methods and social revulsion at his behavior. Hammond, however, had a third and personal motivation that they lacked. The public humiliation attendant upon her husband's dismissal,

Long's frequent references to him as a "double dipper" and "deadhead," and the financial straits into which his situation plunged the family lashed her into greater activity than her colleagues. She wrote with feeling of "the difficulties of housing and clothing and feeding a family when one was slamming the door on prosperity every day" and of "the weariness of swimming always against the tide."[127] That personal motivation doubtless helped to spur her to such herculean efforts of speaking, writing, and traveling.

What effect did Hammond and her committee have on Louisiana? They helped to force Huey Long to return to his state to face a Senate investigation when he heartily wanted to avoid it. She and her committee bombarded the Senate with correspondence and petitions citing his excesses against republican government and earned headlines in the national press for their work. They gathered depositions, hired attorneys, engaged senators in legalistic arguments over senatorial qualifications and constitutional prerogatives. They turned a spotlight of critical public attention on Long when he least wanted it. They were not dilettantes; they persisted with their efforts even when he targeted them with caustic cartoons and false accusations in his newspaper. Indeed, they persisted when men gave up. In doing so, some gained self-affirmation and solidarity that they perhaps had not found in their roles as wives and mothers. Certainly Hilda Hammond found something she needed.

When the Women's Committee was just over a year old, Hammond had received a telegram of encouragement from its members, pledging their dedication to the task and to her as their leader in extravagant terms. From Washington, she wired back a promise: "The Women's Committee of Louisiana shall go down in history."[128]

This has not proven to be the case, however. References to the Women's Committee in histories of the Long era in Louisiana are virtually nonexistent. Both Harnett Kane and Glen Jeansonne limit themselves to one passing reference to Hammond, and Allan Sindler's careful study of Louisiana politics omits her altogether. Henry Dethloff's edition of essays on Long, much employed in college courses, includes no hint that women had any role in Long's political life. Only the recent biography of Huey Long by William Ivy Hair scruples to examine Hammond's leadership role in the anti-Long movement. Although the massive, Pulitzer Prize–winning biography of Long by T. Harry Williams does acknowledge Hammond, Williams adopts a belittling tone in speaking of her efforts, making it clear that he does not intend his readers to take her crusade seriously.[129]

In thirty chapters, Williams mentions Hammond only four times, sometimes calling her "Hammond" and sometimes "Phelps." The first reference is to inform the reader of her unshakable desire for "vengeance" against Long after her husband lost his job. The second reveals that she "and her followers" threatened department stores with cancellation of their charge accounts if they did not withdraw Long's *Every Man a King* from sale. Williams sniffs, "The stores were not frightened."[130]

The third reference to Hammond concerns demands for a Senate investigation of Long and Overton. Williams tells the reader that, in pressing their case with the Senate, "the male conservatives were joined by redoubtable female auxiliaries—Hilda Phelps Hammond, representing her women's committee [note the use of "her" and the lack of capitals] and Mrs. Ruffin Pleasant, representing herself." He adds that Hammond "had gone so far" as to hire attorneys to represent her group's position, but he then drops Hammond in favor of Pleasant. Williams clearly wishes to leave the impression that the protests of Hammond and Pleasant were equal in merit and clarity. He devotes nearly two full pages to quoting verbatim poor Mrs. Pleasant's testimony before Senator Walter George's subcommittee in May 1934, while including not even one quote from any of the countless petitions and letters that Hammond sent to the Senate or from any of the scores of favorable press appraisals of Hammond. He notes that Hammond characterized Mrs. Pleasant's testimony (which Pleasant prepared herself, without benefit of counsel, though he does not share this information with the reader) as "a hodgepodge," and then he cattily labels Hammond as one "who seemed to resent any feminine rivals."[131]

His last mention of Hammond comes in connection with the Square Deal Association, an anti-Long vigilante group formed in Baton Rouge in 1935 "to get rid of Huey Long by whatever means they had to employ." Though he asserts that Hammond was a member, press accounts of the organization of a state women's division of the Square Deal Association fail to mention her in any connection with the group. She was not one of the seven officers nor a speaker at the organizational rally, held in Baton Rouge. Indeed, no published source indicates that Hilda Phelps Hammond joined this body.[132]

All in all, Williams's account of the life of Huey Long would give a reader no cause to suspect that Hilda Hammond had played much of a role in it. He manages to relate a version of the Senate hearings on Overton's 1932 election that omits virtually all mention of Hammond, certainly all serious mention. These were, of course, the same hearings that Hammond's energies helped to force into a second session despite the obvious reluctance of the committee members to take on Huey Long. He tells nothing of her visits to the senators in Washington, of her numerous petitions to them, or of her speaking tours; he omits all mention of the overwhelmingly favorable national press response to the Women's Committee activities.

There is a special irony in Williams's studied coldness toward Hilda Phelps Hammond's role in the Huey Long story. Much of the material he cited is beholden to scrapbooks meticulously compiled by Hammond, the full use of which Williams had in the course of his research, courtesy of Hammond's daughter. His footnotes cite Hammond's scrapbooks. Pasted on their pages were hundreds of yellowed press clippings from all across the nation, chronicling the Women's Committee's anti-Long efforts. The enthusiastic praise that editors lavished on the women's "sacrifice week," the emphatic agreement in many quarters that greeted Hammond's activities, were thus not unknown to T. Harry Williams. Rather, it seems to have been Williams's intent to leave the reader with the impression that the Long opposition was ultraconservative, weak, motivated by spite, and only a minor nuisance to Long. His dismissive attitude toward Hammond and the Women's Committee seems calculated to indicate that the *female* opposition was utterly inconsequential, even though the facts indicate otherwise. His attitude also seems to indicate the inability of an otherwise distinguished historian to take seriously the activities of "club women."

Historians have generally characterized the anti-Long movement negatively, and not without reason. To the extent that any opponent of Long's is linked with Long's predecessors in office, he loses credibility, since the inadequacies of prior state administrations were many. Allan Sindler has noted, "That a majority of the citizenry acquiesced in tyranny because of the benefits it yielded them condemned the conservative predecessors of Huey far more than it did the Kingfish." Judgments about the lack of effectiveness of the anti-Longs are almost unanimously harsh. Arthur Schlesinger Jr. characterized the opposition to Long as "boring, stupid, and reactionary." Even Cecil Morgan, one-time anti-Long legislative leader, conceded upon reflection that "the opposition to Long was inept."[133]

Most anti-Longs unwisely opposed everything Long stood for, a sweepingly catholic repudiation of every Huey-inspired change in Louisiana, never realizing that in comparison with past governors, "Huey gave more to the people, and few... looked, or even cared, to see if he also took more for himself." All that the anti-Longs offered was "the promise that self-government would be returned to a people apparently content without it."[134] An opinion piece in the *New York Times* a year before Long's death enumerated the problems that plagued the anti-Longs, citing their refusal to offer a positive program to the voters, a public perception that they were dominated by "the interests" (i.e., banks, oil, power, and so on), their seeming inability to learn from their defeats at Long's hands, and, above all, the immense appeal of Long's public works program.[135]

Not all anti-Longs fit under the heading of ousted politicians and their cronies. Hodding Carter, one who stood in the front ranks of the anti-Longs, noted "men of dedication and integrity . . . [motivated by] sincere opposition to corruption, ruthlessness, dictatorship and crack-pot economics." He described the anti-Long movement as an assortment of strange bedfellows indeed: "cynical spoils politicians of the Old Regular ring in New Orleans; ardent, idealistic New Dealers; inept leaders of the country parishes, turned out in short grass; nonpolitical gentility awakened from their slumbers by rude knocking; the hitherto secure representatives of Big Business; honestly disturbed, solid bourgeoisie."[136]

Hilda Phelps Hammond and the Women's Committee were of the "nonpolitical gentility" of whom Hodding Carter speaks. Hammond confessed that, throughout the 1920s, "it never entered [her] head that [she] ought to do more than drop a vote in the ballot box."[137] She and women like her would no doubt have gone on in much the same way had not the phenomenon of Huey Long intervened, unwittingly providing fuel for their crusade when he assaulted their assumptions about gender and class.

Any force that threatened to undermine women's sanctioned role as custodians of morality, religion, and culture threatened them seriously, because it menaced their *work*. Middle- and upper-class women's work involved safeguarding the home, setting the tone of family life, rearing virtuous offspring, instilling and maintaining definitions of refinement and rudeness. These women exhibited and demanded standards of deportment, dress, and bearing; they and their children strove for "discretion and sincerity; modesty in claims regarding self; sportsmanship; command of speech and physical movements; self-control over [their] emotions, [their] appetites, and [their] desires."[138] Because Huey Long undermined these standards by being the man he was, women went to war with him.

Complaining "I can't live a normal family life," Long kept a mistress fairly openly and spent most of his days and nights in New Orleans at the Roosevelt Hotel rather than in the home in which he installed his wife and children across town. A man who frequently drank to excess throughout Prohibition and was notoriously unable to hold his liquor, Long often behaved erratically and was given to vituperative speech, insults, and taunts, unrelieved by apology or regrets. He did not attend church services and was notably profane in speech, clearly did not honor his father and mother, and had quarreled publicly with every member of his family. Long lacked refinement and seemed without culture; his taste in music ran either to the vulgar commercial jazz played in nightclubs or the brassy blare of Louisiana State University's marching band; his choices in dress were loud and gaudy, lacking any semblance of good taste. He was loud in speech and in laughter, calling attention to himself whenever he opened his mouth. His table manners were atrocious. Most pernicious of all, Long, in his conduct of office, almost daily violated the standards of honesty, decency, fairness, and restraint that women endeavored to instill in their children.

In short, Long seemed without respect for the things that were the stuff of women's moral, religious, and cultural influence. He made war on the ideals that women were expected to maintain. That women should be affronted by Long is reflective of the values that women were trained to embody and to propagate as part of their feminine roles. Hadn't the great Edmund Burke said, "Manners are of more importance than laws"?[139] Hilda Phelps Hammond and the Women's Committee believed that to exercise moral authority, government and its leaders needed to behave in moral ways.

The maternalist rhetoric that women employed in criticizing Long underscores their acceptance of gender roles and class privilege. Cultural historian John F. Kasson, arguing that manners are "inextricably tied to larger political, social, and cultural context, and that their ramifications extend deep into human relations," sees the once rigid code of behavior of genteel society as supportive of special interests and privilege. Huey Long's flaunting of that code did not bode well for the "better element" and instead symbolized his contempt for them and their concerns.[140]

It is no exaggeration to say that by 1934–35, Huey Long's attitudes and actions had placed republican government in special jeopardy in Louisiana. In two special legislative sessions in late 1934, compliant lawmakers had passed a total of seventy-nine bills in a matter of a few hours, all increasing the power of the state over the local governments. Long won power to remove all elected municipal officers in Alexandria, a recalcitrant anti-Long stronghold where Huey had once been egged, and to appoint their replacements himself. By 1935, he was empowered to approve every fire chief and police chief in the state, to appoint all deputy sheriffs, and, most astounding of all, to have the final say in the hiring, firing, and salaries of all fifteen thousand Louisiana school employees, from principals to janitors. The state tax commission (members appointed by the governor) could change any property tax assessments in Louisiana, thus allowing Long quick retribution against enemies; the bond and tax board could veto any federal grant that a parish might hope to receive, thus allowing Long to deny patronage jobs from any source but the state; the state board of censors could prevent any movie or newsreel from being screened in Louisiana, thus blocking outside criticism of the Kingfish.

Long twice imposed martial law on New Orleans in 1934, sending in National Guardsmen and almost provoking bloodshed when the city's mayor confronted Long's troops with the municipal police force. In 1935, he imposed strict martial law on Baton Rouge, forbidding the sale or possession of firearms to all but city and state police and forbidding the press to print anything that reflected negatively on the state government. The state supreme court voted consistently to sustain these shocking power grabs. Observing from afar, Walter Lippmann wrote, "It is open to question whether Louisiana now has a republican form of government.... Correspondents of unimpeachable integrity ... have described the government of Louisiana as a dictatorship, and they have used the term not figuratively ... but in the literal sense."[141] Not surprisingly, Hammond characterized the struggle against Longism in Manichaean extremes: "It is Right against Wrong, ... Justice against Injustice, ... Truth against Falsehood."[142] The concern of the Women's Committee thus centered on the harmful effects of a system that historians now agree openly displayed a brazen contempt for democracy.[143]

Hammond's behavior represents a real departure from the traditional definition of woman's place. By a conservative estimate, she was away from her home, husband, and children for a total of *at least* six months in a two-year period. Although she cloaked herself in proper dress and morality for every foray to Washington, she adopted a decidedly aggressive and often testy manner that shocked and irritated many senators. Her trenchant attacks on Long show her to have been intelligent and articulate, and her schedule indicates that she was extremely hardworking, but it is likely that many listeners could not accept her absence of "feminine" qualities. Seemingly lacking any semblance of deference, she did not ask advice of senators, play to their egos, humor them, or laugh at their sallies. "Charm," interestingly, is neither an exclusively feminine nor masculine attribute; both sexes can possess and utilize it, without necessarily sacrificing their integrity. Hammond, though petite, well-dressed, and "attractive" by conventional standards, chose not to employ "charm" in her encounters with senators. In the world of 1934, that choice indisputably had greater negative consequences for a woman than for a man.[144]

Hammond did not think as a feminist; she did not seek to change the status quo for women. Her movement to overthrow Long paid her dividends of public exposure, national attention, and leadership of a group, but it is unlikely that her confrontational style of leadership provided a model that many other women could or would want to imitate. Nor did her ability and energy ever lead her to focus on any other cause. She had essentially a one-issue career, a career that was ignited by Huey Long's rise and extinguished by his fall.

Hammond did leave a legacy to New Orleans women, however. Her gift to women was the development of an independent women's movement in New Orleans politics. The women who had first become aware of issues through the Women's Committee, who had gained experience in lobbying and petitioning there, formed the nucleus of large and effective local organizations such as the Woman Citizens' Union, the League of Women Voters, and the Independent Women's Organization and took the leadership roles in them. They consistently saluted Hilda Phelps Hammond as their inspiration. Hammond, who never reached her goal of eliminating Longism from Louisiana, has gone virtually unnoticed in histories of the Long era. The women described in the following chapters owe a debt to her; even though their leadership styles differed from hers, by their own admission, their careers as activists all derived a spark of inspiration from her.

> *We still have the old anti-suffrage attitude in the South, women have been indifferent and their indifference has been preached to them, aided, abetted, and encouraged. They have viewed politics as something they should stay away from. They have been told so and have believed it and the few feminists who have tried to push in have been slapped in the face.* —Sue Shelton White

CHAPTER THREE

"WOMEN OF BRAINS AND STANDING"

THE NEW ORLEANS LEAGUE OF WOMEN VOTERS

UNDONE AND REBORN

In the Jim Crow South of the 1930s, where domestic labor was plentiful and inexpensive, the upper- and middle-class white women of New Orleans routinely hired servants to do their heaviest household labor, such as scrubbing floors and washing and ironing clothes. Many also enjoyed the daily work of full-time domestic servants who freed them from less onerous household tasks such as straightening rooms and cooking meals. By the 1930s, technology and mass production had displaced traditional household labor for women of comfortable means; canned and packaged foods, bread, and clothing were all purchased outside the home, as the housewife came to embody consumption rather than production. The domestic work of economically secure New Orleans women consisted largely of teaching and nurturing their children, supervising servants, and planning meals, household routines, entertainment, grocery orders, and other shopping.

In their world of cheap domestic labor, comfortable incomes, and adequate leisure hours, club work held an understandable attraction for middle- and upper-class women. By the 1920s, they had become widely accustomed to the idea of volunteer service organizations, first by college sororities and later by PTA activity.[1] This kind of activity did not challenge women's traditional role but rather expanded women's sphere to include the public arena. The burgeoning women's club movement and women's expanding role outside the narrow confines of home were logical compensations for diminishing household duties. Their chosen activities allowed them to act "in the name of motherhood and female self-sacrifice for others, without making any direct challenges to traditional arrangements and expectations of women's responsibilities."[2]

Locally, several chapters of national sororities at Sophie Newcomb College gave young women their first brush with rules of order, decisions by consensus, committee work, financial reports, and community projects. Later, as young wives and mothers, many participated energetically in the Parent-Teacher Associations at their children's schools. Women of the New Orleans elite took part in activities at Le Petit Salon in the French Quarter and the Orleans Club on St. Charles Avenue, which provided literary or cultural programs, musicales, and travelogues for members, who could also enjoy luncheon or afternoon tea at the club. Then too, New Orleans boasted a thriving little theater, Le Petit Theatre du Vieux Carre, established in 1917 by enthusiastic women and largely sustained by their dramatic, executive, and financial talents.

Conspicuously lacking among the organizations that attracted the energies of New Orleans women were political groups. The Era Club of the Progressive years had metamorphosed into a chapter of the League of Women Voters in 1920, but as outlined in chapter 1, that body did not flourish. Records make it clear that, by the early 1930s, the New Orleans league had virtually been taken captive by a partisan clique of women identified with the Old Regulars, whose political machine controlled city government. In blatant violation of both the spirit and the letter of the National League of Women Voters (NLWV) constitution and bylaws, which mandated the strictest nonpartisanship, the officers of the New Orleans league, and presumably the rank and file as well, worked openly for the Old Regulars; several league members held positions in city government, theirs by virtue of loyalty to the machine. At the 1930 annual convention, the leaders of the Old Regular faction of women loaded the convention with their partisans and hijacked the election process, prompting heated debates over whether women who owed dues could be elected to office and whether women could vote as delegates if they only paid their dues the day of the convention.[3]

Two sisters married to brothers, Edna Culligan (Mrs. Edward) Pilsbury and May Culligan (Mrs. Albert) Pilsbury, emerged as the dominant forces in the partisan league. Edna Pilsbury's appointment as factory inspector came from Mayor Martin Behrman in 1925; his Old Regular successors Arthur O'Keefe and T. Semmes Walmsley reappointed her until the post was abolished in 1936. An employee of hers in the factory inspector's office recalled it as "a deadhead's paradise," whose "chief use was as a meeting place for Mrs. Pilsbury's cronies."[4] The cronies in question were politicians, for Pilsbury served simultaneously as factory inspector, head of the League of Women Voters, and chairman of the Women's Regular Democratic Organization. Her sister May, also an officer and one-time president of the League of Women Voters, was "lady leader" of the Third Ward and James Comiskey's secretary.[5]

This egregious breach of NLWV regulations allowed the New Orleans League of Women Voters (NOLWV) to endorse legislation based on signals from the Regular Democratic Organization rather than after thorough study of issues as prescribed. The cozy arrangement began to unravel only when a woman whose husband represented another faction in New Orleans politics began making waves within the group. As early as 1930, the national league office indicated its concern over the tardiness of NOLWV in responding to the NLWV's requests for information about its program, which in reality was virtually synonymous with the Old Regular agenda. By 1932, a confidential internal NLWV memo assessed the Louisiana situation warily, noting "the great troublemakers in the Louisiana League . . . , the organizational difficulties . . . , [and] the need for extreme care in correspondence with them."[6] Conditions did not improve. A 1934 report by NLWV investigators assessed Louisiana tersely as a state where "present League pattern probably [was] not workable."[7]

At last, the partisans in the New Orleans league overreached themselves. In 1936, when the Pilsburys tried to reduce the quorum from eleven to five, in an organization with a total membership of fifty, protest ensued. Of greater significance than mere protest concerning the partisan Pilsburys, however, were the letters of inquiry and complaint that unhappy league members wrote to the national headquarters asking if it was legitimate for the local league to alter its bylaws in this fashion.[8]

When rumblings about the unsavory league situation in New Orleans reached national headquarters in Washington, they excited enough concern to precipitate a visit to Louisiana by an NLWV board member. Her fact-finding trip was handwriting on the wall for the errant NOLWV, whose members "had a feeling after Mrs. Anderson's visit that NLWV was going to withdraw recognition."[9] The national office did exactly that in November 1936, when Marguerite Wells, president of the NLWV, informed the New Orleans league that the national board had voted to withdraw recognition from their chapter, closing her letter, "Please believe that I feel very deep regret at the situation that makes such action necessary."[10]

Adopting a pose of puzzled innocence, the NOLWV president, Edna Pilsbury, asked for details of her organization's shortcomings, prompting Wells to reply tersely: "The Louisiana League has not followed the thorough and democratic methods established by the National League for adopting a program of work, . . . it has not avoided the appearance of partisan bias either as an organization or as officers of the Louisiana League, which of course is contrary to the policy of the National League."[11] Evidently Pilsbury expected nothing good to come of her inquiry, for even before she received Wells's adamant reply, she had disingenuously informed the New Orleans press that her group had voted to disband, omitting to mention anything about revocation of its charter by its parent body.

The foregoing saga of the original ill-fated League of Women Voters in New Orleans makes it plain that there were overt ties between the league and machine politics. This situation left many New Orleans women disenchanted with the league; one woman explained in a letter to the national office deploring the decline of the NOLWV, "Women of brains and standing will not mix with anything political."[12] Obviously, though, some women were already "mixing" with politics in the form of the discredited League of Women Voters, serving as women ward leaders for the Old Regulars' organization and earning patronage jobs by their loyal service to the machine. The correspondent evidently meant to imply that their counterparts, women who opposed machine politics, would not become politically involved. But if so, events of the 1930s proved her wrong.

Politically, the anticipated new age that voting women were expected to usher in with their pure ballots simply never materialized. As explored in chapter 1, not only did women fail to vote in a solid bloc to enact reforms, but most women did not vote at all. Orleans Parish records reveal that 14,066 women were registered to vote in New Orleans in 1922 and almost four times as many men.[13]

The women voters' numbers inched upward gradually over the next decade, with women adding a few thousands to the ranks of Orleans Parish registered voters from election to election (see table 1). In 1934, the total of white women registered to vote stood at 47,966, with white men totaling nearly twice that number. Then, in 1936, the registration rolls showed a surprising 70,303 white women voters in New Orleans,[14] a 46.6 percent rise in voter registration among local women in just two years. (Numbers of black women registered, however, had dropped steeply, from a high of 1,797 in 1920 to only 116 in 1936. There were 922 black male registered voters in 1936. Black men thus constituted one-half of 1 percent of the electorate that year, and black women made up an almost unbelievable .0007 percent of the total voters.)

Research by political scientists indicates that women's voting in the early years of suffrage depended on group pressures emphasizing the importance of women taking an active role in politics, coupled with absence of pressures discouraging their participation. Clearly, by 1936, political consciousness among white women in New Orleans was undergoing a significant change. Hilda Phelps Hammond's much publicized crusade against Huey Long certainly contributed to this shift toward higher political consciousness, which nearly doubled the local female electorate. The Women's Committee of Louisiana stirred interest in politics among women, whether they opposed the Kingfish or supported him, and provided many women with the encouragement they needed in order to become registered voters.

Like most southern women, the typical New Orleans woman had been bred to shun anything that could be labeled "unladylike." Well after ratification of the Nineteenth Amendment, politics remained relentlessly male, a world of cigar smoke and spittoons, corner saloons and ward bosses. The key elements of politics, namely, competition, power, aggressiveness, independence, and corruption, were the antithesis of those values commonly used to define femininity, and consequently, most women needed special incentives to become involved in such an unfamiliar milieu.[15]

The necessary catalyst for many came in the form of Huey Long and his perceived manhandling of the democratic process. Outraged by both his actions and his manners, hundreds of proper matrons had joined Hilda Phelps Hammond to work against Long. Women, who as mothers and teachers had spent years admonishing their children to "Watch your language," "Play fair," "Say thank you," and "Share the toys and take turns," were galvanized into political participation by Long, whose excesses against both decency and democracy threatened to undermine every value that women held and transmitted.

Of course, not all women opposed Huey Long. Many had economic reasons to support him. Some twenty-five thousand patronage jobs enabled him to bind large numbers of the population to his machine; if one's father, husband, son, or brother owed his very income to Longism, via the dock board or the levee board, Charity Hospital, Angola Prison, or Louisiana State University, the anti-Long movement held little appeal. Even though circumstances rendered these women's needs greater than their scruples, Long's desecration of the ideals women were expected to practice and to teach must have caused some cognitive dissonance among the female element in the Long faction. The anti-Long movement nevertheless played a role in motivating these same women to register and to vote, as a counterweight to forces that threatened their livelihoods.

The outcry over the allegedly fraudulent election of John Overton to the U.S. Senate in 1932 spurred anti-Long men in New Orleans to form a citizens' group called the Honest Election League (HEL), a typical example of the good government associations common to U.S. cities in the early twentieth century. Seeking to tap the enthusiastic and unpaid labor of their wives and other women, Honest Election League members created a women's division later that year. To lead it, they selected Hilda Phelps Hammond's contemporary and close friend Martha Gilmore Robinson.

The public life of Martha Robinson (1888–1981) spanned a full half century and took her into many areas of urban reform, but it began in earnest in 1932 with the Women's Division of the Honest Election League, which she served as president. Robinson's life was affluent and socially unassailable from the day of her birth, August 18, 1888. Brought up in a large, comfortable house at the corner of St. Charles Avenue and Henry Clay, she enjoyed a serene childhood, romping in the new Audubon Park (where she caused comment by riding her pony astride) and visiting her grandparents' sugar plantation upriver at Donaldsonville.[16]

This eldest child and only daughter of New Orleans city attorney Samuel Gilmore and his wife Martha Nolan grew up with an outspoken bent, an intellectual curiosity, and a strong interest in politics, nourished by her father and his stories of Old Regular associates. At the age of nine, she organized her neighborhood playmates and their pets into a parade for an upcoming city election. When the noted suffragist Maud Wood Park came to speak at Newcomb College in 1908, Martha attended the lecture with classmates and came away a convert to the cause, opposing her father for the first time. While at Newcomb College, she acted in dramatic productions, edited the college literary magazine, and devoted the summer between her junior and senior years to leading the student project of rewriting college rules governing extracurricular activities. She graduated with the class of 1909.[17]

The three years after her Newcomb commencement brought profound changes. In rapid order came her father's election to Congress (1909), his sudden and unexpected death (1910), her courtship and marriage (1911), and the birth of her first child (1912). Moving from her birth family to her procreative family involved no changes in financial or social status, for Martha's husband, Robert Gibson Robinson, was a Princeton graduate (class of 1908) and prosperous lumberyard owner. Their family of four sons and a daughter occupied her time and attentions almost exclusively for the first twenty years of her married life.

Women born in the 1880s spent an average of 35.5 percent of their adult life in intensive child care, or early motherhood, defined as lasting from the birth of the first child until the entry of the last child into school.[18] Robinson's intensive child-care years totaled 29.4 percent of her adult life, stretching from 1912 until 1932. Thus, the intensive child-care years of her life coincided with the first decade of women's political rights. Although essentially a maternal spectator in those years, she did register to vote as soon as she became eligible under the Nineteenth Amendment; among her papers is her poll tax certificate from 1920.[19]

Robinson's outside-the-home activities before the 1930s included serving on the New Orleans Council for National Defense in World War I and helping to found Le Petit Theatre du Vieux Carre, where she occasionally performed in dramatic roles. Her service as a member of the case committee of the local Child Welfare Association gave her a chance to provide help for needy children, though the reports provided by moralizing social workers sent to inspect home conditions tried her patience. One worker, suspecting that the family in question was being supported by a male boarder, concluded, "How the funds were secured to furnish this place and finance it is a question that disturbs the Visitor." In the margin Robinson scrawled, "None of the Visitor's Business."[20] Delivering food to recently discharged Charity Hospital surgical patients took Robinson into parts of New Orleans far removed in space and amenities from her comfortable existence and led her to resolve that if the opportunity should offer itself, she would work to improve "those terrible conditions," which "haunted" her.[21]

Until 1932, her activities beyond home, husband, and children had fallen very definitely into the acceptable Lady Bountiful and cultural roles that upper-class matrons commonly adopted. The 1932 entry of her youngest son into elementary school coincided with the local uproar over the Overton-Broussard senatorial election. When she was asked to assume the helm of the Women's Division of the Honest Election League later that year, Martha Gilmore Robinson was a woman of forty-four, quite attractive, a slightly older version of the Gibson girl, whom her upswept hair, tall, erect figure, and well-defined features had epitomized in college years. The work she was about to undertake had little in common with her experiences urging meatless menus in 1918, delivering soup to poor families, or acting in stage plays. The 262 precincts of Orleans Parish, their poll books and ward bosses, would constitute a new world for her, the world of Louisiana politics.

As Women's Division leader, Robinson soon learned that the machinery governing Louisiana elections (Act No. 130, passed by the legislature in 1916) provided for five election commissioners to preside over the polls in each precinct. Obtaining ballots from the parish registrar, these commissioners verified the eligibility of each voter by checking his or her name and number in the poll book against the name and number on the voter's registration paper and poll tax certificate, both of which the voter had to present. Commissioners kept order at the polls. When the polls closed, commissioners counted the ballots, secured the ballot boxes until delivery to the secretary of state at Baton Rouge, and sent him their precinct's tally. In short, commissioners had total control of the election process in each precinct.[22]

The spirit of the law presumed impartiality in election commissioners, but impartiality was a scarce commodity in Louisiana politics. In the 1930s, commissioners executed their duties in highly partisan fashion in the city of New Orleans. The report of the Connally Commission on the Overton-Broussard election of 1932 revealed physical intimidation of voters, outright fisticuffs at the polls, destruction of ballots, ballot box stuffing, open voting, and more.[23] All of these illegal activities occurred under the eyes of, and sometimes at the direction of, the election commissioners. It was this situation that the Women's Division of the Honest Election League determined to correct, convinced that securing honest elections required securing honest commissioners.

In municipal elections of January 1934, the new Women's Division played a small but significant role. Based on their stated belief that "the presence of respectable and representative citizens at the polls [was] the greatest deterrent against fraud," women offered to serve as impartial commissioners for any candidate who wanted them.[24] They prepared for this new role at schools conducted by attorneys who were Honest Election League members. After being tutored in both election law and the varieties of dishonest tactics that the machine allegedly employed, they received instruction from their president, Martha Robinson, on conduct. Among her admonitions were these: "1. Be on guard against affability. 2. Do not leave Poll or take eyes off box or commissioners. 3. Do not take a drink."[25] Their participation in these sessions placed the New Orleans women squarely in the "citizenship school" movement that Anne Firor Scott has noted as being one of the early manifestations of southern women in politics.[26]

Schooled in election law and armed with Robinson's commandments, the women, mostly from affluent New Orleans neighborhoods, essayed forth to penetrate the masculine confines of the city's 262 voting precincts. They carried a supply of affidavits for voters who wanted to report fraudulent practices they had seen and a telephone number for reporting election law abuses. The number was Martha Robinson's; her home was command central for that early effort by women to participate in politics.

Although generally approving, the press took an amused, rather patronizing tone in reporting Women's Division activities. The mother of one young poll worker was described as "frantic and about to send a squad of policemen to find her daughter," who had not reached home by five o'clock the next morning. A headline reporting the women's experiences—"Women Propose That All Voting Here Be Honest"—provided sad and presumably unintended commentary on the usual state of electoral affairs. To a reporter, Robinson assessed the Women's Division's impact. "Out of what we learned I believe the women will have more to do with assuring honest elections to the city than any other one factor in New Orleans politics."[27] In truth, there was reason to believe that these election returns reflected an honest count of ballots cast.

During the 1930s, Jessie Daniel Ames and her organization, the Association of Southern Women to Prevent Lynching, found that unassailable respectability made progress possible for them. "Secure in the privileges granted family and social standing in the region," they "could act with some immunity" where others could not venture. Their political rights and their husbands' economic positions provided "leverage against county officials and local police. Most importantly, they were strategically placed to make maximum use of the cultural symbol of the southern lady."[28]

Martha Robinson and members of the Women's Division of the Honest Election League enjoyed the same advantages. Respectable female members could act in situations in which the males of the Honest Election League aroused suspicions and hostility. An example in point involves a dispute over qualified voters for the January 1934 election. The Honest Election League's president had asked in December 1933 that the registrar of voters accept his group's offer of extra clerical help, at no cost, to aid his staff in sending out notices to all disqualified voters. The Honest Election League allegedly had found more than ten thousand improperly registered voters on the rolls and, as part of their campaign for honest elections, wanted these purged.[29]

The registrar, frankly suspicious of the offer, felt that the men of the Honest Election League could not be nonpartisan in executing a purge of the voter rolls and declined to accept the HEL offer. Shortly after that, when Martha Robinson offered the services of her female membership, the city allowed women to do what it had refused to allow men, many of them their husbands or fathers, to undertake. The men of city hall had evidently perceived good government, upper-class *men* as either ineffectual nuisances, thus not to be taken seriously (male reformer as weakling) or as men first and foremost, thus steeped in the violent ethos of the masculine political world (male reformer as adversary). However, good government, upper-class *women* were first, last, and always *ladies,* and they were canny enough to make the most of this perception. Nonthreatening because seen as disinterested, they tramped the eight wards in which they were organized, canvassing house to house to compare names and addresses in the poll books with the people who actually lived at those addresses, turning up much evidence of fraudulent registrations in the process. Their work made possible the start of a legitimate cleaning up of notoriously inaccurate voter rolls in New Orleans.[30]

In May 1934, Robinson issued what amounted to a declaration of independence when she announced the intention of the Women's Division to withdraw from the all-male parent league. Her group felt that it could "do more effective work to further the responsible participation of women in government if it [was] an independent women's organization, devoted to the many interests besides election work that [could] be helped by an informed woman vote."[31]

On Friday, June 1, 1934, Martha Robinson presided at a gathering of the leading club women of New Orleans, a meeting to which her postcards had invited a selection of women's groups concerned with social welfare, education, culture, civic improvement, and professional advancement. Those who attended shared certain traits: higher-than-average level of education, civic-mindedness, and previous participation in women's associations. Assembling hatted, suited, and gloved on a warm night in Tulane University's Gibson Hall, the women heard Robinson express her desire to found "a non-partisan organization for promoting women's responsible participation in government." Thus was born the Woman Citizens' Union (WCU), which was a vigorous part of the civic life of New Orleans for the next eight years.[32]

The examples of Hilda Phelps Hammond's Women's Committee of Louisiana and the local League of Women Voters influenced the founders of the Woman Citizens' Union. Unlike Hammond's group, which held the limited and essentially negative goal of seeing Senators Long and Overton removed from office and which was pledged to disband should that condition be met, the Woman Citizens' Union from the outset saw itself as permanent. It held long-range plans for educating women to their citizenship responsibilities and declined to focus its energies on so narrow a goal as defeat or election of any one individual. Because the local League of Women Voters was so fully identified with the machine that ran the city, the better-educated, affluent women of the city shunned it. Thus, the Woman Citizens' Union charter stipulated that anyone holding office in any political party or factional organization would be ineligible for office in the WCU. The new group intended to organize by wards, with the stated objective of educating women socially, economically, and politically and promoting their responsible participation in government.[33]

Eight of the twenty-two women's associations invited to the WCU organizational meeting were clubs for middle-class women who worked, most of whose representatives could not be said to be either affluent or socially prestigious. Martha Robinson thus did not display any particular elitism in peopling the nonpartisan women's political group that she constructed. However, examination of the list of the original Woman Citizens' Union officers reveals that of the seventeen officers elected, ten were listed in the New Orleans Social Register for 1927 and four had husbands in the Boston Club. There was a bias in favor of the city's elite women in WCU leadership positions, but it may have resulted from their greater confidence or polish, from friendships they had formed at Newcomb College, or from other benign factors. It is clear that there was no design to exclude women on the basis of class, except insofar as Robinson's invitations went to club women, and women of the working classes were not likely, because of insufficient time, education, confidence, or wardrobe, to belong to clubs. (Predictably, however, there were no efforts made to include African-American women.)

There was an exclusionary policy where partisan politics was concerned. Although Martha Robinson's press release indicated that the New Orleans Federation of Clubs was among those groups participating in the organizational meeting, other records indicate that that group was omitted. Six months after the WCU's organization, women of the New Orleans Federation of Clubs received an invitation to join the Woman Citizens' Union. Significantly, the federation was indelibly identified with the Pilsbury sisters, both of whom were active and had served as its president. The hostile tone of their group's reply to the Woman Citizens' Union's letter is unmistakable. Stating that they were "ignored when [the WCU] was started," their letter closed haughtily, "As we were not considered in the past we certainly [sic] not consider joining now."[34]

With her election as WCU president in June 1934, Martha Gilmore Robinson inaugurated what became a long-standing pattern for her: taking a room in the Heidelberg Hotel in Baton Rouge and monitoring the state legislature consistently during its regular sessions and frequent special sessions, often for weeks at a time with only weekends spent with her family. (She spent so much time at the state capitol that within the family circle she came to be called "the Senator.") Robinson's focus on politics at the state level coincided with, and was no doubt caused to some extent by, the rapidly deteriorating relations between her native New Orleans and Senator Huey Long that summer.

To Huey Long, New Orleans was the enemy. Its vote controlled by the Old Regular faction, which Long was unable to bring to heel, its lawmakers refusing to back Long's bills, New Orleans was an irritant. The summer of 1934 saw virtual siege warfare against the city as Huey Long grimly determined to bring it into submission by whatever means he could employ. His means included transferring power from the city to the state, especially power of appointment, and drastically cutting city revenues while at the same time increasing city appropriations, thus throwing New Orleans into fiscal chaos.

On August 17, 1934, the last day of an extraordinary legislative session, having observed at close range the Long legislative juggernaut in action, Martha Robinson spoke on three New Orleans radio stations in an attempt to rally local women to action. The streets of New Orleans literally echoed with the tramp of armed guardsmen, dispatched by Long in an attempt to intimidate the city, even as bills that authorized enlargement of Long's secret state police and provided for greater control of elections by the governor drew nearer to ratification in the statehouse. Of these measures Long's biographer T. Harry Williams says: "Huey's purpose in proposing these extraordinary laws was all too plain—they could be applied in any area of the state, but they were aimed immediately at the city that was the center of his opposition, New Orleans."[35]

Echoing the frustration felt by most New Orleanians, Robinson demanded, "Isn't the whole state of affairs a sorry mess?" She urged her women listeners, the mothers and homemakers who had the "welfare of the race at heart," who would "always in the end be the ones to safeguard the morality of the future generations," to protest against "this insane strife." She implored them to wire their state senators to voice their opposition to Long's power grab and closed with an appeal once again to mothers: "And you mothers . . . *demand* that the standard of morality you teach in the home shall be the standard which shall govern public life."[36]

Robinson's plea was to no avail; Long's bills swept through committee in little more than an hour, with Long appearing as the only witness. They passed the full legislature easily. Emboldened by this success, only days before the September 1934 election, Long moved two thousand armed National Guardsmen into New Orleans. What use the Kingfish intended to make of the militia no one knew with certainty, but the very visible presence of armed men had the undeniable effect of intimidating prospective voters, particularly women voters who were only recently registered, many of whom had never before voted, and for whom the very act of casting a ballot under such inflammatory conditions was fraught with anxiety. On September 6, 1934, Robinson again took to the airwaves to encourage women to vote despite the threatening atmosphere: "Do not let talk of trouble frighten you away. A woman who conducts herself with dignity and intelligence will never be molested. In fact the presence of such women at the polls acts as a restraint to lawlessness and disorder. This fact should double the obligation upon women to perform their civic duty."[37]

Clearly intending to reassure first-time women voters and clearly displaying her belief in the moral superiority of women, Robinson instructed women on poll procedure that would be unfamiliar and intimidating. She reminded them that they must present their voter registration certificates and poll tax receipts for both 1932 and 1933. She reiterated the laws governing behavior at the polls.[38] Robinson closed her radio talk with a promise that if a woman, alarmed by all the armed men in the city and the near hysteria about the political war between city and state, should want a Woman Citizens' Union member to accompany her to the polls, she had only to ask and such an escort would be provided.

In an earlier age, tactics intended to discourage women voters had included "threats of reprisal . . . crowded or unsuitable polling premises, uncouth behavior by loiterers and even election officials (some of whom puffed smoke in the women's faces) and actual cases of stone-throwing."[39] As an elderly woman, recalling the experience of voting in the Huey Long era, Robinson declared, with pardonable hyperbole, that "scandalous obstacles existed to make it very unpleasant if not dangerous for a woman to vote. The voting places were located wherever the local authority saw fit to put them. Some were in the very homes of the politicos, or in barrooms or brothels."[40] An editorial in a New Orleans newspaper echoed Robinson's charges: "One of the foul-smelling customs of better machine days was that of setting the polling booths in places that were inaccessible, or places where the machine's hirelings could observe the casting of ballots and perhaps conveniently stuff the boxes, or places of such ill repute that persons of decency, sensitiveness and refinement were reluctant to go there."[41] Other women voters of that era have confirmed the charges, recalling that in many areas of the city, a "nice" woman would not go to the polls unless accompanied by her husband or other male relative. Thus, some precincts remained "male" long after women's enfranchisement.[42]

In the tense election of September 1934, Long's candidates won, but the good-government element in New Orleans took heart from the fact that New

Orleans election procedures were beginning to excite press comment in other sections of the country. Avowing that "woman suffrage [had] been a failure as far as any better influence exerted by women in [the] government [was] concerned," Martha Robinson spearheaded efforts to lead women into full participation in the hope that a women's bloc would at last materialize.[43] Embracing the early suffragist ideology that women were innately more moral beings than men, she asserted that women's influence in elections would of necessity have a purifying impact on government.

> The very fact that they [women] are not politically experienced nor politically practical is their greatest asset here. The problems in government which await solutions must not be approached with a political viewpoint. They must be attacked from the moral, the social viewpoint. Women who through the ages have been the guardians of morality in the home, the bulwark of spiritual humanitarianism and cultural causes in the community, it is your influence which is needed in politics today.[44]

As noted earlier in this chapter, the number of white women registered as voters in Orleans Parish spurted upward between 1934 and 1936. The exact numbers (47,966 registered in Orleans Parish in 1934; 70,303 registered in 1936) reflect a 46.6 percent increase in numbers of white women registered, by far the largest increase among women in any single two-year period. The abolition of the poll tax in Louisiana in 1934 undoubtedly led to greater registration for both men and women, but the advent of no-cost voter registration cannot alone account for such a surge in the number of women voters. The gain in white male voters in Orleans Parish between 1934 and 1936 was only 14 percent, for example. Registered black women increased by 21 percent, from 91 in 1934 to 116 in 1936. Numbers of black males registered actually declined by 10 percent in that two-year period (see table 1).[45]

White women were the only group targeted by civic workers for political consciousness-raising at that time; they were the objects of a great effort by the Woman Citizens' Union in the mid-1930s. Data are not available to substantiate a flat assertion that WCU activity caused the increase in women's registration. If voter registration statistics existed for each of the 262 precincts, or even for each of the seventeen wards, and if those figures were broken down by sex, one would expect to see higher registration of women in those wards and precincts in which WCU influence was greatest. Since such a correlation cannot be determined because of the lack of sufficient voter registration information, the relationship between Woman Citizens' Union activity and women's registration remains conjectural. The formation of the Woman Citizens' Union in 1934 was followed by the climb in numbers of white women registered to vote. The striking increase in the number of white women registered to vote in Orleans Parish is almost certainly related to the efforts of WCU members to awaken political consciousness in the women of their city, but definitive proof is lacking. Robinson herself had no doubts about WCU intentions. She wrote to an acquaintance in another state, "I'm kept so busy trying to get women to vote that I'm not worth a darn as a friend."[46]

The members of the Woman Citizens' Union showed keen interest in reforming the structure of government, with emphasis on greater honesty, greater economy, and greater popular participation. Their activities fit handily under the rubric of "municipal housekeeping," the old idea of earlier women's rights advocates that their special mission in life was to purify, reform, and improve men, children, and society. Such a notion found full acceptance with WCU members, many of whom had absorbed parts of this ideology while studying at Newcomb College. Marion Talbot, dean of women at the University of Chicago in the early twentieth century, had articulated the doctrine of "municipal housekeeping" nicely in a 1911 speech: "The home does not stop at the street door. It is as wide as the world into which the individual steps forth. The determination of the character of that world and the preservation of those interests which she has safeguarded in the home, constitute the real duty resting upon women."[47] Robinson's membership appeal for the Woman Citizens' Union echoed Talbot's reasoning.

> The name implies . . . a union of women who are citizens . . . in the sense that they feel their responsibility to their children, their homes, their city, their country, so deeply that they do not shirk the obligation of casting their ballot for what they consider the well-being of their community. . . . [The woman citizen] can best safeguard her pocketbook, her home, her family by using her vote, . . . to vote is not to be "mixed up in politics," but is simply discharging her obligations as a citizen.[48]

Getting women to turn out at the polls in greater numbers meant countering some long-held shibboleths, namely, "A woman's place is in the home" and "Politics is a man's world." Robinson's words indicate that she realized that many women held the view that the mere act of voting could taint them, possibly rendering voting women susceptible to the charge of being "mixed up in politics." Avoiding such a seemingly innocuous charge was not an unreasonable motivation in a state with a lurid political reputation like Louisiana's. Convincing women to vote meant convincing them to enter a realm, politics, which was, almost by definition, corrupt and foul, and thus, by having contact with it, to risk loss of their special womanly purity.

As the 1930s passed, Robinson's group undertook a serious study of election processes and laws in other states, trying to discover a better way than Louisiana's. They obtained books and statistics from the Brookings Institute, the American Bar Association, and the national office of the League of Women Voters. Robinson herself enrolled in a political science course at Tulane, evidence of her developing fascination with government. The sight of a middle-aged woman in a class of adolescent students excited comment in 1934; her own daughter that semester was a senior at Newcomb. Robinson, undaunted, plunged into the study of local government. In her class notes she wrote: "The idea that when women got the ballot politics would be played on a higher plane and candidates would have to measure up to better standards has not worked out."[49]

The Woman Citizens' Union addressed issues of civic concern throughout its eight-year existence. The group gained a widespread community reputation for effectiveness in achieving its goals. One admirer of its work commented with feeling, "If that bunch of women ever got after me, I'd leave town!"[50] The members interested themselves in an array of progressive issues, among them campaigns to raise the low marriage age in the state, to lower the maternal mortality rate, to combat juvenile delinquency, to adopt child labor and wage and hour laws, and to professionalize the local library system and remove it from political control.

The members of the Woman Citizens' Union reserved their greatest interest and efforts for two issues long dear to progressives: election reforms and civil service laws. The election of Sam Houston Jones to the governorship in 1940 seemed to herald a new era in Louisiana politics. A large segment of the public, reacting to scathing national press coverage about "the Louisiana hayride" and stung by revelations of graft and corruption among Huey Long's inheritors, demanded reforms. The prevailing mood in Louisiana encouraged sweeping changes in state laws and an end to a system that throughout the 1930s had seemed permanently entrenched in the Bayou State. In the momentary revulsion against Longism's excesses, Jones, the darling of the reform element in New Orleans, was able to keep his promises to bring change.

In the first year of its existence, the Woman Citizens' Union had drafted eight proposals for election reform. Prompted by members' vivid experiences as poll watchers and commissioners, the WCU recommended permanent voter registration, the use of public buildings for polling places, requirements for voters to sign a roster at the polls for comparison with a previous signature, and changes in the selection of the registrar of voters in Orleans Parish. It also urged equal representation for all factions in regard to election commissioners, the use of voting machines, restrictions on behavior of police at polls, and poll tax repeal.[51] The women kept up consistent pressure for these measures, seizing every opportunity to educate the voting public on their desirability. Although they found their campaign rough sledding during the unsympathetic Long years, in 1940, the first year of Jones's governorship, the public mood had changed. After the regular legislative session of that year, all but one of the measures they advocated stood as the law of Louisiana, part of the "landslide of administrative and political reform" that lawmakers produced.[52]

The undeniable effect of instituting these changes would be broader participation in elections and a larger vote, goals that departed from the often conservative mainstream of much of progressive reform. In the past, when municipal reformers had dealt with the issue of voter registration at all, they had often favored measures to shrink the pool of eligible voters. The efforts of Robinson and the WCU to broaden the electorate reveal a faith in humanity sometimes lacking in other reformers of the middle and upper classes. These women intended to defeat the machine not by denying some groups the right to vote but by enlisting previously uninvolved citizens and educating them on civic matters. It is true that as the Women's Division of the Honest Election League, these women had helped to identify fraudulently registered voters and to remove them from the rolls. This exercise in reducing the electorate seems less than a purge, however, in light of machine conditions in New Orleans. In fact, the WCU members spent the bulk of their energies not on excluding citizens from the political process but on bringing more New Orleanians, especially women, into political participation.

When New Orleans officials predictably balked at the required use of voting machines in future elections, Robinson and the Woman Citizens' Union mounted a campaign to force implementation of the voting machine law. They picketed Mayor Robert Maestri's office, carrying signs that read, "A Vote Uncounted Is a No-Count Vote—Voting Machines Count 'Em!" and "Voting Machines for Democratic Defense on the Home Front." Shortly thereafter, the reluctant mayor acquiesced and acquired five hundred voting machines for the city. The mayoral contest of January 1942 saw the first use of the new devices in a New Orleans election.[53]

No doubt because voting in corner groceries and neighborhood pool halls had been personally distasteful to women, who disliked encounters with loiterers spending election day on the often filthy premises, the women of the WCU had made special efforts to gain passage of Act 46, regulating the location and administration of polling places. Section 54 of this bill, pertinent only to cities of more than two hundred thousand, meaning New Orleans alone, stipulated that polling places be placed in public schools within the several precincts wherever there was a public school in the precinct. It further stipulated that no liquor could be sold on election days within one mile of any polling place, that police officers, previously a source of trouble, would no longer be assigned to polling places, and that secrecy in voting would be maintained.[54]

The Woman Citizens' Union circulated a petition of support for Act 46 and cited reasons for backing the change. Voting in public schools would "prevent the abuses made easy by the use of private dwellings" and "result in considerable financial savings." Furthermore, the advent of bulky voting machines would render it impractical to continue to vote in cramped tin garages and corner groceries. Not surprisingly, however, their strongest appeal centered on the welfare of their children: "But over and above these practical considerations, the women feel that our children must be made to respect governmental institutions so it behooves us to see that the ritual democratic process of free balloting is conducted in a manner that merits respect."[55] The women found particularly amusing their opponents' weak arguments that elections were unsuitable for children to observe, being, like sausages, something that ordinary citizens should not see being made, and that citizens might be unable to find their way to the public school in their neighborhood.

The passage of Act 46, the election reform law, in June 1940 was particularly gratifying to the WCU membership. From Baton Rouge, where she was, as usual, on hand for the session, Martha Robinson penned a postcard to her cousin. "I am spending lots of time up here protecting 'Democrácy'—happily an easier task now in La."[56]

The second area of Woman Citizens' Union interest centered on a civil service law. In common with most municipal reformers, WCU members saw civil service as democracy's cure. The argument that nonpartisan civil service would flush out spoilsmen and infuse government with honest, disinterested, competent civil servants persuaded them that their goal of seeing good individuals in office could best be won via civil service reform.[57]

Louisiana had had some previous but wholly unsatisfactory experience with civil service. Huey Long had instituted so-called civil service laws, but these were merely devices Long manipulated skillfully to centralize and control state and local bureaucracies. Long mastered the art of patronage dispensation fully, aided by the Great Depression's boost of the value of a state job. For years, those on Long's state payroll were expected to deliver votes for Huey's slate in every election (the usual rule of thumb being "count the payroll boys and multiply by five"), to help get out the vote, and to contribute money monthly to the "de-duct" box as a condition of employment. Forced campaign contributions via set percentage deductions from wages and salaries and mandatory employee political activities were the norm for Louisiana civil servants, who were never allowed to forget their dependence.[58]

To free the city and state from this sort of machine politics became a WCU aim. As early as 1936, members were on record as having interest in civil service laws. "A group of splendid ladies, headed by Mrs. R.G. Robinson, is very anxious to undertake a long, steady and militant campaign for civil service," wrote a male reformer that year, adding, "This group has had considerable experience in dealing with public affairs and getting accomplishments."[59]

In the avalanche of reforms that Sam Jones's election brought, lawmakers adopted a genuine civil service law, drafted by New Orleanian Charles E. Dunbar Jr. A resident of the city's fashionable university section, Dunbar readily enlisted the help of the Woman Citizens' Union, to which his wife Ethelynn belonged. The WCU responded with a public education campaign designed to reach women and convince them of the value of the merit system. Employing household analogies, they reasoned that no housewife would choose a plumber because of the way he voted and then stressed the absurdity of Louisiana choosing highway contractors or hospital employees on such a basis. They devoted countless unpaid hours to addressing and mailing carefully crafted circulars that advocated the civil service measure. In November 1940, the voters ratified the constitutional amendment by a vote of two to one.[60]

When the resurgent Long movement attacked the civil service law in 1941, Martha Robinson and other WCU members journeyed to Baton Rouge to appear at hearings at which the law's constitutionality was challenged. Robinson testified in favor of the civil service law and noted that it provided young women with "the prospect of making themselves a part of the government in honorable careers in public service." She further stated, "We simply cannot let any destructive force interfere with this advancement."[61]

In the civil service fight of 1940, the Woman Citizens' Union of New Orleans enjoyed fruitful cooperation with the Baton Rouge League of Women Voters, led by a former New Orleanian, Emily Price (Mrs. Paul) Blanchard. The two organizations coordinated public education measures, radio talks, and lobbying efforts. Records reveal that Robinson had entered into a correspondence with the National League of Women Voters in 1938 with an eye toward negotiating affiliation of the extant Woman Citizens' Union with the league as its New Orleans chapter, replacing the now defunct and discredited NOLWV.

Subsequent internal memos at the national office made it clear that the NLWV was not inclined to risk another fiasco in Louisiana and intended to grant recognition to a provisional League of Women Voters chapter in New Orleans only upon absolute assurance that the chapter could, as one memo put it, "cultivate the right people in Louisiana."⁶² For Martha Gilmore Robinson to win NLWV approval for the Woman Citizens' Union to affiliate with the League of Women Voters would require proof of her group's solid nonpartisan outlook and seriousness of purpose. The NLWV rules permitted recognition of a state league organization when three functioning LWV chapters existed in the state, with a total of one hundred league members. Robinson and Blanchard had fixed their eyes on a distant goal: *if* the WCU in New Orleans could become a league chapter, and *if* they could stimulate sufficient interest in the league somewhere in Louisiana so that another group of women would form a league chapter, then these two chapters could join with the existing league chapter in Baton Rouge to apply for membership status as the Louisiana League of Women Voters. Very likely, Robinson and Blanchard, both ambitious and strong willed, devoted a bit of thought to who might serve as its first statewide president.

Robinson's way was sometimes to make haste too quickly, but the national office counseled slow progress. No doubt perplexed or even revolted by the lurid political situation in Louisiana, national officers among themselves questioned "whether or not there [was] any ground for believing that a LWV with its nonpartisan purpose could succeed in Louisiana."⁶³ In the wake of disappointment with the limited accomplishments of reform governor Sam Jones, Emily Blanchard wrote optimistically to the national office to plead for faith in a Louisiana league's ability to attract women willing to approach activism from a nonpartisan standpoint. "The 'reform' women in Louisiana have no party now," she explained, "and they will begin to grope for group expression that will be independent and possibly more effective."⁶⁴

The national office correctly perceived that the Woman Citizens' Union had come into existence representing a strong antiadministration bias in the last turbulent years of Huey Long. Although receiving letters testifying to the integrity and ability of the women in the WCU (one observer called them "a group of fine-calibred women representing the best of New Orleans"), and particularly of Martha Robinson as leader ("unquestioned position in New Orleans . . . has done many good things . . . has a personal following"), the national office was frankly suspicious.⁶⁵ Having ousted the old New Orleans League of Women Voters for its blatant proadministration activities, the national league worried that it now ran a risk of welcoming a new chapter tainted with the brush of another political tinge. National League of Women Voters president Marguerite Wells explained that previous attempts at incorporating existing women's associations that pledged to transform themselves into league chapters had not succeeded: "Members who had entered an organization for one or certain specified purposes or were wedded to certain methods were not always equally interested in the new purpose or at home in the new methods of the League of Women Voters.... I have reason to be fearful of success when an attempt is made to consolidate an old organization with a new one."[66]

Although Emily Blanchard avowed that the WCU had been behaving like a league chapter and was "very active in the prosecution of the League program actually," the NLWV flatly doubted the ability of any group of politically aware and interested New Orleans women to function without partisanship.[67] Indeed, nonpartisanship was a scarce commodity in Louisiana.

Ultimately it required a four-year sequence of events, which included earnest pledges of good faith from the Woman Citizens' Union, more testimonials on its behalf, delicate negotiations by mail, and another visit of inspection from a national staff member, before the Woman Citizens' Union was at last allowed to vote itself out of existence in October 1942 and to be reconstituted as the New Orleans League of Women Voters. It received provisional affiliation with the respected National League of Women Voters, with full recognition and affiliation contingent upon the organization's conduct during the first six months of its existence.

Creation of another fledgling LWV in Monroe, Louisiana, meant that three chapters existed, with the requisite total of one hundred members, and thus there could be a Louisiana League of Women Voters, just as Martha Robinson and Emily Blanchard had desired. Although each had insisted that the other should head the new state league, neither did in the end. In October 1942, when Helen Semmerling from the NLWV came to the state to officiate at the birth of the Louisiana league, Martha Robinson was recuperating from gall bladder surgery and "not inclined to be too strenuous." Semmerling observed that she had "serious qualms about Mrs. Blanchard's sincerity and devotion to the methods of the LWV." "I think she is a more serious obstacle to the league's success than is Mrs. Robinson. Mrs. Robinson will lay her cards on the table pretty much whereas Mrs. Blanchard is crafty and wily." A young professor of psychology at Louisiana State University, Ruth Hamill Preston, took the presidency of the new state body, rather than one of "these high-powered women," to Semmerling's evident relief.[68] Martha Robinson accepted the presidency of the New Orleans chapter.

As a world war and the discouragingly familiar brand of politics as usual swirled around them, New Orleans women prepared to launch a strictly nonpartisan organization with ties to a respected national body. The core of the League of Women Voters philosophy was its belief in representative government and the reponsibility of individual citizens to be active and informed participants in the democratic process. In clear distinction to most male political groups, the league's agenda was issue oriented, its pace was deliberate, with months of study preceding any league position, and its enthusiasms involved principles and policies but never candidates. The national office was understandably concerned over whether a body so constituted could succeed in the inhospitable political climate of Louisiana.

The earliest years of the New Orleans League of Women Voters coincided with World War II. From that fateful Sunday afternoon in December 1941 when passersby had observed wisps of smoke curling upward from the Japanese Consulate on St. Charles Avenue, as the consular staff destroyed all records there, the war figured prominently in the life of New Orleans. The local Higgins shipyards hired thousands of area workers, many of them women, and received more than seven hundred million dollars in war contracts. Military installations in the area hummed with activity. The city experienced a 20 percent population increase in 1942 alone, and the growth continued throughout the war.[69] Rationing affected virtually every consumer, but particularly women, who traditionally shopped for the family needs. Indeed, World War II forced New Orleans women to consider public affairs at every level. Martha Gilmore Robinson's war experiences were a microcosm of much that happened to American women in those years. One by one, her four sons entered the armed forces, and all saw duty overseas. The four blue stars in her window were a source of pride, yet her anxiety clearly was great, especially by 1945 when all four sons were at or near the fighting and she knew the war was virtually at an end. Writing in the "Robinson Home Journal," her family newsletter, of which she made multiple carbon copies for circulation, she informed readers that son Jack had been wounded in the South Pacific, and then she admonished all her sons: "Your father and I would very much rather know you were wounded, even seriously, than to have to face uncertainty. . . . Pater and I can take any news. We are not sissies."[70]

Later in 1944, Robinson unburdened herself to Natalie Scott, her closest friend from Newcomb College days. With one son in an engineering corps in France, another flying Thunderbolts in Italy, and another still in the Pacific, her anxiety was very great. "If only I could go to sleep and wake up to find the war over and the boys home. The strain is telling on me." On Mother's Day, 1945, her "Robinson Home Journal" spoke to her boys: "And all day, as indeed most every day, I will be thinking of you and wishing I had you safe in this battered old white house, being able to feed you a good old time meal."[71]

Robinson, a staunch Anglophile, had no doubts about the United States' entry into the war. Even before Pearl Harbor, she was one of several citizens, and the only woman, to address a community mass meeting on the need for "all aid short of war," scorning the "propaganda of isolationist groups" and telling her audience that they should all "be grateful for the chance to sacrifice and help" the British. She fully supported U.S. participation and launched strenuous efforts to do her part for victory; she raised considerable sums for British war relief via an organization called the Silver Thimble League, for which she received the Order of the British Empire after the war, and spoke often at blood drives and bond rallies. Having all four sons in uniform, even though the youngest was only eighteen, pleased her. She noted, "There are no safe places in this war—at least not for men determined to do their share, and I am proud to say that my sons are in this class." Despite the horrible human and financial costs of the war, never at any time did Robinson evince a wavering in her thorough support for the Allied effort.[72]

Scarcities affected everyone, but Robinson felt strongly that all Americans should abide by the rationing guidelines of the Office of Price Administration. Black market buying infuriated her, as did signs of profiteering and tax evasion among her prosperous friends. Even a seemingly innocuous advertisement for hats at a local department store triggered a patriotic response. Writing to her boys about the "wicked and unpatriotic prices," she promised to clip the offending ad and send it to the head of the Senate Banking and Currency Committee, who had been "so vocal in the press about the American people not being able to pay taxes such as the administration ha[d] asked." She favored higher taxes "to pay as much as possible of this war from its profits and not leave the whole debt to [the] boys who . . . fought it." In June 1944, she personally wrote to 115 newspaper editors to urge action "to hold the line in price control."[73]

Robinson cultivated a victory garden and reported regularly on its progress to her offspring. "You boys can know that your family is behind you doing all it can to get this war over with. If you saw us working in the victory garden you would feel proud of your old parents. I enclose snaps of this touching scene," she wrote with self-deprecating humor. She reserved a portion of each Sunday to putter in the garden, noting, "Mother earth always restores me."[74]

Rationing, which caused such irritation for many, seemed to cause no undue problems for Robinson. She managed her household smoothly without the usual supplies and indeed seemed to take a positive delight in making do. Her husband, however, never ceased to grumble over scarcities and never adapted to dietary substitutes. "Peanut butter and brown bread or red beans & rice, with an occasional oyster, keeps me happy, but R.G. [her husband] damns the Democrats and goes on something terrible."[75]

Franklin Roosevelt and his administration had become by the war years a source of serious friction between husband and wife in the Robinson household. Like countless successful businessmen, R. G. Robinson had rejected the New Deal as an overextension of government. By the 1940s, his scorn for Roosevelt led him to blame the president for virtually every inconvenience in his life.

As opportunities in war work opened for blacks, domestic help grew scarcer. Martha Robinson found herself advertising for someone to help the elderly servant who had worked for her for more than thirty years, but she had no luck in keeping a maid. "Pater has gotten so crusty because of his F.D.R. hate that he tries to pick quarrels with me all the time. Says they [black domestics] must all belong to the Eleanor Club. Poor dinks, of course they are taking advantage of the situation as all humans would and do do under the circumstances."[76]

Robinson's reference to Eleanor Clubs brings up an interesting point. White southerners experienced profound uneasiness and frustration over blacks' rising expectations in the 1940s, made possible by employment opportunities in war industries and a growing racial pride and assertiveness. Often they reacted by starting or perpetuating fantastic rumors of disturbances, plots, riots, even a sinister rise in sales of ice picks. Whites self-consciously lowered their voices when black servants were near and whispered in horror their versions of stories concerning bloodshed to come.[77] New Orleanian Edith Stern, daughter of Sears, Roebuck multimillionaire Julius Rosenwald, reported that of all the rumors swirling through New Orleans, the hardest to die was the one concerning Eleanor Clubs, a name bestowed in bitter mockery at Eleanor Roosevelt, who was seen in the South as champion of the Negro cause. Eleanor Clubs, sometimes called Disappointing Clubs because black domestics would disappoint white employers by not showing up for work, represented whites' belief in a black conspiracy to force higher wages and better working conditions for domestics. Stern wrote, "It's hard for the housewives who lose their Negro servants to believe that the reason can be merely the higher wages offered by war industry. Surely housewives often think there must be some sinister organization making dear old faithful Annie act that way!"[78] Robinson seemed to have no difficulty in realizing that economic opportunity explained the dearth of domestic workers in wartime New Orleans, but her husband stoutly maintained his belief in Eleanor Clubs and his conviction that the Roosevelts were somehow to blame.[79]

Martha Robinson's view of the political situation rested in part on her belief in the programs of the New Deal and in part on her utter rejection of what she saw as the Republicans' class prejudice. An incident at a gathering of family and friends, hosted by her son-in-law's wealthy and conservative parents, illustrates the latter.

> I suppose Old Plater [her daughter's father-in-law] thought that Hecht [Rudolph Hecht, president of New Orleans's Hibernia Bank] being a banker, would be for Dewey, so he started the day off auspiciously by remarking that only the "rabble" were voting for Roosevelt. I couldn't resist.... My quick tongue said, "Well, you have three of the rabble at the table with you, as Mr. and Mrs. H. and I all are." You should have seen the old man. He looked as if he wanted to get under the table. But it served him right. That is the typical viewpoint of the bulk of the Republicans, they feel that they are the "elect."[80]

Through the fall of 1944, her domestic disharmony increased. She longed to invite some old friends to dinner but knew she could not have them around her husband: "They are for F.D.R. and he is now savage in his attitude." His irascibility led her to worry that he might be ill, but he blamed it "all on the New Deal" and took it out on her. Finally, she achieved a wry and detached outlook toward his fury. "Our domestic situation is serene. R.G.R. is not yet speaking to me but I ignore that.... R.G. says that if F.D.R. wins he is moving to Guatemala [where his lumber company had business interests]. Sounds like the Tories in 1776. But you will find me ... with my arms and heart open to you," she told her soldier sons.[81]

Roosevelt's win over Dewey did not put an end to the issue. Three months after the election, Robinson wrote, "R.G. is still in deep gloom. He won't talk of anything but the Roosevelt dog and children. You would think I was responsible for them!"[82] That Robinson hoped her sons would somehow develop a broader worldview and more liberal outlook than their father displayed is clear from her letters. "I don't want you boys to be like the narrow minded, ignorant reactionary people in this state. We are in a great social revolution. Whether you like it or not the world can never be the same," she wrote in 1944. After the war, she confided to Natalie Scott, "I hope to have one of my sons with a viewpoint broader and more constructive than the prevailing Business Viewpoint. God save us all."[83]

The Second World War altered Martha Robinson's world drastically, though she never worked on an assembly line or lost a family member. The war years accelerated the pace of personal changes begun by her involvement in the Woman Citizens' Union and saw her transformation into a bona fide public figure in New Orleans. She had honed her speaking talents, her public relations skills, and her organizational abilities while leading the WCU. The days and weeks of monitoring the legislature in Baton Rouge convinced her that she could function superbly on her own, neither seeking nor needing spousal intervention in her causes. She spoke often in public, kept up a voluminous correspondence with friends as well as officials, and gave regular interviews to the local press, all the while maintaining a smoothly running household and meeting the social obligations incumbent upon one of her status in New Orleans. In the press, in her official correspondence, and probably in her own mind, she was not Mrs. R. G. Robinson; she was Martha Gilmore Robinson, at a time when few women of her class in New Orleans styled themselves as anything but extensions of their husbands.

By the war years, Robinson's home was an empty nest, with all her children either married, in college, in uniform, or at boarding school. She acted increasingly as a free agent, going her own way. Some of the material in the "Robinson Home Journal" reveals the emotional distance separating her from her husband by this time; their philosophies on government, business, foreign affairs, race relations, and even pleasure differed wildly. While on an ancestor-tracing expedition to Georgia, she wrote to her family as she prepared to return home, "I think you do not miss me and I know I will not like football and frats any more than you like genealogy." On another extended trip by herself, she evidently felt twinges of guilt and sought to justify herself. "When I get home from this trip I'll not wander away again until June, tho I must say I rest so well when I am away." Again, to her mother, she confided, "Really I am glad to be by myself. I want to collect my thoughts and take a mental rest before descending into the maelstrom that I know I will get mixed up with in New Orleans." Her daughter recalled that Robinson for years suffered with chronic headaches, no doubt stress related. Her pains fitted into a pattern: acute headaches when she was at home and total relief when she traveled beyond New Orleans.[84]

When at home, Robinson wrapped herself more and more in work, rarely seeing friends in purely social settings. Her husband's clear preference for conservative companions disappointed her. She caustically characterized one, the brother of her friend Hilda Phelps Hammond, as having "atrophied into a Bourbon, pickled mostly in Scotch." By the war's end, exhausted by the demands of dealing with her often difficult husband and caring for her ailing mother, in whose room she slept every night, Robinson mused about peace and quiet and described her ideal retirement. "In my old age I'd like to live in the country with a typewriter and an auto and Leila [her servant of thirty years' employment]." Her scenario, while allowing for communication, mobility, and creature comforts, significantly did not mention her husband.[85]

During these years, many New Orleans women busied themselves with "war work," blood drives, scrap collection, Red Cross service.[86] In Martha

Robinson's scheme of things, involvement with the League of Women Voters qualified as "war work." The league's battle to educate the New Orleans citizenry on issues became intertwined in her rhetoric and ideology with the worldwide battle against fascism. She announced a league meeting in the summer of 1943 in a handbill that read, "It's HOT in New Orleans. But not as hot as in Sicily.... Not as hot as in New Guinea. Our boys are fighting there. We must keep working here." When members voted to cancel a summer meeting, Robinson scolded, "When one's sons are fighting through the terrors of the Pacific, in mud and heat unbelievable, it is enough to get under one's skin to have people here take a recess on account of the 'summer heat.'"[87]

By the middle of the war, the fledgling New Orleans League of Women Voters boasted a membership of eighty local women, chiefly from the "silk stocking" district, near the universities or in the Garden District. Indeed, Robinson had gone to some pains to get "the right sort" recruited for the league. She contacted Rosa Freeman Keller, daughter of the wealthy, socially prominent Freeman family, via a long-distance telephone call to Texas, where Keller's husband was stationed with the military. Robinson announced that she expected Keller to join, even though she did not live in Louisiana. Keller, a military wife and the busy mother of three young children, reacted in a way that was indicative of Robinson's standing in the community. "In this setting, a women's good government group was possibly the last place where I might have thought of expending my energies," she recalled. "But tell Mrs. Robinson no—unthinkable, so I sat down immediately and sent my check."[88] (However, the true enthusiasm of the members for their LWV affiliation is somewhat uncertain, since Robinson later confessed that, in her zeal to get enough members for a provisional state League of Women Voters, she had paid the dues for as many as eighty Woman Citizens' Union members and did not know how many were genuinely interested in league work.)[89]

At this time, the general milieu in Louisiana was such that most citizens viewed nearly every group as either for or against the incumbent government; only the most innocuous, such as garden clubs and missionary societies, could escape this suspicion of partisanship. The mere fact that Huey Long was in the grave, some of his cronies in prison, and a self-styled reform administration in office did not erase the ancient tradition of venality in Louisiana. Because the original New Orleans League of Women Voters had been overt in its support of the city machine, many locals identified the successor league as a partisan organization as well. The national office too had shared this doubt about the New Orleans league. Fully two years after its formation, the author of a report on conditions in the New Orleans league noted that local women seemed to focus on the person to do a job rather than on methods for getting the job done and commented, "It is extremely difficult for persons to be active politically and still feel that in the League of Women Voters they might find a common meeting ground on which they can attack problems of government in a nonpartisan way."[90]

In order to make headway with their projects, it was imperative that League of Women Voters members combat this belief in an all-pervading partisanship. Their persistent efforts wrung praise from the editor of one city daily, who observed, "To those steeped in Louisiana's hectic political history, the existence of an organization deeply interested in governmental affairs yet without an axe to grind or favorite son to put in office is rare indeed."[91] Despite this editorial and others like it, the local LWV had always to stress its impartiality and disinterested stance to the somewhat skeptical New Orleans citizenry.

Robinson and the New Orleans League of Women Voters associated local machine politics and corruption with fascist conditions abroad and sought to rouse the local citizenry, particularly the female citizenry, with images of a battle of good versus evil. The league's most sustained project of the war years targeted voter registration, especially registration of women, even though Robinson was far from sanguine about women's affinity for politics. Like most of the female reading public, she had seen the pessimistic articles that appeared in 1930 on the tenth anniversary of passage of the Nineteenth Amendment. They labeled woman suffrage a failure, because a mere ten years of women voting had not yet reformed the world into a utopian community! In the 1940s, Robinson was fond of saying that more than twenty years of the ballot had not seriously challenged the view that politics was a man's world, among southern women in particular. Studies support her opinion.[92]

Nationally, women voters outnumbered men for the first time in November 1942. A Gallup poll taken in the summer of 1943 predicted that between seven and eleven million men in service would fail to cast absentee ballots, thus rendering women the majority of voters again in 1944. Inaugurating the New Orleans league's voter registration drive, Martha Robinson told the press, "The League believes that ballots on the home front are as vital as bullets on the firing line. We must preserve at home the democracy we fight for abroad."[93]

Traditionally, a city machine through its precinct leaders saw to it that citizens linked in any way to the machine registered to vote. In return for cutting through the red tape of city government and doling out small political jobs, the machine garnered strong support at the polls from those who called it friend. This ability to deliver votes was basic to the success of the machine.

Thus, an increase in registered voters ran exactly counter to the machine's interests. The smaller the electorate, the more easily the machine ward leaders could assure an election's outcome, for they knew with practiced accuracy the total of votes they controlled. As one politically active woman put it, "That's the way the Old Regulars were—the harder it was to vote, the better they liked it!"[94]

The state League of Women Voters adopted voter registration as its special wartime project, but politicians displayed a decided coolness toward the idea of getting more voters on the rolls. Their tepid response rested on two basic Louisiana premises: first, that a small electorate benefits the incumbent, and second, that nothing should be done to risk even an infinitesimal increase in black voter registration.[95]

When the New Orleans league undertook a voter registration drive, it targeted no specific neighborhoods and no particular class. Instead, league members conducted an exhaustive canvass of the entire city, house to house, to identify unregistered individuals and distributed pledge cards that read, "To take the place of a voter gone to war, I promise to register at once and do my part as an American citizen by taking an active interest in government and voting in elections." They did, however, bypass black neighborhoods and made no effort to boost black voter registration.[96]

Between 1942 and 1944, the years of the league registration drive, the number of women registered to vote in Orleans Parish increased modestly. The exact gain, 6 percent, reflected a climb from 73,587 to 78,110.[97] Registering several thousand women voters constituted only half the battle, however. Persuading them actually to exercise the vote and not to succumb to the traditional Louisiana viewpoint—"politics is a dirty business and ladies shouldn't get mixed up in it"—was the other half. Among first-time women voters, "for females to vote at all required a substantial break from their conventional role. To ask that they oppose their husbands or fathers in the process entailed a commitment which only the most dedicated could sustain."[98]

It was this viewpoint that Martha Robinson, a skillful speaker animated by a strong ethos of personal responsibility, strove to change. She was fond of citing Lincoln Steffens, who wrote in *The Shame of the Cities*, "The misgovernment of the American people is misgovernment *by* the American people.... Are the people honest? ... Isn't corrupt government after all representative? ... The people are not innocent."[99] Through public speeches to civic groups and schoolgirls, and in many radio addresses during the war, Robinson hammered home the point. "Ask yourself—Why is politics a dirty business? Why should the business of managing the most idealistic form of government the world has ever known be a dirty business? Ask yourself—Is it any fault of mine? Could I do anything about it? Is it my business? Yes, it is your business—your most pressing and immediate business. . . . There is nothing that touches your home, your family that is not touched by politics. It is up to you to see that politics is clean."[100]

Jury service for women was another project undertaken by the NOLWV but one that local judges and the jury commissioner rebuffed. Amid a flurry of press stories lamenting the wartime manpower shortage and imploring women to do their part, league members contacted judges to offer their services as jurors and polled the magistrates to discover their feelings about women in the jury box. They were disappointed when only one judge welcomed them with enthusiasm. Another was distinctly cool to the idea, and the remainder did not even deign to respond to their questionnaire. Thus rebuffed, league members dropped the issue; not until 1949 did a woman serve on a Louisiana jury in a criminal case.[101]

During the war and in the years immediately after, the League of Women Voters attained great stature in New Orleans. Members frequently presented educational programs on radio, and their activities drew positive media attention.[102] Robinson, presumably aided by her position at the pinnacle of New Orleans society, consistently received generous coverage. The league's patrols of precincts to check for violations of election law earned respect from political figures, because, after meticulous inspections and record keeping, Robinson was certain to inform reporters of specific violations uncovered by league members. Not content with merely documenting illegalities at the polls, Robinson provided the names and addresses of buildings that should have served as polling places under the law and of bars that remained open in violation.[103]

A 1944 election revealed the effectiveness of league members' diligence. Obtaining a list of polling places one month before elections, they checked each address, 262 places in all, and found that two were "in objectionable neighborhoods" and three were "illegally selected." Robinson then penned a gracious note to the chairman of the parish Democratic Executive Committee. "We cannot believe that your committee is deliberately violating the law, nor that it desires to flout public opinion by placing polls in neighborhoods where women citizens are reluctant to go," she wrote in informing them of the league's findings.

When this ladylike remonstrance brought no assurances of action, Robinson escalated the league's involvement by requesting police protection for league members who planned to picket the offending polls. The gentlemen of city hall surrendered rather than face women on the picket line and endure the negative press coverage that was sure to result; the league won its point and the polling places were moved to more acceptable buildings.[104]

Robinson excelled at garnering publicity for the league's activities, usually managing to attract coverage once a week in the local press. Answering a national league questionnaire that asked if newsworthy LWV stories were ever relegated to the women's page, she wrote candidly, "Not if it is given to city editor and you know him." In New Orleans, the daily newspapers unanimously praised Robinson and the League of Women Voters for their work. An editorial, "Woman Has the Answer," mused that if women voted in numbers, government would be safe from "the elements that [had] debased, disgraced and plundered" Louisiana. "Many women would stand against this even against the influence of their men." Mentioning Robinson and the LWV by name, it urged readers to help them "to get Louisiana's womanhood to take its rightful place and exert the influence . . . proper to it."[105]

Calling Robinson "a fearless, sane and sensible leader" whose plans would "mean a greater and a happier Louisiana," another editor opined: "More and more, the women are taking a dominant part in the affairs of our state. . . . The day of the racketeer seems doomed. It may take a long time, but never again will the kind of machine politics Louisiana once cowered under be able to crush our people and entrench itself in government."[106] Yet another editorial stated explicitly the effect of the increased voter registration and the reason for political opposition to it, noting that the league's registration drive was "increasing the ranks of independent voters who [stood] out in bold contrast to voters hidebound by party and shackled by machine."[107]

In 1944, Martha Robinson assumed the presidency of the state League of Women Voters, a post that gave her wider visibility. Because the National League of Women Voters advocated education of the electorate on the necessity of adequate postwar planning and supported U.S. participation in a United Nations organization, Robinson undertook tours around the state to argue for international cooperation after the war. In New Orleans, league members studied the Dumbarton Oaks proposals, the Atomic Energy Commission, the United Nations plan, and various trade bills, all traditionally terra incognita for women. Their foray into foreign policy and defense issues was sufficient to raise male eyebrows in amusement or dismay, as this editorial about the local league makes clear: "If a determined looking woman, with the light of a crusader in her eyes, walks up to you, a perfect stranger, and begins discussing international affairs, don't get alarmed. . . . They discuss present problems and postwar problems with taxi drivers, elevator tenders, manicurists; with doctors, lawyers, policemen."[108]

Kate and Jean Gordon, c. 1890.
Courtesy of Jacob D. Dresner Collection, Manuscripts Department, Howard-Tilton Memorial Library, Tulane University, New Orleans.

Huey Long gives instructions to a compliant legislator, c. 1930.
Courtesy of Leon C. Trice Collection, Manuscripts Division, Howard-Tilton Memorial Library, Tulane University, New Orleans

A disheveled Long embraces cronies, 1935.
Louisiana Division, New Orleans Public Library

Hilda Phelps Hammond addresses members of the U.S. Senate Investigating Committee, November 1933, as members of the Women's Committee of Louisiana look on.
New Orleans Times-Picayune

Martha Gilmore Robinson

Three League of Women Voters members picket Mayor Bob Maestri's office in favor of voting machines, 1941. Martha Gilmore Robinson carries sign "A Vote Uncounted Is a No-Count Vote—Voting Machines Count 'Em!" The other two women's signs read "Voting Machines for Democratic Defense on the Home Front" and "We Want Voting Machines—We Demand Voting Machines."
New Orleans Times-Picayune

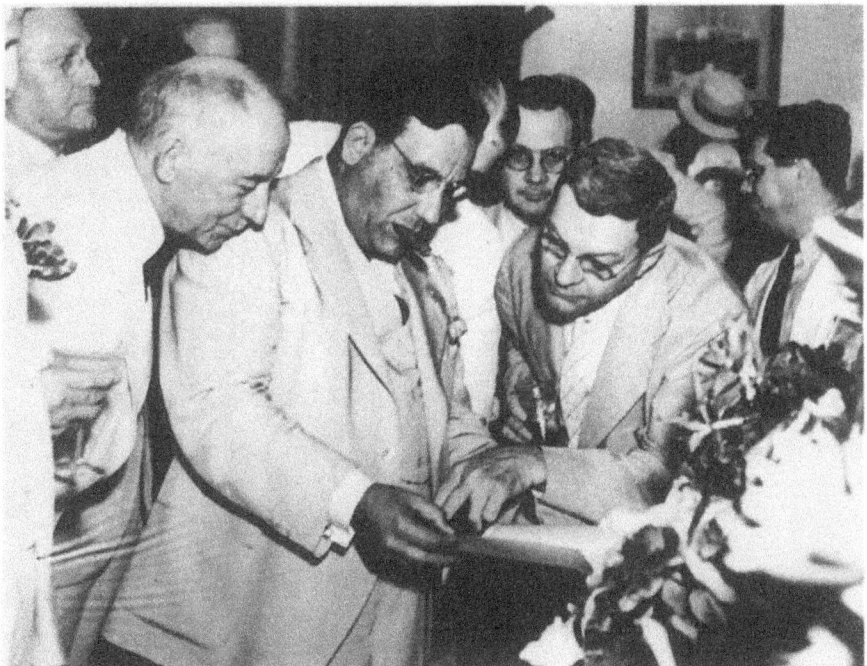

(Above) Emily Blanchard campaigning with Henry Wallace in New Orleans, 1948. *Courtesy of Mrs. Carver Blanchard*

(Below) Mayor Robert Maestri, with cigar, looks the part of a city boss in this undated photo, c. 1940. *Louisiana Division, New Orleans Public Library*

A recently married Mary and Jacob Morrison, New Orleans, 1938. *Courtesy of Mary Morrison*

July Breazeale Waters, c. 1950. *Courtesy of Mrs. Harcourt Waters*

Anti-Longs All: Three big names in New Orleans politics.
Left to right: deLesseps "Chep" Morrison, Corinne "Lindy" Boggs, Hale Boggs. (Morrison had just been reelected as mayor at the time this photo was snapped [1950], and Hale Boggs was serving in the U.S. House of Representatives. In 1971, upon Hale Boggs's disappearance in a plane crash in Alaska, Lindy Boggs replaced him in Congress, from which post she served her New Orleans district until 1990.) *Louisiana Division, New Orleans Public Library*

Mayor Chep Morrison with "cooperator" Vic Schiro, 1961. *Photo by J. R. St. Julien. Louisiana Division, New Orleans Public Library*

Rosa Freeman Keller, on the program honoring her for eighteen years of service as chair of the board of administrators at Flint-Goodridge Hospital, 1971. *Louisiana Division, New Orleans Public Library*

The southern preoccupation with race presented the league with problems during the 1940s. The New Orleans league at its inception was of course not integrated racially. In 1948, a gentle suggestion from one league member to establish a "Colored Chapter" ran afoul of traditional attitudes.[109] Any league interest in electoral reform raised hackles in Baton Rouge, for legislators possessed a well-developed sense of alarm triggered by anything that might open the way for black citizens to vote in greater numbers. Thus, although the league had favored permanent voter registration since 1940, it risked its high standing in the community when members broached the subject with legislators. On many occasions, even their usual allies among the good-government elite fell silent or counseled delay when leaguers urged a permanent registration law.

In 1943, amid alarmed talk that black New Orleanians were mounting a voter registration drive and persistent rumors that the leader of the effort was a Communist, some in the league favored quietly shelving plans to back permanent registration. "I do think that it would be unfortunate for the League at this point to become associated in people's minds with the campaign for the registration of Negroes," wrote a New Orleans member.[110] Martha Robinson, however, favored proceeding at full speed with the effort to educate the public on the benefits of permanent registration, which had long been a part of the national league's progressive platform. She explained her rationale: "People who know us will not impute to us improper motives—people who do not believe in governmental reform along progressive lines may attack us—but they would anyway. I think only people who do not understand what permanent registration is could mix it up with encouraging registration of negroes. It does not seek to alter the method of registration and it retains all the safeguards now in the law."[111]

Robinson, with strong ties to rural Louisiana and its plantation economy, had no qualms about throwing obstacles in the path of blacks trying to register to vote; she was of the old regime in that regard, as the previous passage, with its reference to "safeguards," makes clear. However, her energetic persistence on the permanent registration issue dismayed legislators and many league members alike because it seemed likely to amplify blacks' interest in registration. The status quo position seemed to be that if whites did not remind blacks of it, blacks would not conceive a desire to vote. Robinson impatiently maintained that the system regarding blacks would remain just as unyielding as it had ever been and that arguments based on racial fears should not be permitted to stall a much needed campaign for permanent voter registration.

In the long run, Robinson prevailed on permanent registration, with the

League of Women Voters working in every legislative session for twelve years in behalf of this issue. The progressive argument held that requiring regular reregistration by its nuisance value discouraged voting and actually promoted a controlled vote, since the incumbent machine saw to it that its friends remembered to reregister at the correct intervals. The League of Women Voters agreed that permanent registration would increase the number of voters. The permanent registration law, as written, would remove the annoying requirement that the voter present a registration certificate each time he or she voted and would leave each registered voter's name on file until death. It had the support of political scientists around the country.

Robinson recalled that when she first broached the subject of a permanent registration law with friends in the legislature in 1940, their response was, "You're crazy—you couldn't do that kind of thing in Louisiana!" However, league members persisted with their campaign of educating the public to the bill's merits. Finally, after having seen it defeated in five consecutive sessions of the legislature, local league members decided to accept half a loaf, which came in the form of a bill mandating permanent registration in the state's urban areas: Orleans, Caddo, and East Baton Rouge Parishes only. Passage of this measure in 1952 signaled a special triumph for the members of the League of Women Voters, who had been virtually alone in championing such a move when they began their efforts for it in the early 1940s. Despite the dire predictions of many conservatives, permanent registration did not bring significant increases of registered blacks.[112]

In 1948, the New Orleans league stumbled over another racial issue fraught with divisive potential. At the center of the controversy was the Southern Conference for Human Welfare (SCHW). Ten years earlier, President Roosevelt had requested a report outlining the South's major economic problems. As the nation grew accustomed to hearing the South called "the nation's number one economic problem," southern progressives and moderates formed a coalition of reform groups to attack southern ills and lift the region out of its backwardness. Meeting in optimism in Birmingham in November 1938, the new Southern Conference for Human Welfare, according to a charter member, "was just full of love and hope.... The whole South was coming together to make a new day."[113] Its delegate list read like "a who's who in Southern liberalism," featuring Virginius Dabney, Mark Ethridge, Frank Porter Graham, Brooks Hays, Lister Hill, Ralph McGill, and many others. Eleanor Roosevelt, Claude Pepper, and Hugo Black all addressed the convention. In attendance were clergymen, educators, contingents from the American Federation of Labor (AFL) and the Congress of Industrial Organizations (CIO), representatives of the League of Women Voters and the Women's Trade Union League, and prominent black leaders. The declared purposes of the SCHW were to promote the general welfare of the South and to improve the economic, social, and cultural standards of the southern people. The first convention adopted resolutions favoring shorter hours for women, liberal workmen's compensation laws, civil service laws, state Wagner acts, and women's bureaus in state labor departments. It also advocated abolition of the poll tax, freedom for the Scottsboro boys, and a federal antilynching law. This emphasis on labor and racial issues reflected the large delegations of CIO members and blacks.

At the time of its inception, major newspapers generally viewed the SCHW favorably, but small southern papers denounced it for its attacks on southern institutions. As a result, most southern politicians, among them Lister Hill, John Bankhead, and Claude Pepper, soon severed connection with the SCHW. The onset of World War II diverted popular focus from domestic troubles, and the SCHW did little during the war years. However, after FDR's 1944 reelection, the group began a voter registration drive throughout the South, designed to recruit "small farmers, tenants and workers" who "would, if given the vote, return progressive candidates." Clearly, this campaign, if effective, would seriously alter the status quo in the South. In Savannah, for example, SCHW workers in 1945 boasted an increase in black registrants from nine hundred to nineteen thousand.[114]

As the New Orleans League of Women Voters carried out its voter drives in 1944 and 1945, the SCHW registration effort also went forward, obviously without League of Women Voters cosponsorship. Cooperation would have violated the league's emphasis on nonpartisanship, since the SCHW had a political agenda and its stated objective was to recruit voters of a particular economic status who would vote for certain candidates.

By 1946, the CIO had broken with the SCHW because SCHW liberalism on race relations hampered CIO efforts to unionize southern whites. An SCHW resolution against segregated meetings alarmed its remaining white moderates, who were accustomed to approaching racial matters with great circumspection, and cost the SCHW its unity and more of its white membership.[115] When the SCHW held its convention in New Orleans in November 1946, more than half of the delegates were black. By this time, Mrs. Roosevelt and President Truman had disavowed the SCHW completely, as had many other former allies. At the 1946 convention, the SCHW went on record to condemn racial discrimination in housing, in education, in employment opportunities and wages, and in transportation accommodation.

By 1947, the Southern Conference for Human Welfare, which had begun with the enthusiastic support of the leading southern white progressives, was unrepresentative of the white South and had ceased to speak with unity for even that small segment of enlightened white southerners who had founded it. Nineteen forty-seven was a year of purges in U.S. organizations, as they anxiously policed themselves for Reds. "The NAACP purged, the unions purged, everybody purged," remembered one southern liberal.[116] As the Cold War chilled the American scene, the SCHW defiantly defeated a resolution condemning the Soviet Union and refused to bar Communists from its ranks, convincing many that it was a hotbed of fellow travelers and prompting many resignations. Later that year, the House Un-American Activities Committee (HUAC) branded the SCHW a "deviously camouflaged Communist-front organization." Although the HUAC report was called "a masterpiece of logical fallacies, quotations out of context, and guilt-by-association techniques," it proved the coup de grâce for the SCHW in public opinion.[117] Even such a devoted liberal as Ralph McGill, editor of the *Atlanta Constitution,* turned against the group.

At this point, strands of the story of the Southern Conference for Human Welfare and the New Orleans League of Women Voters intertwine. Emily Blanchard, the state chair of the Louisiana SCHW committee, had long been an active member of the Baton Rouge LWV and an officer of the state LWV. Martha Robinson had known Blanchard for years and had worked closely with her on projects of civic improvement both while Blanchard lived in New Orleans and later when she and her husband had moved to Baton Rouge. It is clear that they regarded each other with mutual respect and affection and ranked among each other's closest colleagues in league and PTA work.[118] In New Orleans, where the press had spread stories of the SCHW's left-wing affiliations even before the HUAC report, release of the report made the SCHW a target for constant media criticism. Although Robinson had at one time subscribed to the SCHW newsletter, the *Southern Patriot,* and had initially favored the organization, by 1947 she was disaffected by the group's pronounced leftward drift. Concerned that the public might come to believe the League of Women Voters was associated with the highly unpopular SCHW if Blanchard continued to serve on the state LWV board while chairing the state SCHW, she talked with Blanchard about the advisability of her not taking another term on the state league board. Their conversation was friendly; Robinson came away believing that Blanchard would in fact not seek reelection when her term on the league board of directors ended.

Instead, Blanchard allowed her name to be put in nomination for another term on the board when the league met in annual convention. Robinson's refusal to support her and subsequent coolness prompted Blanchard to write a fond letter to explain herself. "Martha, darling . . . I missed your warm, affectionate approval yesterday. . . . I am not choosing S.C.H.W. as against the program of the League . . . [and I] would not consciously embarrass you or the League." However, Robinson allowed the breach to remain between them. When Blanchard suggested consideration of black membership in the league, the chill intensified.[119]

In the summer of 1947, a New Orleans newspaper reported erroneously that the local League of Women Voters and the Southern Conference for Human Welfare would be working together in a voter registration drive, which prompted Robinson to issue a vehement denial. Blanchard then requested that she be allowed to address the next meeting of the state LWV board of directors with information about the SCHW. Robinson demurred: "We are not at all interested in the same way in influencing public opinion. There is no reason for any association between these two organizations. These are very critical times, and unless the League follows a very wise & well balanced course its effectiveness will be utterly nullified."[120] To another correspondent, she explained herself more fully.

> I felt it would nullify all League efforts to be associated in the public mind with a group pushing a program which is considered radical by the mass of people in the south. . . . The League would have no more chance of passing anything in the coming Legislature than a flower would have in a furnace. . . . Lord knows, the League program is very progressive, to put it mildly, to most Louisiana communities. If we try to get too far ahead of their ideas we will repel them and be unable to get them to take any more liberal point of view.[121]

Robinson read the situation correctly, in her practical assessment of the state legislature and public opinion in New Orleans and in the state. At the same time, this pragmatic approach also coincided with her own personal feelings on the issue; one suspects she would have steered a different course had she felt strongly that the SCHW deserved a hearing.

There are numerous examples of state leagues that mirrored the conservative climate in their states and caused the progressive National League of Women Voters to despair of making progress there.[122] The Louisiana LWV, however, had been out ahead of the state legislature on many progressive issues and had vigorously supported measures to make politics more responsive to the popular will. Its members time and again had worked for changes in the status quo, in particular, electoral reform and civil service. Martha Robinson, unlike many New Orleanians, was actually acquainted with the circumstances surrounding the inception of the SCHW, knew some of its members, knew its program, and had read its newsletter regularly. Her conclusions cannot be said to have been uninformed. Moreover, she had read the

Harvard Law Review article on the HUAC report that denounced the House Un-American Activities Committee for ascribing "to every member of an organization the character of its least desirable member" and that concluded, "The Committee has been either intolerably incompetent or designedly intent upon publicizing misinformation."[123] It left her unmoved.

The situation degenerated rapidly into a breach between Martha Robinson and her former staunch liberal allies in league work, Ruth Hamill Preston and Emily Blanchard of Baton Rouge and Louise Meyer and Ruth Dreyfous of New Orleans. Preston, who held a Ph.D. in psychology and taught at Louisiana State University, made one last effort to persuade Robinson to relent and let Blanchard explain SCHW principles at a league board meeting.

> Since there seems to be gross misunderstanding concerning the SCHW (which also is in the interest of the public good with a governmental orientation—in attitude, if not in fact), it seems like a grand opportunity to hear the Chairman . . . who would be able to give us firsthand knowledge. . . . I do hope the Board will reconsider this action with apologies to Mrs. Blanchard and a request for her to come before the Board as one of us—but with a special knowledge that the rest of us can little afford to brush aside.[124]

In April 1948, the board of directors for the state League of Women Voters finally considered Blanchard's request to be permitted to speak to the board concerning the Southern Conference for Human Welfare. By this time the SCHW had had a year-long flirtation with Henry Wallace and had sponsored his speaking tour of the South, during which, in New Orleans, Wallace had predicted the death of the Democratic Party if it failed to abolish segregation.[125] With Robinson formally recusing herself from the vote, the league board, by a two-thirds vote, declined to hear Blanchard extol the SCHW. This vote brought to an unhappy end a drama that had been playing for a full year, causing serious dissension among league members.[126]

In a letter written nearly thirty years after the events of 1947–48, Emily Blanchard alleged that it was her advocacy of membership for blacks in the LWV that, in combination with her association with the SCHW, severed her connection with the league: "Mrs. Robinson brought to my home a letter from the N.O. League which deplored my position concerning membership for negro women and stated concretely that unless I resigned from the Southern Conference for Human Welfare, I would be stricken from the The League's membership."[127]

The New Orleans league lost some key members because of the liberal-moderate split in 1947–48. One was Louise Meyer. President of the New

Orleans league after Martha Robinson, a native New Orleanian and Newcomb College alumna, Meyer, unmarried and unorthodox, served as head of social services at Charity Hospital. She cut a notable figure in the 1940s as she pedaled about the city on her bicycle, often bare-legged and shod in sandals. Another charter member of the LWV who left it in 1948 was Ruth Dreyfous, a local leader in educational psychology and child development, whose brother George Dreyfous was a pioneer in defending civil liberties in Louisiana. Although she and Meyer had been officers in the New Orleans league from its inception in 1942, increasingly they found the local league less able to satisfy their sense of social justice. Forty years later, Dreyfous characterized the League of Women Voters as "a pokey sort of an organization," which continually frustrated her in its refusal to take stronger stands on issues without "studying them to death." She averred that in its first five years the league had done great good, but she felt that the Southern Conference for Human Welfare manifested an outlook much more in harmony with her own liberal sentiments, which were increasingly out of place in the more moderate league. Both Meyer and Dreyfous abandoned the League of Women Voters.[128]

Disquieted by the controversy that surrounded the Southern Conference for Human Welfare and unsettled by her friend Emily Blanchard's close association with it, Robinson had in effect participated in a purge in 1947–48. Yet under her leadership, the League of Women Voters steered a definitely progressive course, intent on governmental reforms and greater citizen participation in government. It did not, however, support changing the racial status quo in the South. The incident is indicative for what it reveals about Robinson's attitudes on race and Communism, attitudes that the bulk of southerners, even those of a progressive cast of mind, shared at that time. After Blanchard's exit, the most markedly liberal league members drifted away and found organizations where they were more philosophically comfortable.

By 1948, the New Orleans League of Women Voters had undergone a traumatic year of dissension. From monthly unit meetings, and board meetings two, three, or even four times a month, the organization drifted into stagnation; it did not meet at all from November 1947 until June 1948. A state official reported the situation delicately. "Due to circumstances beyond control the N.O. League had become almost inactive. The retiring State President, Mrs. Robinson, feeling very keenly the responsibility of reviving interest and getting the League organized, is being urged to take over the Presidency."[129] During this period of inactivity, some members drifted away and never returned. Others no doubt abandoned the league because it had been tarred in some minds with the brush of extremism and controversy.

The intimate association of the League of Women Voters with one woman,

Martha Gilmore Robinson, had left the organization poorly prepared for life without her. After having led the New Orleans group successfully as president for a full decade, Robinson moved on to head the Louisiana League of Women Voters in 1944. It is not surprising that this identification with one strong leader for such a long period rendered the New Orleans league somewhat unready to stand alone under the leadership of others when the time came. As had been the case with Hilda Phelps Hammond and the Women's Committee of Louisiana, the institution was too much identified with one person; its fortunes rose and fell with that one woman's efforts and successes. The loss of a handful of strong members over the issue of the Southern Conference for Human Welfare in 1947–48 further weakened the local league chapter. Thus, when Robinson assumed the presidency of the New Orleans LWV for the second time, in 1948, she faced a major task of rebuilding.

From this watershed onward, an important change was apparent. The New Orleans League of Women Voters, which had begun as an outgrowth of the Woman Citizens' Union, ceased by midcentury to be a provincial, inbred organization dominated by the city's elite. It became instead more representative of the city's population. A survey taken in 1951 revealed that of twenty-five members of the NOLWV board, only seven were lifelong residents of New Orleans; eight had lived in the city less than five years. The education levels of these women differed vastly from the norm for that time and place. Of significance is not only the fact that they were all college educated but also the fact that the colleges they had attended represented many geographic areas and approaches to education. In addition to Newcomb College in New Orleans, board members held degrees from Barnard, Berkeley, Northwestern, Radcliffe, Sweet Briar, and Wellesley, rendering them a very cosmopolitan group.[130]

With its infusion of new blood, the New Orleans League of Women Voters experienced a rapid growth in membership. It had begun with an initial roster of 80 members in 1942, of whom 30 were either listed in the Social Register or connected via husband to the Boston Club. Thus, 37.5 percent of the initial membership came from the city's elite. The league's numbers hovered around 100 for several years thereafter. By 1950, under Martha Robinson's recruitment efforts, its membership had climbed to 513, an increase of more than 500 percent. Expanding out of its original stronghold in the neighborhood near Tulane and Loyola Universities, where many upper-class New Orleanians lived, the NOLWV established "unit groups" in the neighborhoods of Algiers, Gentilly, Lake Vista, the Central Business District, Carrollton, and the Garden District. With the exception of the Garden District, all were distinctly middle class. The new units acknowledged members' needs by scheduling night meetings for the first time, a tacit recognition of the fact that not every member had household servants or was a full-time homemaker.[131]

The New Orleans League of Women Voters had prospered in its early years chiefly through the exertions of an exceptional leader, Martha Gilmore Robinson. Many documents and individuals bear witness to the fact that she was commonly regarded as phenomenal in ability and in energy. Robinson, state league president from 1944 until 1948, had labored conscientiously to awaken interest in the LWV in communities around Louisiana. She took great pride in the chapters of the LWV that she had helped to start and nurture in Lake Charles, Shreveport, Tallulah, Lafayette, West Monroe, Abbeville, and Alexandria. Her repeated visits, frequent encouraging letters, and generous portions of time and attention succeeded in encouraging fledgling leagues and in sustaining tender shoots of progressivism in various inhospitable corners of the state. She provided the support and the reinforcement many women needed to grapple with policy issues that had traditionally been the province of men and to back programs that were seen as quite liberal in much of 1940s Louisiana. Under Robinson's stewardship, membership in the League of Women Voters in Louisiana climbed to 1,018 by the end of her tenure as state president. Her whirlwind trips around the state in "Solace," her Studebaker; the nickname "Senator," which she earned by her hours spent in the legislature; the acclaim she received for her public efforts; the boundless good humor, much of it aimed at herself and her friends, which comes bursting through in her letters: all testify to an impressive woman.

She accomplished a major change in attitude at an age when she could have been collecting Social Security checks, had she ever held a paying job. Robinson had begun her work in the league with a provincial view of "transients," or people living in Louisiana who were not natives, as this excerpt from a blunt letter to Ruth Preston in Baton Rouge demonstrates. "I do not suppose you *transient* Louisianians can understand how we feel about going to the Roosevelt Hotel. It is . . . a moral issue with all those in N.O. who care for good government," she wrote, referring to the fact that the Roosevelt Hotel, which had served as unofficial headquarters for Huey Long, stood as a symbol of Longism to the anti-Long element in the city; for years, this group refused to patronize it. Her letter continued, "I wonder if you have ever read 'Let Freedom Ring' [Hilda Phelps Hammond's book]. That would perhaps let you understand how we who have fought for good government in this community for many years, still feel on this subject."[132] This letter was sent to an educated, progressive woman who, with her husband, had been a resident of the state for ten years.

Through her association with the League of Women Voters, Preston herself was fully aware of the local elite's attitude toward those women not born in the state. She once confided to a national LWV staff officer, "I find that even among liberals in Louisiana an outlander is still treated suspiciously!"[133]

It is to her credit that, well past the age of sixty, Martha Robinson was able to change, to become less chauvinistic about her city and state, and to accept those she had once called "transients." In her original lexicon, a "transient" was a newcomer, whose roots did not go very deeply into New Orleans and Louisiana and who could never achieve the status of a "native." Robinson's attitude typified the outlook of many New Orleanians, male and female. A noted historian of the city has commented that "in no other American city does birth, as opposed to achievement, count for so much. Such values and the social intimacy of the group," he writes, "mean that newcomers . . . have a great difficulty circulating in the city's highest circles."[134] However, the burgeoning of the league after it began energetic recruitment efforts and attracted hundreds of new members, many of them newcomers to New Orleans, gave Martha Robinson genuine pleasure. Contact with educated women whose backgrounds were varied and outlooks broad stimulated Robinson. She wrote of the new members, "They are good, live gals!"[135]

Of this growth and rebuilding, a staff member from the national LWV office wrote, "They are doing a tremendous revitalizing job under Mrs. Robinson and if they will only let more new people get in . . . it should be wonderful." In 1950, Robinson noted appreciatively that Mathilde Dreyfous, herself a recent newcomer to the city, had rendered the league "a true cross-section of [the] community," through her work as membership chairman.[136]

In truth, the NOLWV was distinctly *not* "a true cross-section of [the] community." It was not racially integrated, although in this it differed not at all from league chapters in many parts of the United States. Furthermore, a scholar of the League of Women Voters has commented that it might more accurately have been called the "League of Affluent Women Voters," since members "lived in the best neighborhoods of their communities, had exceptionally high levels of education, and had incomes well in excess of the national average." This pattern held true in New Orleans, but it is significant that by 1950 the NOLWV was actively recruiting women who were not New Orleans natives. Although the membership continued to be characterized by a privileged status, it was no longer insular and clannish.[137]

To what is Robinson's change in outlook attributable? The League of Women Voters and its predecessor, the Woman Citizens' Union, had occupied her energies for a decade and a half when the liberal-moderate schism ripped the New Orleans group. The loss of a handful of key members, left liberals who had endorsed the policies of the Southern Conference for Human

Welfare and who had supported Henry Wallace's 1948 presidential ambitions, deprived the league of some of its most capable women and threatened its very existence. Robinson apparently saw two options: either find replacements for the departed members and rejuvenate a stagnating organization, or preside over the slow decline of the League of Women Voters, the organization that was at the center of her life and that she regarded as a desperately needed force for political enlightenment and moderation in Louisiana. Faced with such a stark choice, Robinson adapted.

Martha Gilmore Robinson was no reactionary. She had consistently supported Roosevelt and the New Deal. In her leadership of the League of Women Voters, she worked for reforms to end the dominance of the machine, the cronyism, and the corruption that had long characterized Louisiana politics. She enthusiastically subscribed to league policy promoting greater internationalism, ardently backed the new United Nations, and advocated sharing U.S. atomic technology with the Soviet Union.

The schism that rent the league in 1947–48 shows that women's groups were not immune to the Cold War fears that plagued the nation; the split between Blanchard and Robinson is an echo of national patterns in the late forties. When prominent New Dealers formed the outspokenly anti-Communist Americans for Democratic Action (ADA) in 1947, they had the support of such liberals as Eleanor Roosevelt, Walter Reuther, and Arthur Schlesinger Jr., who, in pulling away from the so-called progressivism of the left liberal Henry Wallace, left him to the Communists and fellow travelers.[138] Quite simply, anti-Communism was in vogue for liberals; in the South, it was equaled in popularity by persistent support for racial segregation. The course that Robinson steered allowed the League of Women Voters to retain its influence with the extremely conservative state legislature, a body that viewed the league, even as reconstituted after the split, as shockingly liberal.

As the New Orleans League of Women Voters moved into the second half of the twentieth century, it was not racially integrated; the first halting steps in that direction would come in the 1950s. Nonetheless, it was indisputably a much stronger organization, improved because of its diversity, its broader base of support in the city, and its greater numbers. But, despite these changes, and possibly *because* of these changes, the League of Women Voters was not the political organization of choice for the majority of middle- and upper-class women.

Some parted company with the league in order to work actively for political candidates. As always, because of its constitution and bylaws, the league abjured partisan stands; it endorsed policies and philosophies but never candidates. This principled forswearing of partisan politics struck some locals as unsatisfactory. Robinson recognized this, noting, "With feeling high, many people will feel that League work is ineffective. But when the smoke of battle clears the League will be found respected & secure, ready to carry on its continuous job of getting citizens interested & active in their government."[139] As staff members from the national LWV headquarters office in Washington visited Louisiana to assess league works and progress there, they came to realize what an uphill struggle league women had against partisanship.

Proud of its independence from electoral politics and constitutionally prohibited from mobilizing its members to work for political candidates, the league provided a superb training ground for women in politics, allowing them to gain familiarity with the issues by keeping its focus away from personalities. Because its rules forbade any precipitous endorsement of a cause, every league position resulted from thorough study and consideration. A charter member of the NOLWV summed up the disciplined league methods: "Know your facts, stand your ground, keep your temper and become an expert on the issue."[140]

This circumspection brought criticism as some women rejected the league's aloofness from partisanship and its slow, methodical approach to issues. Jessie Daniel Ames once characterized the league as an "organization for conservative people who always look many times before they leap."[141] Women intent on working actively for candidates to bring the progressive changes that the League of Women Voters supported could not do so under league auspices. The austere nonpartisanship of Robinson and her organizations, first the Woman Citizens' Union, then the League of Women Voters, baffled and sometimes infuriated them. If the problem plaguing New Orleans was "dirty politics," their solution was to defeat the politicians on their own playing field. In particular, many of the city's elite women sought to support a candidate of background similar to their own, to boost his candidacy with their considerable talents and energies.

Dissatisfaction with nonpartisanship coupled with the desire to elect a reformer as mayor led to the formation of another women's group in New Orleans. Two decades after attaining suffrage, local women ventured into local politics in an organized fashion. Their group, the Independent Women's Organization (IWO), would make a name for itself in the 1940s, to the point of being lauded for having changed the entire political climate in the city of New Orleans. Meanwhile, the local chapter of the League of Women Voters continued its trademark activities, conducting exhaustive studies of issues, polling candidates to ascertain their views on a broad range of issues, and attempting to educate the public to matters of public concern.

Thus, by the 1940s, there were two distinctly different organizations for

New Orleans women interested in political issues, the League of Women Voters and the Independent Women's Organization. Both groups began with a central core of women leaders from the city's upper class. The LWV, however, changed its composition by broadening its membership and becoming more representative of the city as a whole. The IWO, by contrast, as will be shown in the following chapter, was throughout the 1940s a stronghold of New Orleans elitism.

Men who work hard in party politics are always recognized, or taken care of in one way or another. Women, most of whom are voluntary workers, . . . are generally expected to find in their labor its own reward. —Eleanor Roosevelt

CHAPTER FOUR

❑

THE PLEASURES OF PARTISAN POLITICS

❑

THE INDEPENDENT WOMEN'S ORGANIZATION

The roots of the Independent Women's Organization reach back to 1939, a year that looms large in historical perspective. Nineteen thirty-nine gave the public Superman comic books, the New York World's Fair, the debut of television, and goldfish swallowing as campus sport. Cinematically, the year brought Judy as Dorothy, Gable as Rhett, the unforgettable Joad family struggling west on Route 66, and newsreels of the king and queen of England picnicking on hotdogs and beer with Squire Roosevelt at Hyde Park. An ailing Lou Gehrig hung up his Yankee spikes for good. Death claimed Freud and the pope. Shirley Temple turned ten; Hitler, fifty. Europe danced a stately minuet of futile diplomacy, edging ever closer to the abyss of war, finally falling headlong in September of that year.[1]

In the state of Louisiana, too, 1939 was a fateful year, the year of "the Scandals." As Huey Long had once prophetically observed, his successors lacked sufficient gifts to carry on without his guidance. Nineteen thirty-nine brought a special prosecutor from the U.S. Department of Justice into the state. Tall, thin O. J. Rogge became the hero of reformers and the scourge of Long's inheritors. Saying tersely that "major criminals ought not to commit minor crimes," he flailed key government figures with charges of mail fraud, tax evasion, and embezzlement of more than one hundred million dollars in state funds. A welter of indictments stung more than one hundred Louisiana officials, including Governor Richard Leche. The nation applauded.[2]

Men who once sat at Huey Long's right hand went to prison. It was remarked of the state during this period that Louisiana had "more men who [had] been in jail, or who should have been, than any other American state."[3] Long's chosen successor, Leche, who had swept the state in 1936, winning the gubernatorial election by a larger margin than Huey had ever enjoyed, received a ten-year sentence for fraud. The men bound for prison had built the electoral bandwagon that rumbled to such a smashing win, but, three years later, the wheels had come off. Miraculously, Earl K. Long escaped unscathed, save in the opinion of skeptics who noted that either he had been so close to the transactions that he must have known about them and thus was implicated and unfit to serve his state or, on the other hand, as he asserted, he had not known and was thus too dumb to serve. As Huey's brother Earl Long prepared to carry the banner for the somewhat chastened Long inheritors, anti-Long strategists were meeting, scheming, and yearning for the tantalizing brass ring of the governor's office.

The anti-Long element, who had endured lean years, now saw a golden opportunity. They felt that a reform candidate for governor would have a greater chance for election in 1940 than at any time in well over a decade. As campaigners, the reform element tended to offer nothing more than good government, feeling that it alone should be sufficient inducement. They viewed political activity as a matter of civic duty and appeared to believe that voting for clean government should be reward enough to voters. Consequently, when offered inducements from the ringsters' grab bag, which ranged from pensions to pavement to a place on the state payroll, voters not surprisingly tended to perpetuate the machine in office. Reformers had success only "when the machine became outrageously venal."[4] Thanks to the conduct of Huey Long's successors and the tenacity of the federal prosecutor Rogge, public perception by 1939 was that the state machine was in fact "outrageously venal."

For the first time in Louisiana's history, women were about to play a well-publicized role in a statewide election. Women's awakening interest in political reform proved timely, for by 1939 the public mood in Louisiana endorsed the belief that the time for change had come. The anti-Long sentiment in New Orleans had prompted Huey Long to employ some of his most extreme tactics, but the city stubbornly refused to be converted. Among the city's population, anti-Long feelings ran high; old-fashioned good-government conservatives, businessmen who wanted businesslike government, women disgusted with Long's crass behavior, citizens repelled by corruption and waste, ousted politicians and their relatives—all set their faces like granite against Longism. The daily newspapers in the Crescent City maintained a staunch anti-Long editorial posture. A large segment of the bourgeoisie, outraged at stories of flagrant dishonesty at their state's highest levels, rallied to the anti-Long cause, as did certain pragmatic spoils politicians of the powerful Old Regular ring. Prominently represented among all of these anti-Long elements were women.

In 1939 there emerged three serious candidates for governor: Earl Kemp Long, incumbent by virtue of having assumed the office when Governor Richard Leche had resigned earlier that year as the scandals broke about his head; James A. ("Jimmie") Noe, north Louisiana oilman and erstwhile ally of the Kingfish, now stung into denouncing the Long regime by the Long camp's refusal to back him for governor; and Sam Houston Jones, a gentlemanly attorney from Lake Charles and a reformer in the progressive tradition of former governor John Parker. Noe was expected to split the Long vote, since some loyal Longites, believing the disgruntled Noe's tale of having been chosen by Huey to be his anointed successor, preferred him to Earl Long. Hopes ran high among reformers. They hailed Sam Jones as a savior who would surely slip into the second primary while the Long forces battled each other in the first.[5]

In the wake of the scandals ripping the state, a group of "young Turks" formed the People's League that year in New Orleans. Decrying the corruption being revealed in daily headlines, this group of young professionals, led by future congressman Hale Boggs, hoped to seize the moment to elect an anti-Long governor in 1940. Among the People's League members was Jacob H. ("Jake") Morrison, an attorney who developed the idea of using, in the coming campaign, a virtually untapped source of power: women. In the fall of 1939, Morrison instigated invitations from his wife, Mary Meek Morrison, to a small group of local women to attend an evening meeting at their Royal Street home, in the still unfashionable French Quarter of the city. Jake, not Mary, chose the women who would be invited, and he chose

TABLE 3. *Upper-Class Affiliations of Women Who Met to Organize Support for Sam Jones, 1939*

Name	Social Register, 1927	Male Relative in Boston Club
Bruns, Bland Cox	yes	yes
Boggs, Corinne Claiborne	no	yes
Dinkins, Cecile Airey	yes	yes
Favrot, Charlotte	yes	yes
Labouisse, Catherine	yes	yes
Moore, Catherine	yes	yes
Morrison, Mary Meek	no	no
Reily, Gladys Weeks	yes	yes
Waters, July Breazeale	yes	yes
Westfeldt, Kate Monroe	yes	yes

Source: New Orleans Social Register, 1927; Landry, *History of the Boston Club.*

them because of their husbands, whom he knew to be affluent and anti-Long. (Mary Morrison, from Jackson, Mississippi, later to be a respected local activist, had married only the year before and did not know any of the invited women well.)[6]

Among those who assembled in her home were Corinne Claiborne ("Lindy") Boggs, Bland Cox Bruns, Cecile Airey Dinkins, Charlotte Favrot, Catherine Labouisse, Catherine Moore, Gladys Reily, July Breazeale Waters, and Kitty Monroe Westfeldt. Many were veterans of Hilda Phelps Hammond's crusade and had been aroused to political action by the events of the Long years. All were of the city's elite. Every woman except the hostess was connected to the Boston Club through male relatives. Eight, all natives of the city, were listed in the city's 1927 Social Register; the two who were unlisted were not native New Orleanians and had not resided in the city in 1927 (see table 3). The group represented an excellent sample of the dispossessed elite, alienated by the Huey Long regime. One woman was the daughter of a former chief justice of the Louisiana Supreme Court; one was related to former governor John M. Parker; one was the daughter of a former Louisiana congressman; one a descendant of the first American governor of Louisiana; one the daughter-in-law of a former state legislator and reform delegate to the 1921 constitutional convention. Several had strong family connections to the planter elite that had ruled Louisiana for more than a century. All had experienced dismay and revulsion as the state government scandals associated with Long became public in 1939; all wanted higher standards of conduct in their officeholders.

Jacob Morrison addressed the small group, speaking of the unique opportunity that existed to expel the Long regime in 1940. He spoke of Sam Houston Jones as the candidate who could oust the grafters and restore integrity to state government and asserted that women who valued integrity in government had an obligation to enter into political activity with vigor. His pep talk to the intent audience of women had exactly the effect he had desired; they voiced an eagerness to begin.[7]

This nucleus of ten women aggressively recruited others for the coming gubernatorial campaign; they organized throughout the city and elected officers and ward leaders. Many enlistees were middle-class women, some of whom worked at jobs outside their homes. In age, they ranged from a few who were too young to vote to some who were elderly. In unprecedented numbers, these women — numerous housewives, a switchboard operator, a Newcomb professor, a bridge teacher, the owner of a pressing shop, and an architect among them — joined the effort. Although the group of women for Jones and reform broadened to include women from the middle class, it appears that the elite founders retained the leadership.[8]

Politically, the state of Louisiana at this time consisted of three parts: the north, the south, and the city. It seemed a foregone conclusion that Earl Long would carry the country parishes and poor lands in north Louisiana, locus of his brother's greatest strength. Sam Jones expected to take much of the region in southern and western Louisiana around his home of Lake Charles. The cities of Louisiana (Shreveport, Lake Charles, Monroe, Baton Rouge, and Alexandria) would also provide Jones votes, since urbanism was strongly associated with anti-Longism. The more prosperous agricultural parishes were potential sources of Jones strength as well, since analyses revealed that the richer the farm land, the less likely were the voters there to support Longism.[9] Barring an act of God, the New Orleans vote was Earl Long's. Through their staunch ally, Mayor Robert Maestri, the Longs controlled the election machinery in Orleans Parish, determining who registered, who voted, and even which votes were counted. Facing this array of Long advantages in the city, the Jones faction chose to counter with a small group of handpicked New Orleans women. Referring to their confidence, their ability, and their eagerness to participate in effecting change, Lindy Boggs commented, "We were a rambunctious group."[10]

Once they were organized, the first mission of the women involved cleaning up the voter registration, much of which they believed to be fraudulent.

A Gallup poll taken in late 1939 revealed that fully 60 percent of Louisianians believed that elections in Louisiana in recent years had been conducted unfairly.[11] Certain precincts in New Orleans always mustered a suspiciously large total for the Long ticket. Thus, checking the poll books in the Office of the Registrar of Voters was essential. But simply obtaining the poll books presented difficulties the women had not imagined. The officials frankly stalled them, alleging that the books were being "worked on" and were not available. Day after day, contingents of determined women returned to the registrar's office across the street from Gallier Hall and politely repeated their request. Getting access to the poll books was only the beginning, however. Copying them meant standing for hours at a tall counter, painstakingly writing by hand every name and address on the rolls, working under the baleful glare of city officials. "But," one veteran of the effort recalled with obvious satisfaction, "we kept on, by golly. We got those poll books copied."[12]

Next came the more demanding, time-consuming task of canvassing, personally visiting each address on a block to discover if legally registered voters actually lived there. This canvassing effort differed from the earlier nonpartisan effort of Martha Robinson's Woman Citizens' Union in that these women distributed Sam Jones literature as they called house to house. Their purposes were twofold: to expose any fraudulently registered individuals, and to boost Jones's candidacy with everyone to whom they spoke. In the "silk stocking" districts of New Orleans (the Fourteenth Ward, in the university section, for instance), they went about their project unmolested; no one interfered with their activities as they knocked and asked the names of those who lived in the houses. But in other wards, notably the Fifth and the Tenth (in the French Quarter and the Irish Channel, respectively), things often got rough. The Long organization all over the city knew that the women were up to something. In some neighborhoods, ward leaders gave the okay for harassment measures. Some women were jostled on the streets; others reported having dogs loosed on them.[13]

> It was so bad that down here, a couple of Longs would follow us around. And when the door opened, they would be standing across the street. And the minute the occupant of that house would see those men standing over there, even if they had been interested in Jones, they would quietly close the door or just get rid of us. We were trailed around like that. Everything you can think of was used to intimidate us. Occasionally, they might even cross our path and say something like, "You're wasting your time."[14]

Such intimidation did not deter the women. One recognizes strong convictions motivating them to persevere in the face of unpleasant incidents and their genuine belief in the cause for which they were working. Their knowledge of practical politics often failed to match their motivation, however. Lindy Boggs, who later represented Louisiana's Second District in the U.S. Congress for nearly twenty years, responded to a request that she serve as precinct captain by asking naively, "Don't the police do all of that?" In 1939, *precinct* evoked only a memory of accompanying a friend to pay a traffic ticket. Like most New Orleans women, Boggs had a great deal to learn about politics.[15]

Among the women canvassers, the opinion was common that people in working-class neighborhoods feared to express openly their opposition to the current administration. They reported being asked repeatedly by householders not to tell anyone that they were anti-incumbent.[16]

The appeal of machine politics generally eluded the middle- and upper-class women who worked for Sam Jones. They failed to understand why anyone would expect to "get" something for his or her vote other than the satisfaction of having put in an honest administration that would work for the public good. Among these women reformers, the concepts of honesty, purity, and integrity were very real. *They* needed no specific inducements when they considered these ideals; they bridled when less-affluent or less-educated voters wanted tangible rewards for doing their civic duty. Their lives were such bedrocks of economic security that the motivation of quid pro quo in relation to a vote was foreign to them.

One leader of the Jones women recalled her ineffectual naïveté in trying to convince women whom she canvassed that she personally would not benefit from a Jones victory and was only interested in good government. "Boy, that was a mistake. I was immediately suspect. I could tell; they would look at me and say, 'Yes, she's a liar. Nobody would be out on the street like this, ringing doorbells, for nothing.' So after that, when they would ask me, I would say, 'If Mr. Jones is elected governor, I'm gon' be his secretary!' [Laughs] They accepted that, they understood that."[17]

In early January 1940, O. J. Rogge, the assistant U.S. attorney general who had brought indictments against several Long associates, publicly invited citizens to report voting frauds to his office. In an effort to reassure anti-Long voters that this election would be different, the campaign ads of Sam Jones, headed "Uncle Sam Protects Your Vote," reminded citizens that a copy of each precinct's vote tally had to be mailed to the secretary of state in Baton Rouge and that federal law forbade anyone to mail any matter intended to defraud (i.e., falsified voting returns).

The grateful anti-Long element in New Orleans viewed the federal government as a shield against a state government drunk with power, but key figures in the Long machine felt differently. Senator Allen Ellender, with no sense of irony, hotly denounced Rogge for "tactics intended to intimidate the citizens of a sovereign state" and accused him of "persecution." Grumbled Ellender prophetically, "If you people don't watch out, in ten or fifteen years, the federal government will be in charge of all your elections and the darkies will be voting," demonstrating again the southern propensity to lunge at the race issue when the subject of voting practices arose.[18] Finally, the furious Louisiana senator thundered that a *Times-Picayune* headline, "Vote Thieves Warned by Rogge," and its accompanying story that Rogge had pledged to investigate any charges of fraud served to intimidate Louisiana voters. Martha Gilmore Robinson voiced the exasperation of many when she wrote to the U.S. attorney general, "The senators who are crying 'States Rights' in this issue . . . have put themselves in the position of defending election stealing."[19]

The conservative New Orleans press solidly supported Sam Jones, whom the Long forces derided as "High Hat Sam." In his effort to delineate the election as a battle between the classes and the masses, Earl Long delivered a classic of rich-versus-poor campaign rhetoric when he characterized Jones as "High Hat Sam, the High Society Kid, the High-Kicking, High and Mighty Snide Sam, the guy that pumps perfume under his arms."[20] Long correctly perceived that "the better element" had rallied to the Jones campaign and hoped to rekindle the embers of class resentment in Louisiana. Many average citizens, however, were moved more by evidence of corruption in the incumbent regime than by sneers at the challenger for having ties to the elite.

On the day of the first primary, January 16, 1940, the *Times-Picayune* printed on its front page a long list of instructions to voters on how to avoid having their ballots invalidated for technicalities, a common device employed by the machine to minimize the nonmachine vote. The editorial admonished voters to use pencil only; to mark their choices with Xs only; to refuse to allow anyone to stuff the ballot into the slot with a pencil (which could leave a stray mark and spoil the ballot). Also printed in the election day issues of New Orleans papers were Rogge's reassurances that his office would investigate irregularities and Jones's appeal to his supporters to go to the polls with cameras to photograph any irregularities they saw.[21] Quite striking is the newspapers' assumption (correct, as it happened) that such irregularities would occur at the polls.

In the face of harassment, the women recruited by the reformers' campaign had persevered. Day by day, they had matched the names and addresses in the poll books with those they gathered on the street, noting discrepancies. When election day came, they were ready. Armed with their information, many of them reported before daylight for duty at the polls to serve as volunteer poll watchers as the law permitted. One woman explained to a reporter, "Most of my precinct captains were new at it too, and they were so anxious to do everything right they were at the polls before dawn."[22]

Election law required one of the five official commissioners in the polling place to call out in an audible voice the name and address of the person presenting her- or himself to vote. Straining to hear and consulting their lists simultaneously, the women verified the authenticity of the registration. If the person named was not legally registered, one of the women would call out in a loud voice, "I challenge that vote! I challenge that vote! He doesn't live there!" There were challenges to their challenges, of course, and efforts to disrupt the women's monitoring, such as the Old Regular precinct captain who ordered a large cabinet radio brought out on the balcony across from the polls and played at full volume to drown out the voices of the commissioners as they called voters' names.[23]

On occasion, a challenge alone would cause a fraudulent voter to vacate the polls. For those who voted in spite of a challenge, a poll watcher filled out a challenge slip, naming the allegedly illegal voter, and placed it into the ballot box with the voter's ballot. Theoretically, the commissioners would disqualify these votes upon proof of illegal registration. In practice, however, challenges were consistently overridden in precincts with a majority of three or more Long commissioners.

The women felt great pride in those of their number who had been selected in the random drawing to serve as election commissioners, for they would actually administer election procedure at the polls. Those selected felt keen responsibility to stay on the job, which meant thirteen or fourteen hours at a minimum. Often they relied on orange juice, which was believed to lessen dehydration while having less of a diuretic effect than any other beverage.[24] Nearly fifty years after the fact, one veteran of that election recalled with admiration tinged with wonder how a friend of hers, drawn as a commissioner for Sam Jones in her precinct, had vowed not to leave the polls for any reason whatever, from opening till closing through ballot counting. To make possible this stoic marathon, she wore four sanitary napkins and declined to drink any liquids the entire day.

The women faced other impediments to their work in the two primaries. Both election days, January 16 and February 20, 1940, had dawned unusually cold for winter by New Orleans standards; for the first primary, the temperature never rose above thirty-nine degrees, with snow flurries reported. Both times, the weather stayed painfully cold throughout the day. Since only commissioners and voters were officially permitted to enter the polling places, the volunteer women watchers depended on the kindness of strangers (the commissioners) if they wanted to seek relative warmth in the polls. Many commissioners kept them at bay, forcing them to watch and listen under the windows or from porches all day as a sharp wind gusted relentlessly off the river. Occasionally they huddled around fires kindled in metal drums on the streets, but only occasionally, for they were remarkably faithful to their task. Other women had the assignment of bringing sandwiches and hot coffee to the poll workers. In some precincts, in middle- and upper-class neighborhoods, order reigned; in others, along the riverfront or in the French Quarter, chaos prevailed, as party loyalists bristled at the unprecedented challenge to their hegemony by bluestocking do-gooders. Partisans exchanged insults, fistfights erupted, sound trucks blared. The women fortunate enough to be inside the polls remarked on the chill; those less fortunate hunched shoulders inside coats and turned backs to the wind. Slowly, the cold hours passed.

The women watchers lasted through the day and into the night. Night brought the counting, a time for special vigilance. At their schools, run by local attorneys such as Jacob Morrison and Burt Henry, the women had learned both election law and the opposition's ways. Their instructors admonished them to take flashlights to the polls with them, in readiness against a fairly common trick of turning the lights out long enough to switch ballot boxes. They warned that though the women would see things that would outrage their sense of fairness and inflame their tempers, they must refrain from antagonizing the election commissioners, who could oust them from the polls if they chose. Their mission was to observe and document everything illegal that occurred, in the hope that possibly their forces could seek redress in federal court later. As one woman remembered, " 'Don't antagonize anybody, and get arrested, and get carted away where you'll do nobody any good.' We were warned about that again and again. 'Whatever happens, take it.' "[25]

Mary Meek Morrison discovered firsthand just what it meant to "take it" when, within sight of a uniformed policeman at the polls in her precinct, she received a roundhouse blow to the side of her head from an infuriated female Long supporter, who, on overhearing Morrison make a slighting remark about her faction, had swung her large and heavy purse at Morrison's head with terrific effect, almost knocking her unconscious. Although the officer witnessed the incident, he said nothing to the attacker. Promising to jail Morrison if she complained again, he then turned his back on the two women. Morrison's comment to the local press about the incident captures a New Orleanian's characteristic insouciance, "Well, if someone blacks the other eye, I won't have to buy a mask on Mardi Gras."[26]

July Waters too had an encounter with the law enforcement officials patrolling the polls and carrying a mandate to assist the Long candidates. When the sheriff ordered her to move away from the polls, she replied that she was not breaking the law, since she knew what it stipulated about distances. He then threatened to haul her off in the "paddy wagon." "Well," she replied placidly, "I've never ridden in one of those." Seeing that she was undeterred, he abandoned his effort.

Another incident involved a Garden District woman who challenged an Old Regular as he lowered the window shade so that the watchers outside could not see the activities inside the poll. "Don't you think we ought to leave that shade up?" she asked sweetly. "Lady, I've been running this poll for fifteen years and now you come along and tell me how to do it!" "Yes, but *the law* says the voting shall be visible from the street, so there's no reason to pull the shade down," she insisted, still sweetly. Seeing a policeman inside, she further inquired, "And don't you think the policeman ought to be outside? The law is that the policeman must be outside the barrier unless needed by a commissioner." The result was not long in coming: shade up, officer out. Having been repeatedly admonished to know the law and to stand their ground without antagonizing anyone on election day, the women activists did just that. They did not so much as raise their voices, much less use rough language; they consistently said "please" and "thank you," "could you" and "may I" when addressing the Old Regulars and the policemen on duty. And this gentility, combined with their solid knowledge of election law, prevailed in many, many cases.[27]

These incidents illustrate the threatening and decidedly masculine atmosphere still prevalent at the polls in the 1940s. In places where swaggering policemen boldly flaunted their allegiance to one faction, where mayhem was not uncommon, where the simple act of placing a paper ballot into a wooden box could be accompanied by taunts, leers, threats, or even fisticuffs, numbers of women certainly hesitated to cast votes. Having other women physically present at the polls served to allay hesitations and fears in many women voters. For this reason, the women activists of New Orleans deserve credit for changing with their very presence the threatening atmosphere at the polls and making it possible for all women to vote with greater peace of mind.

New Orleans newspapers carried reports of a few election irregularities: someone had poured ink into a ballot box; fistfights were commonplace at precincts all over the city; some individuals had their cameras snatched and smashed as they tried to photograph proceedings at the polls.[28] For years, the Old Regulars had routinely hired "goon squads," rowdies who could be mobilized to disrupt polls long enough to destroy ballots or steal boxes if precinct captains felt that the vote was not going their way. One veteran of such a squad recalled episodes of setting fires in the kitchens of homes where balloting was done, using grease from boxcars to make a great deal of thick, black smoke in order to get the reformers to flee outside. In their absence, the toughs did whatever was necessary to assure the election's outcome.[29] Candidate Jimmie Noe told his followers, "When one of our loyal supporters comes to vote and some bruiser goes jostling that woman, I want our men to hit him in the jaw," but he later relented somewhat, requesting that his men at least not carry shotguns to the polls.[30]

The returns from the January 16 primary showed that the reformers' efforts had fallen short in New Orleans; Earl Long had carried only nine of Louisiana's sixty-four parishes, but Orleans, with its reliable machine, was one of them. Long led Sam Jones in the city by a margin of two to one, carrying fourteen of seventeen wards. However, the total vote received by the four candidates aligned against Long exceeded Long's total, giving hope to the reformers that Sam Jones could prevail in a second primary.[31]

When James A. Noe finished third in the first primary, he endorsed Sam Jones in the runoff. Jimmie Noe's support did not come cheap, however. The high price he exacted required that Jones would pay his campaign debts and give Noe supporters half of all state jobs under a Jones administration.[32] This deal cut with a one-time Long loyalist upset some of the women who were participating in the Sam Jones campaign. Repelled by political expediency as practiced by a campaign, many disliked seeing their candidate abandon the moral high ground and instead wanted Sam Jones to remain "pure." Dissatisfaction raged among the women. However, the leaders of the women's movement for Sam Jones recognized the essential arithmetic behind such a deal and adopted a pragmatic attitude, realizing that without it, Sam Jones would not become governor and reform would lose again. Said one woman, "That election taught me a great deal about politics. It's all a compromise; you've got to compromise. To know when to compromise or not compromise is the crux of the matter."[33]

In the five weeks between the first and second primaries, the surreal headlines bespoke chaos. While the Soviet Union methodically devoured Finland, New Orleanians frolicked through another Mardi Gras, the masked holiday that Mary Morrison had mentioned in her statement to the press. The charms of Carnival revelry distracted but did not deter the women from their mission. Only five days after the first primary, women workers for Jones assembled in a huge citywide meeting at the Sam Jones headquarters, to which they had invited all women who had supported Noe in the first polling. In a pragmatic move, and over the objections of the purists among them, they consolidated their resources and emerged united in their goal of defeating Earl Long and the hated Long machine.³⁴

Six weeks later, the results of the February 20 election showed that Louisiana had chosen a new governor, the reform candidate Sam Houston Jones. In the state, Jones defeated Long, 283,470 votes to 261,790. But in Mayor Robert Maestri's city of New Orleans, Jones managed to carry only four wards, all in the more affluent sections, missing capturing a fifth ward by only 81 votes.³⁵

Analysis of the gubernatorial elections of 1936 and 1940 reveals that in 1936, the anti-Long candidate, Cleveland Dear, polled more than 33 percent of the vote in only four Orleans Parish wards, more than 40 percent in only one ward, and a majority of votes in none. Four years later, after the efforts of anti-Long women of the city, who pruned illegally registered voters from poll books and boosted support for Sam Jones by widespread and effective personal contact with voters, the anti-Long candidate polled more than 33 percent of the vote in thirteen wards, more than 40 percent in ten, and a majority in four.

Although the Long-Leche-Maestri machine still held sway in the city, the reform element had mounted a stout challenge. Figure 1 shows that the percentage of the New Orleans vote won by the anti-Long candidate increased strikingly from 1936 to 1940. In the areas of the city where the anti-Long women lived and were most active (Wards 10, 11, 12, 13, 14, 16, and 17), the anti-Long vote increased, respectively, by 12, 10, 21, 23, 22, 23, and 25 percentage points. Although organized anti-Long women had not carried the city for their candidate, they had made a decent start, and their organization would fight again another day.

The wild celebrations that swept New Orleans on election night had counterparts all across the state as hundreds of thousands of people exulted in victory over a government they had long feared and despised. Citizens wept, prayed, orated, and drank. Celebrations were termed "the biggest since Armistice Day." A massive eight-column headline in the *New Orleans Times-Picayune* proclaimed, "MACHINE RULE ENDS!" while a front-page editorial, "Let Us Give Thanks," warned against wild exultation and urged a time of solemn thanksgiving. The *Times-Picayune*'s admonition notwithstanding, the women who had labored strenuously for a change in state government did celebrate. Decades after that election night, they still remembered vividly their victory parades, some on foot, some in automobiles with horns blaring, their victory waltzes and jitterbugs, and, of course, their victory toasts.³⁶

Clearly, the women of the anti-Long elite in New Orleans who had first

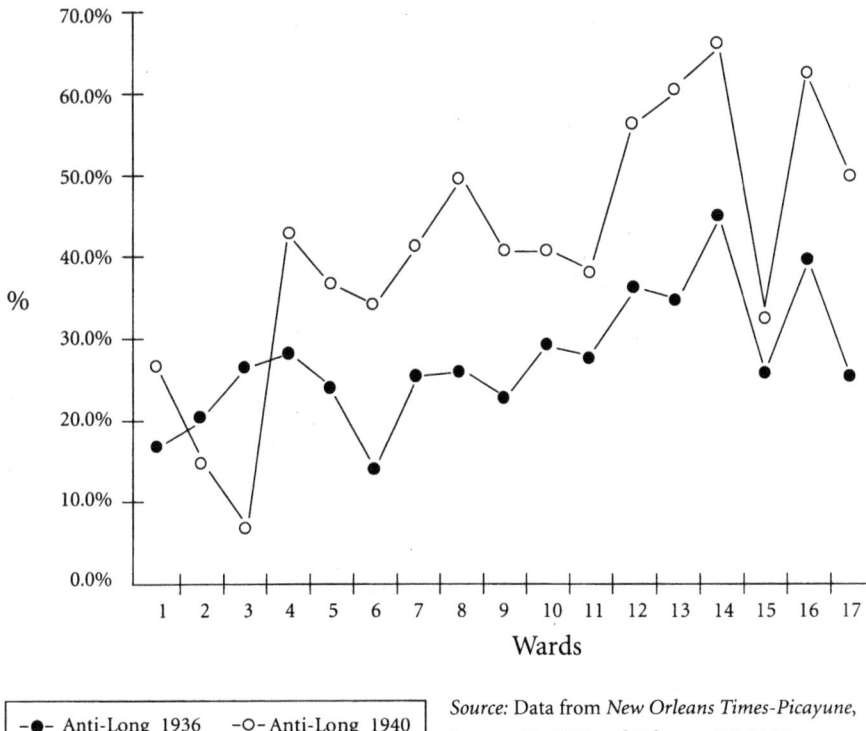

FIGURE 1. *Anti-Long Vote in New Orleans in Gubernatorial Elections of 1936 and 1940, by Wards*

met in Mary Morrison's home in 1939 were numerically unable to deliver the city to Sam Jones. It was cooperation from voters of all classes that allowed them to carry even four wards and to make a respectable showing citywide. They became allies for good government with people whom they did not know socially. A victory celebration in the Tenth Ward, a neighborhood that included both the exclusive Garden District and the working-class Irish Channel, mingled the disparate Jones voters in a social setting. One woman reformer commented on what she perceived as the incongruity of it. She recalled leading off the dancing at the victory party with the Jones men's leader, an Old Regular Irishman of humble origins, saying of the situation, "It was simply killing."[37]

Victory telegrams poured in to the governor-elect, many of them from the state's women. A sampling of wires shows that they had high ideals and high hopes for the future. In voting for Jones, they felt they were choosing someone who shared those ideals and hopes. One saw "the dawn of a new era," another "the glorious rescue of Louisiana," and yet another spoke of throwing off "the yoke of oppression" with "the victory of the people over the gangsters." "Thank God Louisiana is at last redeemed." One suggested that February 20 be made a state day of independence, and another echoed the idea, saying simply, "Fourth of July in February." Another was "Happy as a June bride," and others commented on the relief they felt at showing the rest of the country a new Louisiana. "Your overthrow of the corrupt Long political machine will convince the outside world that all of the citizens of Louisiana are not crooks." "Can again be proud to be a Louisianian."[38]

The idea that there was such a thing as "the women's vote" had not crossed the minds of politicians since the early 1920s, when events had proved that women did not bloc-vote and thus need not be appeased in their demands. Absent any objective analysis of the 1940 vote, the subjective perception common at the time was that a women's vote had accounted for the stronger anti-Long showing in New Orleans. Local women received public recognition for their role in the Jones victory. One New Orleans paper headlined, "Women Prove Factors in Primary," and an editorial cartoon depicted a horrid creature labeled "Gangster Politics" being barred from a doorway marked "Future of Louisiana Democracy." Blocking the way were three saber-bearing stalwarts, "Sam Jones, John Citizen and *Women's Vote*."[39]

The assessments of women who participated in the anti-Long campaign clearly reflect a consciousness of having played an important role. Bland Cox Bruns, later to become New Orleans's first woman legislator, wrote that women had not realized what "enormous power" they had until 1940, asserting, "Undoubtedly the work of our women was a tremendous factor in the victory."[40] Her neighbor, July Waters, a Newcomb graduate and daughter of a former U.S. congressman, maintained that years of corruption in politics had readied women to participate in a cleansing of state government. When Sam Jones, a candidate "of vision and courage," offered himself, they were ready.

> At that time they [women] little realized what a power they were to become. . . . In the hearts of women of all ages and of all walks of life was a burning, driving conviction—they must work tirelessly and ceaselessly until the crooks and thieves and rascals who were despoiling this State and undermining the morals of the people were turned out. No woman among them could rest while there were such conditions for her children to grow up in. The Louisiana that they and their forebears had revered and honored must be their children's heritage—not the degraded Louisiana that the past twelve years of vice and corruption had made.[41]

Waters's maternalistic words echo the theme of "republican motherhood," the idea that women must act to assure that their children will become honest, responsible, moral citizens of the Republic. Believing that the future safety and well-being of the Republic rested on responsible motherhood and rejecting any notion that motherhood was a passive activity confined within the walls of home to the exclusion of the larger world, the good mother concerned herself with the larger world, for its pernicious influences, if unchecked, could undo all that she did for her children at home as soon as they ventured into that larger world. In 1940, Waters herself was mother to three teenage sons, young men who stood poised on the threshold of the real world as it teetered on the brink of war. She surely had reason to wish for a better world for them.[42]

After her candidate Sam Jones's election, Waters assumed that women could be instrumental in ensuring the implementation of moral policies. In the ward newsletter that she had undertaken to publish monthly for the anti-Long element, she exhorted women readers to learn about government's actions and to accept their share of responsibility in governing Louisiana. "We must play our part in politics!" she insisted.[43]

July Waters's statement in 1941 that women had become a power in politics claimed too much, since most New Orleans women still lived and died in traditional roles. Few, if any, were questioning a system that permitted their political activity only in the form of the tedious, grassroots work necessary to get a male candidate into office but that never encouraged their political activity to take any other forms. Periodically the press threw verbal bouquets to women, praising their herculean and unpaid labors to get out the vote and alluding to their activity as "a highly valuable example to [the] men," but such praise hints at the severely limited role in politics that was envisioned for women.[44] New Orleans women did not hold office, because they did not seek office; they did not rebel against their position but instead strove to shine within it. In short, they were feminine, not feminist. But the long years of World War II, a watershed in so many ways, left many New Orleans women to cope with larger responsibilities than ever before, and by 1946, many of them were prepared to assume what would be their biggest role to date in electoral politics.

The New Orleans mayoral election of 1946 featured a classic contest of reformer versus machine politician. Anyone living in New Orleans before the mid-twentieth century had vivid firsthand knowledge of machine politics. Since 1897, the Regular Democratic Organization had enjoyed a half century of control, with one four-year interlude of a reform administration. The Old Regulars, in common with all effective urban machines, depended on tight ward and precinct organization, dispensed services with unapologetic favoritism, and knew exactly where to get votes and how many they could muster.[45]

The rise of Huey Long had challenged Old Regular domination in New Orleans, since the unwillingness of the Old Regulars to form a coalition with him led Long to attack them with energy and originality. With the carrot of patronage and the stick of reprisals, he lured many Old Regulars into defections. The political history of New Orleans in the 1930s is a story of bitter warfare between state and city, as Long attempted to crush Old Regular resistance to his programs by punishing the people of New Orleans. In this drama, the local reform faction was a very weak third voice.

Ultimately, the Old Regular mayor, T. Semmes Walmsley, resigned in the face of municipal bankruptcy brought on by Long's financial squeezing of the city through denying it revenue sources while increasing its financial obligations. Although a special election was called to fill his office, it was never held. To the Longs' delight, their machine's grip was perceived as being so dominant and absolute that no opponent could be found to sacrifice himself electorally to the Long mayoral candidate, Robert S. Maestri. Thus, in 1936, the city's new mayor, one of the late Huey Long's inner circle, took office without the annoyance of facing the voters.[46]

Maestri, a second-generation Sicilian, has been likened to a Damon Runyon character. Armed with a third-grade education, a thick accent, shrewd managerial sense, and financial independence acquired through wise investments, Bob Maestri assumed his new post as mayor of New Orleans. A measure passed by the Long faction then dominating the legislature simply canceled the mayoral election of 1938 and gave Maestri six full years in office before he ever faced the electorate. During that time, aided by the fact that the state had ceased to make war on his city, Maestri brought fiscal order to New Orleans, reduced city debt, improved the city's bond rating, and restored investors' confidence.

Although Mayor Maestri made the trains run on time, so to speak, an essential part of his effectiveness rested on his role as boss of a powerful urban machine, a machine that at last enjoyed peace and harmony between the Longs and the Old Regulars. At election time, familiar machine practices prevailed. Padded payrolls, forced payroll deductions for the campaign, and voter intimidation were commonplace and highly effective in perpetuating the incumbents in office. After Maestri won reelection in 1942, his style of governing changed radically. Seemingly detached from municipal operations, he allowed city services to deteriorate; street maintenance and garbage collection suffered in particular. The vice and corruption that had long infested the city attained a new public prominence. Gambling and prostitution flourished; slot machines, racing handbooks, and bawdy houses operated boldly, especially in the French Quarter, spurring a torrent of citizen complaints.

An alert Maestri would have detected trouble brewing in his fief, but he had become increasingly detached from city government. Although he nonetheless wanted a third term, conditions prevailing in New Orleans in 1946 differed significantly from the circumstances of earlier years. First, the end of World War II had left voters in a reforming mood, mindful of their wartime sacrifices, inclined to throw the rascals out; incumbents everywhere, from Winston Churchill on down, felt their sting. Second, the election of Sam Jones to the governorship in 1940 left a legacy of encouragement to Louisiana reformers. Third, a group of New Orleans women, with the experience of working for Jones in 1940 behind them, formed a solid phalanx of experienced political activists, adept at canvassing voters, getting out the vote, and monitoring the polls for dishonesty and unfairness, the tasks that Lindy Boggs called "the chores of politics."[47] They had an organizational framework ward by ward, virtually intact from 1940. Moreover, they had the inner flame that burns within the true believer. In common with reformers for the better part of a century, they viewed an election between a machine candidate and an antimachine opponent as a crusade, and they acted accordingly. One woman spoke for most when she quoted self-deprecatingly, "'Our strength was as the strength of ten, because our hearts were pure.'"[48] Most would have vehemently disputed another quote, this one from Walter Lippmann: "Before you can begin to think about politics at all, you have to abandon the notion that there is a war between good men and bad men."[49]

Despite all signs of encouragement to reformers, it looked in December 1945 as though Robert Maestri would again coast to another term without even the nuisance of opposition. In a shocking eleventh-hour development, Maestri's announced opponent, J. O. Fernandez, withdrew from the race only three weeks before the last day for qualifying and coolly endorsed Maestri. Stunned reformers muttered angrily about a sellout. Their mutterings were correct; the price, Fernandez's campaign debts, was reportedly thirty-five thousand dollars, which Maestri blithely paid.[50]

A coterie of alarmed reformers, calling themselves the Independent Citizens' Committee (in distinction from the "nonindependents," by which term they meant machine-aligned citizens) cast about frantically for a replacement candidate in time to meet the qualification deadline. In December 1945, July Waters's son, returning home from a country club dance, mentioned to his parents that he had seen young deLesseps ("Chep") Morrison, just home from the service. Preparing to retire, Arthur Waters, member of the Independent

Citizens' Committee, sat on the edge of the bed to remove his shoes; he let one shoe drop, but its mate did not follow. His wife looked across the room inquiringly to see him waving the other shoe in his hand, saying, "That's it! That's it!" He announced triumphantly, "We'll run Chep Morrison!" Arthur Waters phoned the club, spoke with the young officer, and arranged a late-night meeting in their living room, where, before the crackling fire, July Waters plied the returned veteran with coffee while her husband sounded him out about his candidacy.[51]

DeLesseps Story Morrison, thirty-three years old, a graduate of Louisiana State University and its law school and a native of New Roads, Louisiana, had practiced law in New Orleans for several years before the war, in a partnership with his half brother, Jacob Morrison, and a family friend, Hale Boggs, whose wife Lindy was Morrison's cousin. In 1940, he had won a seat in the state legislature on the Jones ticket, representing the anti-Long Twelfth Ward of the city. Clearly identified with the Sam Jones reform faction, he had directed passage of two significant measures, the civil service law and the voting machine act. When war interrupted politics, Morrison entered the U.S. Army as a first lieutenant; he reached full colonel by 1945, and, during the latter part of his tour, acted as mayor of the large German port of Bremen. The decorated veteran was handsome and in excellent physical condition, married and the father of a young son.[52]

Morrison jumped at the chance of a mayoral campaign. Despite pundits' prediction of Maestri's inevitable reelection, Morrison, a young man with strong political ambitions, saw an ideal opportunity. If he ran an energetic campaign and lost, his expected defeat would not cost him credibility or damage his future. If, however, he ran and managed to win, people would call it phenomenal. Running for mayor as standard-bearer of the reform element was in some ways a no-lose situation for deLesseps Morrison.

The Sunday papers of December 9, 1945, carried enthusiastic headlines announcing Morrison's mayoral candidacy. The *Times-Picayune,* the *States,* and the *Item* all endorsed him. Lamented the *States,* however, "The Independents have not much time to get their lines drawn, their precinct captains and their workers deployed."[53] The newspaper was not alone in its pessimism. The feeling that Maestri was unbeatable was so well established that more than a dozen men, all of them reasonably promising candidates, had rebuffed the reformers' earlier importunings to make the race. Insiders in the reform camp admitted later that nobody, including Morrison, felt that there was more than the slimmest thread of a chance for victory.[54]

The incumbent himself behaved with supreme confidence, seldom bothering with public appearances, making very few speeches at gatherings and only one by radio, frequently dispatching surrogates to appear for him.[55] The Morrison campaign offered a strong contrast to the Maestri approach. The vigorous young candidate eagerly spent eighteen hours daily in campaigning, honing skills of winning people with an engaging personality and ready smile. His manifest desire to meet the voters at every turn stood in bold distinction to the reclusive Maestri's behavior. Despite the advantages of youthful stamina and a willingness to forgo the comforts of food, sleep, and family, Morrison was only one man; he relied on the efforts of supporters to boost his campaign, and no supporters did more than the women of New Orleans.

In 1945, women who had participated extensively in the Sam Jones campaign of 1940 shaped themselves into a formal association that they called the Independent Women's Organization (IWO). The group's single purpose was to elect deLesseps Morrison mayor of New Orleans. Leading the new political association was July Breazeale Waters (1895–1989), the woman who had emerged as leader of the Sam Jones effort among women in 1940. Originally from an old town of old money, Natchitoches, the oldest settlement in Louisiana, Waters was the daughter of Phanor Breazeale, a country lawyer who had served several terms in the U.S. House of Representatives earlier in the twentieth century. From their youngest years, Breazeale had regularly included his four daughters in his public world. Waters's childhood had included animated conversations around the dinner table featuring the family's frequent political houseguests, endless talk of political matters and personalities, and summertime trips to political speakings at the popular resort of Hot Wells, the traditional spot for launching a campaign in the state of Louisiana. It was there that she heard a very young Huey Long speak for the first time. When her father had occasion to argue a case before the Louisiana Supreme Court, he habitually took rooms in New Orleans's Roosevelt Hotel for his young daughters so that they could observe the court proceedings. Waters consumed a steady diet of politics, issues, and personalities all her life and seemed to thrive on it.

July Waters received a degree in music from Sophie Newcomb College in 1915, taught violin there for a short interlude until she married, and then spent the decade of the 1920s fully immersed in the domestic sphere. The world shared by Waters and her husband, Arthur, an investment banker listed in the city's Social Register, was Protestant, prosperous, well mannered, well tended, and socially elite. Home was a handsome Greek revival house in the city's exclusive Garden District; leisure hours often involved the Southern Yacht Club and their sailboat, the *Vanguard*.

The mid-1930s, when Waters's children were all of school age, coincided with her friend Hilda Phelps Hammond's anti-Long crusade, which Waters joined with alacrity. She thus came to the Independent Women's Organization as a veteran of Hammond's battle against Longism. She had also enjoyed a brief affiliation with the local League of Women Voters, joining at the invitation of her friend Martha Gilmore Robinson. However, she found her long-standing inclinations stifled by the league's insistence on nonpartisanship and, significantly, did not renew her membership when it expired. Waters, more comfortable viewing the world in Manichaean terms and acting on those views, drew from the devil image of Huey Long and his successors the inspiration to act rather than discuss. In 1946, as July Waters, an angular, intelligent woman of fifty, with ice blue eyes and a charming manner, took the helm of a new body established by women to oust the machine and elect a reform mayor in New Orleans, she must have felt as if she had been in training for the post for years.[56]

Because the women who established the IWO had one specific goal, to elect Morrison mayor, they viewed their organization as short-term. That they revised their expectations shortly after the election and made their organization permanent indicates the invigorating effect of the campaign upon them. The campaign and their role in it changed the way in which these women viewed themselves and advanced them a step further toward political maturity.

The 1940 women's effort on behalf of Sam Jones had featured primarily women from the city's elite. In 1946, the elite again dominated the positions of IWO leadership and policy making. Morrison's family connections attached him to uptown New Orleans and the city's elite, meaning that, though not a native, the candidate was one of them. A woman of Morrison's age remembered him as "a debutante's delight."[57] However, his attraction stretched far beyond the cotillion and the country club.

Middle-class women participated in great numbers in the Morrison campaign. Morrison's appeal to women crossed class lines in much the way that John Kennedy's had done, as women of varying backgrounds viewed the young candidate as what they would like their sons or husbands to be. Aides to JFK remembered the reaction of an audience of women to Kennedy, also running in 1946 for his first office. "I heard those women saying to each other, 'Isn't he a wonderful boy, he reminds me so much of my own John, or my Bob.' They all had stars in their eyes," recalled one Kennedy associate.[58] In that first year of peace, women voters in New Orleans identified strongly with deLesseps Morrison. His status as a decorated war veteran, reunited with a loving wife and a baby whom he did not know, struck responsive chords in the electorate. With young bobby-soxers who had never voted, with war brides adjusting to returned husbands, with middle-aged women who had sent sons to war, and with older women charmed by his unfailing courtesy, the Morrison style had its effect. The image of a war hero stepping forward to do his civic duty, redeeming a city mired in neglect and corruption, had great appeal for women voters in 1946.

After throwing his hat into the ring on a Saturday, Morrison signaled the importance he assigned to women in his campaign when he appeared before the inner circle of the Independent Women's Organization on the following Tuesday. Assembling at Kitty Westfeldt's home, in the same large comfortable room where Hilda Phelps Hammond had launched her crusade against Overton and Long thirteen years earlier, Morrison reminded his small audience of women of their effectiveness in Sam Jones's campaign and urged that they again use their influence to achieve good government.[59]

After a vigorous pep talk, the candidate departed. During the next month, women volunteers hosted dozens of coffee parties to which they invited their female friends and neighbors to meet the candidate, whose good looks, charm, and ability to deliver brief, energizing messages stood him in good stead. As the campaign unfolded, Morrison's strength with women manifested itself and became a bedrock of his strategy. At that first IWO meeting, however, July Waters, though inspired by Morrison's style and message, felt pessimistic as she reminded her members that only forty-one days remained until the election. She urged all of the women to see immediately to their crucial registration certificates, without which no one could vote. These minutiae of suffrage in Louisiana gave extra leverage to the ruling machine, since the machine loyalists received timely reminders about updating registrations and address changes, whereas the reformers sometimes had their voting strength diluted by a tendency not to have all documentation in proper order. In addition, the legal necessity of reregistering every election meant that voter registrars in league with the machine had numerous opportunities to toss out independents' voter registration forms for being improperly completed, not an unlikely eventuality when the law required the applicant to state his or her age in exact years, months, and days.

At the first IWO gathering, Waters and the members mapped strategy. They wanted to influence both the electorate and the election machinery. To reach the voters, women arranged for rallies, coffee parties, and receptions at which voters could meet and hear the candidate. They renewed a voter registration drive, canvassed with vigor, and distributed Morrison literature and signs to any householder who would take them. They wielded the telephone as a most effective campaign tool, methodically contacting voters in all wards and speaking with vivacity and intelligence on Morrison's behalf. Their efforts to reach the voting public personally succeeded spectacularly.[60]

Voter registration for the January 1946 mayoral election closed on December 22, 1945, exactly two weeks from the day Morrison announced his candidacy. Recalling the IWO's strenuous registration efforts, a charter member said with emphasis, "We worked like beavers!" An editorial cartoon depicting their efforts showed a frowning, dispirited woman reading of New Orleans's plight in a newspaper whose headlines spoke of uncollected garbage and poor schools. Approaching her was a smiling, attractive woman labeled IWO, poised to make a pitch for voter registration. The caption read, "Hey Thinker, It's Time for Action!"[61]

One week from the deadline for registration, the local registrar of voters reported the hiring of twenty additional clerks for the last week of registration to deal with the anticipated crush of citizens turning out to register. The actual total of registered women voters in 1946 hit an all-time high of 83,621. Of those in Orleans Parish who could cast a ballot on January 22, 1946, 44.9 percent were white women, with white men claiming 52.4 percent of the eligible electorate, black men not quite 2 percent, and black women less than 1 percent.[62]

The voter totals for women in 1946 were not record breaking in percentages. Women had constituted a greater part of the whole in both 1942 (45 percent) and 1944 (46 percent) because of the absence of so many men in military service. In absolute numbers, however, registered women voters had increased significantly in 1946. Their strength shows up as a smaller percentage of the total only because thousands of returning servicemen also registered as voters. The 1946 election for mayor of New Orleans differed significantly from previous elections in having two unpredictable elements of voters largely unsusceptible to the blandishments of the machine: women and veterans. Both groups gave strong support to Morrison.

Although waging a vigorous "friends-and-neighbors" campaign, the Independent Women's Organization acknowledged the impossibility of contacting every voter personally and employed the mass media's help. One IWO project involved having a daily letter from a prominent woman citizen appear in the local papers under the heading "I Want a Change Because." The letters targeted women, trying to break the still powerful prejudice against women being "mixed up in politics." The women's letters stressed that women "who love[d] their homes and families" bore a responsibility to register and to vote. Echoing Montesquieu's argument that the stability of a republic rests upon the persistence of virtue among its citizens, they reasoned that mothers who had patiently labored to instill virtue in their offspring were seeing a corrupt city administration, in its very public disregard for virtue, undoing all that their years of efforts had sought to establish. Lambasting the Maestri administration for everything from abstract evils ("dictatorship" and "the lowest type of civic morals") to specific problems ("rats," "garbage," and "foul smells"), the writers, appealing to still high patriotism, called for "freedom from fear," a familiar phrase in 1946. They reminded readers, "A vote for Mr. Morrison is a vote for those boys who cannot vote, but who registered with their lives, their protest against dictatorship." The war motif sounded prominently through their rhetoric as they called on women to face up to the irony of a world war fought to eradicate conditions abroad, which, in their view, still existed in their own city.[63]

By far the most memorable event in the brief Morrison campaign, one totally planned and executed by women, came on the frigid Saturday night before the January election, with the so-called March of Brooms. A clever word association with the well-known March of Dimes (an annual event held in late January to coincide with Franklin Roosevelt's birthday), the March of Brooms involved hundreds of New Orleans women massed in ranks, each shouldering a common household broom and marching shoulder to shoulder for blocks. Impervious to the cold winter night, united in exhilarating camaraderie, they strode down Canal Street and onto St. Charles Avenue, then on toward Lee Circle and their ultimate destination, a Morrison rally at the Jerusalem Temple. Led into the hall by their president, July Waters, the broom-wielding members of the Independent Women's Organization prompted deafening applause.[64]

Their theme, "A Clean Sweep with Morrison," reflected clever and familiar use of household imagery to gain a political goal. Women in politics had long used such rhetoric. As far back as 1888, Frances Willard claimed a women's mission "to make the whole world homelike." The *Ladies' Home Journal* in 1920 had heralded the advent of women voters by commenting, "Let them shake the dust off from a few of our political fixtures and see what is underneath. Let them drive the rats out of the public pantry." Such language, when coupled with the symbolism of brooms in 1946, posed no threat to traditionalists, whether male or female. This imagery reassured onlookers that voting women were still creatures of the home, wielding the emblem of their sphere in a rather endearing statement of support for the right candidate, who of course happened to be male.[65]

The "Broom Brigade," attracting attention and major publicity, proved effective in reaching the electorate. Members of the IWO sported broom lapel badges, some featuring real wooden handles, tiny broomstraws, and red ribbons, others cardboard brooms proclaiming, "A Clean Sweep for Morrison." The symbolism of the broom became fully identified with the women's good-government movement and was used often in subsequent campaigns. "Wearing the broom" became synonymous with opposing the machine and with backing reform candidates. New Orleans women were not alone in 1946 in adopting homely household imagery, however. In Alabama, the successful gubernatorial candidate, Big Jim Folsom, had won votes that year by brandishing a corn shuck mop as emblem of his pledge to clean up the government.[66]

An event such as the March of Brooms gave its participants solidarity, a sense of sisterhood, and an identification with a larger cause. Women with distinctly different experiences and backgrounds had joined together in response to the IWO appeal to any woman who favored a clean and honest administration. They felt a surge of empowerment from this march and from the serious attention being paid the women's vote by the press and candidate Morrison. Some responded to an item that appeared in the classified ads. Asserting "IT'S FUN TO FIGHT / FOR WHAT'S RIGHT," it extended an invitation to all women volunteers eager to work in the Morrison campaign to report to Morrison headquarters downtown or to telephone for information on how they could help.[67]

The second part of IWO strategy, to influence the election machinery, involved scheduling scores of women to serve on election day as poll commissioners, alternates, and poll watchers. The society section of the *Times-Picayune* reported accurately, "Social engagements will take second place on Election Day."[68] But not all society women in New Orleans were focused on politics that year. A local matron, serving as head of the Colonial Dames of Louisiana, an exclusive organization with eligibility based on birth and family connections, unwittingly scheduled the annual state meeting and reception on election day, completely oblivious to the coming election. However, once she was contacted by dismayed IWO members, she postponed the meeting and encouraged her membership to become more politically aware and active.[69] The potential contretemps resulting from scheduling a society function on the same day as a mayoral election had actually worked to the women's benefit; older society women, who rarely voted, received word of this election from the Colonial Dames organization, a source they relied on, and possibly took to heart the state president's admonition that women should take more interest in politics.

No longer novices at politics, women outdid themselves in 1946; recruited by the IWO, four hundred of them served as poll workers for Morrison.[70] Veterans of the Sam Jones effort found volunteer newcomers swelling the ranks of women at the polls on election day. As a result of measures passed in the flush of reform when Sam Jones took office, New Orleans in 1946 used voting machines instead of individual paper ballots in most precincts, and voters thus entered with the knowledge that their votes would be secret and would be counted. The use of voting machines, plus the presence of so many women, made the precinct atmosphere considerably less volatile in 1946 than in years past.

Few in New Orleans would have gone so far as a local editor who, in a preelection bouquet entitled "To the Ladies," wrote, "We would be willing to let the verdict next Tuesday be rendered by the women." On January 22, 1946, another bitterly cold election day arrived, and with it, not the female domination desired fancifully by the editor, but local women's largest political involvement to date. "I've been around voting polls for about 15 years now, and I've never seen so many women out voting," commented one experienced commissioner.[71]

The Maestri organization had no polling data to predict an outcome, but the wisdom of long years' experience with the machine's efficiency led everyone to expect the incumbent's reelection. Maestri had reason to feel optimistic, as he explained confidentially to a local reporter. "Don't you know it ain't the voters that win elections for you, Gillis?" he demanded once. "It's your commissioners!" Then, with a comment foreshadowing coming events, he added grimly, "But it's getting harder all the time with these damned voting machines!"[72]

However, the validity of that wisdom had evaporated in 1946, victim to a combination of voting machines, genuinely secret ballots, the appeal of a particularly attractive challenger, the incumbent's lethargy, and the reformers' energetic campaign efforts. In addition, a civil service law now shielded city workers from arbitrary dismissal for failure to support the incumbent and, by removing fear of unemployment as a stimulus to force votes for Maestri, clearly fogged the machine's customary calculations. Morrison predicted, "When they sit down with their figures and start the old system of adding up the jobs in each precinct and ward and multiplying by five, they're going to get badly jolted."[73]

Voter turnout reached an unprecedented 80 percent despite a colder-than-average day. Again women stuck to their posts for long hours under adverse conditions, and again they endured abuse from machine politicians still unresigned to women's presence at the polls. When the counting was done, challenger deLesseps S. Morrison had defeated Mayor Robert S. Maestri by 4,372 votes, out of just over 133,000 cast—a margin of only 3 percent.

Had the intense voter registration drive mounted by the IWO in the brief interval between Morrison's announcement and the deadline reaped dividends? It is impossible to say exactly how each of the 4,183 newly registered women cast their first-time ballots, but every indication points to the fact that they were overwhelmingly pro-Morrison. In addition, it appears that women voters across the board gave strong support to the challenger.

Voter registration data by sex are not available at the ward level for 1946. However, because there were no major voter registration drives by women, for women, between 1946 and 1954, one is not mistaken to assume that the figures of registered women voters by ward in 1954 are valid as rough estimates of the proportion of women voters in each ward in 1946. (The absolute number of women registered would not be the same, of course.) Using the 1954 voter registration data as a guide to 1946, one finds that in the five wards with the greatest percentage of women voters (Wards 10, 12, 13, 14, and 16), the winning candidate was Morrison, who took majorities of 51.7 percent, 60.4 percent, 65.7 percent, 74.1 percent, and 63.0 percent, respectively. (Morrison also carried two other wards, neither of which had a majority of women as registered voters.)

There does appear to be a clear correlation between women voters and Morrison support. Table 4 shows the percentage of the 1946 vote polled in each ward by candidates Maestri and Morrison; it also includes the data for percentages of 1954 registered voters in each ward that were female. It will readily be seen that the wards with more women voters were more likely to vote for Morrison, the anti-Long, antimachine candidate. The Old Regulars and their Long allies, accustomed to mastery of the small voting populace, found themselves done in by a seemingly innocuous movement of women who had methodically gone about the chore of registering previous nonparticipants, expanding the electorate, and mobilizing the "independent" (antimachine) vote.[74]

To label the outcome "surprising" fails to convey the enormity of the shock. A well-known local hotelier commented, "The two most surprised individuals in New Orleans were Maestri and Morrison." The ousted incumbent and his victorious challenger, as well as hordes of reporters, both local and national, awarded major credit to the dynamism of women. The soon-to-be former mayor was quoted on the morning after as saying, "Them widder women beat me." (Private versions of his assertion are considerably saltier.) In remarks to jubilant supporters at his headquarters, Morrison named women first among the groups he recognized as he meted out praise.[75]

Press coverage solidly credited the women with being the single most decisive factor in Morrison's election. The *Times-Picayune* lauded "the tens of thousands of women who worked unceasingly from the campaign's start to its finish, to end intolerable conditions and establish clean, competent and democratic government in the city." The *Item*, in a feature called "Never

TABLE 4. *Relationship of Registered Women Voters and Morrison Vote, by Wards, 1946*

Ward	Morrison Vote (% of Total)	Women Voters, 1954 (% of Total Registered)
1	33.0	46.7
2	35.6	46.7
3	32.8	48.4
4	50.2	48.9
5	43.0	47.5
6	31.7	48.6
7	44.0	45.8
8	54.6	40.5
9	46.1	45.5
10[a]	51.3	50.4[a]
11	44.4	48.6
12[a]	61.0	51.7[a]
13[a]	65.2	51.0[a]
14[a]	73.4	51.2[a]
15	47.8	47.8
16[a]	67.0	53.7[a]
17	53.9	49.0

Source: Data on Morrison vote from *New Orleans Times-Picayune*, January 24, 1946; data on women voters from Leonard Reissman, K. H. Silvert, and Cliff Wing Jr., "The New Orleans Voter: A Handbook of Political Description," *Tulane Studies in Political Science* (1955).

Note: Figures for 1946 voter registration are not available by sex.

[a] Indicates majority of registered voters were women.

Underestimate the Power of a Woman," told the melodramatic tale of a woman whose husband had fallen dead of a heart attack on election day. She walked into the polls that afternoon, "red-eyed but determined," and voted for Morrison. Her two brothers voted with her. The feature, noting that the vote count showed a Morrison edge of exactly three votes in that precinct, was accompanied by photos of seven prominent Independent Women's Organization members and an enthusiastic account of IWO activities in Morrison's behalf.[76]

One woman poll worker for Morrison told of her day: "It was a miracle when our Mayor Morrison was elected. We canvassed the whole ward, and election day we stood in the cold at the poll. It was bitter cold, and we stood outside. About three o'clock it began to snow, and the Old Regular ladies, they said, 'Go home, Mrs. Bruder, you know you are whipped.' 'No,' I said, 'we will be dancing in this snow at 3 o'clock in the morning to celebrate our victory,' and we did dance in the streets. It was a miracle."[77]

Outside the Crescent City, the verdict was unanimous on the role of women. Writing of the "tremendous part" women voters played in Morrison's victory, the *Shreveport Times* noted, "All reports from New Orleans indicate that women were the real spearhead in his campaign, that they went to the polls regardless of weather, and that their votes were a substantial portion of the Morrison total." The *Memphis Press-Scimitar,* published in a southern city with a noted machine tradition and dominated by "Boss" Ed Crump, awarded considerable coverage to the upset and asserted, "The women ... led the revolt. ... Many things beat the machine. And the women led all the rest." Even the *Christian Science Monitor,* with its nonpartisan reputation, reached a verdict that women were the deciding factor, maintaining flatly, "The women of New Orleans elected deLesseps S. Morrison."[78] July Waters received notes of thanks lauding the achievements of the IWO. Read one, "Certainly, the men of this community have the ladies to thank for this victory, and you deserve full credit."[79]

No one thought it important to record the unpaid hours worked day after day by women volunteers in the tedious tasks of electoral politics. No one noted the numbers of telephone calls made, addresses visited, or pieces of literature distributed by women; certainly no one counted the dozens of finger sandwiches they made or hundreds of cups of coffee they poured at "meet the candidate" rallies. It is thus impossible to quantify exactly what women did to elect Chep Morrison. It is known that Morrison won an upset victory in 1946 and that unprecedented numbers of women worked for his candidacy. There are, of course, other factors that contributed to the outcome: Morrison was an attractive, well-educated candidate and a vigorous campaigner, whereas the middle-aged, uneducated Maestri did little to woo voters. Returning veterans identified with candidate Morrison the former soldier. Ultimately, however, the factor that calls for most attention is the pathbreaking participation of women in the campaign. To assume that their activity made a crucial difference is not unwarranted.

Figure 2 indicates that the percentage of the vote won by the anti-Long candidate had increased significantly since the 1940 gubernatorial contest. Morrison polled at least one-third of the vote in every ward but one and bettered the 1940 Jones showing in sixteen wards. Morrison carried six of the seven wards in which the Independent Women's Organization was most active.

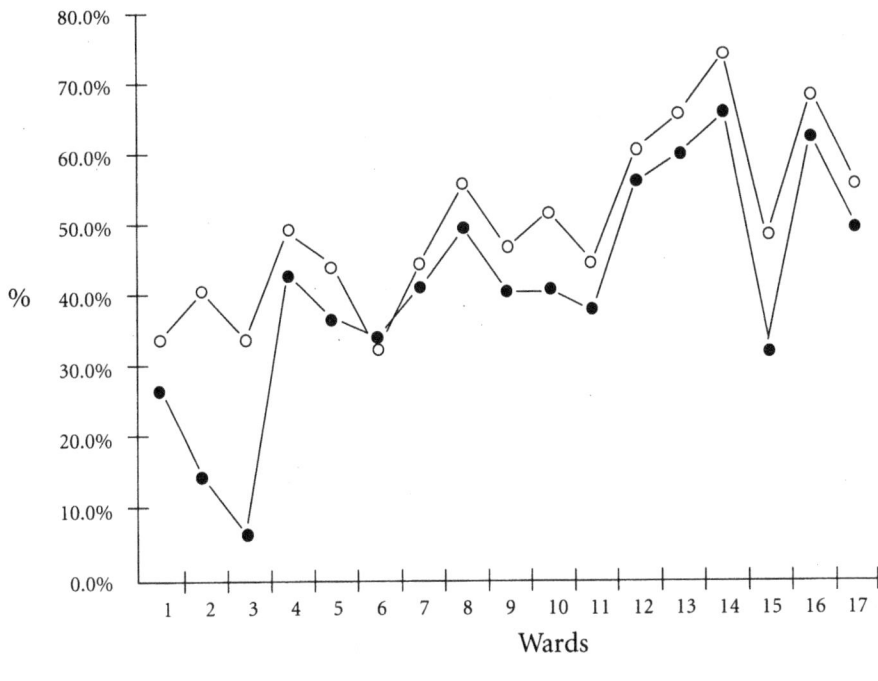

| -●- Jones 1940   -O- Morrison 1946 | Source: Data from *New Orleans Times-Picayune*, February 22, 1940 and January 24, 1946. |

FIGURE 2. *Anti-Long Vote in New Orleans in Gubernatorial Election of 1940 and Mayoral Election of 1946, by Wards*

Figure 3 depicts the steady growth of anti-Long strength in New Orleans during the decade from 1936 to 1946. During these years, women's organizations were at work expanding the small electorate by actively recruiting new voters to erode the machine's control.

The women themselves were vocal in their own behalf in 1946, displaying a healthy regard for their contributions. No longer the shrinking violets of 1940 who had demurred when praise came their way, they now showed readiness to assess their worth positively. They still maintained the womanly attribute of sharing credit easily, as in this statement from IWO president Waters. "No one group of women did it. Every woman who helped did it, and as the world has seen, there were plenty who helped."[80]

Growth of confidence among the women engendered a change in the Independent Women's Organization. After Morrison's election, the young association voted to transform itself into a permanent body; Waters appointed a committee to draft a constitution and bylaws. The acclaim the members had enjoyed in the wake of Morrison's upset victory over Maestri convinced them

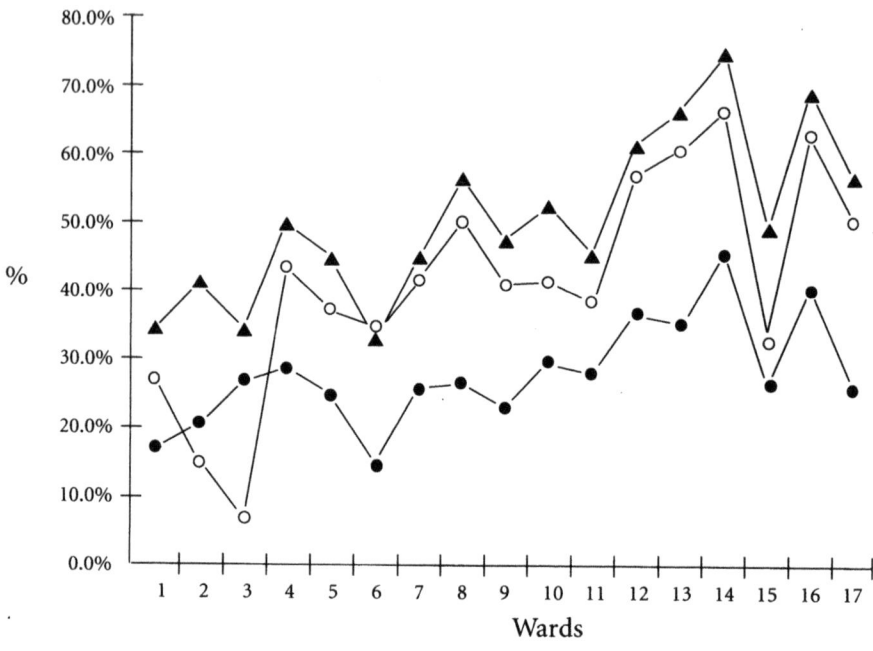

-●- Dear 1936
-○- Jones 1940
-▲- Morrison 1946

Source: Data from *New Orleans Times-Picayune,* January 23, 1936, February 22, 1940, and January 24, 1946.

FIGURE 3. *Comparison of Increase in Anti-Long Vote in New Orleans, 1936, 1940, 1946*

that they could not only be effective in subsequent campaigns but could also exercise a positive influence on city affairs.[81] Accomplishing their electoral objective had given them a heady feeling of competence, and they sought to perpetuate it.

The local press applauded the IWO's decision to become permanent, crediting the women with superior morality. "All power to them! And may every corrupt, grafting, squandering knave in public office promptly feel the power of their righteous wrath," crowed an editorial, noting women's "conspicuous role" in Morrison's win and commenting pointedly on "indifference on the part of the masculine herd." The press seemed inclined to designate the IWO women as keepers of the flame of decency in government while excusing men ("too occupied with their various concerns to keep properly watchful") from such an exercise.[82] For its part, the IWO readily accepted this time-honored version of the gender-appropriate political role for women.

The 1946 constitution of the Independent Women's Organization opened

TABLE 5. *Upper-Class Affiliations of Original Board of Governors, Independent Women's Organization, 1946*

Name	Social Register, 1927	Male Relative in Boston Club
Baker, Mrs. Robert	yes	?
Bruns, Bland Cox	yes	yes
Demarest, Mrs. Francis	yes	yes
Friend, Ida Weiss	yes	no
Goodspeed, Mrs. Lawrence	no	no
Labouisse, Catherine	yes	yes
Moore, Mrs. Edward	yes	yes
Morrison, Mary Meek	no	no
Oliver, Mrs. Norvin	no	?
Ott, Mrs. Lionel G.	no	no
Reily, Gladys Weeks	yes	yes
Ricau, Mrs. Gustave	yes	no
Waters, July Breazeale	yes	yes

Source: New Orleans Social Register, 1927; Landry, *History of the Boston Club.*

membership to women voters, registered in Orleans Parish, "upon approval of the Board." The general membership included around one thousand white women in 1946. Because of the IWO's size, general meetings were infrequent, usually four a year. Although they had been invaluable as foot soldiers in the Morrison campaign, the rank and file did not wield the clout that the IWO could deliver. That privilege lay with the board of governors, a body of twelve members, plus the president, chosen by a nominating committee, elected for two-year terms, and eligible for reelection. It was the board that had the power to speak for the IWO. It was the board that took positions on public matters and then used radio and the press to advise the public of these positions.[83]

Just as they had been in Hilda Phelps Hammond's Women's Committee and Martha Gilmore Robinson's Woman Citizens' Union, the women of the New Orleans elite were heavily represented among the leadership of the Independent Women's Organization. The roster of the first board of governors for the IWO consisted of twelve prominent local women, of whom nine were listed in the Social Register and at least five had husbands or other male relatives in the Boston Club. (Table 5 lists the first IWO board members and their upper-class affiliations.) This inner circle met at least monthly, sometimes more often, at July Waters's home in the Garden District, typically spending two morning hours in IWO business.[84]

This influential inner core of the IWO enjoyed ready access to deLesseps Morrison, especially in the first years of his administration. Recalled a charter member, "We could *always* get in there to see him, any time we wanted to." Indeed, Morrison's official appointment books reflect numerous meetings with IWO board members as well as engagements to address the group or to appear before the board to answer questions. On an official basis, it appears that Morrison met with IWO women at least monthly in the late 1940s, and certainly more often than that unofficially. Traveling in the same social circles of the New Orleans gentry, Morrison and the IWO power structure frequently came face to face at dinners, receptions, weddings, and the like. A few minutes on the dance floor with the mayor often proved sufficient to transact a piece of business. This sort of casual access to Morrison was worth a great deal to the women and was owing strictly to their being inhabitants of the same social community.[85]

In politics, access traditionally translates into something concrete: a minor position for one's nephew, favors for one's friends, passes to the racetrack, special paving on one's street, perhaps. The greater the access, the greater the rewards, culminating with influence on major appointments and key policies. The old-style pols who had abandoned the Old Regulars for the Morrison camp commonly desired a say-so in patronage matters, whereas the so-called Cold Water Committee, a highly influential body of the city's social and economic elite that financed Morrison's campaigns and consequently carried heavy weight with him, preferred influence on policy and policy makers. This arrangement replicated the situation that had existed while Martin Behrman headed the city administration earlier in the century.[86]

The women of the IWO, new to the role of political insiders, initially plunged in with gusto, helping themselves to the spoils of political victory. The first president remembered, "That was a lovely thing, the reward afterwards, being able to get jobs. We'd just put in for them and we could get 'em, Bland [Bruns] and I. And Mr. Gray, too," she added, referring to the former Old Regular who became Morrison's man in the Tenth Ward. "But," she went on in a confiding tone, "a lot of it through me, because I had access to *all the higher-ups* that he didn't have."[87]

Morrison's biographer Edward Haas, in a study indicatively titled *DeLesseps S. Morrison and the Image of Reform*, posits that Morrison, the consummate political animal, "all too often . . . was content with the illusion of reform" and that he "frequently allowed his ambitions and penchant for expediency to override his belief in good government."[88] Waste and corruption resulted; discrimination and spoils politics reemerged. And as time passed, Morrison the opportunist disappointed the idealists of the IWO.

New Orleans had long tolerated more vice than other southern cities. An 1853 observer had commented, "From certain flagrant features of open abandonment . . . among a population so little American in its composition, it is not strange that an impression extremely unfavorable to the morals of the city should be produced."[89] Through long decades of multicultural familiarity with varieties of "sin" unknown in primmer regions, the local mores had stretched to permit jazz, honky-tonks, B-girls, prostitution, suggestive dancing, unorthodox expressions of sexuality, high consumption of alcohol, and many kinds of gambling establishments in Orleans Parish. Not all of this was legal, but as Martin Behrman had allegedly said of prostitution, "You can make it illegal, but you can't make it unpopular."

Early in his first term, deLesseps Morrison found himself caught between the reforming mentality of some of his most vigorous supporters, particularly the IWO membership, and the prevailing ethos in the Crescent City, which wanted to preserve the illicit activities. Morrison's personal proclivities led him to side with the "live and let live" school. Martha Gilmore Robinson said of him: "He was a real south Louisianian in that gambling wasn't bad; it was a good; people had to amuse themselves and it didn't do any harm. It was in his background. . . . He wasn't interested in cleaning up the French Quarter. . . . He had that Latin way, that attitude toward gambling and drinking."[90]

During the campaign, Morrison addressed a huge rally of women workers at the Monteleone Hotel and pledged himself to getting rid of "the vicious gambling syndicate" in the city, a stance that he knew would please his audience. After his election, however, legalized gambling arose as Morrison's solution to a potential political problem with vice. Many of his financial backers supported this choice. Within days of his election, Morrison proposed authorizing 3,000 slot machines and 250 racing handbooks. He urged licensing private clubs and permitting roulette wheels, dice, and card games, thus satisfying the public appetite for gambling while giving the city control and income. Said he, "Remove the objectionable features from gambling but leave it to provide revenue for the city."[91]

Implementation of these drastic proposals required an act of the legislature, a body dominated by rural interests and not likely to view gambling favorably. To give his bills any chance of passage, Morrison needed to approach the statehouse in Baton Rouge with a monolith of support in New Orleans to buttress his position. But Morrison's gambling plan roused immediate opposition from religious groups, particularly the New Orleans

Council of Church Women, a body that represented fifty-nine Protestant women's societies. The vigorous rejection of his scheme by churchwomen could not have come as a surprise to the mayor. However, he counted heavily ("just dying to have it," one IWO member recalled) on an endorsement from the Independent Women's Organization, which was by this time a prestigious, highly respected group identified in the public mind with good government.[92]

Within the Independent Women's Organization, local millionaire Edith Rosenwald Stern was the most vociferous advocate of the gambling proposal. The IWO board of governors opposed the plan, citing the association of gambling with organized crime and juvenile delinquency. The IWO constitution allowed the powerful board of governors to decide whether to award IWO endorsement to the gambling proposal. But, because the issue had sparked controversy all over the city, and because Stern, a heavy financial contributor to Morrison's campaign but not an IWO board member, was insistent about allowing the general membership to vote, the board decided to take its stand and then to convene a general IWO meeting. At this meeting, two IWO members would speak about the mayor's plan, one pro and one con. After ample discussion, the full membership would vote on the question.[93]

On May 20, 1946, deLesseps Morrison, still in his first month as mayor, came before the IWO board, at the women's request, to answer their questions about his proposed gambling plan.[94] The board members formed the core of Morrison's strong support among local women; barely four months earlier, they had stood for hours on his behalf in freezing weather to work at the polls on election day. They knew Morrison and his wife socially; there were significant bonds between him and these women. No prigs themselves, decidedly not provincial, the IWO board members nonetheless had serious objections to his plan to legalize gambling. Morrison, a master at persuasion, appearing before a pro-Morrison audience, had every reason to expect to convert the IWO board. His arguments centered on the reduction of police corruption, increased revenues for charities, hospitals, and general improvements, and a reduction of city taxes, all of which he alleged legalized gambling would make possible. Members of the IWO board, however, harbored very strong antigambling feelings; most knew well the familiar boasts of the benefits gambling could bring their city and knew even better the lurid history of the corrupt Louisiana Lottery of the late nineteenth century. In the end, Morrison's arguments failed to win them.

Morrison at this meeting evidently made a pitch for the IWO to incorporate itself with his political organization, the Crescent City Democratic Association (CCDA), as a sort of women's auxiliary. In return for giving the IWO more leverage in patronage matters, his group would subsume the IWO within itself and give Morrison more control over the women's group. As a lure, this bait was extremely obvious, and Morrison's timing was maladroit. The women were outraged at Morrison's indiscretion in resorting to what seemed the outright bribery of a patronage offer to win them. They truly valued their autonomy and had no intention of surrendering their eponymous independence, feeling that they best served good government by remaining an independent group. Morrison's blatant tactics repelled the women, who had no intention of playing Jonah while the mayor played whale. Their vote to oppose his gambling measures dealt Morrison a severe and unexpected blow.

The day after the meeting, July Waters wrote Morrison a formal refusal of his patronage offer. Her reasoning reflects an awareness of the IWO's perceived position as arbiter, a disinterested good-government group above the quid pro quo that characterized politics at the precinct level, and indicates political astuteness. "Since the Independent Women's Organization has no control over appointments and no say in all appointments, we feel sure you will understand our decision that we cannot assume responsibility for isolated parts of patronage, and confuse the public as to our responsibility for patronage at large."[95]

Although the IWO board members exerted themselves on occasion to secure particular appointments, they appear to have done so on a purely ad hoc, situational basis and not as a matter of routine. If the IWO allowed itself to be taken into the Morrison tent, it would forfeit its greatest strength: the widely held belief that it was "a watchdog for civic virtue."[96] The majority of IWO board members agreed that their watchdog function could best be fulfilled by their keeping entirely clear of obligations and preserving their valuable freedom to criticize the incumbent whenever circumstances warranted. Thus, the IWO decided to remain independent, in fact as well as in name. Having begun life as a separatist women's group, its members elected to continue in that vein, rejecting a chance to become more fully integrated into factional politics.

The IWO rejection of Morrison's gambling plan won front-page headlines. "Women Rap Gambling Plan," announced the *New Orleans Item* in a page-one article that left the clear impression that the group's stand had great significance. In Baton Rouge, Earl Long prowled through the legislature, newspaper in hand, shaking the story at his listeners and growling, "Why, even his *women* don't support him on this thing!"[97]

Morrison had another chance to win the support of this very influential group of women, however. Knowing that the IWO would meet in general session on Friday, May 24, to conduct its open forum on the gambling issue, he began badgering the leadership to allow him to appear and speak to the entire membership in behalf of his plan.[98] The board steadfastly adhered to its original agenda, which allowed for one IWO member to argue for the Morrison gambling plan, followed by another IWO member to speak against it. Faced with adamant refusal, Morrison, with his next move, lost some credibility with his most fervent group of supporters.

On the night of the meeting, July Waters had an importunate phone call from Victor Wogan, a close Morrison aide, who pleaded with her to relent and let the mayor address the women. Citing the board's feeling that an address by the mayor would carry too much emotional baggage to allow for a decision on the merits of the issue, she refused. Arriving at the school to preside over the gathering, she was met by an IWO member who brought unpleasant news. "Chep is in the building! He's hiding down in the principal's office!" Feeling keenly that to allow Morrison to address the group would be to give unfair advantage to his proposal, a very nervous Waters, wondering what the mayor had in mind, walked onto the stage of the auditorium of Sophie Wright High School to face a crowd of hundreds of interested women.

Informing the group that two IWO members would present reports on their findings for and against legalized gambling, Waters announced that the general public was welcome but would not be allowed to participate in the discussion or to vote. Having concluded her explanation, Waters was taken aback to see the mayor of New Orleans striding up the center aisle toward the stage. As he walked, applause began at the back and followed his progress forward, until the entire room was thunderous with clapping. Realizing that the women believed his entrance to be a part of the script, Waters clapped politely while consternation reigned within her.

When Morrison reached the stage, he proceeded straight to the microphone, greeted Waters, and, in a breezy, confident way, said that he could not resist talking a bit to "all these ladies." While Waters courteously stood aside for the interloper, he began to berate the IWO board, which she headed, for having taken a public stand against his gambling proposal. After a few moments, Waters recovered her composure and interrupted the mayor, who was confidently selling his proposal to a rapt and unsuspecting audience. "Mayor Morrison," she recalled saying, "I hate to do this, but I must tell you that you are not supposed to talk today. I can't have you address this meeting. And I don't think it is proper for you to make those remarks against us that you are making."

Waters recalled a tense pause, after which Morrison, "with a hang-dog expression," turned and silently walked off the stage, down the aisle, and out the door. His wife, an IWO member, rose and walked out, as did some other members, to protest his not being allowed to finish. Since all plans had gone awry, Waters, appalled at the turn of events, called a recess in the meeting to consult the parliamentarian. They decided to resume the meeting, adhering to the arranged format for presentations and discussion, but concluded that there had been undue influence and that they should not take a vote.

Waters chose not to reveal to the general membership exactly what had gone before between the mayor's office and herself, how he had tried to get clearance to speak, had failed, and had taken it upon himself to force his way in and be heard. "I just didn't want to tell them; I didn't want to put him in that light," she said with regret in her voice, forty years later. Feeling disappointment and anger at Morrison's behavior, she nonetheless felt that as the first nonmachine mayor of her city in a quarter of a century and one pledged to reform, he deserved her group's continued support. She decently forbore to say anything that would cost him popularity or credibility, even at some risk to her own.

Subsequently, the state legislature defeated one gambling bill, and Morrison withdrew the other. Many factors contributed to the gambling rejection, but Morrison's failure to secure the endorsement of the Independent Women's Organization, with its sterling reputation and influence, must rank high among them. Thereafter, relations between the mayor and his previously most loyal supporters cooled a bit, as he was deeply displeased with them. Waters explained, however, in a frank and accurate assessment of IWO status, "He had to have us. He needed us." The IWO members remained strong for Morrison in general and backed him when they felt he was right, which was often. He had been their candidate; among both IWO members and political observers, the feeling was strong that women had virtually delivered his upset election in 1946. Despite the rift over the gambling issue, IWO members continued to have access to the mayor. As a past IWO president put it, "We spent an awful lot of time going down to the mayor's office and telling him what to do. . . . And he did do a good many things we wanted."[99]

Despite this breach with their candidate early on in his administration, the Independent Women's Organization developed a reputation in some quarters for being blindly supportive of any Morrison measure. Martha Gilmore Robinson, not herself a part of the IWO, scoffed, "The Independent Women's Organization? They weren't independent. They were *Chep's* Women's Organization!"[100]

A list of their mutual causes is much lengthier than a roster of issues on which they found themselves taking opposite positions. The IWO members generally endorsed most of Morrison's CCDA ticket when elections rolled around. They unanimously sanctioned a controversial bond issue, worth $23.5 million, without which Morrison's ambitious program of city improvements, particularly construction of a union railroad terminal and a new city hall, would not have been possible. With the women's influential support, the bond issue squeaked by the voters with a slim margin of just over one thousand votes.[101]

The women of the IWO worked for Judge Robert Kennon, the Morrison-backed candidate, in his 1948 race against young Russell Long for the U.S. Senate seat vacated by the death of the once controversial John Overton. Long eked out a very narrow victory in the state, carrying it by fewer than ten thousand votes. In New Orleans, however, Kennon carried fourteen of the seventeen wards and won the city by a large majority. One suspects that in this case the IWO members had campaigned with particular vigor, with the motive of working against the son and inheritor of Huey Long, against whom large numbers of them had worked in the Women's Committee in the 1930s. A Russell Long candidacy, activating all the old memories and prejudices against his father, would have helped to mobilize the women fully.[102]

The Independent Women's Organization excelled in getting out the vote, a labor-intensive task that required hours of patient personal contacts and follow-up. Politicians of every faction acknowledged its influence and effectiveness, although Morrison exaggerated when he said of the IWO, "Even the dyed-in-the-wool Old Regulars will tell you that whoever gets the women's vote is a cinch to win." He came closer to accurate description when he asserted, "Women have the kind of push and pep needed to put over a campaign."[103]

The impression was strong that women, by their sheer hard work, had engineered Morrison's first election. Their uncounted hours of canvassing, envelope stuffing, and telephoning, their hostessing of coffee parties and "meet the candidate" occasions before the election, coupled with their service at the polls on election day, were of course made possible by the fact that those involved expected and received absolutely no remuneration for their work. Their valuable labor was free. The overwhelming majority of IWO members were not employed outside their homes. In general, the upbringing, education, and temperament of IWO leaders had left them unsuited for any paying job that they might have been able to secure, had they sought to work. Political activism provided a welcome outlet for their genuine talents of speaking, organizing, fund-raising, planning, and motivating. Their participation received sanction from husbands, parents, friends; working for Morrison (whom they, or their daughters, had voted "most popular escort" in the 1936 debutante season) was socially and personally acceptable in a way that taking paid work would not have been.[104]

As the years unfolded, the major source of IWO dissatisfaction with de-Lesseps Morrison centered on public education and what women perceived as his calculated attempt to politicize the local board of education to his advantage. During Robert Maestri's years as mayor, school board posts had been plums given to loyalists for services rendered, and the schools had naturally suffered. A new law forbade Morrison to endorse officially any school board candidate or to place candidates on a sample ballot as part of a ticket that he approved, though he could with a wink and a nod let everyone know whom he supported.

Historically a "women's issue," education naturally appealed to many women because of their role as nurturers and teachers of children. From the late 1940s through the 1950s, the Independent Women's Organization played a key role in reforming the public schools of Orleans Parish. In its first year of existence, the IWO created a committee on school improvement that produced a thoughtful report deploring the fact that "the best talent available for a school board [would] not run because individuals, particularly women, [were] not willing to undergo the rigors and expense of a campaign."[105] The IWO favored a law mandating appointment of the school board by the mayor, but the state legislature rejected such a measure. Subsequently, IWO member Sarah Heath Sharp announced her candidacy for the school board. Although Sharp, a wife and mother, graduate of Randolph-Macon College, and former president of the Louisiana Parent-Teacher Association, was superbly qualified, her campaign spent little money and attracted little media attention; the major newspapers failed to endorse her.[106]

Sharp assumed energetic IWO support for her candidacy. However, a disappointing ruling by the state attorney general that the IWO was "political" prohibited the group from actively supporting any candidate in school board elections, which had been assigned new "nonpolitical" status by recent legislation. Members of the IWO then voted to work individually for Sharp, but predictably, their individual efforts lacked sufficient energy and direction. Sharp's prospects were not aided by the fact that, although she was one of three independent challengers seeking to oust the Old Regular school board member, the press backed another candidate and scolded her for not withdrawing in order to avoid splitting the good-government, antimachine vote. It could, of course, have scolded the other candidates for not withdrawing to leave her a clear field, but a female candidate was still a new and possibly threatening idea in 1946. The Old Regular was reelected to the school board.

However, the combined votes for Sharp and the closest challenger totaled well over his. An I-told-you-so editorial nagged, "The outcome was regrettable but no surprise. We twice predicted it would be just what it was unless one of the independent candidates retired from the fray." The editors' choice for dropout was Sarah Sharp.[107]

Morrison had done nothing whatsoever to aid Sharp's candidacy, placidly allowing himself to be bound by the letter of the new law. He soon acted to name Sharp to a spot on the City Planning Commission and further flattered the IWO by choosing another of its members, Gladys Reily, to serve as the only woman on his eleven-member advisory commission. Of course, service on advisory bodies as token women members diluted whatever impact the women might have had, as Morrison may have intended.[108]

The IWO drew a lesson from Sarah Sharp's defeat in 1946. Even though forbidden to work as a group, the members vowed to make their influence felt in future elections for school board. Barred by the state attorney general's ruling from using the IWO name for endorsement of any school board candidate, they ingeniously utilized the nonpartisan American Association of University Women (AAUW), to which many IWO members belonged, to lead the effort. Ultimately, they formed a group called Citizens for Progress in the Public Schools; a look at its membership reveals chiefly IWO members.[109]

Various ills plagued New Orleans public schools in the post–World War II period. Under Robert Maestri, all school jobs, from principal to janitor, had been distributed as patronage. No new school had been constructed in more than ten years, and the existing buildings were in deplorable condition, crumbling firetraps with falling plaster and dark corridors. The baby boom caused such overcrowding that split sessions by shift were necessary to cope with the numbers of pupils. Revelations of a horse meat scandal, wherein the wieners bought by the school system for school lunches were of seriously poor quality, outraged the public. This confluence of circumstances helped focus attention on the school board to an unprecedented degree. In 1948, a reformer, Jacqueline T. McCullough, successfully ran for a seat on the school board, winning by a margin of more than ten thousand votes. Although she credited the hard work of women for her victory, McCullough did not cite the IWO by name, because legally it could not participate. In reality, IWO members had taken up her cause and delivered their patented hard work.[110]

The women of the IWO had been unable to interest a man to seek a lowly school board seat as a reform candidate, and after Sarah Sharp's failure, no woman from the IWO had really wanted to make the race. McCullough, an outsider in every respect, was a divorcée, a native of Oklahoma, part Cherokee Indian; it appears that she had absolutely no connections with the New Orleans establishment. Her 1948 election marked what the local press chose to call "a victory for Mayor Morrison." However, he had neither endorsed her nor assisted her campaign. In fact, Morrison would in short order be working behind the scenes to prevent the election of candidates like Jacqueline McCullough.[111]

McCullough proceeded to set the school board on its ear. Her resentment over its closed sessions had led her to run in the first place. Now she warned that if the board continued to meet clandestinely, she as a board member fully intended to make public every detail of board business. The board relented and held open meetings. When she discovered that, one by one, the four men were excusing themselves to go to the men's room, where they clearly remained to transact school business, she called their hand on that tactic and promised to tell the public if they ever did it again. They stopped. Suddenly, public education was a hot issue.

In the school board election of 1950, the IWO and the AAUW sponsored well-attended public forums at which school board candidates aired their views about New Orleans schools. These forums met in area churches after the angry school superintendent, wincing under the barrage of criticism loosed in the meetings, refused to allow the use of public schools for such sessions, intending to deny the reformers a hearing. In one session, an incumbent board member whom the women wanted to unseat charged that "a small group" was trying to take over the board. Furious because numbers of women, many from the IWO, had been been attending school board meetings regularly and posing tough questions, he asked voters to elect "native persons" to serve. This was a reference to the fact that the elected reformer, McCullough, was an Oklahoman by birth and that Clarence Scheps and C. P. Besse, the challenging reformers whom the women backed in 1950, originally hailed from out of state as well. "Will you let . . . a foreigner from Oklahoma [McCullough], the Johnny-come-lately from Texas [Scheps] and Mrs. Moneybags control your public schools, or will you re-elect R. E. Mahoney?" he thundered. The reference to "Mrs. Moneybags" took surly aim at every middle- and upper-class woman engaged in the endeavor to oust him and put in progressive citizens instead.[112]

Three hundred uptown women made an estimated sixty thousand phone calls to get out the vote. With this extensive assistance, Scheps and Besse won their school board posts handily, despite the fact that the school superintendent had campaigned for their opponents. The innovators by 1950 held a majority on the school board and used it to effect numerous reforms. They implemented a central purchasing system, regular audits, and modern accounting methods; they instigated construction of eleven badly needed new schools and renovations of forty-one others. On a more long-range level, they began to lobby for public support in appointing a truly professional school man to serve as superintendent, with no weight given to his nativity.[113]

At the first school board meeting attended by new members Scheps and Besse, the board elected a new president, Jacqueline McCullough (who had remarried and was by this time Jacqueline Leonhard). Leonhard had gone several rounds with recalcitrant school superintendent Lionel Bourgeois, who had flatly refused to allow her to read an evaluation of the school system that severely criticized his administration. She responded by coming to his office with her attorney, who told Bourgeois that Leonhard was prepared to file charges immediately unless he gave her the report. What she read convinced her that Bourgeois should step down. Presiding over her first meeting as school board president, she and the newly elected reform faction passed a resolution accusing the superintendent of incompetence and inefficiency and calling for a hearing into his conduct of office. Clearly, the revolution had begun.[114]

The mayor, who had kept hands off the school board in the races of 1946, 1948, and 1950, suddenly took an interest in 1952. Unfortunately, his interest proved negative. The innovators were attempting to secure two more members who embraced their progressive outlook about school governance. In a face-to-face private meeting with the reformers Besse, Leonhard, and Scheps, Morrison allegedly stated bluntly that unless they would approve his choice for superintendent of schools and appoint a CCDA ward leader to serve as school board attorney, he would throw his weight publicly to two school board candidates whom they found regressive and unacceptable.[115]

Upon learning of this, the IWO passed a resolution at its general meeting, attended by 650 members, regarding the mayor and the school situation. The IWO statement excoriated Morrison for meddling. Noting that the IWO had twice worked strenuously for his election and had always accepted his assurances that he would enforce separation of politics and schools, the IWO members cried foul in a resolution urging the voters to "reject all efforts at political control of the school board." They then released their stinging statement to the press, which printed it on the front page.[116]

With this resolution, the Independent Women's Organization rapped its protégé's knuckles, publicly and hard. He made no public rejoinder to the IWO message but opposed its two candidates anyway. Although clearly upset with Morrison, the IWO chose to go no further with criticism directed at him.

The local press, however, published a letter from the Citizens for Progress in the Public Schools calling deLesseps Morrison a liar; those who signed this critical letter were all IWO members.[117]

Ultimately, the women's candidates, Theodore Shepard and Emile Wagner, won easily despite Morrison's backing their opponents. Their election gave the New Orleans school board five progressive, disinterested citizens highly acceptable to that portion of the population with an educated, good-government outlook. The average age of a school board member after the 1952 elections was under forty, a drop of nearly thirty years since 1946. It appears that women were the prime movers in this school board overhaul, fully responsible for awakening public interest in school board elections and for reforming school governance. After 1952, Morrison abandoned his ill-advised efforts to dabble in school board politics.[118]

Having succeeded so well in reforming local school politics, the IWO next trained its sights on a much more formidable target, the bête noire of progressive educational practices in Louisiana, state superintendent of schools Shelby Jackson. Early in 1954, a group of education specialists from George Peabody College had released a comprehensive report on the state of public education in Louisiana that the Louisiana Legislative Council had commissioned. Although critical of many inferior aspects of Louisiana public education, the outside evaluators reserved their strongest criticism for an autocratic structure that allowed the state superintendent to exercise one-man control of his state's schools. Jackson, an elected official firmly allied with the Long faction, routinely ignored the state board of education when making policy and when disbursing education funds to the sixty-four parishes, the Louisiana equivalent of counties. The Peabody Survey recommended an independent staff to serve the board of education, whose members were totally dependent on Jackson for any and all data regarding his policies and expenditures and who consequently often lacked same, having been "totally nonentitized" by the dictatorial Jackson. Jackson's strenuous arm-twisting scotched a 1954 bill intended to fund such a staff and bring the light of inquiry into his personal fiefdom.[119]

Infuriated by Jackson's high-handedness, the IWO swung into action, with an IWO member, Margaret Polk (Mrs. Paul) McIlhenny, chairing CAPS, the Committee for Action on the Peabody Survey. The women gathered facts, disseminated them, and proselytized energetically about the merits of an appointed state school superintendent. In 1955, the IWO joined the state PTA in backing a bill for a separate budget for the Louisiana State Board of Education, which Jackson branded as a measure sure to lead "only to disunity, duplication, and confusion." He much preferred the status quo, which enabled him to bypass an impotent and uninformed state board of education and to disburse unilaterally four dollars out of every ten spent by Louisiana's government.[120]

In 1955, the IWO and the New Orleans League of Women Voters endorsed Alice Stringer of Baton Rouge, a former president of the state PTA, when she announced her candidacy opposing Shelby Jackson. A good campaigner but a political neophyte, Stringer won endorsements from all three New Orleans daily newspapers. She repeatedly scored Jackson for abusing his office, building a political machine, and attempting to intimidate state school board members, charges that forced him to expend unaccustomed financial and personal resources to win reelection. With the advantage of running on the Long ticket in a year when voters swept Earl Long back into the governor's office, he defeated Stringer by a margin of five to one. New Orleans women nevertheless continued to work actively for years for Shelby Jackson's defeat and removal from virtual czardom in Louisiana public education.[121]

The decade of the 1940s brought New Orleans women into political participation in significant numbers, with much of the leadership for reform movements coming from them. Through their work, they developed strategic and tactical skills, speaking talents, organizational methods, and, most important, confidence in their own abilities. Their fledgling and unsuccessful efforts for Sam Jones in 1940 matured to pay dividends when they backed deLesseps Morrison six years later. A longtime leader of the Independent Women's Organization summed up her feelings about the elections of Jones and Morrison: "We were such neophytes. [Laughs] We had such fun doing it. I say fun, because those elections were really thrilling, because it was black and white. . . . The line was drawn; it was Right and Wrong. . . . It was so pronounced and so evident that you were inspired to work, and to win it. . . . It was the most thrilling, exciting, interesting thing to work in those campaigns!"[122]

Her words make clear the sheer exhilaration felt by participating women. They derived pleasure from playing their parts in a moral crusade wherein Right jousted with and, in the cases of Sam Jones, Chep Morrison, and the public school situation, unhorsed Wrong. For women reformers, Wrong meant corruption, bribery, waste, vulgarity, inefficiency, plunder, and dishonesty, conditions they always opposed. Their cause took on additional intensity when Wrong was personified by a devil image. Huey Long had been the best devil image imaginable; his successors, the rustic Earl Long, the corpulent Richard Leche, and the Runyonesque Robert Maestri, carried on the tradition by words, deeds, demeanor, and personal habits inimical to the genteel reformers. An educated, affluent southern woman, noting that the South was "absolutely class-ridden," recalled: "'Common' was a great word. If anything was common it was just terrible. Mother used that word often.... That meant it was just vulgar.... There was a great distinction between what 'proper' people did and what 'common' people did."[123]

The crude, alcohol-abusing Huey Long, his buffoonish brother Earl, the porcine Leche, and the inarticulate Maestri all qualified as "common" in the lexicon of many New Orleans middle- and upper-class women. By their definition, Sam Jones and deLesseps Morrison were not "common." But the further away from Huey Long's era they moved, the fewer were the people of that so-called common type who offered themselves as candidates. The further the devil images receded into memory, the less passionately voters responded to the appeals of good-government groups, and, indeed, the good-government groups themselves seemed to feel less passionate about political contests. July Waters's comments about politics in the 1940s being "black and white ... right and wrong ... so pronounced and so evident" began to be less applicable to politics as New Orleans moved into the second half of the twentieth century. The devil image that had initially galvanized many women into reform political activity was disappearing, and loss of a devil image seemed to render them less effective and less active politically. The 1950s would see a change in the type of candidates who offered themselves for office.

Candidates after 1950 would be less obviously associated with either the upper echelons or the lower classes. There was a great middle-class metamorphosis in Louisiana after World War II as mass marketing, mass communications, and mass transportation caused a homogenization of the public. If every candidate seemed to dress and speak more and more like every other candidate, how could an election be a crusade, as in days of old between "common" and "proper," Long and anti-Long? Virtually every candidate would pledge to keep Huey Long's material changes in place, for who could argue with the popularity of bridges and roads and free school textbooks? Virtually every candidate would pledge to run an honest administration, for, after the scandals of 1939 and the upsets of 1940 and 1946, who could afford not to castigate nepotism, venality, and waste?

In the 1950s, the women of New Orleans were to have a unique opportunity to support one of their own, a well-educated, privileged woman who moved in the social circles of the elite. After two decades of trying to elect progressive *men* to important political offices, New Orleans women decided to elect a *woman*. But ironically, when a candidate from the increasingly effective clan of politically interested women stepped forward to run for office, there was no devil image in the race against her. After two decades of emotional political crusades pitting Right against Wrong, Martha Gilmore Robinson's turn at jousting would pit her not against an evil inheritor of Longism but against an innocuous candidate whom some in her circle called the "Little Man on the Wedding Cake."

We must pick out women in our own communities, in our states and in the nation. We must urge them to become candidates for public office. And then we must stand behind them and work for them as women.

—Emily Newell Blair

CHAPTER FIVE

❏

"THE CITY FATHERS NEED A MOTHER"

❏

MARTHA GILMORE ROBINSON'S 1954 CAMPAIGN

❏

FOR CITY COUNCIL IN NEW ORLEANS

The idea that woman's place is in the home has enjoyed sturdy longevity as a mainstay of American culture, but in the post–World War II years it was trumpeted with a special shrillness. Heavy emphasis on gender stressed that unless individuals accepted their "natural" roles (men as breadwinners, women as homemakers and mothers), confusion, discontent, and chaos would result. Advertising, music, movies, and television, joined by a chorus of "experts," relentlessly touted what Betty Friedan later labeled "the feminine mystique," the notion that true fulfillment for women would come only through dedication to domesticity, marriage, and motherhood. The explicit antifeminism that characterized the late 1940s and 1950s led much of society to take a negative or even hostile view of women who pursued options outside the home with too much enthusiasm. Such a climate of opinion obviously created serious obstacles to any woman seeking elective office in this period.[1]

However, though the antifeminist mood of 1950s America was real enough, some scholars now argue that Friedan overstated the case for the pervasiveness of this domestic ideology. The most strident antifeminist rhetoric emanated not from the mainstream but from a conservative fringe. "Not only was the feminine mystique not a phenomenon unique to the postwar world, but many women managed to lead active and interesting lives even at its height."[2] Postwar women's magazines encouraged increased participation of women in politics, including office holding; in one six-month period in 1952, the unquestionably centrist *Ladies' Home Journal* printed articles entitled "It's Time Women Took Direct Action," "Women Like You and Me in Politics," and "Busy Women Have Time Enough."[3]

In New Orleans, the League of Women Voters and the Independent Women's Organization continued to exert an appeal to middle- and upper-class women, pulling them beyond the family-centered life and into political life. In the years immediately after World War II, women led efforts to reform the local schools via electing more progressive individuals to school board posts, as discussed in the previous chapter. In 1950, Bland Cox Bruns, an integral part of the Independent Women's Organization since its origins in 1939, won election to the state legislature, representing the House district composed of Wards Ten and Eleven in New Orleans. Her district was home to July Waters, the IWO's first president, whose efforts had made the neighborhood a stronghold of IWO activity and organization. Bruns's sponsorship of a permanent voter registration bill, support for state civil service laws and home rule for New Orleans, and attention to issues affecting the welfare of women and children ensured her the continued backing of progressive women's groups, while her ability to adapt to the "impurities" of politics, such as the realities of spoilsmanship, solidified her position with Mayor Chep Morrison's forces. Indeed, Bruns served as chairman of the women's auxiliary of the CCDA (Crescent City Democratic Association), the Morrison organization at ward and precinct levels.[4] Bruns's reelection in 1952 convinced the IWO that the time was right for a woman candidate to crack the citadel of city politics, and thus, two decades of women's increased political awareness and activity culminated in Martha Gilmore Robinson's 1954 candidacy for the New Orleans city council.

In 1953, deLesseps Morrison was concluding his second term as mayor of New Orleans. A new city charter, written by a citizens' committee and adopted by the local voters in November 1952, stipulated that no mayor could serve more than two consecutive terms, but its provisions were not retroactive. Morrison, who had won two terms before the charter took effect, had a clear field to continue as mayor of New Orleans until 1962, and it surprised no one when he announced as a candidate for reelection.

The municipal election of January 1954 was the first held under the new city charter. To replace the old commission council, whose members had come from gerrymandered districts both under- and overrepresented, the charter committee had created a city council with two at-large members and five members to be elected from reapportioned districts. Having had little opposition from the council in his first two terms, Morrison intended to employ long coattails to sweep into office with him a city council of "cooperators" who would not oppose his plans, plans that were often extravagant and increasingly under fire from his critics.

As mayor, Morrison had built the Crescent City Democratic Association, an apparatus designed to perpetuate him and his supporters in office. Organized tightly along precinct and ward lines, the CCDA dispensed patronage, resolved grievances, and got out the vote for Morrison. Candidates actively courted a CCDA endorsement and held a spot on the Morrison-CCDA ticket in high regard. In short, the CCDA was a political machine, constructed by the man who had flailed the incumbent mayor, Robert Maestri, for having such a machine when he challenged him in 1946.[5]

The other New Orleans political faction existing in the 1950s with precinct and ward organization was the Regular Democratic Organization. Defections to the CCDA had decimated the RDO ranks, as the Old Regulars responded to overtures from the mayor and rallied to the cause of reform — if the price was right. Contemporaries felt that the Regular Democratic Organization was, by 1954, a weak organization, a relic of another day. Turned out in the short grass since Maestri's defeat in 1946, the RDO, though still intermittently effective, was no longer the power it had once been in city politics.[6]

Morrison benefited to a great extent from the contrast between the Old Regulars and his own CCDA, which he successfully depicted as a collection of energetic good citizens united in support of an upright reformer. In reality, both bodies were urban political machines, skillfully employing similar tactics, but Morrison's snug relationship with the New Orleans press insulated him from close scrutiny and negative evaluation. Morrison's biographer Ed Haas concluded that the mayor was "a politician, gregarious, ambitious, and astutely expedient." Although not the overweight, undereducated, cigar-chomping manipulator of caricature, Morrison was, despite his education, good looks, and sense of style, the head of a machine. He was very much a big-city "boss."[7]

Morrison enjoyed the enthusiastic support of the local press. Just past his fortieth birthday, the mayor retained his popularity after eight years in office. Among his accomplishments, creating the widely admired—and highly photogenic—New Orleans Recreation Department (NORD) program, with its welter of new playgrounds, swimming pools, athletic fields, and recreation buildings, ranked high. In addition, plans for a new, modern city hall were proceeding, as well as for consolidation of all rail and bus lines into one efficient, centrally located terminal.[8]

Although Morrison was universally credited with making physical improvements for the city, his detractors questioned his tendency to think in terms of bricks and mortar at the expense of less visible but equally important parts of civic life. Some criticized him for what they saw as his friendly attitude toward vice elements entrenched in New Orleans, his meddling in police business, his rumored associations with organized crime, his tendency to give priority to high-visibility projects, his massive ego and ambition, his cavalier attitude toward the truth, and his great reliance on public relations experts at a time when image makers were largely unknown. By 1953 a citizens' body called the Metropolitan Crime Commission had instigated a full-scale police probe in New Orleans, employing former FBI agent Aaron Kohn to conduct the investigations. Although publicly supportive of the action, behind the scenes a furious Chep Morrison was working vigorously to resist the inquiry and discredit its evidence of a far-reaching network of graft and an unsavory relationship between law enforcement and politics. He enlisted his CCDA ward leaders to hinder the investigation as well. Some disillusioned loyalists in the reform element thought they detected a disquieting lust for power in the mayor.[9]

Evidence of Morrison's desire for control surfaced in 1950 when the legislature at last granted New Orleans home rule and permitted creation by citizens of a municipal charter. Although initially loud in his praise of the idea of the charter, the mayor cooled when he learned that he would not appoint the twelve members of the charter commission. The Morrison-dominated council would name two members, but the other ten would be chosen by ten organizations that would each submit three names to the council, leaving it to choose the ones it favored. However, when the organizations learned of Morrison's desire to stack the charter commission with individuals of his own choosing, they thwarted him by displaying an unusual unanimity; each group submitted only one name. Morrison thus had no leeway in selecting the individuals who wrote the city charter.[10]

Among the twelve New Orleanians on the charter commission, there was one woman, Martha Gilmore Robinson.[11] Robinson's unanimous selection by the League of Women Voters surprised no one; she had led that body since its first incarnation as the Woman Citizens' Union in the 1930s and was arguably the leading woman activist in New Orleans. She brought to the task of writing a city charter a bias against the strong-mayor type of government (a legacy of her political science study at Tulane) and a decided coolness toward the mayor himself.

Robinson had earlier served one term as the only woman on the Louisiana Board of Institutions. A Sam Jones appointee in 1940, she had inspected state facilities, given meticulous attention to reports and audits, and showed herself a diligent reader who devoured printed material, eagerly dispatching the homework associated with the position. In 1945, she was named to the board of the New Orleans Bureau of Governmental Research, a private nonpartisan watchdog group dedicated to reviewing municipal government performance and offering intelligent suggestions for improvement. On that important body, she was again the only woman.

At the start of Morrison's first term in office, the Bureau of Governmental Research submitted numerous carefully considered recommendations to him. Morrison embraced suggestions concerning reorganization of financial administration and expansion of the Recreation Department, but he ignored recommendations that he place more city employees under civil service protection and that he abolish the mayor's permit fund, a vast slush fund entirely at the mayor's disposal for which only the scantiest records were kept and for which he was accountable to no one. Martha Robinson, who had had a role in drafting these recommendations, felt strongly that they were in the interest of honest, efficient government and that Morrison's rejection of them did not bode well for the city.[12]

Unlike the Bureau of Governmental Research, which had no power to implement its suggestions, the twelve-member charter commission of 1951–52 produced the document that literally made the rules for governing New Orleans. Martha Robinson was the *only* individual to have contributed to both the 1946 Bureau of Governmental Research recommendations to the mayor and the 1952 city charter. Robinson assisted materially with the tedious and demanding task of writing the charter. Harry McCall, charter commission chairman, said of her that no member took a keener interest or made a greater contribution to it.[13]

The new charter contained the exact elements of reform that Morrison had rejected when the Bureau of Governmental Research had first raised them in 1946. It abolished outright the mayor's permit fund and placed more city workers under civil service protection. Martha Robinson was identified as one of the strongest supporters of the "little Hatch Act," the provision that protected municipal employees from being forced to engage in political activity in behalf of the incumbent mayor. Mayor Morrison had disliked these provisions in 1946, and he objected strenuously in 1952 to their inclusion in the charter. Robinson's long-standing antipathy to machine politics led her to oppose a mayor's unregulated special fund and a mayor's ability to deploy brigades of city employees as campaign workers. Her persistence in behalf of these measures made it more difficult for an urban political machine to operate out of the mayor's office, exactly as she intended. Her experience in drafting recommendations for the new mayor in 1946 had clearly influenced her input into the city charter six years later.[14]

For more than twenty years, Robinson's political activism had fed her growing mastery of issues in state and local government. Her activities during World War I on the women's division of the Council of National Defense and her later service on the case committee of the local Child Welfare Association had initiated her acquaintance with city bureaucracies. Beginning in 1934, she had headed two groups, the Woman Citizens' Union and its successor, the New Orleans League of Women Voters, that were fact finding, educational, and nonpartisan in nature. Although her WCU and LWV work had taken a great deal of time and had required intelligence and tact, it was of course unpaid.

In 1953, the board of the Independent Women's Organization, the association that had contributed grassroots labor to deLesseps Morrison's campaigns, concluded that the time was right for a woman to serve in city government. July Waters, the IWO's first president and a lifelong friend of Martha Robinson's, approached her about running for a post on the new city council, and the two friends discussed the possibility of a Robinson candidacy. The stereotypical woman's response of coy demurral and protestations of inadequacy was not forthcoming. Instead, in a response reminiscent of John Kennedy's version of how Lyndon Johnson accepted the vice presidential spot on the 1960 ticket ("I just held it out like this . . . and he grabbed at it!"), Waters recalled, somewhat disapprovingly, that Robinson "leaped at the chance." With her friend, Robinson scorned false modesty and did not scruple to admit openly her ambition.[15]

The IWO had good reason to feel optimistic about a Martha Robinson candidacy. With impeccable credentials as a civic activist, Robinson had won wide recognition for her recent service on the city charter commission, as well as for earlier, well-publicized projects with the League of Women Voters.[16] Member of a prominent family, Robinson had always received favorable and ample publicity in the local press. The New Orleans public already knew her as the leader of causes—efforts to obtain voting machines for Orleans Parish, to locate polls in public buildings, to enlist women to monitor polls on election day, to institute a system of permanent voter registration, to save the city's Charity Hospital from massive budget cuts, to professionalize the public library staff and remove it from political control, and to save historic buildings from demolition. At a luncheon in her honor, Anna Many, dean of Newcomb College, said of her, "Mrs. Robinson, I think, was born clutching a banner for a good cause."[17]

Robinson's wealthy and conservative husband agreed, although without notable enthusiasm, to bankroll her race, removing campaign financing as cause for concern. Her name recognition was high, both via her own accomplishments and those of her father, the late Samuel Gilmore, one of the few socially elite individuals in the inner circle that had advised Old Regular Mayor Martin Behrman. Robinson herself was an engaging speaker, witty, energetic, well informed; to those who heard her, she projected a love of her city and an intense desire to serve it well.[18]

Mindful of these assets, the Independent Women's Organization voted unanimously to issue a formal request to Martha Robinson to run for office. A recent study reveals that women candidates cite "encouragement by women's organizations" as the most important factor in their decision to run.[19] Robinson valued the IWO encouragement and accepted its request with alacrity. In February 1953, nearly a full year before the election, she announced her candidacy.

Clouds appeared on the horizon immediately. With surprising political naïveté, the IWO had failed to consider Mayor Morrison's wishes in the matter, evidently assuming that support from his powerful CCDA would be automatic for the candidate whom they backed. On the contrary, "it was common knowledge," according to local political columnist James H. Gillis, that Morrison planned to run Victor Schiro and Glenn Clasen, both then serving on the commission council, for the two at-large slots. Furthermore, by the time he heard from the women, the mayor had already determined his choices for the five district seats as well. When three IWO stalwarts rushed to the mayor's office to tell him of their success in drafting Robinson to run, they got immediate access to Morrison, as usual. But when he heard their news, "his face dropped." It was clear that the idea of a Martha Robinson candidacy held no appeal for him.[20]

In fact, though she had voted for him, Martha Robinson had never supported deLesseps Morrison with great enthusiasm. Her daughter recalled that her mother felt that Morrison "was compromising instead of sticking up for his principles." Robinson commented often that Morrison opposed a full-scale police cleanup in New Orleans, which troubled her; she felt that his image as a tough law-and-order reformer was only a pose that masked a willingness to adulterate impartial law enforcement with blatant favoritism and to tolerate a massive and malignant system of payoffs in the police department. In that view, Robinson was not alone. Morrison's biographer alleges that the local press corps "saw the contradictions, deficiencies, and outright flaws in the Morrison administration," and numerous Morrison contemporaries recall evidence of his hypocrisy. Robinson's correspondence with her friend Natalie Scott reveals that the two women saw Morrison as one who needed "a few doses of sound opposition" and "a bit of taking down."[21]

Added to Robinson's position as a sometime Morrison critic was the fact that she had forced bitter medicine on the mayor with the city charter. The revocation of his private fund and the institution of prohibition of political activity among classified employees had infuriated Morrison. Despite the fact that good-government advocates, his chief financial supporters, and the New Orleans press supported these measures fully, the angry mayor was only narrowly dissuaded from publicly repudiating them. Robinson's part in insisting on these changes was well known at city hall.[22]

Should she be elected, Martha Gilmore Robinson, an affluent homemaker with no children at home, would be the only council member without a profession or job to compete with city affairs for her time. She would be able to devote all of her energy and ability to overseeing city business with the utmost care, a situation of scrutiny not to the mayor's liking, especially since she had been outspoken about her dismay over police corruption. Thomas Brahney, a city councilman in the early 1950s and a Morrison opponent, summed up the situation bluntly. "Oh, my God, he didn't want that woman on the council. Martha Robinson had been up and down his back like a window shade!"[23]

At the outset, the Independent Women's Organization had reason to feel sanguine about Robinson's chances at victory. One cloud of doubt arose when the IWO discovered that Morrison adamantly rejected the idea of putting her on his ticket in 1954. Another took shape when Robinson informed the IWO of her intention to seek election to an at-large post rather than to run for a seat in District A, her home district near Tulane University. The IWO felt tremors of doubt over Robinson's chances in a citywide race. The expenses would be greater, as would the effort involved in meeting the entire electorate. Accordingly, some IWO members tried to persuade Robinson to change her mind and seek the District A post. Arthur Waters, husband of July Waters and an intimate of deLesseps Morrison, and Bland Cox Bruns, a charter IWO member, met with Robinson and spent a long but fruitless session trying to prevail against her determination to run at large. Waters and Bruns left angry and frustrated, in a portent of troubles to come.[24]

Robinson's chief reason for an at-large race centered on her belief that she could draw an overwhelming women's vote citywide. Convinced that women in all wards knew and admired her and would be her staunch supporters, Robinson chose to give women of all classes and backgrounds an opportunity to rally to her; the women's vote was integral to Robinson's plan for winning. Having worked with women in politics for two decades, she naturally had a high opinion of what women could do to advance an issue or a candidate, and she believed that registered women voters would be strong in her support. (In 1954, there were 84,324 white women registered to vote in Orleans Parish, 88,146 white men, 11,352 black women, and 14,172 black men.)[25]

Enthusiastic friends who urged her to try for the more impressive post and spoke encouragingly of her chances also contributed to her decision to run at large. The prestige attached to an at-large seat no doubt carried weight with her as well. Under the new charter, the two at-large council members would alternate as acting mayor when the peripatetic Morrison was unable to preside at civic functions, and one of them would serve as president of the council. It appears that her own ego may have been a factor in her choice to make a citywide race even though more detached advisers counseled seeking the post from District A.

Finally, her friend and neighbor A. Brown Moore held the seat from District A. A fellow councilman described Moore as "a real honest-to-God reformer," and Robinson shared this opinion. She respected Moore, felt he deserved reelection, and simply declined to oppose him, even though informed opinion held that the seat in District A was hers for the taking.[26]

Finding its candidate adamant about following a difficult path to victory, the IWO requested that the Crescent City Democratic Association give its all-important endorsement to Robinson. Not surprisingly, it refused. Although CCDA leadership theoretically existed as a caucus of seventeen individuals acting as a board of directors, in reality the mayor dominated them.[27]

Thus rebuffed, the women astutely turned to the Cold Water Committee, a group so called because it consistently threw "cold water" on Morrison's desires to run for governor. The Cold Water Committee was a small inner circle of patricians who provided Morrison's principal financial backing and who accordingly exercised great influence with him. Martha Robinson and the Cold Water Committee occupied the same social world. They attended the same Carnival balls; they were veterans of good-government fights together over the years; in some cases, though not actually kin, Robinson's children knew them as "Uncle" and "Aunt."[28]

The Cold Water Committee intervened with deLesseps Morrison on Robinson's behalf after it heard from the IWO. Because these valuable allies supported Robinson stoutly, and because he could ill afford to alienate them,

Morrison reluctantly consented to accept the candidacy of Martha Gilmore Robinson. His agreement meant that her name would appear on the sample CCDA ballots along with names of "the entire Morrison ticket." The ticket carried indisputable weight with the electorate. Thus, Morrison, swayed by arguments from a group too powerful to be ignored, agreed to endorse a candidate whom he viewed with hostility.

Triumphant and flushed with their coup, IWO members rushed to Robinson's home to tell her their news in person. Her unexpected response crushed them. Robinson calmly stated that while she would *accept* the mayor's endorsement, she would *not* endorse him. Thunderstruck, the women demanded to know her reasons. Robinson maintained that Morrison was devious and unprincipled; her strong conviction that he was working behind the scenes to block an honest investigation of his police department while publicly trying to be seen as supporting it dictated her coolness toward the mayor.

"We were horrified, because, I mean, you just couldn't expect him to have her on the ticket if she was going to be working against him. So, it just queered the thing," recalled Carolyn Gay Labouisse, who as IWO president in 1953–54 played a key role in the IWO overture to Robinson about her candidacy. Although various IWO members tried to persuade her to change her stance and endorse Morrison, Martha Robinson was adamant in her refusal because principle was involved. When she subsequently proceeded to endorse the mayoral candidacy of Councilman Thomas Brahney, her action left the IWO board "really very put out with her."[29]

The predictable upshot was that Martha Robinson did not receive the Morrison-CCDA endorsement. As a conciliatory gesture toward the IWO and Cold Water Committee, however, the mayor did agree that his CCDA ticket would maintain neutrality in the matter of the at-large seat Robinson sought, pledging that all CCDA ballots would list Robinson and Victor Schiro, with the message "vote for one."[30]

Robinson's chilly reaction to the IWO news of Morrison's willingness to endorse her identifies her as an amateur in politics who placed principle above result, a variation on the theme "I'd rather be right than president." She spurned the help of a powerful mayor whom she personally did not respect. Morrison's endorsement, coupled with her own name recognition, popularity, and ability, was tantamount to victory, yet Robinson could not bring herself to accept it. She rejected outright the counsel of those who urged her to take the pragmatic, expedient course, stood resolutely by her convictions, and refused to compromise. This display of stubbornness dismayed even her most loyal supporters. As July Waters later characterized it, shaking her head, "Martha had got the bit in her teeth, all right."[31]

A peculiar situation had developed. The civic group that had urged Robinson's candidacy initially, the Independent Women's Organization, also supported deLesseps Morrison unswervingly. The mayor valued and needed IWO support, because the group "carried a certain reform aura which helped to offset the diminished reform image of the administration, an inevitable result of the building of an effective political machine."[32] In the city elections of 1954, the women of the IWO had the unenviable task of backing both Robinson and Morrison, who were rather like two scorpions in a bottle.

When the IWO delegation had first approached the mayor about their enthusiasm for Robinson's candidacy, he had informed them that he preferred someone else for the at-large post, someone who was simply unacceptable to the IWO. Morrison's choice was Victor Hugo Schiro, an insurance salesman whose leadership of two civic clubs in the late 1940s constituted his first public service. With his pencil-thin mustache and natty sartorial style, Schiro looked rather like an attenuated Adolphe Menjou, and indeed, he had acted in a few movies in the late 1920s before beginning a radio career in New Orleans. From radio days, he went on to open a profitable insurance agency. Seated at a civic club dinner between Mayor Morrison and guest of honor Franklin D. Roosevelt Jr. in 1949, he was astounded to hear Morrison ask him to consider a run for a seat on the commission council. Schiro's candid reply that he did not know what ward he lived in indicates his level of political awareness.[33]

With no strong qualifications save that the mayor liked him, Schiro made the race in 1950 on the CCDA-Morrison ticket. When he failed to win outright, timely blandishments from Morrison to Schiro's opponent led the opponent to withdraw and spared Schiro the exertion of a runoff. Thus, the affable Vic Schiro, inexperienced in public life, assumed a place on the council. According to an associate, behind his back Morrison referred to Schiro sarcastically as the "Little Flower," a double slap at his dapper haberdashery and his ethnic heritage. (Fiorello LaGuardia, Italian mayor of New York, was called the "Little Flower.")[34]

Schiro loyally supported his mentor throughout an uneventful term. The contrast between the pleasant, pliant Schiro, son of a Sicilian immigrant and an admitted novice at government, unencumbered with strong convictions about municipal administration, and the confident, assertive activist Martha Robinson, a fixture within the city's upper class who believed that she knew as much about city government as anyone, could hardly have been greater. DeLesseps Morrison had no doubts about which one he preferred in office.

The public rapidly learned Morrison's sentiments. The CCDA had endorsed one candidate for an at-large seat (Glenn Clasen), but, because of effective pressure from the Cold Water Committee and the IWO, it made no recommendation for the other at-large post. Supporters of the CCDA were to be free to vote for either Robinson or Schiro. However, keenly desiring a council of men who had previously given strong support to his plans, Morrison opted to take an active role in electing Schiro. Despite earlier promises, he abandoned his reluctant neutrality in the Robinson-Schiro race and, on January 4, 1954, issued a brief statement to the press. "I intend to vote for Commissioner Vic Schiro," he said, "and I urge all my friends to do likewise."[35]

Robinson herself "was in a rage about it," but there was nothing she could do. The combined influence of her friends in the elite had in the end failed to overcome Morrison's antipathy to her candidacy. From January 4 until January 26, the date of the election, she faced the strength of a very popular mayor, who had decided to bend every effort to elect her opponent.[36]

Robinson ran a high-energy campaign, with George Tessier, a legislator from her 14th Ward neighborhood, serving as campaign manager. Robinson's first efforts aimed at securing a large base of women's support, via the "friends-and-neighbors" approach. Throughout the summer of 1953, she appeared at coffee parties two or three times a week, meeting small groups of women in friends' homes, speaking informally about her vision for New Orleans.[37]

In December 1953, Robinson opened a campaign headquarters in the business district of New Orleans; volunteers from the IWO staffed it daily. In a radio address that month, Robinson issued her platform. Maintaining that New Orleans *women* wanted and deserved a woman in city government, the candidate pitched her appeal squarely at women voters. She pledged to work to improve health and moral conditions, to improve the public library, and to attend to the problems of youth and the elderly. She promised to give special attention to historical preservation, "especially [the] irreplaceable Vieux Carre," and to give careful study to the city tax structure.[38] With the exception of the point about taxes, all these issues reflect an emphasis on quality of life issues that women had traditionally addressed, an indicator of her quest for women's votes. It appears that Robinson accepted the commonly held belief that women had elected Morrison against great odds in 1946 and believed that their support could elect her in 1954. She failed to consider, however, the effect her repudiation of the mayor might have on these very women voters.

During the campaign, the word *independent* assumed a great importance. Vowing to represent independent citizens on the city council and styling herself Martha "No Deals" Robinson in radio and print ads, the candidate served notice at the outset that she opposed the concept of the Morrison-

CCDA "team." Indeed, Robinson maintained that the idea of a Morrison ticket worked diametrically against what the citizens' charter commission, on which she had served, had intended when it created the city council. She reminded audiences that a system of checks and balances, so vital to democratic government, functioned only when the legislative branch, the council, was truly independent of undue influence from the executive, the mayor.[39]

The mayor's forces quickly seized on Robinson's use of the word *independent* and sought to make the term synonymous with *obstructionist*. Calling Schiro a "cooperator," Morrison cleverly implied that Schiro's opponent was *not* a cooperator. In a radio address, Robinson's campaign manager maintained that while his candidate did indeed have a mind of her own, it was "a fair mind," and she was "always willing to listen to reason." Robinson herself was initially inclined to make no apologies for the "independent" label and tended to flaunt it, as this passage, in which she referred to herself in the third person, shows: "There are no strings on Martha Robinson. She can't be bulldozed and she can't be bamboozled. She does not want one favor for herself. She only wants to do a good job for you."[40]

When events revealed that the opposition's use of the term *obstructionist* to describe her was having a negative impact on her chances, Robinson tried to counter. "I am no obstructionist. . . . I do not let my personal feelings influence my decisions. I *can* work with the Mayor. . . . Only on those occasions when my conscience and considered study make it necessary to say 'no' (and I anticipate those times to be not too frequent) will I take an opposing stand. Yes, I *will* obstruct graft, corruption, collusion, and dictatorship."[41]

Vic Schiro's forces energetically attacked on the so-called obstructionist issue and stressed the concept of "the Morrison team." Mayor Morrison bought television time to imply that he would interpret a vote for an "independent" as a vote of no confidence in him. Reminding voters that, under the new charter, he had no vote on the council and could find his plans stymied by an uncooperative council, he declared, "My opponents . . . are saying that we must have an independent council. But what in reality they are asking for is that you elect a hostile or opposition council."[42]

By rejecting a chance to run *with* a popular incumbent mayor, Robinson herself had unwittingly fomented the issue of "obstructionist versus team player." When the opposition raised the point, she fought back with vigor.

> During this campaign there's been an attempt to make the word "independent" ugly—bad—nasty, and . . . to substitute the word "team" for political machine. . . . [Independent] means freedom to cooperate with others in the public interest as well as to oppose them. . . . Yes, I am independent. I

am not a "team" candidate. When you elect me, I will be free to serve each and every one of you equally well—to the best of my ability . . . cooperating with others for the common good—opposing those who serve other masters.[43]

It was rapidly apparent to observers that the incumbent Schiro did not intend to run on his own meager record. In answer to a reporter's question about his greatest accomplishment as council member, he had cited, after some thought, "the new kitchen in the city jail."[44] Nor did Schiro often mention his plans or thoughts about New Orleans. Instead, the Schiro strategy rested squarely on attacking Robinson. In addition to the "obstructionist versus team player" issue that his forces highlighted, the Morrison-Schiro campaign found other Robinson negatives and targeted them with an ugly whispering campaign, occasionally going public with attacks via radio or at rallies. Among the negative issues that the Schiro-Morrison forces raised about Robinson were her age, her sex, and her class.

At the time of her campaign, Martha Gilmore Robinson was sixty-five years old. Her opponent, Vic Schiro, at age fifty, was hardly on the cusp of youth himself, but he stressed the fact that her advanced age rendered her unfit to serve. The Schiro-Morrison forces addressed the age issue chiefly informally, not going on the record through newspaper ads or in public forums, but nevertheless, the word got around to the wards and precincts of the city.

For years, Martha Robinson had routinely maintained a strenuous pace, attending a plethora of meetings, presiding at some, participating in all, keeping up a voluminous correspondence, taking care of the household's ordered maintenance by supervising a domestic staff, entertaining almost constantly. Robinson stood ever ready to host a tea or reception for a notable occasion and opened her home frequently for entertainments. Her daughter commented of her mother's frequent houseguests, "She ran a hotel! People were coming and going all the time at our house." Guests came from her husband's business world, frequently including visitors from Central America, where he had lumber interests, as well as from her world of women's organizations. For example, she regularly entertained representatives from the state and national League of Women Voters. One visitor recalled brushing up on proper etiquette before she embarked for Robinson's home, leafing through her copy of Emily Post in preparation for the style in which she would be entertained. In addition, there were often extended stays by family members at 26 Audubon Place with various young offspring in tow. In pursuit of her duties as state League of Women Voters president, and, later, in association with her historical preservation interests while leading the Louisiana Landmarks Society, Robinson undertook frequent road trips around the state, driving herself in her Studebaker. She traveled out of state often, by rail and air, and kept up a pace of interviews and appointments that seems to have been unaffected by her age.[45]

A close reading of her correspondence reveals no evidence that would allow a conclusion that Robinson's age restricted her activities in any way. At age sixty-five, she presented a picture of an intelligent, healthy, and vigorous individual whose age had no bearing on her schedule. Indeed, her closest friend Natalie Scott offered some sound advice from Mexico. "As for the flip gentleman who said you were 70, you should just send him the itineraries of your various trips in the past few months; that would fix him."[46]

Nevertheless, Robinson had to counter a relentless whispering campaign about her age. She did not help herself by her decision to feature in campaign literature a flattering photograph that was at least ten years old. When people actually saw her at a rally or on television, they noted the difference between the campaign photo and the woman running in 1954. On the night before the election, she received a strange special delivery letter from a furious correspondent brimming with anger at what he called "her faking her age impression on the public." The sometimes incoherent anonymous writer railed, "We all saw her on TV as an old, fat, growling fog-horned fat frog woman instead of the vibrant young woman depicted in her years-ago photos." After a few more references to "old lady fat-frong [sic] Robinson," the writer closed by scrawling, "Martha, you are a fake."[47]

One of motherhood's standard consequences had affected Martha Robinson, who bore her last child at the age of thirty-eight. Her intense civic activity commenced only after that child reached school age in 1932, for society and custom dictated that for a woman to undertake time-consuming civic projects with a preschooler still at home was unnatural and unwomanly. In 1932, when young Samuel Gilmore Robinson turned six and entered elementary school, his mother had eagerly entered the mainstream; she spent twenty productive years immersed in the details of local and state government, but she was forty-four years old when she began this phase of her life. She herself said forthrightly, "When I was a young woman, I did not know enough to be your Councilman." She reminded voters of Churchill's age when he assumed power in Britain in 1940. She asserted her strength and health. These reminders and assertions evidently availed her little in the face of comments about her age. There is a rather pathetic quality to her offer late in the campaign to submit to physical and mental tests to determine her fitness for office. Having successfully planted the doubts about her age and fitness, her opponent of course did not reply to the offer.⁴⁸

If Robinson was vulnerable on the age issue, she was defenseless on the issue of sex. The traditional view of the "weaker sex" attributed qualities of passivity, jealousy, submissiveness, vanity, and a limited sense of justice to women. Any political woman with personality traits of independence, assertiveness, a sense of justice, and ability to engage in abstract, theoretical thinking was "atypical," even "abnormal." In many minds, traits of political leadership and "femininity" were mutually exclusive. Indisputably, Robinson was a woman, and many voters, women as well as men, still honored the old shibboleths about woman's inferiority. Notwithstanding the support for a woman's candidacy exhibited in some quarters, a woman political candidate in 1954, particularly a postmenopausal one who flaunted her independence by styling herself Martha "No Deals" Robinson and who had refused the shelter of a capable man's "team," faced an uphill battle.

Internal memos from the Robinson campaign shed light on insiders' thoughts on countering the sexist opposition. Urging the candidate to remind voters that the modernization of the home, via frozen foods, washing machines, and the like, had given women sufficient time to give to the community, one adviser argued that a woman's active service should surely rank higher than a life at the bridge table or in front of the television set. Another suggested reminding voters that Franklin Roosevelt and Dwight Eisenhower had included women in their cabinets. More than one stressed the need for a powerful organization of *men* behind Martha Robinson's candidacy, to demonstrate that she was *not* strictly the women's candidate.⁴⁹

The fact that there had never been a woman in city government in New Orleans meant that the voters had no frame of reference for a woman on the council. Role models of political women were virtually all "Yankees," Clare Booth Luce, Frances Perkins, Margaret Chase Smith, and the much reviled Eleanor Roosevelt, for example. As late as 1971, a local study found that in New Orleans, elite women did "not normally run for political office or aggressively engage in politics," noting that their effectiveness came behind the scenes.⁵⁰ Phoning, writing, and canvassing, the unpaid and inconspicuous chores routinely done by women's groups, were within the realm of the appropriate. The canon of notable New Orleans women whom speakers regularly lauded included Sophie Wright, a frail, unmarried educator who taught poor children at night school; Josephine Louise Newcomb, a benefactress who gave more than one million dollars to found a college to memorialize her daughter; Dorothy Dix, a women's advice columnist; Kate Chopin and Grace

King, genteel ladies of letters; and Kate and Jean Gordon, the redoubtable sisters who conquered a variety of civic ills via the usual volunteer work of women. None had been "political" in the sense in which Martha Robinson now proposed to be political.[51]

To explain why a woman would be an asset to the city council, Robinson reverted to arguments first used in the nineteenth century by feminists intent on getting the vote. Like many before her, she likened city government to municipal housekeeping, as in this speech. "These major problems are all well within the province of being understood and coped with by a woman. In fact there is nothing difficult to understand in municipal finance and municipal housekeeping that a woman who has run a household and been purchasing agent for a large family, that has organized and directed civic organizations and important boards and committees cannot handle with ease and efficiency."[52]

Employing the slogan "The city fathers need a mother in government," the candidate focused on issues that were traditionally a woman's concern—education and housing, libraries and historical preservation, the care of the young and the needs of the elderly. Robinson pledged to be a conduit for the concerns of all the women of the city. Unfortunately, she was attempting to coax bloc voting from a female electorate that had never been united along gender lines.

A political contemporary of hers alleged that "women didn't like women in politics in those days."[53] In 1954, surely as much as today, women were split over such basic values as political ideology and factional or party preferences; they differed on lines of race, class, religion, and income. When they went to the polls, they carried with them beliefs about gender roles that they had learned in early childhood, long before they had contact with the political world. Despite revisionist history that holds that the impact of 1950s antifeminism was less virulent than Betty Friedan and others have alleged, a woman voter in 1954 had not experienced the transforming effect of years of reborn feminist outlook from which her daughters would benefit. Her ideas about "masculine" and "feminine" were still likely to include stereotypical views concerning politics.

On the issue of class, Robinson undeniably enjoyed an affluent, privileged status, made possible in part by her husband's business success. Servants cooked meals and cleaned house for "Miss Martha," whose days of active housekeeping were long behind her. Her social status in New Orleans was unassailable, for by being born into one of the city's well-connected families, she had assured that for herself. Her marriage had only strengthened that status. Moreover, she was educated, with a degree from a highly regarded women's institution, and articulate, with unmistakable patrician inflections in her speech.

Vic Schiro's supporters gleefully circulated a tale that Robinson's house servant had remarked that Miss Martha rarely ate breakfast before ten o'clock. They repeated this fiction at every chance to working-class voters, and though his wife claimed that Schiro "felt very badly" about the use of the story, he did not disavow it.[54]

Had she chosen, Martha Robinson could have insulated herself somewhat from working-class voters by running from District A (Wards 13, 14, 16, and 17). Although no wards in New Orleans were homogeneous in socioeconomic terms, those in her uptown area included a preponderance of home-owning voters with higher-than-average educations. However, Robinson believed that she could be effective with all classes of voters and particularly wanted to court the votes of women in every ward.

To capture the women's vote, Robinson relied to a great extent on coffee parties, hosted or arranged by IWO members, where she met small groups of women in relaxed settings. Observers recall her as an effective campaigner, combining intelligence with a delightful ability to be very funny, but such functions overlooked the schedules of working women, who seldom could attend. Evidence indicating her plans, if any, for meeting women in the labor force does not exist. Early mornings often found her on the Mississippi River docks, greeting longshoremen on the waterfront. With working-class audiences, she emphasized her Irish heritage (her family lines, Gilmore and McGinniss, were thoroughly Irish) and regaled Irish Channel rallies with tales of her father's Old Regular friends, often employing an Irish brogue to good effect. On such occasions, crowds of blue-collar Irish Catholic voters received candidate Robinson favorably. But the middle-class, middle-brow Schiro, son of an immigrant, had natural advantages with the masses of voters. Fred Cassibry, a candidate for a council post in 1954 who admired Robinson, stated, "She was a dignified, intelligent woman and she couldn't hide it. And I think it turned off a lot of people." In short, if the voters wanted a candidate like themselves, Schiro, a perfect monument to nonthreatening ordinariness, had advantages that Robinson lacked.[55]

"Old." "Fat." "Blue-blood." "Obstructionist." "Woman." These epithets were flung at a well-qualified, widely endorsed candidate for city council in 1954. The candidate devoted valuable resources to refuting a quiet campaign of barely stated but potent charges on issues of age, sex, and class, parrying allegations that she preferred not to dignify with comment. On the "obstructionist" issue, the only one on which the opposition went public with explicit radio and print ads, the candidate devoted her energies to defining repeatedly what was meant by "independent."

The fact that the Schiro-Morrison forces singled Martha Robinson out for attack in the primary indicates that they viewed her as their principal opponent. There were ten candidates in the field, vying for two at-large seats. One race lacked all suspense; Commissioner Glenn Clasen was a certainty to win easily. Although Lionel Ott, an incumbent commissioner, was also in the field, Schiro clearly was most concerned with Martha Robinson, as his negative campaign makes clear.

Robinson emphasized her record of unpaid service, stressing that she, in contrast to Schiro, had a list of solid accomplishments. For her audiences, she always outlined the distinction between experience *in* the legislature and *at* the legislature. "When I hear these young candidates cite two years as a legislator as their chief qualification," she commented in a radio broadcast, "I am tempted to tell of my over twenty years of experience *with* the legislature." She went on to read the agenda of issues she had studied and for which she had lobbied in Baton Rouge—a women's wage and hour bill, a child labor law, a juvenile court system, voting machines, polls in public buildings, better election laws, permanent voter registration. But her work for these issues was that of an unpaid volunteer activist and thus in danger of being undervalued.

On the night before the election, Robinson delivered a radio address, stressing again her community service. She emphasized her selflessness in striving for the greater good of her city and took pains to show that she had never placed class or neighborhood above the general welfare.

> My activities for a quarter of a century have centered around what is good for New Orleans and *all its people.* Whether I was fighting for better schools or better housing or better health conditions or better libraries—and I have fought for all of them—I was fighting for every citizen of this community, my beloved New Orleans. When I sat on the charter committee, its only woman member, I was working for the entire community.[56]

Stung by Schiro's use of "vicious rumors," Robinson bluntly juxtaposed her solid civic accomplishments against Schiro's leadership of businessmen's luncheon organizations in the hope that voters would recognize the qualitative difference between their activities.

> I helped push through laws for the betterment of child labor conditions. I helped make the lot of women in industry easier. It took me 12 years to push through the legislation that finally gave us permanent [voter] registration, the best bulwark against dishonest elections this country has ever

known. I defy my opponent to match this. . . . By contrast, his presidency of a civic club or two, his collecting in several fund drives, and other minor achievements pales into insignificance.⁵⁷

Martha Robinson had a strong sense of her own capabilities. In her words, one hears assertiveness and a tinge of anger, transgressive qualities in a woman, which no doubt dismayed or shocked some voters. She prided herself particularly on her contributions to the city charter, contributions that she made to an otherwise all-male body. "I am a woman, but I submit that I understand this Charter as well as any man now a candidate for the Council," she asserted forthrightly. Then, acknowledging that voters might feel such claims violated gender proprieties, she said, "And if you would not think it too cocky, I know I understand it better than many of them." Yet because of strictures still placed on women, particularly southern women, some listeners did think such statements "too cocky" to be seemly in a woman. Certainly, some men, long accustomed to women's public deference, preferred a bantering conversational style rather than a common sense approach buttressed by a sturdy ego. Assuredly some women voters felt the same way.⁵⁸

The three local newspapers endorsed Martha Robinson's candidacy. She garnered a brace of endorsements from small neighborhood political organizations and from prominent individuals, among them Councilmen Thomas Brahney, Brown Moore, and Lionel Ott and council candidates Fred Cassibry, Guy Deano, and Fred Donaldson. All of these individuals called themselves "independents" and, like Robinson, sought to serve on the council without being obligated to Mayor Morrison's organization.⁵⁹

Not all support came without complications, however. The largest association of black voters, the Orleans Parish Progressive Voters League (OPPVL), supported Robinson. Its president, the Reverend A.(Abraham) L.(Lincoln) Davis, pastor of one of the largest black Baptist congregations in New Orleans, was so thoroughly supportive of Chep Morrison that Earl Long groused that Morrison "had a Baptist preacher that didn't preach nothing but Morrison."⁶⁰ Speaking for his OPPVL, the Reverend Davis noted that Robinson was "close to the pulse of people of the city" and praised her "years of experience in dealing with social and civic problems." The OPPVL women's auxiliary also endorsed Robinson. In a radio address, a black woman who knew Robinson personally, by virtue of having worked with her on the Social Services Committee at Charity Hospital, urged black citizens to turn out for someone who had "kept the common touch" and called Robinson the type of representative they wanted and needed in City Hall.⁶¹

Attracting support from black voters was a mixed blessing in the South of the 1950s; such support, if much publicized, could offend conservative white voters. The same was true of the endorsement Robinson won from the CIO, one that she called "particularly gratifying." On the day before it ran the story of the CIO's decision to back Robinson, the *States* had printed a cartoon depicting John L. Lewis, whose United Mine Workers was a part of the CIO, scattering handfuls of cash along the New York docks, out of a barrel labeled "Dough for Strikes." Captioned "I Cover the Waterfront," this drawing reflected a commonly held negative view of union activity and certainly foreshadowed the fact that union support would be objectionable to some.[62]

Highly objectionable to some was the support that Robinson received from a group called the Teachers' Committee for Martha Robinson, organized by Sarah T. Reed. Reed, an attorney who taught American government and law at Fortier High School in New Orleans, was considered radical by the education establishment. She had organized teachers into the New Orleans Classroom Teachers Federation and affiliated them with the AFL in the early 1930s. Opponents, especially her principal and the superintendent of schools, wanted to fire her for her political activity in behalf of teachers. Reed regularly attended school board meetings at which she questioned and challenged board members relentlessly. A firm advocate of equal pay for *all* teachers, male and female, white and black, married and unmarried, Reed was charged with practicing "unAmericanism" in her classes and suspended in 1948, but she won acquittal in court and was reinstated. Reed's group printed handbills urging Robinson's election, and Reed herself mailed letters of support to twenty-four hundred teachers.[63]

The Young Men's Business Club, with Vic Schiro as its president, denounced Sarah Reed vehemently in 1948 and had consistently taken a hard line on matters of organized labor and Communism. Although there is no evidence indicating that the Schiro forces spoke out *for the record* against Robinson's support by black New Orleanians, organized labor, and a militant schoolteacher, it seems not unreasonable to assume that the Schiro camp in the 1954 election made the most of Robinson's "tainted" support, in view of its pernicious and effective "whispering campaign" tactics.

What emerges as one tracks the record of endorsements is a picture of a patrician candidate who appears to have been skillfully broadening her base beyond her natural uptown constituency. A citywide race required Robinson to break out of her insular upper-class world, a process already begun during her last years of leadership of the New Orleans League of Women Voters. As the league had altered its structure to include members from beyond the affluent university neighborhood and as it changed to accommodate working women by scheduling night meetings and welcomed newcomers from all corners of the country, Robinson had changed too. Her experience in dealing with women from a variety of backgrounds helped her in politics.

Of all the disparate elements in her coalition of support, the most problematic for Martha Robinson was the Regular Democratic Organization. As the organized opposition to incumbent deLesseps Morrison, the Old Regulars had endorsed Councilman Thomas Brahney for mayor. Their support of Martha Robinson caused consternation and dissension among the Independent Women's Organization, which she had counted as her bedrock of support, and even produced doubts about her suitability as the IWO candidate.

Reformers, Martha Robinson among them, had always castigated the brand of politics the Old Regulars played. When the New York writer A. J. Liebling visited New Orleans a few years after the 1954 campaign, he described the individuals who attended an Old Regular meeting: "They are home-bred descendants of the famine Irish who came in '47, their assimilates, the German Catholics who came in '48, and their political feudatories, the Sicilians, who came much later. They intermarry. . . . [They] could have been coming out of a Jim Curley meeting in Boston or a gathering of Paddy Baulerites in the Forty-third Ward of Chicago."[64]

Early in the twentieth century, the Old Regulars had seemed the epitome of bossism and the urban machine, but with the advent of Longism, they were eclipsed. The Long faction was by far the more adept at use of force and fraud, by far the more powerful adversary. When a web of indictments and convictions crippled the powerful Long machine in 1939–40, the ordinarily weak and disorganized reform element succeeded in putting Sam Jones into the governor's office. Their astonishing 1946 upset victory over Mayor Bob Maestri meant that reformers had bested the Long inheritors twice in six years. By 1954, with the Long faction seemingly vanquished in New Orleans, the chief organized opposition to the "reform" element came from the weakened but still surviving Old Regular faction.[65]

Although Chep Morrison was still the young Galahad to many of his supporters, some early backers had lost their enthusiasm. Disillusioned with the mayor, who through astute use of municipal patronage had built himself a formidable political machine, they said he was "terrifyingly ambitious, a complete egoist, and willing to trade for votes anywhere." The Old Regulars, though greatly weakened by defections to Morrison's CCDA and the loss of patronage jobs, nevertheless had the only extant organization capable of taking on Morrison. Thus, anyone who had ceased to view deLesseps Morrison as a reformer, who saw him instead as a poseur, "cold as ice and devoid of conviction," might be prepared to accept Old Regular help.[66]

Robinson's willingness to take the RDO blessing outraged the women of the IWO, who still supported Chep Morrison overwhelmingly. Robinson, who had never been an IWO member and who had viewed Morrison with something less than their giddy enthusiasm even in 1946, had shocked them when she spurned the mayor's grudgingly given agreement to place her on the "Morrison team." She shocked them almost beyond redemption with her willingness to allow her name to be associated in any way with the Regular Democratic Organization.

The IWO refused to recognize that by making expedient deals, dangling patronage plums to construct a political machine, and impeding reform of the city's notorious police department, Morrison had come to resemble the predecessor he had ousted. When a longtime Louisiana congressman compared Morrison and Maestri, he concluded, "Chep had a bigger machine than Maestri, and I think he was much more ruthless than Maestri. Chep was cold-blooded as hell." Seen in retrospect, Morrison turned out to be more of a promoter, both of himself and of his city, than a reformer. Morrison's biographer scores Morrison for tolerating "public waste, police corruption, arbitrary rule, spoils politics, and racial discrimination" and concludes that despite bringing some real improvements to his city, "all too often he was content with the illusion of reform." The reasoning within the Independent Women's Organization, however, seemed to be once a reformer, always a reformer.[67]

Carolyn Gay Labouisse, daughter of a U.S. senator, a member of the city's elite, and president of the IWO in 1953–54, regularly worked long hours in Robinson's downtown office throughout the campaign. Losing patience with the candidate over her Regular Democratic Organization connection after observing a meeting in the headquarters between Robinson and Captain William ("Billy") Bisso, a ferryboat captain and Old Regular stalwart, Labouisse heatedly told Robinson that she was quitting her campaign. Robinson subsequently mended that fence by promising Labouisse not to be so overt in taking Old Regular help. "But she was still doing it," Labouisse recalled.

To what extent she was "still doing it" is unclear. In Robinson's campaign literature for door-to-door distribution, she listed the RDO as endorsing her candidacy. Yet, in RDO advertisements in the press, her name is not among its endorsed slate of candidates. Clearly, there was some Old Regular tie-in, but the extent is uncertain.

In the last days of the campaign, Labouisse got word of Robinson's plan to appear at an Old Regular rally in the heart of the Irish Channel. Outraged that she would actually take the stage with politicos whom the IWO had for years regarded as enemies, and that she would pursue this course of action without discussing it with the IWO, Labouisse went incognito to see for herself what would happen. She wore old clothes, eyeglasses, and a hat pulled low to shield her face. From the rear of the hall, she watched. "I saw the whole thing. She came marching in with two men that I didn't know and went up on that platform and they handed her a huge bouquet of red roses and she grabbed the roses and she said, 'I have come *home!*'"[68]

As she recounted the incident thirty years later, tones of disapproval tinged Labouisse's voice. She and other IWO members felt that Robinson had betrayed the Independent Women's Organization, the body that had instigated her candidacy initially. A difficult situation resulted, with Labouisse, Waters, and other IWO mainstays unhappy with Robinson. Doubts plagued them: could Martha Robinson be a bona fide reformer if she refused the imprimatur of Morrison and took Old Regular support? Was she the candidate they really wanted to back? Officially, they continued to work for her. Members of the IWO staffed her headquarters, worked the phones, stuffed the envelopes. Although news of this internal tempest never reached the public, multiple doubts about Robinson dampened IWO enthusiasm and kept IWO members from working with their trademark vigor for her.

Unlike the women who had worked to elect Morrison in 1946, Robinson did not view him sentimentally or fondly. His attitude and conduct often offended her sense of virtue; she doubted his veracity and distrusted his ambition. Contemporaries had noted his tendency to pass off a convenient fiction as truth if such would help him. To some, the mayor was a "con man," "an educated Maestri," "a pathological liar [who] . . . never let himself be governed too much by the truth if it would interfere."[69]

It was a belief that a ruthless, unscrupulous deLesseps Morrison was hiding behind a mask of reformist respectability that led Thomas Brahney to oppose the mayor for reelection in 1954. A respected attorney and city councilman, Brahney accepted Old Regular endorsement though he had never been a part of their organization. Robinson too accepted their support, which gave her a base in the world of the working class, essential in a citywide race. Once in office, she intended to function as an independent watchdog for the general good, beholden to no faction or ward, unfettered by special relationships, free to speak and act as her conscience dictated. In Robinson's lexicon, acceptance of Old Regular support did not connote acceptance of old-style bossism. Because she distrusted the mayor, she never fully comprehended the opprobrium that the true believers of the IWO attached to her association with their old adversary, the Regular Democratic Organization.

The women of the IWO, for their part, adopted an unbending attitude that allowed them to see only the positive side of Mayor Morrison. If Robinson could not embrace Morrison, they felt sure that the fault lay in her, certainly not in him. They reacted negatively to Robinson's efforts to get votes from the Old Regular camp and to her strong-willed determination to run her campaign as she saw fit.

By running as Martha "No Deals" Robinson and spurning the "Morrison team," the candidate risked losing the good will of the small reform element and of women, the groups that ranked as the staunchest of Morrison's supporters. Ironically, Robinson had counted them to be among hers as well. Losing them was costly.

Custom in New Orleans called for political organizations to issue sample ballots with a roster of candidates whom they endorsed, distributing these on election day. Observing election day behavior in New Orleans in the late 1950s, bemused journalist A. J. Liebling noted that "the gutters leading up to most polls were ankle-deep in sample ballots."[70] Louisiana law permitted voters to take sample ballots into the voting booth, and indeed, many relied heavily on the printed ballot of a political organization when making their choices, since the long ballot (the so-called bedsheet ballot) made it difficult to vote knowledgeably in every race. In New Orleans with its heritage of machine politics, voter reliance on someone else's suggestion of how to vote was strong. In the absence of a bona fide two-party system, a potent factionalism provided a near substitute in the Crescent City as voters identified themselves with either the CCDA or the RDO. Many who counted themselves in the Morrison or the Old Regular camp relied passively and exclusively on their organization's sample ballot for instruction on how to vote. A candidate running independently and eschewing either faction's ticket risked being overlooked entirely save by the most intelligent, aware, and independent voters.

Although restrained by the influential Cold Water Committee from aiding Schiro to the extent of omitting Martha Robinson outright from the CCDA sample ballots, Morrison was far from hamstrung. He announced to the public his personal support of Schiro. Then he explicitly told his seventeen CCDA ward leaders that he favored Schiro's election and won from most a pledge that they too would work for Schiro despite the earlier CCDA decision to give CCDA loyalists a choice between Robinson and Schiro. The result, according to a reporter, was that "a lot of Morrison workers [were] wearing badges with Schiro's name along with their Morrison campaign buttons, which [drew] more attention to his [Schiro's] candidacy in many places than to that of any candidates on the mayor's official ticket."[71]

The importance of the sample ballot explains the resultant uproar in 1954 when deliberately misleading sample ballots materialized. Sample CCDA ballots marked "Vote the Straight Morrison Ticket" appeared at the polls in several wards on election day, January 26. Schiro workers energetically distributed these bogus ballots, which omitted Robinson's name entirely and depicted the lever pulled down beside the name of Vic Schiro. This violated Morrison's agreement that the CCDA would give equal treatment to Robinson and Schiro via the so-called straddle ballot on which both names were to be listed with the instruction "Vote For One."[72]

The blatant, widespread distribution of phony CCDA ballots promoting Schiro brought bursts of indignation from the Robinson forces. Gervais Favrot, a wealthy Cold Water Committee member who supported both Morrison and Robinson, called Scott Wilson to account for the unfair tactics. Wilson, in tandem with Dave McGuire, handled public relations for Mayor Morrison. In a disingenuous response, Wilson contended rather lamely that *some* CCDA-Morrison ticket sample ballots were inadvertently printed with Schiro's name on the Morrison team; he blamed this on "limits of staff and . . . printer's carelessness." He maintained that "someone" took seventy-five thousand defective ballots to the city dump, where they were deposited but not burned. "It is unreasonable that any appreciable number either escaped or were salvageable," he wrote. This was patently untrue, since numerous voters reported having had the deceptive CCDA ballots thrust upon them on election day. Robinson poll workers had noted the bogus ballots, as had members of the press. In some wards, these phonies were the only CCDA ballots available for voters to consult.[73]

The implications of the sample ballot situation merit emphasis. Virtually any voter who favored Mayor Morrison would be a willing recipient and user of a CCDA sample ballot. Voters long accustomed to voting a "ticket" needed to know only the name of the man at the top—in this case, Mayor deLesseps Morrison. Only voters who had actually followed the campaign via the press would know without reading a sample ballot that Robinson and Schiro officially had the joint endorsement of the CCDA.

There were other questionable tactics by the Schiro-Morrison forces. On the eve of the election, the mayor and Schiro appeared at the Central Fire Hall. There they addressed off-duty firemen who had been summoned by a ruse when the fire chief had ordered them to gather on a Sunday afternoon to hear a speech from a member of the National Board of Fire Underwriters. In actuality, the occasion was purely political, as the mayor's remarks made clear. After a promise to work for a raise for the firefighters, Morrison stated that, in order to get it, he needed "cooperators" on the city council. He then introduced "cooperator" Vic Schiro. Although the Robinson faction pointed out that this meeting was a blatant violation of civil service regulations, no action against Morrison ensued.[74]

Schiro had such legitimate advantages that taking unfair advantage seemed superfluous. Morrison's public relations team arranged extra public exposure opportunities for Schiro in the month before the election. He cut ribbons, welcomed dignitaries, and appeared with a beauty queen and at a movie premiere. Moreover, in joint television appearances with Morrison, he basked in the reflected glow emanating from the popular mayor. On the night before the primary, Morrison spoke on television for half an hour, followed by Schiro for fifteen minutes. No other council candidates received such pointed assistance from Morrison.

For her part, Robinson took the advice of her friend Bland Bruns, who urged her to take the high road. "Forceful aggressive stating of past record," the state legislator advised, "appealing to the *best* in the voters." However, Bruns also counseled "steering away as far as possible" from alignment with any faction—the CCDA or the Old Regular ticket. Another strategist recommended having respected local *men* to proclaim how well Robinson had worked with them on important committees as a countermeasure to Schiro's "obstructionist" attack. On the woman issue, the adviser urged, "Don't apologize for Martha's Womanhood. Capitalize on it!" He or she went on to counsel emphatically that Mayor Morrison should not become an issue; his popularity made it "strategically unwise to attack him."[75]

Yet "attack" seemed to be the key to the Robinson-Schiro race. There were three CCDA rallies scheduled, huge affairs at which all CCDA endorsees spoke. Piqued at Morrison's personal endorsement of Schiro, Robinson did not attend the first rally but sent her son to observe the proceedings. He reported that the individual introducing Schiro drew roars of approval when he referred to Robinson as "the old bag." Robinson steeled herself and went to the second rally, only to be irritated by Schiro's comic, ostentatious courtesy in conspicuously rising to hold out her chair for her, courtesy that drew titters from the audience. At the third and final rally, in what must certainly have been an unpleasant and unexpected ordeal for Robinson, the pro-Schiro crowd booed her, unchecked by anyone on the "Morrison team."[76]

Robinson, a veteran of service at the polls in numerous past elections, coordinated election day logistics for her campaign workers. Her precinct captains received printed instructions from her on everything from lunch breaks to the placement of posters, with emphasis on the necessity of scrupulous observance of election laws. Even as her camp stressed integrity, still traveling the high road, the Schiro forces, certainly with the knowledge of the mayor, were distributing their illicit version of CCDA sample ballots, wherein Robinson's name did not appear.

DeLesseps Morrison easily won reelection, polling 94,314 votes out of the

158,483 cast. His coattails lacked length, however; in the council races, only two of the "Morrison team" won outright. Five CCDA favorites faced runoffs. To the consternation of Morrison, who had confidently expressed the belief that Schiro would run ahead of the field, Vic Schiro was among them. He had polled 64,887 votes to Martha Robinson's 53,091, with neither taking a majority.[77]

The sources of Robinson's strength in the primary were two—the Old Regulars and the Uptowners. Robinson made her best showing in the Third Ward, the bailiwick of James A. Comiskey, an Old Regular chieftain with twenty-five years of experience in politics and the last warhorse in the tradition of Martin Behrman. Comiskey proudly told the press that, though he was disappointed in the citywide outcome, he felt "comfortable and pleased with the perfectly marvelous support" that he had received in the election.[78] Within his ward, the two Morrison favorites, Clasen and Schiro, polled their worst totals in the entire city, whereas Robinson polled her best there. Although she outdrew Schiro in six wards, Wards 1, 2, 3, 10, 13, and 14, three of these, Wards 1, 2, and 3, were in the orbit of Comiskey. It appears indisputable that her decision to take Old Regular support bore fruit.

The other bedrock of Robinson support was Uptown. Robinson amassed more votes than Schiro in Wards 10, 13, and 14, all of which numbered a majority of women voters. Initially, this outcome seems to indicate that Robinson succeeded in her quest for women's votes. However, in Wards 12 and 16, which also had a majority of women voters, Schiro outpolled her, taking 22.7 percent of the vote in Ward 12 to her 19.6 percent and taking 24.1 percent of the vote in Ward 16 to her 21.7 percent there. Thus, of the five wards with a predominance of women registered voters, Robinson carried three and Schiro two. Across the city, from precinct to precinct, there is a positive correlation between female registration and the Robinson vote in the primary. A regression analysis of the primary returns reveals a correlation coefficient of .247 between women voters and Robinson's votes. Multiple factors affected Robinson's chances of garnering the votes of women. The women whose votes had helped Morrison into office in 1946 faced a choice in 1954 of supporting Morrison *and his team* or supporting Morrison and someone whom he made clear he did not want on the council.

Analysis of the outcome of the 1954 primary allows a partial testing of the assumption held by many that Robinson would have "just walked in" had she sought a seat not citywide but from District A (Wards 13, 14, 16, and 17). In District A, she trailed Schiro by more than 7,000 votes, polling 13,532 to his 20,994. These results certainly cast doubt on the assumption that the District A seat was "hers for the taking," as her contemporaries had it.

Dave McGuire, Morrison's public relations wizard and chief administrative officer, felt that the lesson to be drawn from the returns was that voters wanted Morrison as mayor but rejected his "team" concept. "On the Schiro-Robinson matter, it becomes obvious that Vic did not have the degree of popular support we all assumed," he commented candidly. "Martha, on the other hand, had much more than we anticipated." McGuire recommended that Morrison concentrate on other runoffs and emphatically urged "strict and definite neutrality" in the Robinson-Schiro runoff.[79]

Robinson's chances in the runoff hinged on her ability to attract the losing candidates' votes in a runoff. In a fairly strong showing, Councilman Lionel Ott had polled more than 40,000 votes in the at-large race, made possible to some extent by his Old Regular support. If Robinson could hold her support and garner a sizable portion of Ott's votes, she had a good chance of being elected.

Robinson's hopes for Old Regular help in the runoff were dashed quickly, as James Comiskey, the Third Ward leader, issued a statement in which he expressed the hope that the candidates would "spare the people of [the] city what appear[ed] to be a hopeless and useless second primary," adding, "Let the high men be declared the nominees."[80] One week after the election, the Old Regulars caucused at the Choctaw Club and announced to the press afterward that they would take no active part in the runoff. Referring to the RDO's depleted treasury, their leader declared, "We lack the sinews of war." The once powerful Regular Democratic Organization lacked the funds to mount meaningful campaign efforts twice within six weeks. Each of the seventeen RDO ward leaders was authorized to do as he saw fit in the matter of endorsements.[81]

Robinson had in effect fallen between two chairs. Having spurned a spot on Morrison's ticket, she opted to build a coalition of support wherever she could find it, including the Old Regular organization. Now that body abandoned her, in what must have seemed a betrayal. Indeed, some observers felt the Old Regulars made a mistake in forsaking Robinson, seeing her as a still viable candidate who could win election with their continued backing.[82]

The next betrayal came at the hands of the Orleans Parish Progressive Voters' League, the largest organization of black voters in New Orleans. Although the OPPVL had backed Robinson in the first primary, it withdrew its support for the runoff, allegedly because she refused to meet the price it set for its continued support.[83] It is likely that "persuasion" from the Morrison forces led to this development, since the Reverend A. L. Davis, OPPVL leader, was Morrison's leader in black New Orleans. Indeed, the OPPVL endorsement of Robinson in the first primary was a rather surprising gesture of independence on the part of black voters, in view of Morrison's known preference for Schiro.

Meanwhile, even the support of the Independent Women's Organization appeared shaky. Not until three full weeks after the primary did the IWO issue a public statement of support for Robinson in the runoff. In the interim, a visit from July Waters, who came as emissary for Mayor Morrison, stung Robinson deeply. The message Waters brought crystallized Robinson's thinking, as she told a radio audience. "The last straw was when a dear woman friend of mine was sent to me by the mayor's office to ask if I would see the mayor, that there perhaps was some honor he could persuade me to accept—that a second primary would cost a lot of money that he knew I would like to save the city. . . . It was then that my Irish really boiled over."[84]

Abandoned by the Old Regulars, cold-shouldered by the largest African-American organization, shocked that her erstwhile allies in the IWO would urge her to accept "some honor" and withdraw from the race, and still facing the powerful opposition of a popular mayor, Robinson made the decision to soldier on. She refused to see Morrison and sent word that, in regard to his offer of "some honor" to her, the only honor she wanted was from the voters, hotly calling his talk about saving money "an insult to intelligent citizens [who had] a right to have offices decided by votes and not by deals."[85]

Insiders recall that this was a difficult time for Robinson. Pessimism set in; the candidate felt deserted. Her daughter commented that the Independent Women's Organization "really didn't support her and really didn't work the way you have to work to win." Fred Cassibry, the only non-CCDA candidate elected to a council post that year, felt that Robinson could have won with Old Regular help in the runoff and that it was a mistake for the RDO to pull out. Although three RDO ward leaders did endorse Robinson, their support fell far short of what was needed. Commented veteran political analyst James Gillis, "It was apparent to me that Morrison pulled out all the stops to elect Schiro. Toward the end . . . I think she [Robinson] felt she had been badly treated."[86]

For his part, Morrison ignored his adviser's counsel to adopt a neutral stance in the Robinson-Schiro runoff. Instead, he threw great effort into boosting Schiro's candidacy, thus displeasing his public relations team of McGuire and Wilson. They correctly discerned that Robinson had popular support and admiration that the mayor needed to respect, if for no other reason than that many Robinson supporters were the financial backbone of Morrison's own operation. But the mayor could not be restrained. Columnist Gillis reported, "Mayor Morrison is working as hard to put Schiro over in the second primary as he did in the first." Having won his own race, he vigorously stumped for Schiro, touting the "Morrison team" concept and reiterating the idea that a vote against Schiro was a repudiation of his own recent electoral triumph. Joint appearances at rallies and on radio and television ensued.[87]

In order to avoid antagonizing the influential Morrison contributors who were Robinson supporters, Morrison's CCDA adopted *official* neutrality in the runoff for the at-large council seat. However, behind this ostensible neutrality again lay energetic support for Schiro. Again, the CCDA printed sample ballots endorsing him for councilman at large. When the IWO telephoned for a supply of ballots, which contained the name of Leon Hubert for district attorney (Hubert had the backing of both the IWO and the CCDA), Morrison's close assistant Dave McGuire had to pretend ignorance on the matter. In reality he knew that a sample ballot containing Hubert's name would also reveal CCDA endorsement of Schiro and the IWO, despite its misgivings about Martha Robinson, would "certainly not want to be handing out a Schiro sample ballot which may [have contained] Hubert's name."[88]

Robinson was by no means without support. Brown Moore, the reformer reelected from District A, endorsed her stoutly and repeatedly, as did Fred Cassibry, an independent council candidate in a runoff. However, the Old Regular support had evaporated; many RDO loyalists opportunistically backed Schiro in the runoff. Ott, the defeated candidate whose vote she needed, declined to endorse her. There was a public perception that the results of the runoff were a foregone conclusion, a perception that Robinson sought to counter by saying, "Don't let propaganda that my chances are hopeless deter you. This is deliberately done to discourage voting."[89]

Voter turnout was 56 percent for the runoff on Tuesday, March 9. The day's results ended Martha Robinson's brief season as a politician, with the final tally showing that Schiro had carried every ward except two—her own, the Fourteenth, and the neighboring Thirteenth. Despite there being fewer total votes cast, he boosted his total vote in nine wards (Wards 2, 3, 5, 9, 10, 11, 12, 16, and 17); Robinson's total declined in every ward except the working-class Seventh and Ninth. In the wards that she had carried in the primary (Wards 1, 2, 3, 10, 13, and 14), Schiro polled runoff percentages of 59.4 percent, 72.1 percent, 58.9 percent, 62.9 percent, 48.3 percent, and 45.6 percent, respectively. His total runoff vote exceeded his total in the primary, whereas Robinson's plummeted by more than seven thousand. There was a desertion of Robinson across the city, as her totals were lower in the runoff than in the primary in every ward but two. It was a very thorough defeat.[90]

A postmortem on Robinson's defunct campaign leads to the conclusion that the candidate made mistakes that cost her dearly. Although arguably better qualified than Schiro, she also had stronger negatives and was wounded when her opponent exploited them. As he used her age, her sex, and her social class to sow doubts about her fitness to serve, Schiro steered Robinson away from talking about her positive program for New Orleans and forced her to continue to spotlight personal characteristics rather than issues, ability, and vision. She might have been better served to ignore the whispering campaign, but the allegations were so irritating that one can certainly sympathize with Robinson's decision to refute them.

Robinson's decision to take the support of the Old Regulars, around whom hung a lingering aura of ill repute, alienated many in the IWO. Her father had been an Old Regular and a friend of Martin Behrman's. Although she felt comfortable in taking their help (she even performed a clog dance when she appeared at an Old Regular rally), her doing so alarmed the IWO. Her propensity for dealing with Old Regular politicians discouraged the women reformers, and her doing so without consulting them angered the women's group.

The conclusion is inescapable that the greatest factor in Martha Robinson's loss was not her age, her sex, or her class. It was her perception of deLesseps Morrison as a dangerous fraud whose pulsing ambition and tendency to brook no opposition were detrimental to New Orleans. She perceived him in this way, and she let it be known. Morrison at this time was still highly popular, especially among the IWO membership and in the uptown areas. Robinson's criticisms of the mayor, well founded as later events would show, offended the women. This capable corps of politically aware women, who had worked for reform in New Orleans for at least fifteen years before this race, lost their unanimity. It is ironic that this occurred when one of their own was seeking office.

The irony extends further yet. Robinson had the chance to run *with*, rather than *against*, this popular mayor. Her strong convictions intervened, and she refused to take the expedient course. In deLesseps Morrison, the public in some ways had elected an unknown quantity, a deceiver capable of seeming to be in agreement with his audience, but, as a longtime city employee recalled, "When you hit the door, he was going to do what he wanted to do."[91] In Martha Robinson, the voters had a veteran of countless causes, who had ever been willing to have her exact views known. Too blunt for some tastes, she was nonetheless a known quantity. Her convictions put her on a collision course with a man of keen political instincts who was eternally shifting and adapting. The very quality that had won Robinson her citywide reputation, that of doggedly insisting on what she thought was right, may well have cost her the election.

Like most genteel reformers, Martha Gilmore Robinson agreed that "right and wrong were the most important categories" and that "all good citizens knew one from the other,"⁹² and therein lay some of her trouble. When she identified deLesseps Morrison as part of the problem, not part of the solution, her attitude splintered the middle- and upper-class women of New Orleans who had previously exhibited such joyful solidarity on things political. As her friend July Waters had remarked of earlier campaigns, "The line was drawn, it was Right and Wrong. . . . It was so pronounced and so evident that you were inspired to work, and to win it."⁹³ The 1954 elections featured less black and white and more shades of gray, to Robinson's disadvantage.

For reformers, the machine was always the enemy. Yet in New Orleans in 1954, a situation had developed in which a large component of the reform phalanx refused to acknowledge the existence of a machine under the aegis of their favorite son, deLesseps Morrison. Each Robinson criticism of him and his administration made it more difficult for the women of the IWO to support her enthusiastically. Each assertion of "independence" made them increasingly uncomfortable with the candidate whom they had drafted. Their experience with politics had accustomed them to campaigning against a "devil image," but the city council race of 1954 lacked any such figure. Unwilling to allow Martha Robinson to cast the mayor in that role, and unable to see the affable Vic Schiro as a villain of the Huey Long–Robert Maestri type, the Independent Women's Organization could not enter the 1954 campaign as crusaders.

Robinson's insistence on principle led her to assume a ludicrous position, that of attempting to receive the votes of a very popular mayor's supporters while running a campaign unaligned with that mayor and in support of his opponent—a virtual political impossibility. By making such an issue of the "Morrison team," Robinson unwisely ran almost as much against Morrison as against Vic Schiro. Although reflective of her convictions, this was a tactical mistake.⁹⁴ The chief consequence of her criticism of the mayor was to create a political enemy of Morrison himself, an enemy whose skilled opposition ultimately proved decisive. Even though Morrison seemingly lacked respect for Schiro, he viewed him as useful. In the end, he risked offending his financial backers, the Cold Water Committee, and the adoring women of the IWO when he first boosted Schiro's candidacy. He opted to ignore their pleas, to ignore his advisers, and to let the chips fall where they might. On the second primary day, the returns gave him the councilman he desired.

Less than a week after the election, Dave McGuire, the public relations man ever conscious of appearances, wrote to his employer: "I would suggest that you consider appointing Martha Robinson to some important board or commission in the near future. I think your appointment of her would be accepted as a generous gesture of recognition and would do much to heal the situation."[95] Significantly, deLesseps Morrison ignored the advice.

The Independent Women's Organization was a strong body, strong enough to demand that women's interests be served, as it demonstrated in its initial drafting of Martha Robinson as a candidate over the objections of Morrison. There is every reason to believe that the IWO's brand of political separatism, an organization of *women* working for a *woman* candidate, would have yielded Martha Robinson a victory had not Robinson herself fomented division by her rejection of their standard-bearer Chep Morrison. In its coldness to the mayor and its warmth to the Old Regulars, her campaign simply did not follow the script they had envisioned. Ironically, Martha Robinson's focus on good government led her to neglect good politics, and consequently, she never won the post she coveted.

Southerners, though tenacious of social traditions ...
are chivalrous toward a woman who wishes their
cooperation provided that she comes to them as a lady.
—Belle Kearney

CHAPTER SIX

❏

IN TWO WORLDS

❏

ROSA FREEMAN KELLER,

❏

RACE AND REFORM

The ugly outline of race relations that emerged in mid-twentieth-century New Orleans took casual observers by surprise, since the city's history and demography had seemed to indicate that New Orleans could never be another Little Rock. A prominent news magazine, headlining an optimistic 1959 article "New Orleans Knows Better," predicted the city would be a leader in "peaceful integration." It was true that antebellum relationships between blacks and whites, fostered in part by the large number of free people of color and the steady influx of immigrants from France and the French-speaking West Indies, had been "more elaborate than those in any other city in the United States." And true, there was the looming presence of the Catholic Church and the pronounced Latin influence in the culture, both assumed to be factors promoting racial tolerance. Perhaps truest of all, there was, as one African-American woman put it, "all that decadence . . . all together." Over the decades there had developed a significant population of educated, prosperous blacks who displayed traits of assertiveness and pride; there were black business owners, doctors, dentists, attorneys, teachers, funeral directors, insurance salesmen. Nevertheless, New Orleans did not escape Jim Crow, for the stifling strictures of racial segregation existed in the Crescent City to bind behavior, and the white majority seemed to accept the status quo with equanimity.[1]

Conditions in New Orleans at midcentury were grim indeed. The 1950 census found that although African Americans were almost a third of the city's population, black males accounted for only 3 percent of all New Orleanians aged twenty-five or older who had four or more years of college; black women in that age bracket held not quite 5 percent of all college degrees. The median black family income was less than half that of whites. White men outnumbered black men as professional or technical workers by fifteen to one, and more than 68 percent of all employed black women labored as domestic servants. In the state of Louisiana, from 1900 to 1950, forty-one black men had been executed for the crime of rape; in the same period, only two white men drew the death penalty for that offense. The city's police force employed no blacks at all, and complaints of police brutality against African Americans were common. Blacks made up a minuscule 0.054 percent of the workers in city government. They viewed movies only from theater balconies ("buzzard roosts," in the vernacular of the era), rode in the backs of streetcars and buses, and attended inferior, segregated schools. Even though postwar overcrowding in the schools affected all children, the sacred calculus of race demanded that no improvements be made on black schools until all white schools were renovated to house their pupils comfortably.[2]

Largely deprived of education, security, jobs, respect, justice, and the vote, New Orleans blacks also lacked effective communication with the white community. Many whites imagined that they communicated well with blacks, but they were commonly talking to maids, cooks, and gardeners; between superior and inferior, honesty is rare. Jim Crowism's separations caused a great ignorance about blacks' lives among whites and "allowed whites to believe patently false things about blacks."[3] Chief among the falsehoods embraced as an article of faith in the white community in New Orleans was a belief that blacks and whites had long enjoyed good relations and that contentment characterized blacks' emotional landscape. However, periodic outbreaks of panicky rumors among whites, reports of a sinister rise in sales of ice picks to Negroes or belief in the approach of "push day" (on which whites believed blacks would systematically push everyone they encountered on public sidewalks), belied whites' confident claims that they knew blacks' needs and wishes.[4]

The ultimate test of the white southern liberal was a willingness to criticize his or her society's racial mores. Under the liberal banner were included "those white Southerners who perceived that there was a serious maladjustment of race relations in the South . . . and who either actively endorsed or engaged in programs to aid Southern blacks in their fight."[5] By this definition, Rosa Freeman Keller (1911–   ), an affluent and privileged white New Orleanian, ranks as a racial liberal; moreover, because of her particular combination of education, wealth, status, and personal warmth, she came to be the most effective white liberal in her native New Orleans. For more than two decades, Keller occupied a unique role, that of informal liaison officer linking the black community and the white power structure.

On a warm night in May 1956, Rosa Keller learned from a reporter's phone call that Leander Perez, leader of the region's segregationists, had just addressed a huge local crowd. Keller had known of the planned rally of the Greater New Orleans Citizens' Council (GNOCC) on this second anniversary of the *Brown v. Board of Education* decision. Governor Marvin Griffin of Georgia was slated to deliver the main address, but the evening would have been incomplete without remarks from "the Judge," the unquestioned boss of Plaquemines Parish and a long-standing figure in state politics who, in 1954, had publicly dedicated the rest of his life to maintaining segregation. She *was* surprised, however, to hear that the ultrasegregationist Perez had denounced her personally for fostering desegregation through her work as president of the New Orleans Urban League. She was horrified to learn that he had given the crowd her address and phone number and had added his opinion that "every time they bought a bottle of Coca-Cola [they were] putting money in [Keller's] pocket." Perez's implied suggestion for a boycott of Coca-Cola did not result in a mass renunciation of the beverage, bottled in New Orleans by Rosa Keller's family. But the crowd had loudly booed her name, and later that evening someone erected a fiery cross on Keller's lawn, seemingly a signal that neither social standing, wealth, nor gender would shield her from segregationists' frenzy.[6]

At this point, Keller had behind her nearly fifteen years of steadily increasing activity on behalf of racial justice. Her life by the mid-1950s featured frequent meetings with concerned citizens, travels outside the state to attend conferences, reading in a wide variety of sources, and considerable correspondence. Working to change the racial climate in her native city had become the functional equivalent of a career for Rosa Keller. In her struggles to chip away at the conditions of segregation then prevailing and to improve life for others, she, an unemployed, affluent woman, was unconsciously improving life for herself.[7]

There was little in Keller's early life to suggest that she would one day suffer the particular slings and arrows that outrageous fortune cast at southern liberals: a cross burning on her lawn, threats against her children, anonymous epithets spoken low over the telephone, thick spittle spattering her, shots fired at her, an enraged bigot pulling a gun on her in her own home. Keller's experiences became more and more the dividends earned by those who challenged racial mores, as the erosion of Jim Crow drove many white southerners to madness and violence. W. J. Cash's "savage ideal" of conformity of thought loomed like a lurid nightmare over the South in the 1950s, smothering options and eliminating flexibility.[8]

Born in 1911 in New Orleans, Rosa Freeman enjoyed a pleasant and secure early life. Although not born to wealth, her father, through hard work and business acumen, made a fortune with the Coca-Cola Bottling Company. By the early 1920s his growing affluence allowed him to move his family from a modest house on Hickory Street to a splendid one located on fashionable Palmer Avenue near Tulane University. As A. B. Freeman's fortunes rose, so did his civic prominence. In the summer of 1927 he sent his wife and sixteen-year-old daughter abroad, where Rosa and her mother flew across the English Channel. "That was the Lindbergh summer, you know," Keller said by way of explanation, noting that it was her mother who had insisted on the flight "for the adventure, the experience."[9] In 1932, A. B. Freeman, the boy who had had to go to work before he completed high school, reached the pinnacle of social success in his adopted city, being selected to reign as Rex, king of Carnival.

His daughter Rosa was educated first in the New Orleans public schools and then at private high schools. She attended Sophie Newcomb College but did not thrive there. Troubled by the sorority system and the competitive social atmosphere that she encountered, she nonetheless pledged a sorority but found the whole process "distressingly silly" and felt pain over the fate of the young women who were excluded. After one unhappy year, she persuaded her parents to send her to Hollins College in Virginia, chosen solely because she had learned that Hollins had eliminated sororities altogether.[10]

Keller already had a well-developed sense of honor and discipline, but at Hollins, by her own account, she "did foolish things in order to break foolish rules." Reading by flashlight after lights out, skipping chapel, and, on occasion, leaving campus for a date without signing out earned her a suspension at the close of her junior year. She never returned to Hollins. Instead, once settled in New Orleans, she threw herself into the gaiety of the social season, capping the whirl by making her debut during the 1932 Carnival season when her father ruled as Rex.

In less than a year she wed Charles Keller Jr., neither a native Louisianian nor a Protestant like herself but a midwesterner and a Jew. A West Point graduate working in Louisiana with the Army Corps of Engineers, he met and married Rosa in 1932. Recognizing her daughter's genuine happiness, Ella West Freeman was warmly supportive, but A. B. Freeman, though he did not actively oppose the marriage, indicated plainly that he thought the couple would face difficult times because of anti-Semitism, commenting gruffly that he supposed his daughter was "tough enough to take it." A few years later, when the young officer decided to leave the army and settle his family in New Orleans, his wife acquiesced but thought it unwise, "fearing he might be overwhelmed . . . by social customs" that might not include him. Her comment refers obliquely to the socially significant Carnival krewes, which barred Jews and which, as her instincts told her, refused to make overtures to her husband.[11]

Chuck Keller unwittingly provided the catalyst for his wife's metamorphosis into a civil rights liberal, both through his cultural-religious background and his choice of profession. It was as the Protestant wife of a Jewish husband, learning about anti-Semitism from him and his family, listening with new ears to the ugly thoughtlessness of casual anti-Semitic remarks that were common in the 1930s, that Rosa developed a heightened sensitivity to prejudice in all its forms. It was as an army officer's wife that she experienced life outside the South; over the next decade, the couple lived in Massachusetts, Panama, Michigan, and Colorado, giving Keller slices of life without de jure segregation. An unorthodox marriage liberated Rosa Freeman Keller from the conventional life that New Orleans had intended for her.

In the years before the United States' entry into World War II, three children were born to the Kellers. In 1941 Chuck Keller returned to uniform, and when the military ordered him to Europe, Rosa returned to New Orleans with her children to wait out the war among family and friends. Life on the home front was not pleasant for her.

> We were sick of the whole damn thing! There was nothing in it for women — nothing! You're sitting home, keeping the home fires burning and taking care of the kids and the old folks and the jobs and everything else, and living with rationing. Rationing was a *serious* problem. If you had three little children and one shoe coupon every six months — shoes didn't last six months. We didn't have sugar, we didn't have meat, we didn't have coffee, we didn't have booze, we couldn't go anywhere — the gas was in short

supply. Now, you endure those things but there's nothing in it for you. There's no glory in it. You're *expected* to do it, but nobody rewards you for being a good war wife. We were sick of the whole shebang.[12]

Keller was an able woman, coping competently. Yet as this outburst makes clear, she craved meaningful work and thirsted for appreciation. As a privileged woman of the New Orleans elite, she had no encouragement to pursue a career that might have met those needs. The prevailing wisdom assumed that fulfillment for women would come through service to husband and family, supplemented by volunteer work, "keeping the home fires burning."

Predictably, New Orleans drew Rosa Keller into a web of appropriate organizations and activities: League of Women Voters, Independent Women's Organization, PTA, Girl Scouts, civil defense blackouts, air raid drills, scrap collecting, poll watching. The most significant affiliation that Keller made during the 1940s, however, was one she undertook out of filial duty. In memory of her mother, she agreed to serve on the board of directors of the local YWCA. An extraordinarily close mother-daughter relationship led Keller, for decades after her mother's death in 1941, to follow a pattern of asking herself, when making a decision, whether her mother would have approved of the action she was taking. Because Ella West Freeman had served on the YWCA board and had felt strongly about the good being done there, her daughter followed.

The YWCA endeavor changed Rosa Keller's life. In 1942, Keller attended her first biracial meetings when the YWCA board of directors met monthly at the local Y. Her initial pleasant surprise of encountering black women whom she described as "very attractive women with educational backgrounds equal or better than [her] own and charming manners" was followed by a rueful realization: "We couldn't eat lunch together; we couldn't ride the streetcar together—the normal things that friends do, we could not do." Keller had become aware of the total lack of social contact between the races. After more than thirty years of life in the South, surrounded by the barriers of Jim Crowism but oblivious to their cruelty, she was at last perceiving what she called the "small world" to which segregation restricted most blacks. "My outrage was enormous the more I learned about what a small world. I wondered how they could tolerate this and still keep the genial attitude."[13]

As a girl, Keller had known African Americans chiefly as servants and as the drivers of her father's Coca-Cola wagons; as a young married woman, she dealt with them as domestic servants in her own households. It was during the war years that she began seeing things differently. The irony of black troops serving in World War II only to face humiliating segregation when they returned ate away at her. She brooded over the situation in Europe. "Suppose," she later wrote, "that my own family was German. I would be the pariah, then." Marrying a Jew would have placed barriers in her path, would have narrowed opportunities for her children, would ultimately have been life threatening. Learning of the horrors of genocide just at the time when she was meeting able, attractive black women who were barred from "public" places such as parks, schools, libraries, and restaurants for no other reason than the accident of race awakened in Keller recognition of the inhumanity of a caste system that she had been bred to accept unquestioningly.[14]

There was no blinding conversion experience for Rosa Keller; rather, bit by bit, her eyes and her heart were opened. Her involvement in race relations grew steadily after the war with one affiliation or activity seemingly leading logically to the next; she began to establish an "invisible career" for herself as an agent of reform. Over the next decade Rosa Keller became chair of the board of management of Flint-Goodridge Hospital and a member of the board of directors of Dillard University, both institutions that served the African-American community in New Orleans, and a charter member of the small local Committee on Human Relations. After the war she and her husband invested heavily in developing Pontchartrain Park, the city's first subdivision for black home owners. It was as the only woman member of the United Fund that she first heard of the Urban League and expressed interest in its work. In no time she found herself on its board as well; by 1953 she was the Urban League's president. At decade's end, she was spearheading efforts to effect peaceful desegregation for the New Orleans public schools. All this activity had its start in the seemingly innocuous integrated working luncheons she helped to instigate at the YWCA in the 1940s, meeting around a table to consume simple meals with African-American women who, like herself, were YWCA board members. Although her girlhood in segregated New Orleans had taught her the intricate code governing southern racial etiquette, the adult Rosa Keller found that code odious.[15]

However, her changing attitude and growing interracial work discomforted her husband, provoking him to try to bar the subject of racial discrimination from their home. His edict triggered a heated declaration from his wife, who had reached a turning point. "I said, Chuck, if you're serious about that, you're gonna have to bar me too, because I have come to the place where I cannot walk out now. You fought your war—I was very helpful to you—I took care of your children; you were gone for two years. This is my war, it's got to be done, somebody's got to do it."[16]

Ultimately Rosa Keller became a conduit through which messages flowed from the black middle-class community to the white power structure and back again. More than a mere intermediary, she became an advocate, articulate and well placed. The relationship was an unequal one; whereas she was economically, socially, and racially unassailable, the black elite with whom she dealt almost exclusively did not enjoy anything approaching her security in 1950s New Orleans. In unsympathetic terms, it might be described as a maternalistic relationship, involving her doing *for* blacks. Arnold Hirsch has delineated the "dogged persistence of paternalism" in New Orleans race relations, documenting the black community's dependence, for much of the twentieth century, on white patrons to dispense favors to it.[17] Yet Keller was a highly consistent patron and advocate. She did not waver; she was reliable, even when being so became first inconvenient, then controversial, then dangerous. Some white liberals were summer soldiers and sunshine patriots, but an examination of Keller's activities over two decades reveals nothing of the dilettante in her. The price of advocating racial justice escalated dramatically in the strife-filled 1950s, and she faced strong incentives to abandon her work. Instead, she stayed the course.

Rosa Freeman Keller did not lead or even organize a political movement. Her efforts were usually indirect, discreet, inconspicuous — the antithesis of direct politics. One must, of course, ask whether her indirection was motivated by tactical or ideological considerations. Some moderates evinced interest in racial justice largely in order to avert black protest and forestall militance, never offering a condemnation of segregation but rather endeavoring to take the rough edges off the treatment accorded blacks in a segregated system, thus allowing the continuation of that system.[18] Keller's polite gradualism owes more to tactical considerations than to convictions on her part about African Americans' "place." If she did not lead marches or preach fiery sermons, she contributed what she could do best — gentle efforts, courteous prodding, well-placed suggestions — made potent because of the standing she enjoyed in her city.

Although Keller's first contacts in the African-American community were the women whom she met at the YWCA, it was the men of the community with whom she dealt most frequently. One may question why this was so. The answer is that although black women occupied strong positions in both the home and the cultural and religious life of their community, few black men would have classed them as community leaders. According to Daniel C. Thompson, it was unusual for women to "initiate, stimulate, coordinate, or direct the activities of the Negro masses in the solution of major social problems affecting them." Yet this male monopoly on positions of formal leadership in black community organizations has obscured the importance of women, who often wielded considerable authority without titles.[19] Although

Keller genuinely valued her connections with women in the city's African-American community, she pragmatically reasoned that to rely too heavily on them would mean challenging generations of gender relations, offending black men and diluting her effectiveness.

A prime example of how she functioned lies in the story of the desegregation of the New Orleans public libraries. In 1949, prominent local citizens asked the library board to make a policy change. Specifically, they suggested "*approaching* the board . . . with the *suggestion* that *consideration* be given to adopting a policy permitting all citizens, regardless of race, to use—on a non-segregated, integrated basis—the . . . Public Library."[20] Their caution appeared understandable, in view of the reactionary attitudes of board members. Rules limited black readers in the city's main library to the librarian's office only, where, isolated from contact with white patrons, they read under his watchful gaze. The use of the card catalog was forbidden them entirely. In response to prodding, the board grudgingly voted to set aside one table in the main library for "adult colored patrons." But even this slight change drew stout opposition from at least one board member, who wrote a testy letter to John Hall Jacobs, the city librarian. "The negroes in this community are receiving too much rather than too little and to a sizeable extent they are not taking care of what they receive," he groused. Defensively anticipating criticism for his views, this writer informed his correspondent proudly that he had two old family retainers buried in family plots in North Carolina and Kentucky, which made him feel he knew "as much as the average philanthropist."[21]

As a payback to the Independent Women's Organization for its staunch support, Mayor deLesseps Morrison appointed Rosa Keller, a charter IWO member, to the library board in 1953. By this time her feelings on race were well known in the city; she was chair of the board of management of Flint-Goodridge Hospital and president of the New Orleans Urban League. Her views clashed with those of the nervous library board members, all men and quite conservative. The men worried that imminent completion of a new branch library near Dillard University would lead blacks to press for unrestricted use of that branch, which was intended for whites. The mayor, a racial realist but also a politician anxious not to appear too moderate on the race issue, almost certainly appointed Keller to accomplish what he saw as the inevitable desegregation of the libraries.[22]

To Keller, the libraries constituted the ideal starting place. "What better place than the library where people don't get very pugilistic," she commented.[23] Her pressure for desegregation immediately drew hostile responses from board members, many of whom openly resented a woman's presence on a city board. In February 1954 this body received a letter from a group of black educators requesting that the Latter Library, a branch located in the uptown-university area and noted for its collections of jazz and art, be opened to all. Keller had known in advance about the request, since the group had informed the Urban League of its plans. She was able to relay to the Urban League the mood of the library board and to the library board the black community's talk of legal action to force desegregation. Repeatedly she tried to persuade the board to vote to desegregate, but to no avail. Advised by the city attorney to make "no attempt . . . to enforce segregation in . . . the libraries" and informed by the mayor of his belief that they should desegregate, the recalcitrant board instead voted, exactly one week after the historic *Brown v. Board of Education* decision, to instruct all librarians to continue to enforce segregation.[24]

Keller submitted her resignation in disgust, prompting Mayor Morrison to convene the men of the board for a heated session that concluded after midnight with their grudging consent to open all libraries to all patrons. The mayor himself telephoned a sleeping Keller to press her to withdraw her resignation, which she did. In return Morrison wanted a favor from Keller: would she use her contacts in the black community to announce and implement the library decision?[25]

Morrison did not want the desegregation decision trumpeted in the local press; the angry rhetoric sparked that month by the *Brown* decision had had its effect on him. He was by this time consumed with his obsession to become governor of Louisiana and feared offending conservatives, who viewed a moderate segregationist (which Morrison was) as no segregationist at all. He asked Keller to spread word of the new policy informally. Accordingly, there was no public announcement. Keller, working with Albert Dent, president of Dillard University, arranged to have the news circulated and scheduled contingents of circumspect well-dressed blacks to be the first to integrate the libraries. When she contacted black associates to arrange for the desegregation to begin, she had no doubts about the kind of blacks who would be deployed; they sent "their most beautiful people," as she put it.[26] Keller subscribed to Gunnar Myrdal's assimilationist views about blacks, assuming, as he did, that it was "to the advantage of American Negroes . . . to acquire the traits held in esteem by the dominant white Americans."[27] Like him, she felt that blacks could do themselves some good by fitting in, by eliminating traits that made them offensive or conspicuous to whites. Thus, her choice of individuals to integrate the library reflects what might be called cultural arrogance by some and pragmatism by others.

This appears to be the only consequential gain made by the black community through quiet negotiation rather than through public protest, litigation, or political action. Long after 1954, however, the library drinking fountains remained segregated, and restrooms were simply unavailable to black patrons.[28]

After the library victory, Keller suffered a setback in her role as gradualist go-between when she approached the medical establishment of her city on behalf of New Orleans Negroes. Prior to the 1932 construction of the Flint-Goodridge Hospital of Dillard University, New Orleans blacks had had scant access to decent medical care. As one local African American had put it, "Most places there isn't any hospital for Negroes, and when they take you into one for white folks they put you in the basement or in a ward out in the barn or some such place."[29] Indeed, the segregated facilities of the city's sprawling Charity Hospital and one small, underfinanced infirmary (Flint-Goodridge's forerunner) had constituted the only options for the hospital care of blacks.

Dillard University, founded in 1930 through a merger of all-black New Orleans University and Straight University, operated Flint-Goodridge Hospital to serve the medical needs of the African-American community in New Orleans and the surrounding area. Opened in 1889 as a black medical college, with a generous donation from John D. Flint, a Massachusetts textile manufacturer, the hospital had changed its name early in this century to reflect the bequest of another wealthy northern benefactor, Caroline Goodridge Mudge of Boston, who made a $25,000 donation in honor of her mother, Sarah Goodridge. When the American Medical Association's Flexner Commission demanded higher standards for medical education in 1911, the medical college expired, but the hospital continued to operate, straining to meet state and national standards, providing much-needed service by treating both paying and charity patients. In 1930, in the wake of the merger that wrought Dillard University, the Julius Rosenwald Fund, denominational boards, and other foundations pledged $1.75 million to a hospital building fund, stipulating that the local community raise $250,000 as a match. The local drive netted $304,000, leading Edwin Embree of the Rosenwald Fund to call the effort a record "for any southern city both in the sums involved and in the spirit of partnership between the races in working for a common civic purpose."[30]

At the 1932 dedication of the modern four-story structure, remarks by Dr. James Hardy Dillard (head of the Phelps-Stokes Fund, a former dean at Tulane University, and the individual for whom Dillard University was named) revealed an unblushingly utilitarian justification for the hospital's construction. "In improving the health of the negro," he said, "the white people are protecting themselves, since negroes are necessary to the community and must be taken care of properly."[31]

The Board of Trustees of Dillard University, headed by Edgar B. Stern, selected the administrator for the new facility. On Will Alexander's recommendation, they hired young Albert W. Dent, a Morehouse College graduate, to serve as Flint's first superintendent.[32] As superintendent, Dent thoroughly impressed Stern and the Dillard trustees, particularly with his detailed financial reports and administrative skills. However, Dent left hospital administration to assume the Dillard presidency in 1941, and Flint-Goodridge entered a period of rocky times. In the heady climate of the immediate postwar years, when many African Americans pressed more insistently and confidently for application of the American creed to their lives, black physicians, especially the younger among them, deserted New Orleans for better opportunities elsewhere. In the three years after 1950, Flint-Goodridge lost 48 percent of its black physicians and numbered only eighteen black M.D.'s on its staff, down from a high of forty-five in the early 1940s. In addition, the military's demands for physicians contributed to the hemorrhage of talent, with nine black doctors at Flint inducted into the armed service during the Korean War. None of the remaining doctors was board certified in any specialty. Such a mass exodus of skill presaged dire consequences, which were not long in coming. In 1954, an accreditation committee revoked the hospital's accreditation, citing deficiencies of medical care, high infant and maternal mortality statistics, and poor management.[33]

Galvanized into action by the loss of accreditation at Dillard's hospital, Edgar Stern moved to create a hospital board of management, to be composed of black and white citizens. Black members were Dillard's president Albert Dent, Fannie C. Williams, a schoolteacher, the Reverend Robert Hill, a local minister, T. L. Miller and James Gayle, businessmen, and Dr. W. R. Adams, a longtime staff physician at Flint. Monte Lemann, an attorney, Bruce Brown, a businessman, and Stern himself were the white members. Seeking for chairman a tactful individual who could command respect in the black community, Stern turned to Rosa Keller. When she protested her inadequacy and inexperience, Stern reminded her of the confidence the black community had in her, of the solid reputation she enjoyed in racial matters, born of her biracial contacts at the YWCA and the Urban League. Keller accepted the post reluctantly.[34]

In acquainting herself with the problems the hospital faced, Keller uncovered a vicious cycle: the black doctors of the Flint-Goodridge staff were denied membership in the Orleans Parish Medical Society and access to the library of the state medical school in New Orleans and were then scorned for professional inadequacies. Medical society membership conveyed more than opportunity for camaraderie with one's professional peers. Under the auspices of the society, physicians had access to monthly scientific meetings at which the latest findings on a variety of topics were discussed, often with clinical demonstrations, since the sessions met in area hospitals on a rotating basis. In the first year of Keller's association with Flint, for example, sessions were held dealing with proctologic examinations, medico-legal problems, the nature of toxemia in pregnancy, problems in gastrointestinal bleeding, and surgery of the common bile duct. Under the auspices of the National Foundation for Infantile Paralysis, members viewed a closed-circuit telecast on the new polio vaccine. Whereas white physicians could affiliate with any hospital that suited their needs, black doctors could admit their patients only to Flint. Although the prestigious American Medical Association had no color bar regarding membership, the Jim Crow practices of Orleans Parish served to keep local black doctors out, since the AMA accepted only doctors who were members in good standing of their local medical societies.[35]

To Rosa Keller, the steps for remedy seemed clear: enroll black physicians in the local medical society, upgrade their clinical skills through the free monthly seminars, improve the quality of care at Flint-Goodridge Hospital, and restore its accreditation. Using personal contacts and moral suasion, she quietly began to work toward desegregation of the Orleans Parish Medical Society. In so doing, however, she seriously miscalculated the readiness of that group for racial change, later explaining ruefully that she had "hoped for a measure of compassion from doctors more than from businessmen, but their prejudices were as bad as anyone's."[36]

In the months following the *Brown* decision in 1954, a heady climate prevailed in the black community, spreading contagiously to white moderates like Keller. The signs of change were everywhere, signifying growing confidence and diminishing patience among blacks: a successful boycott of segregated McDonogh Day ceremonies, an integrated banquet at a local Democratic National Committee fund-raiser, public criticism of the mayor when his proudly unveiled union railroad terminal was found to contain segregated facilities, and the desegregation of public libraries.

In this climate, in late 1954, Keller contacted Dr. Edgar Hull, president of the Orleans Parish Medical Society, regarding the situation at Flint-Goodridge Hospital, and Hull arranged for Keller and a contingent representing Flint-Goodridge to meet with the Hospital Committee of the local medical association. Accompanying Keller, Edgar Stern, and Albert Dent were Clif Weil, the black administrator of Flint-Goodridge, Dr. Franklin McLean, former dean of the Medical School of the University of Chicago, and Dr. Peter M. Murray, a Louisiana native who was the first black president of the New York County Medical Society.[37] Prior to this conference, Keller had traveled to New York to meet Dr. Murray. Establishing a warm relationship with him, she felt that "because of his prestige in New York, he might be listened to" by the white medical establishment in New Orleans. In this hope she was mistaken.[38]

Noting the frosty attitude of the local doctors, who "made it quite clear that they had been designated to be there," Keller assumed her go-between role at the meeting's outset, trying to state pleasantly some of the barriers black doctors faced. Dr. Murray gently tried to explain the flight of good black physicians away from New Orleans, stating,

> If a boy puts in six or seven years studying, working, training, he is not going to come back to a community where he can't keep up with his intellectual development. If he does come back, as things now are, he will only slump, because he doesn't have the mental stimulus of attending medical lectures and talking with other professional men. . . . We must create an atmosphere where a negro can look forward to joining in on lectures and other intellectual activities.

The local physicians countered that black doctors had refused opportunities offered them in the past by the white medical establishment, an assertion that the Flint-Goodridge contingent disputed, prompting the committee chairman rudely to state his belief that "the colored people could get educational facilities here if their desire was strong enough." Keller interjected soothingly, "Maybe you can tell us what is the best thing to do," and again reviewed some of the problems. Ultimately, it was the white outsider, Dr. McLean of Chicago, who put into plain words what Keller wanted, saying bluntly that the first step was "to make negro doctors eligible for membership in the local medical society," which meant that race or color was not to be "a barrier to membership." Clearly disgusted at having had to listen to a Negro, a woman, and an outsider assert themselves, the committee chairman turned to Edgar Stern, who was white, male, and a New Orleanian, and said pointedly, "Mr. Stern, if you have any concrete requests to make in the future, I wish *you* would make them."[39]

Keller recalled that the meeting ended with the chairman announcing that "niggers" preferred white doctors, although the remark was sanitized in the minutes. The doctors left by one door and the Flint-Goodridge group by another. Keller's pain over this incident was considerable, not for herself, for "these rude rebuffs had gotten to be a way of life" for her, but because she had "subjected [her] Negro friends to a disagreeable insult, and Dr. Murray had come all the way from New York for it."[40] Keller's sense of etiquette cast her in the role of hostess, for she had in fact initiated the meeting to which she invited Dr. Murray; Dr. Murray, her guest, had been treated rudely by others at the gathering and she felt a personal responsibility.

Keller and the board proceeded with plans to recruit young, well-trained black doctors with certification in specialties by subsidizing their practices. By mid-1955 four young M.D.'s had relocated to take privately subsidized residencies at Flint-Goodridge, which guaranteed them a monthly salary of one thousand dollars and the possibility of establishing private practice after fulfilling their hospital commitment. This tactic did upgrade the skill level of the staff but also antagonized older black physicians by importing competition and to a certain extent factionalized the staff between "young turks" and "the old guard."[41]

A centerpiece of Keller's approach involved increasing the contacts between the Flint staff physicians and the most prominent and respected white doctors in the city. As she had discovered in her own life, contact across the color line between individuals with common interests and similar levels of education acts as a powerful solvent to dissolve prejudice.

Keller decided to approach the city's most esteemed physician, Dr. Alton Ochsner, then in his late sixties, in the hope that he might lend his prestige to her efforts by heading an advisory board. Founder of the Ochsner Hospital, which provided sophisticated treatment for an international clientele of patients, Ochsner possessed a massive ego that expressed itself in abrasive, intolerant, and often obnoxious behavior toward family and colleagues. An irreverent couplet about Ochsner composed by his medical students at Tulane ("Early to bed and early to rise / Work hard and publicize") hints at his passion for headlines. The earliest physician to link cigarette smoking and lung cancer (characteristically, though, on a hunch and without empirical data), Ochsner became widely recognized as an authority on lung cancer and garnered national recognition, serving as president of the American Cancer Society and of the American College of Surgeons. He also took the most prestigious duo of local social-civic honors, winning the *Times-Picayune* Loving Cup in 1945 and reigning as Rex in 1948.[42]

Despite such accolades and the public perception of him as a saintly healer, Ochsner never enjoyed really good relations with the medical establishment in New Orleans. Although approached about building a hospital jointly with Ochsner and his partners, the staffs at Tulane, Touro, Mercy, and Southern Baptist Hospitals all refused because of their anti-Ochsner feelings. Ochsner's sympathetic biographers speculate that other physicians were jealous of his fame. Another explanation might address his thoughtless personality and the accusations of incompetence that he routinely flung at colleagues. In addition, his anti-Semitism could not have gone unnoticed; he was known to believe Jews could not make good surgeons.[43]

By the 1950s Ochsner was increasingly interested in politics; his biographers report that "every instinct was right-wing conservative." He defended Mussolini and Perón as "benevolent dictators," loathed FDR and his legacy of social welfare concerns, and preached a virulent anti-Communism. His racial beliefs were such that he refused to allow the black cooks and custodians employed at Ochsner Hospital to receive medical treatment there and instead sent them across town to Flint-Goodridge Hospital for care. In successful efforts to attract wealthy Latin Americans to his hospital, he cultivated the Perón and Somoza families and established lasting friendships with them. When his fear of Communist advances in Latin America became an obsession, Ochsner accepted the presidency of the Information Council of the Americas (INCA), a right-wing propaganda body that distributed "truth tapes" to counter Castro's popularity.[44]

All these aspects of Alton Ochsner's personality were unknown to Rosa Keller when she arrived in his office for her meeting with him. Although she had encountered Ochsner socially, she did not know him well; his alleged belief that "women really should amuse themselves frivolously and stay away from anything of importance" led her to anticipate a polite refusal when she asked his help, but nothing had prepared her for the scene that ensued. She did not expect to witness what she later called "his crack-up." She had hardly broached the subject of the advisory panel at the city's black hospital when the doctor changed from an affable, ingratiating person into a maniac who reminded her of Humphrey Bogart's portrayal of Captain Queeg in *The Caine Mutiny.* "His face began to twitch, his hands nervously moved things around on his desk, his eyes darted around quite strangely, and he mumbled incoherently." Shifting suddenly from uncertainty to an explosion of abusive rhetoric linking civil rights, Communism, blacks, and venereal disease, he found himself overcome and literally unable to continue. Rising, he ordered his visitor out. Shaken by his diatribe, Keller went home in tears and was physically sick. This reaction from one of the city's best-known and most respected men had shocked Rosa Keller deeply. "He spoke to me as *no* gentleman should speak to a lady," she recalled. "I expected Dr. Ochsner to be better than *that.*"[45]

Keller persisted with attempts to upgrade the hospital, persuading prominent physicians from the medical schools at Tulane and Louisiana State University to sit on the medical advisory board. Recognized authorities whom she consulted urged expansion and modernization of Flint-Goodridge. Because the needed improvements (a four-story addition, a 60 percent increase in beds, a recovery room, air-conditioning, blood bank services, new boilers, new furniture and bathrooms for patients, modernized dietary services) bore a price tag estimated at one million dollars, Keller familiarized herself with guidelines governing distribution of federal Hill-Burton funds for hospital construction and then organized a campaign that netted half a million dollars from black and white donors. Her skills as a racial diplomat led her to name cochairmen for the drive, one black and one white, and to encourage each to raise money from his respective community by using the methods that worked best. "I felt that we should have a Negro chairman, but realized that most of the white donors would not give appointments to this kind of chairman," she said candidly.[46]

Keller traveled to Baton Rouge to meet with Governor Earl Long, at his request, taking Flint-Goodridge administrator Clif Weil along because of his expertise regarding hospital conditions and regulations. To her dismay, Governor Long refused to see the African American, who could only wait in an anteroom during the interview.[47] Keller and Weil had more success meeting with officials about Hill-Burton funds in Washington; they also enjoyed a shared taxi ride and a casual cocktail at the bar in her hotel, innocent pleasures not to be had by a "mixed" couple in Louisiana.[48]

In addition to health care issues, Keller's attention encompassed housing. The well-documented postwar housing shortage affected all New Orleanians, but blacks were hit especially hard. Mayor Morrison's ambitious urban renewal and municipal construction projects resulted in the razing of whole blocks of African-American neighborhoods. Although many black families lost their dwellings to Morrison's slum clearance energies, fierce opposition from white property owners stalled construction of black housing projects, and rents on existing properties soared. The National Urban League equated "urban renewal" with "Negro removal," and the local black newspaper printed statistics indicating that, in a city that was one-third African-American, forty-six thousand new homes had been built since V-J Day but fewer than five hundred of them were occupied by blacks. Discontent among blacks was rising. Rosa Keller commented of the situation, "Chep was scared. We were all scared."[49]

A casual dinner party conversation about the difficulty of her host's servant in finding adequate housing led to plans for Pontchartrain Park subdivision, a development for middle-class blacks, which Rosa and Chuck Keller and Edith and Edgar Stern would finance. The plans became reality in 1955, when 241 modern homes, ranging in price from $9,500 to $25,000, were built by Keller Construction Company, sold, and occupied by local black families.[50]

In both Pontchartrain Park subdivision and Flint-Goodridge Hospital, Keller's efforts promoted a distinctly middle-class—but undeniable—version of "separate but equal." In her world, attractive, comfortable housing and adequate medical care were basic necessities. Her acquaintance with professional black men and their well-educated, stylish wives forced her to see that even with wealth and education, black citizens could not always obtain housing and health care that met her standards of quality. She took pleasure in watching the burgeoning suburban sprawl in Pontchartrain Park and beamed over the landscaping award the development won when it opened, recalling that white friends had scoffed that blacks would not make their mortgage payments or maintain their yards decently.[51]

In her work to obtain better housing and a good hospital for the black community, Keller undeniably perpetuated segregation. Some local blacks, such as A. J. Chapital, president of the New Orleans NAACP chapter, pointed this out. Black civil rights attorney A. P. Tureaud and Daniel Byrd of the NAACP objected for the same reasons. Others, virtually all of the middle-class "racial diplomats" whom Keller knew, such as Albert and Jessie Dent, Dr. Leonard Burns, J. Westbrook McPherson, and Revius Ortique, supported her because they knew and trusted her, because her indirect gradualism was bringing benefits to segments of black New Orleans, and because the need for middle-class housing was unmistakable.[52]

In the realm of education, however, Rosa Keller was an early and public advocate of desegregation who abandoned any faith in the "separate but equal" approach. Ignoring the implications of *Brown v. Board of Education*, the Orleans Parish School Board stubbornly refused to plan for change. In 1955, Keller circulated a petition, written by Rabbi Julian Feibelman, that urged compliance with the Supreme Court decision. She and Rabbi Feibelman attended a school board meeting at which he addressed the board. When Keller read the petition, school board members responded rudely and abusively. "We were practically thrown out of the place," she recalled. "Such howling and screaming you never heard."[53]

The punitive backlash from a disapproving community began immediately. On the morning after the school board meeting, a *Times-Picayune* headline declared, "School Board Hears Desegregation Plea," setting in bold type the petition's request that "desegregation in schools of Orleans parish . . . go forward as soon as possible." Rabbi Feibelman noted wryly that he "awoke to find [himself] infamous." Keller could have said the same. Her telephone rang with a stream of denunciations, anonymous abuse, and profanity. Attending a League of Women Voters meeting later that week, she found herself treated with cold disdain.[54]

In all New Orleans, Keller and Feibelman had found only 179 whites willing to sign their petition; they made no effort to circulate it in the black community. But in the climate of heightened racial consciousness then prevailing, this minuscule stimulus elicited a disproportionately large response. In only two weeks, the Greater New Orleans Citizens' Council responded with a petition signed by nearly 15,000 citizens, all of whom supported segregated schools and implored the board to take action to prevent race mixing.[55] Subsequently, both Keller and Rabbi Feibelman were the targets of shots fired from speeding cars. Again came the opportunity to abandon her work, this time because of legitimate fears for her safety. Again, Keller was undeterred. Not cowed, she attended every school board meeting for the next two years, monitoring their discussions and reporting to the Urban League.[56]

Rosa Keller's wide variety of contacts included many in the New Orleans establishment. She informed her friends in the Urban League of how various influential figures felt about certain issues, thus ensuring wide dissemination of their views and comments to local blacks. Her associates in the black community knew, for example, about Dr. Ochsner's rabid reaction to her visit; they knew about the school board's hostile response to the desegregation petition. From Keller they also learned that the medical society had only narrowly defeated a measure resolving that school desegregation was a public health threat because black children allegedly carried venereal disease. From her they learned that the graduate faculty at Tulane University wanted to admit black applicants. They learned of the first integrated meeting of the local League of Women Voters, held in Keller's home. They heard of her progress, appallingly slow, at persuading local businesses to hire qualified blacks as employees. They heard of the warm reception that J. Westbrook McPherson, the black executive director of the Urban League, had received from a group of white teenagers when he spoke to Keller's daughter's group at the St. Charles Avenue Presbyterian Church, but learned also that adult men in the church had responded to his visit with hostility and had charged that his motive was interracial sex. A respected church elder had brought the youth meeting to an abrupt end by shouting to the visiting McPherson, "Why don't you just tell these kids that all you niggers really want is our white women?"[57]

Conservative middle-class blacks of the Urban League in essence had a mole in the white establishment, one who was working steadily for causes that were important to the African-American community and faithfully reporting developments to them. In the 1950s, the black elite in New Orleans was frankly accommodationist and preferred negotiation over protest, litigation instead of confrontation. A preference for change through gradualism characterized these "racial diplomats," who displayed social polish, skill in dealing with white leaders, and disgust at anything ill mannered. Their genteel attitudes and Keller's were perfectly compatible.[58]

The gradualism of the New Orleans black middle class stands in stark contrast to other local events that signaled a coming mass activism. In 1956, for example, the *Louisiana Weekly*, serving the black community, reported a local mass meeting of support for the Montgomery bus boycott, at which thirty-five hundred dollars was collected for that cause, and a visit to New Orleans by Emmett Till's mother, who spoke to a large audience about her son's murder at the hands of white men the year before in Mississippi. But New Orleans "racial diplomats" were not yet ready to speak forcefully for themselves. The black executive director of the Urban League said candidly in 1959: "I believe it is necessary to get white support. . . . These people must be in positions of influence with the respect of the community. We work through and with them."[59]

In time, however, it appeared that good manners and polite prodding worked to no avail. The mood after the *Brown* decision and the Southern Manifesto was increasingly embattled; the middle ground eroded as militant segregationists equated moderation with Communism. Any willingness to envision change in the racial code sparked furious denunciations. Because she challenged racial orthodoxy, Keller was frequently branded a Communist. Keller's daughter summed up the polarizing effect of the Citizens' Council rhetoric: "You've got to go or not go. At that point, you're either one of them or one of us. Especially when it turned the corner where it wasn't just 'you're a traitor to our race' but now 'you've become a Commie.' If you ever had any sympathetic thoughts, then you might as well go whole hog." Noted white liberal Anne Braden expressed similar sentiments more succinctly: "You can't be neutral. You are either part of it or you are against it."[60]

Serving as president of the New Orleans Urban League allowed Keller to show which side she was on. Founded in 1910 with a biracial middle-class membership, the National Urban League functioned as a social service organization to advance the economic and social conditions of blacks in cities. It left civil rights issues to its counterpart, the NAACP, and was considered so tame that some black activists derided it as "the Bourbon League."[61] The New Orleans chapter had twenty-five years of service to its credit when Keller took the helm in 1953, just as a crisis was brewing.

Like all local affiliates, the New Orleans Urban League received most of its funding from the Community Chest (United Fund). In 1954, Gerald L. K. Smith's National Citizens' Protective Association branded the Urban League a "subversive" organization because of the National Urban League's endorsement of the *Brown v. Board of Education* ruling and attacked Community Chests for supporting Urban League branches. By 1955 the White Citizens' Council had begun an anti–Urban League crusade in the South, calling it an integrationist organization. Pressure mounted against local affiliates in Atlanta, Little Rock, Louisville, Memphis, Miami, Richmond, and Tampa, and in response, several southern Community Chests suspended their funding of local Urban Leagues.[62]

In April 1956, the crisis reached New Orleans. Leaders of the United Fund of New Orleans requested that the local Urban League withdraw voluntarily from the United Fund, because, they alleged, many of their former campaign leaders had refused to participate in the 1956 fund drive, citing their displeasure that the integrationist Urban League was a recipient of United Fund financing. The leaders feared for the success of their fund-raising unless the tainted Urban League withdrew. Rosa Keller "jumped on this proposition with both feet," in the memory of one African American who attended the session, parrying the idea by pointing out that this would set a highly dangerous precedent. Criticism might next be directed at Catholic agencies or Jewish agencies or the YWCA, she warned; did the United Fund want to give the Citizens' Councils the power of judging the worthiness and orthodoxy of all potential recipients of United Fund largesse? Chuck Keller, who attended the meeting, was vocal in support of his wife's reasoning. He suggested that the New Orleans Urban League might remain a part of the United Fund without requesting funding for 1957 and volunteered to take responsibility for finding twenty corporate sponsors to raise money for its 1957 budget.[63] Nothing was resolved at the meeting.

A month later, the Greater New Orleans Citizens' Council turned up the heat. At a massive rally held in Pelican Stadium, Dr. Emmett Irwin, the group's president, denounced the Urban League: "I have evidence here the Urban League is working for integration in all walks of life—is working to have Negro physicians admitted to the Orleans Parish Medical Society and to place Negroes on a higher level in the telephone company and the Esso Standard Oil Company."[64]

Thundering that the Urban League wanted "total and complete equality for the Negro," Irwin announced that the organization was "almost totally supported by the Community Chest, a subsidiary of the United Fund." Judge Leander Perez informed the crowd that Rosa Keller was president of the despised group. Charging that unnamed members of the National Urban League board were Communists, he urged a boycott of the United Fund if the Urban League remained a member. From that point on, Keller's life was never the same. Her role in race relations took on a much more public dimension thanks to the vitriol of Irwin and Perez.[65]

When Keller stepped down after three years as Urban League president to take a position on the National Urban League Board of Trustees, many acknowledged her as the most effective white liberal in New Orleans. In a report to the National Urban League, the local executive director had praised the "bolder approach" of Keller's leadership, citing particularly her ability "to rally support." In 1959, a leading black activist singled out Keller when asked about white leaders whom he regarded as influential in race relations. He commented that she had been "consistent in expressing liberal views in spite of opposition" and seemed always "able to draw a following."[66]

Her unique status does much to explain her success. The Urban League's other white members were priests, rabbis, social workers, educators, and a few Jewish housewives, all sincere and caring but only marginally associated, if at all, with the New Orleans elite. Keller was Presbyterian, a member of a prominent New Orleans family, wealthy, and socially secure. Of the power structure, she once said, "They just couldn't tell me 'no.'"[67]

Beyond her status, Keller's quiet consistency earned trust. Intuitively she seemed to know the consequences of unreliability. "There were times when I would have quit this whole thing, from just fatigue and loneliness over it. But I couldn't disappoint people. Black people had had some friends in this city, but they didn't stay there. When the going got tough, and it always did, the people would leave. I could have done that, very easily. That was my hardest struggle."[68]

Her beloved father never supported her efforts. To maintain any kind of relationship with him, she avoided the subject of race altogether, even though it now was at the center of her life. Occasionally he related to her the substance of conversations at the exclusive Boston Club, where leading New Orleanians groused to him, "Can't you make that daughter of yours shut up? She's just outrageous." Nor did her husband, at least during the first twenty years of their marriage, encourage her work to improve race relations in New Orleans. Telephoned messages stating "Your wife is sleeping with ———— ————" (various black men were named) could only have added to the burden. Her only brother stoutly opposed everything she did on the racial front. Friends did not want to hear about her feelings on race. She worried about ostracism for her three children, who were in high school during the 1950s and felt all the usual adolescent concerns over peer acceptance. Of even greater concern was their physical safety; telephoned threats came regularly and gave rise to uneasiness. Indeed, her consistency did not come cheap; she purchased it at a great personal price.[69]

Keller established a pattern of social contact with black New Orleanians. She attended weddings and graduations, programs on the Dillard University campus, "that lovely green and white world." She took her Girl Scout troop to hear Eleanor Roosevelt speak there in 1953, opting not to ask parental permission because of the likely refusals. The contact was not reciprocal, however; Keller did not invite black associates to her daughters' weddings or to social functions in her home if white friends were attending. She was guaranteed a warm reception in their world but knew she could not guarantee them the same in hers. When she did once invite Sybil Haydel Morial to bring a group of black women to her home to meet with members of the all-white Independent Women's Organization, she was shocked and pained when the white women spoke rudely to her guests. She had believed, wrongly, that the IWO was ready to embrace integration.[70]

In her writings and comments, Keller frequently referred to walking "in two worlds." Her life was compartmentalized; she knew black people and white people, with no overlap. There was a satisfying personal life with her family and a life built around her invisible career, two separate circles that rarely intersected. The apparent broad-mindedness of her peers, manifested in the women's movements in New Orleans for honest, responsible government, deserted most of them in racial matters. Wrote one affluent woman, a veteran of Hilda Phelps Hammond's anti-Long movement and long association with good-government efforts,

> I do not wish to get involved or identified with any movement which solicits the Negro element in New Orleans.
>
> Let me explain that I not only believe in better housing and better schools for both white and Negro but I do not advocate integration which, to my mind, is the logical outcome of social and personal contacts. I believe primarily in the purity of the race and, fortunately, I hope that I will only live long enough for this condition to remain.[71]

The New Orleans school desegregation crisis of 1960 provided bitter proof of the ineffectiveness of gradualism and demonstrated conclusively the weakness of white liberals. Keller's well-meaning efforts at moral suasion, her appeals for fairness and justice, appeared anemic indeed in comparison with the menacing rhetoric and actions of the Leander Perez–led Citizens' Council. In the face of massive resistance, the old coalition of the well-mannered black middle class and well-placed Keller working quietly together for racial progress was no longer viable.

Shortly after the desegregation order of July 1959, Rosa Keller had begun organizing to build white support for integrated schools. Convinced that an all-white pressure group could produce the best results, Keller consulted black community leaders, who not only concurred but even made a contribution of one thousand dollars to finance her segregated group. Composed chiefly of women, with a handful of men, the group unanimously adopted the name SOS, for Save Our Schools, and began meeting weekly. In their pamphlets and press conferences, SOS members took pains to avoid saying anything that could characterize them as "integrationist," fearing that in the racial climate then prevailing, such a label would discredit them with the whites whom they hoped to sway. Thus, SOS deliberately refused to offer an opinion on the merits of the *Brown* decision.[72]

After months of delays and assurances by irresponsible officials that segregation would not be breached, unprepared white New Orleanians were thunderstruck when, in accordance with Judge Skelly Wright's reviled order, four little girls integrated the first grade in November 1960. The howling legislature in Baton Rouge postured in rage, enacting an array of laws designed to thwart the inevitable. Indeed, "no southern state matched the vigor, imagination, and frenzy displayed by Louisiana in battling to maintain segregated public schools."[73] Mobs roamed New Orleans, rioting whites attacked school board offices, and television cameras captured it all.

Long before the crisis, Keller had approached the school board to urge its members to select for the trial two schools in an affluent area whose PTAs had voted to support the change. She received a peremptory hearing and then was dismissed with cavalier assurances that everything was "under control." Unknown to her, board members had already made their choice: two schools in the most neglected, least prosperous area of the city. White parents in that district, chiefly blue collar and working class, many living in public housing, reacted angrily and predictably to the implementation of desegregation by taking their children out of school altogether.[74] Keller's small group organized car lifts to transport the few white children whose parents did not withdraw them from the two targeted schools, but the violence and abusive rhetoric took such a toll on the children, their parents, and the women drivers that soon federal marshals assumed the task of driving.[75]

In the summer of 1961 Keller's group hoped to persuade white parents to end their boycott, which had been almost total, and to reenroll their children, nearly three hundred of whom had not been enrolled in any school during the 1960–61 year. Save Our Schools published literature to inform citizens of successful desegregation efforts in other cities and to acquaint them with the extent of negative press coverage on New Orleans outside the Deep South. A mass mailing went to parents of children in the desegregated schools. Many were returned by the next mail, covered with hostile remarks. One recipient returned his letter with this scrawled note: "My children is white and I wont send them to no nigger school. I would rather have them ignorant, you nigger lovers. I wiped my ass with this and you can wipe your ass with it too." Unmistakably, the writer had indeed done that.[76]

Analysts of the school crisis in New Orleans universally remarked on the absence of leadership from elected officials and the business community.[77] Mayor Chep Morrison never endorsed Skelly Wright's desegregation order and steadfastly refused all entreaties to meet with an SOS delegation; city councilmen maintained silence; the *Times-Picayune* opined glumly that desegregating the schools and closing them to prevent it were equally undesirable; the Catholic Church remained on the sidelines. Although worried over the mounting financial impact of continuing racial unrest, the business elite worked to maintain "the maximum possible degree of segregation consistent with their city's progressive image."[78]

Only one month after the riots, state superintendent of education Shelby Jackson, an intimate of segregation stalwarts Leander Perez and Willie Rainach, addressed a large Citizens' Council rally in New Orleans's Municipal Auditorium, invoking the name of an ancestor to claim that he would "stand like a stone wall" on the issue. "Don't let anybody tell you the fight is over," he urged. "It has just begun. Let's see to it that we are not controlled by the National Association for the Advancement of Colored People in the state of Louisiana."[79]

The Orleans Parish School Board included four members who, though moderate segregationists, were at least realists who wanted to keep the schools open even if that meant that a handful of black children enrolled in previously all-white schools. But the stark results of a special survey the school board conducted in May 1960 unnerved them: nearly 82 percent of white parents responding voted to close the schools entirely rather than accept any breach of segregation.[80] The survey results left school board members badly shaken and demoralized, facing the unwanted task of implementing a federal court order for which the city's officials and press took no steps to build support.

In such a vacuum, New Orleans women were notable for their innovative efforts to promote peaceful implementation of court rulings. But for the quiet and persistent efforts of women, the beleaguered school board initially would have had virtually no public support from whites in managing desegregation. Approximately forty SOS members traveled to Baton Rouge to support fellow members Betty Wisdom, Mary Sand, and Katherine Wright as they testified before a hostile legislature concerning school desegregation. When school board member Matthew Sutherland ran for reelection in November 1960, only days before the scheduled implementation of desegregation, the contest was seen as a referendum on open versus closed schools.

Save Our Schools women established the Committee of 100, made up of business and professional men who endorsed Sutherland in a full-page newspaper ad. Sutherland, the only candidate who favored open, desegregated schools, was reelected. A month later, another large ad in the *Times-Picayune* called for an end to street demonstrations and urged community support for the school board. Again, women were the motive force behind the action, having initiated the project and gathered the signatures of the community men. At the end of January 1961, a well-attended testimonial dinner, instigated and organized by women, was held at the Roosevelt Hotel to honor the embattled school board for its work to preserve public education.[81]

The politically astute Independent Women's Organization read in the words of their old nemesis, Shelby Jackson, something more menacing than rabid segregationist rhetoric. After the state superintendent's appearance at the Citizens' Council rally in December 1960, the IWO wrote to Orleans Parish school board members in an attempt to stiffen their resolve to implement the federal court order. The IWO ascribed an ulterior motive to those who were so vehemently attacking the school board.

> As a political organization we recognize that the attacks against you have much more significance than is conveyed by public pronouncements. . . . When the smoke and fire have cleared away, there are those who would like to see control of the Orleans parish schools directly in the hands of the state department of education and under the direction of Shelby Jackson, superintendent of education. . . . We believe that state control of school funds and personnel is the real objective of leaders who continue to attack you. Only you, our elected board . . . can save us from state control of our schools.[82]

There was nothing remotely equivocal about IWO support for the school board and its plans for desegregation; IWO members submitted this letter, in which they pledged "the active support of the Independent Women's Organization in any manner in which [it could] be of assistance," to the press for publication.

Women of the League of Women Voters, the Independent Women's Organization, and Save Our Schools worked to involve city leaders of business and government and to buck up the resolve of the isolated school board members. They nudged, prodded, and cajoled the city's leading men into taking a reluctant public stand in favor of the inevitable desegregation of schools. Ironically, as the crisis waned and tensions eased, the *States-Item* editorially lauded the efforts of leading New Orleans *men* but offered no recognition of women's role in prompting the reluctant men to act.[83] Even though a small group of liberal to moderate women prodded the city's leadership into taking public stands on the necessity of keeping the schools open, the women themselves seemed to understand that in the social climate of 1960, their signatures on a public statement would command insufficient respect to effect a significant alteration in the public mood. Women were still seen as essentially private people. Even after three decades of political activism and increasing visibility, they wielded insufficient clout to sway public opinion on such an emotionally charged issue. Thus the women of SOS, the IWO, and the League of Women Voters exercised indirect influence to obtain their goal of saving the public schools of New Orleans.

Keller never appeared to think in explicitly feminist terms. Yet some of her comments indicate her clear recognition of the chauvinistic nature of many men and her dissatisfaction with a system that paid "nice rewards to simple-mindedness in females." Of her dealings with Mayor Morrison, she remembered, "You could put on your pretty hat and dress and get what you wanted from him. That sounds silly but it's true." Recalling her frustrations with condescending men, she said, "You'd have to dress up and look nice and keep your mouth shut a lot of the time," noting, "Most men to this day don't expect women to have good sense."[84] Even though she perceived that ideas of female inferiority were hollow, she never challenged prevailing assumptions about gender in any direct or overt fashion.

Desegregation proceeded, albeit at a glacial pace, and by early 1962, the second year of token integration, the crisis atmosphere in New Orleans had abated. Indeed, tensions had so diminished that SOS voted to become inactive.[85] Keller happily laid down that commitment of time and energy, because by 1962 she was thoroughly immersed in efforts to desegregate higher education in New Orleans, efforts that would bring down the wrath of the white establishment upon her.

Tulane University, a selective private university with an enrollment of seven thousand in 1961, located in the shady heart of the most exclusive residential area in New Orleans, was held in high esteem by the white elite of the city, many of whom were alumni. This number included Rosa Freeman Keller and her brother Richard West Freeman. Some New Orleanians fatuously referred to Tulane as the "Harvard of the South," but in truth the university had, through a purposeful program of building and hiring begun in 1937 under the presidency of Rufus C. Harris, raised its standards and reputation immensely over a twenty-five-year period. In the South its peer institutions were Duke and Vanderbilt Universities.[86]

Tulane's admissions policy still barred blacks. Apologists pointed to benefactor Paul Tulane's will, which stipulated a college for "white young persons,"[87] but the university's practice of accepting Chinese, Indonesians, Latin Americans, and other people of color seemed to show that Tulane's definition of "white" meant simply "not Negro."

In the late 1950s, Rosa Keller began serving as Tulane's liaison between international students and the community, arranging in-home visits and wider contacts with New Orleans families, providing advice and offering assistance. She enjoyed telling the story of being rebuffed by the management at the Roosevelt Hotel when she tried to schedule a luncheon there for a racially mixed group of international student advisers. The manager agreed, provided the guests would wear "native garb." Replied Keller, "Their native garb is a grey flannel suit!"[88] Her work at Tulane proved sufficiently valuable for the dean of students to find space for a campus office for her. Through her campus contacts, Keller was heartened to discover a racial liberalism among some faculty and students that was not in accord with the highly conservative stance of the Tulane board of administrators, one of whom was her brother, Richard Freeman.

As far back as 1954, the university had received prodding to desegregate. In that year, the hundred-member graduate faculty overwhelmingly adopted a resolution recommending admissions without regard to race, and the campus newspaper echoed the sentiment editorially. Tulane clung to segregation, however, even though it became increasingly difficult and often embarrassing. The Athletics Department had problems formulating schedules, since more and more opponents' teams included black athletes; a chagrined university president had to apologize profusely to Dr. Albert Dent of Dillard, whose wife, a classical pianist, had been turned away when she tried to attend an orchestral performance on campus at McAlister Auditorium; university officials found themselves in the galling position of justifying the arrangement of campus plumbing facilities in response to a Citizens' Council complaint that the school had insufficiently segregated provisions for the needs of "White" and "Colored" employees.[89]

However, it was not football schedules or water fountains that finally focused the attention of the Tulane board of administrators on the desegregation question; it was money. In March 1961, Tulane received notification that the Ford Foundation had rejected its application for a lucrative grant that the university had desperately hoped to get. Its earlier approach to the Rockefeller Foundation had also failed. Board president Joseph M. Jones candidly told troubled board members that, in his judgment, "these denials were prompted solely by [the university's] admissions policy."[90]

Tulane's board of administrators in 1961 was still composed of native Louisianians, all reared to acceptance of the racial code of segregation. Rosa

Keller knew many board members personally and sensed their profound reluctance to lower the color bar at their beloved university. She concluded that "it was quite obvious that the Tulane board would not make the decision to admit Negroes unless goaded." In her view, "they needed help. A lawsuit was the only way." With Henry Mason, a professor of political science at Tulane, and John Furey, a Dillard sociology professor, both of whom were white and both of whom she knew through Urban League membership, Keller formed a team to turn up the heat on Tulane and force the issue. The three concocted a plan by which Furey would locate well-qualified black plaintiffs to apply for admission to Tulane. If, as they anticipated, the university rejected their applications on the basis of their restrictive admissions policy, they would sue. Rosa Keller agreed to finance the coming lawsuit.[91]

Furey identified two outstanding Dillard alumnae, Pearlie Hardin Elloie and Barbara Guillory, who expressed a desire to attend Tulane to obtain graduate degrees. Knowing that the ordeal ahead would likely be long and complex, Furey had approached the selection process "with the same care with which the Brooklyn Dodgers selected Jackie Robinson for big league baseball." After receipt of Elloie's application, the board voted that Tulane would admit qualified students regardless of race "if it were legally permissible." Deeply divided on the issue, however, with only a minority who truly wanted to desegregate, and scarred by the frenzy of local resistance to public school desegregation less than a year before, the Tulane board did not intend to take steps to ascertain the legality, evidently, but seemed to hope that such a statement might restore the university to the good graces of the grant-giving foundations. Indeed, in the same meeting in which they voted for opening admission to blacks "if it were legally permissible," the board, realizing that rejection of Elloie's application likely presaged a lawsuit, also voted to hire outside counsel to assist its attorney "in the vigorous defense of same."[92]

As the desegregation troika of Keller, Furey, and Mason had expected, Tulane did reject the applications of the women, noting that their educational qualifications were acceptable and alleging that Tulane would admit them "except for the fact that [the university did] not believe it [was] legally possible . . . to do so." The stage was thus set for a courtroom drama. Their request for legal representation rejected by noted black attorney A. P. Tureaud (who cited other commitments but also seemed to believe such a suit was unwinnable), the three approached a young white lawyer, John P. Nelson, who was deeply committed to racial justice. With some misgivings about taking on such a Goliath of prestige and resources as Tulane University, Nelson, a graduate of Loyola Law School, agreed to represent the plaintiffs. After meeting with Tulane's legal representatives during the summer, he filed suit for Elloie and Guillory in Judge J. Skelly Wright's federal district court in September 1961.[93]

In the weeks before Nelson filed suit, Rosa Keller girded up her courage to have a series of unpleasant but necessary conversations with those members of the Tulane board who were her lifelong friends. Her sense of decency insisted that she must inform them of what was afoot and of her role in it. Joseph M. Jones, the board chairman, assured her that he would never question her motives, to which she responded prophetically, "You will before we get through." Darwin Fenner, prominent businessman and civic leader, was "patently unhappy" but took the news like a "complete gentleman." Her brother Richard Freeman "blustered a bit." One by one, her acquaintances heard from Keller about the suit and her role in instigating and financing it; almost universally, they "deplored" her actions.[94]

John P. Nelson brought an innovative suit, and one that terrified the Tulane board. He crafted the startling position that Tulane University was not a private university at all but was rather a state university that, in the late nineteenth century, had been transferred to a corporation by contracts made between the state of Louisiana and Paul Tulane. Nelson's careful searches of the Tulane records revealed that in 1884, the state legislature had passed Act 43, turning over the buildings and meager resources of the anemic University of Louisiana to the Tulane Educational Fund, which nourished it with donations from philanthropist Paul Tulane; the result was the Tulane University of Louisiana. Act 43 provided for various degrees of state control and influence over Tulane, namely, the rule that the governor, the state superintendent of schools, and the mayor of New Orleans be ex officio members of the Tulane board, the tax-exempt status of the university, the stipulation that each legislative district in the state have one free scholarship to Tulane, and the requirement that Tulane seek legislative approval before selling any property acquired from the University of Louisiana. The voters of Louisiana had ratified this arrangement in 1888 by approving a constitutional amendment, making these stipulations part of the organic law of the state. Furthermore, in 1886 the Louisiana Supreme Court, ruling unanimously that the erstwhile University of Louisiana was a public institution, had granted all property of the Tulane Educational Fund a tax exemption. In the ensuing decades, Tulane University had never challenged this ruling.[95]

Thus, the crux of Nelson's case was that Tulane University, because of its peculiar relationship to the state, was not in reality a private institution at all and was thus subject to the full impact of the Fourteenth Amendment. This approach offered the plaintiffs the advantage of avoiding trial in a state court, where Tulane Law School graduates exercised great influence, and allowed

Jack Nelson instead to demonstrate to a sympathetic federal judge, J. Skelly Wright, the logic of his argument that the constitutional rights of Elloie and Guillory were violated by the Tulane Educational Fund Board of Administrators, who denied them admission to the university. He sought to have all regulations that kept blacks out of Tulane declared unconstitutional. To achieve this, he had to demonstrate that Tulane was sufficiently affected by the state of Louisiana to make it vulnerable to the provisions of the Fourteenth Amendment. Having presented his case with force and logic, Nelson at last asked that Judge Wright grant relief by summary judgment. To the utter consternation of the Tulane community, J. Skelly Wright did just that when he declared Tulane University public for the purposes of the Fourteenth Amendment and ordered the board to admit the plaintiffs.[96]

Skelly Wright had already endured more than five years of being reviled, cursed, and isolated in his hometown because of his rulings on desegregation in the Orleans Parish public schools. In the summer of 1961, Rosa and Chuck Keller and another couple spirited Wright and his wife away for a much needed vacation in New England. Keller agonized over the ostracism meted out to the family, which weighed particularly heavily on Wright's wife Helen; Keller saw that it was nearly crushing her. That the hotel staff, without prompting, brought out a bottle of champagne on a silver tray for the judge and his party was immensely satisfying to Keller, demonstrating that he was honored elsewhere for actions that had earned him infamy at home.[97]

The pending lawsuit's threat to Tulane's status as a private institution made Keller infamous herself. An aggressive blend of McCarthyism and racism, fueled by an insistence on conformity to community norms, had led to the creation of a state legislative body, the Unamerican Activities Committee, that investigated activities on Louisiana campuses of higher education for the purpose of exposing and eliminating any deviations from the expressed orthodoxy on race relations. The group's blistering criticism had already forced the resignation of a Louisiana State University professor who had condemned the state's segregation laws. Assuming that the legislature would view Skelly Wright's ruling as an invitation to interfere, many in New Orleans were horrified at the possibility of the state silencing liberal voices on Tulane's campus and trampling principles of academic freedom. If a court ruling held that Tulane was a state institution, could meddling by reactionary state lawmakers be far behind? Many outraged New Orleanians blamed Keller for Tulane's predicament; the actions that she had instigated and financed could lead to the wreck of their university. Numerous old friends were perfectly furious with her. With her usual understatement, Keller noted that things "got pretty unattractive."[98]

The ultimate resolution of the Tulane case involved Skelly Wright's removal from New Orleans to assume a seat on the Second Circuit Court of Appeals in Washington and Tulane University's motion for a new trial on grounds that Wright had erred in granting relief by summary judgment. Wright's replacement, Judge Frank Ellis, was a much more conservative jurist than his predecessor. To the intense relief of the Tulane University administrators, Ellis vacated Wright's decision and granted Tulane a new trial. In the end, Judge Ellis ruled that Tulane University was not a state institution at all; thus the plaintiffs were not entitled to the relief that Rosa Keller's suit had sought. However, Ellis's ruling also removed the barriers to desegregation, in the form of Louisiana Act 43 and the legal objections of the Tulane heirs, leaving the way clear for the Tulane board to admit black students, should it so desire, but at the same time making it clear that it was under no compulsion to do so. In December 1962, board members unanimously voted to admit black applicants, heaving a collective sigh of relief at having the university's cherished private status restored in court and at having avoided what they saw as the insult and ignominy of being coerced on the subject of desegregation.[99]

Rosa Keller had gladly assumed the financial burden of the Tulane suit. She later wrote: "I thought that I might find a few people who would *want* to contribute funds for this lawsuit, but I did not discover any. Some times it is very pleasant to have money; that time was surely one of them." Actually, the records show that she did receive some contributions from the local Unitarian Church, which had solicited donations from Unitarians nationwide to assist in the effort. Their gift notwithstanding, it appears Keller spent at least ten thousand dollars of her own money.[100]

In the course of the Tulane suit, Keller found herself the target of criticism from black friends and white friends alike. Rising expectations led some in the black community to feel unhappy because progress was slow; their frustrations at the seemingly glacial pace of legal action found a target in Keller. Outraged white friends berated her for endangering the private status of Tulane and, with it, academic freedom on campus. But at last, in February 1963, the victorious plaintiffs entered Tulane University.

Keller's involvement continued. With the still vivid memory of jeering crowds howling at the six-year-olds who integrated the public schools seared into her brain, Keller felt genuine concern over the safety of the young women students who would venture onto the shady Tulane campus, a bastion of class privilege and segregation. In a sincere and generous gesture, she gave Elloie and Guillory keys to her home, situated near the campus, and invited them to view it as a refuge should they ever need or want to escape from Tulane for a few hours. Worried about the possible incendiary effects of television cameras and trucks on campus, Keller hoped to minimize news coverage of the first few days of integration. She telephoned Bill Monroe, a former New Orleanian then working with NBC News in Washington, who interceded with the NBC affiliate station in New Orleans, and paid a call on the publisher of the *Times-Picayune* to wring from him a similar promise to show restraint in coverage. Things went smoothly at Tulane; there were no riots or hostilities for absent cameras to have recorded. Unmolested and serene, Elloie and Guillory returned Keller's house keys within a week.[101]

In the emotional aftermath of the Tulane decision to admit black students, though Keller's role in the process had not been publicized, congratulations came her way from insiders. John Furey of Dillard University wrote, "While everyone is being praised and congratulated, it is difficult to know what to say to you. I will simply say this: I think you are wonderful." From a vacationing Edith Stern came a postcard: "I feel so guilty basking in this relaxation while you faced the firing squad.... You never cease to amaze me, my love. My congratulations—you have made history. We are all grateful." And from Pearlie Hardin Elloie came an acknowledgment of Keller's efforts and a tribute: "This little 'guinea pig' appreciates your interest and wishes every Southern city had a lady such as yourself."[102]

In a supreme irony, the Tulane student body chose to dedicate the 1963 yearbook "with pride, respect, and admiration" to the Tulane board of administrators, lauding its "bold and courageous action" in voting to desegregate the university. Their choice of dedication ignored the fact that it had required two costly, hard-fought lawsuits, which Rosa Keller financed, before the board took the "bold and courageous action" that the students praised. Keller never shared the view, advanced by the old guard of the Tulane board in later years, that it had been "a friendly lawsuit" all along and that Tulane merely needed legal certainty before breaking Paul Tulane's will, an action that they asserted the university in actuality had long wanted to take. Keller maintained that this revisionist interpretation contained not "a particle of truth." Attorney Jack Nelson heartily concurred. Historian Adam Fairclough agreed, noting that the Tulane board of administrators "churlishly bowed to the inevitable."[103]

Four months after the first black students entered Tulane, Keller penned a letter to President John Kennedy on the day after his historic, nationally televised address on civil rights.

> I wish to congratulate you most heartily on your statement to us last night, and to cheer you on in your effort to build a fire under the Congress. As one of those whom you mentioned who tries and has tried for years to change racial patterns, I can tell you of my own experience that it is getting

very late for anything but the strongest kind of leadership in this field. Surely, if my position needs any emphasis, it was given by the brutal murder of Medgar Evers. You may hear all kinds of rumblings from the Deep South as a result of your remarks, so I did want you to know of some who salute you.[104]

It was late indeed. The turbulent events of the sixties lay ahead. The civil rights movement in New Orleans was assuming a more militant character, epitomized in the blunt challenge of Ernest N. ("Dutch") Morial (who would become the city's first black mayor in 1978) to the city's mayor in 1963, "Negro citizens of New Orleans will no longer tolerate the spoon feeding of their rights. We want all of our rights now."[105] Direct action was replacing the indirect gradualism of Keller and the racial diplomats. Keller's letter indicates that she, as well as local black leaders, had lost hope of improving the status of African Americans through local politics and was looking to Washington for remedies.

Still, her contributions to justice and progress were far from insignificant. In addition to earning the esteem of black New Orleanians for her quiet consistency, she had raised the consciousness of white New Orleanians about racial injustice, and through her activities she had helped to keep public attention fixed on matters of race.

Keller had reaped benefits of her own. In the course of pursuing racial reform, she had carved out a virtual career for herself, from which she derived personal fulfillment. "Society ladies" are routinely patronized, fondly or derisively; their motivations and their accomplishments are frequently disparaged by men and sometimes by women. Rosa Freeman Keller deserves better. She made a mature choice to work for change in New Orleans and, as a result, found herself fighting not only the local establishment but also long-standing friends and even some members of her own family. Measured in terms of commitment of time and energy, her work clearly approximates what society commonly calls "a career." She felt satisfaction in seeing change come and knowing the part she had played. An "invisible career" rewarded her with prestige, experience, civic power, a sense of virtue, and feelings of efficacy. Speaking of that invisible career and what it meant to her, she once said, emphatically and candidly, "What would I have been without it?"[106]

Keller's comment illustrates her self-effacing, self-deprecating style. Public recognition seemed to be of remarkably little importance to her. John Nelson, the attorney she retained to challenge Tulane's admissions policy, assessed her in this way: "I never did consider Rosa a leader. Rosa *was* able, though, to get other people to do things, very subtly.... Rosa didn't want any glory. Rosa's style was to get other people involved. That was very much needed. The Rosa Kellers of the world come very seldom."[107]

If not a "leader" in Jack Nelson's sense of the term, Rosa Keller was certainly a quiet, consistent agent for change. Perhaps the best analogy is scientific: she was like a colorless, odorless vapor, virtually undetectable to the average observer but possessing certain catalytic properties, able by her presence to effect various actions and changes. Rosa Keller seldom called attention to her involvement in community race relations. Instead she worked inconspicuously but reliably to bring needed changes. In the judgment of others, Rosa Keller's involvement in race relations changed her city for the better. In her judgment, it did the same for her.

All history resolves itself quite easily into the biography of a few stout and earnest persons.

—Ralph Waldo Emerson, Self-Reliance

CONCLUSION

In tracing the convoluted course that New Orleans white women of middle- and upper-class origins followed from indirect to direct political participation, this book has related a story of change over time that broadened the public role for women. Throughout the years of depression and world war, anti-Communist hysteria and early civil rights activism, political activity among New Orleans women increased steadily. The new political day for women dawned rather inauspiciously in the Crescent City, however, as contradictory messages from the woman suffrage movement's leader in New Orleans created confusion locally and, by raising the specter of black equality and federal intervention, served to diminish political fervor among women. When initial excitement over suffrage waned and the much vaunted but unrealistic "women's bloc" failed to materialize, local women in the 1920s displayed a decidedly tepid attitude toward political involvement, not an unremarkable response in light of the peculiar history of woman suffrage in Louisiana.

In the 1930s Franklin Roosevelt responded to the ravages of the depression by annexing to government many functions formerly executed in the private sector by women's associations. So great was the national emergency, however, that there was work enough for both public and private sectors. When Eleanor Roosevelt, strategizing over ways to combat the economic and social effects of the crash, stated flatly, "It looks like it's up to the women," many in New Orleans responded in the time-honored tradition of women's benevolent associations. Two examples of their efforts to ameliorate the harshest effects of the economic crisis on area women and girls involved raising funds for the local YWCA to increase services for the female working poor and redoubling efforts, via the Christian Woman's Exchange, to provide opportunities for the sale of handiwork of women otherwise unable to help themselves.[1] Thus traditional patterns of women's activity continued.

On the other hand, the 1930s saw a clear departure of local women from the purely private sector and a rush of middle- and upper-class New Orleans women into politics, caused almost exclusively by the specific conditions in their city and state known as "Longism." The spectacle of the state's most prominent political figure mocking the standards that genteel women held dear proved stimulus enough to impel many women to action. Once organized and active, they could not be easily ignored, because to justify their demands and petitions, they invoked the name of a most revered institution—motherhood. The activities of the anti-Long women's movement proved them to be rational and hardworking.

The Long/anti-Long division of politics within the state spanned a period of some thirty-five years, roughly 1928 to 1963. During these decades, when the Republican Party was virtually as alien to the American South as Marxism, this two-sided alignment gave Louisiana the functional equivalent of a two-party system.[2] State and local candidates adhered to factions and formed slates of like-minded hopefuls, voters identified strongly as either "Long" or "anti-Long," and a rough approximation of party discipline prevailed. As long as this situation lasted, which is to say as long as issues of class remained the dominant motif in state politics, women's politics in New Orleans was molded into the familiar Long/anti-Long form. The women scrutinized in these chapters hewed to anti-Long principles with a Manichaean vengeance. Like the anti-Long element at large, they generally represented the haves in opposition to the have-nots, a reflection of class-based politics. They were prone to demonize the opposition, sometimes describing rival candidates' unfitness for office in energetic ad hominem attacks. Like their male counterparts, they deplored the Long faction's profligate spending and erection of a mammoth welfare state. However, much of the women's rhetoric indicates a lasting concern with demagoguery, demeanor, and democracy.[3]

Their staying power is apparent in the continuity of membership and activity of the independent women's political movement in New Orleans over the next three decades. Clear linkage exists between the earliest anti-Long women's movement and the later so-called independent women's movements of the 1940s and 1950s. Before Huey Long's death in 1935, his expansion of social services and state programs solidified his political base and discouraged Hilda Phelps Hammond and the Women's Committee from pursuing electoral politics because their chances of defeating the Long ticket were remote. But at decade's end, the anti-Long movement received a transfusion of hope as federal investigations led to indictments and convictions of key figures in the Long faction and emboldened women to enter partisan political activity as never before.

Women's entry into the murky domain of electoral politics required abandonment of their pure and womanly stance above it all in exchange for the impurities of partisan politics. Nothing could have sufficiently prepared women, political neophytes that they were, for the cynical and corrupt landscape of Louisiana politics. The art of the deal, the necessity of compromise in politics, the resort to pragmatic but unsavory alliances shocked many novices. Lindy Boggs, who later served nearly two decades in the U.S. Congress, was in 1940 a politically naive wife and mother in her twenties when she enlisted in the anti-Long women's movement backing Sam Jones's gubernatorial aspirations. Her eager report that she had won a promise from a rival candidate's female precinct captain to back Jones in the runoff did not elicit the enthusiasm from her friends that she expected. "Honey, haven't you ever heard of patronage?" asked a more pragmatic woman, who, unlike Boggs, understood that such support from a rival camp would come not as a gift but only in return for a quid pro quo arranged via a backdoor deal.[4] Through episodes such as this one, women learned the realities of politics.

In their quest for good government, women sometimes overlooked good politics, as Martha Gilmore Robinson's unsuccessful campaign in 1954 illustrates. Her rejection of a place on Mayor Chep Morrison's ticket cost her the election. Not until more than forty years after that failure did New Orleans voters place a woman on their city council. Bland Cox Bruns, a founding member of the IWO who in the 1950s was the only woman in Louisiana's state legislature, likewise placed principle over politics when she quit Morrison's Crescent City Democratic Association to protest his shabby treatment of her friend Martha Robinson in the matter of sample ballots in 1954. Her resignation from the Morrison organization had serious repercussions and contributed to her defeat at the polls in 1956, as did her unpopular decision to vote against the segregation measures rammed through the legislature in the wake of the 1954 *Brown* decision. Rejecting the counsel of political advisers who urged the expedient course, Robinson and Bruns acted on principle and suffered electoral defeat as a consequence.[5]

The rising determination of African Americans during and after World War II to abolish the degrading racial status quo is well recognized, but perhaps less recognized is an echo of this feeling among women, some of whom saw their wartime experiences as grounds for defining a different relationship to the public world.[6] Expected to shoulder new responsibilities in men's absence yet given little more than perfunctory and patronizing expressions of gratitude from their government and their men, women on the home front had no choice but to deal with the inconveniences of rationing and shortages, nonexistent or inadequate child-care arrangements, travel restrictions, loneliness, and boredom. Men could win medals for serving their country even in the motor pool or behind typewriters, but there were no ribbons for being a good war wife. Is it far-fetched to posit that World War II gave women something in the way of self-confidence, perhaps intensified by resentment, that they needed in order to become more assertive and confident in 1946? Certainly, Rosa Keller's pithy words (see pp. 207–8) indicate that this was the case.

Many New Orleans women experienced a steadily growing sense of self during the war years, made possible by enhanced opportunities for public service and the greater legitimacy accorded women's public activities in the crisis atmosphere. Certainly, some women workers yearned to drop their blue-collar "men's" jobs, but this appears to have been an age-based phenomenon, with younger workers eager for a revivification of traditional gender roles, having been deprived of domestic security for close to two decades by the interruption of depression and war. Even though the postwar words and actions of middle- and upper-class women, who lived lives of relative comfort and even of privilege, show them to have been unready to challenge male dominance overtly, they nonetheless reached new levels of political participation in New Orleans in the immediate postwar years. For the growing numbers of local women who devoted their best energies to politics, such involvement assumed the dimensions of a career.

Like the world war, the Cold War left its imprint on women's political activities in New Orleans. Women's organizations enjoyed no immunity from the relentless Red-baiting of the era, as Martha Gilmore Robinson discovered.

Purging the League of Women Voters of suspect members was her response to the climate of orthodoxy prevailing in Louisiana in 1947–48. In the hysteria then current, nothing was innocuous, as the Orleans Parish School Board was made to realize when it received criticism for having painted the doors on an elementary school *red*. Certainly the local women who engaged in efforts at building better race relations knew well the experience of being Red-baited, not only by members of the far-right fringe, but by public officials as well.

The burgeoning civil rights movement posed a special challenge: would the perennially active political club women of New Orleans who had worked for "reform" for three decades embrace the racial aspects of reform, or would the racial code they had learned as children of the South prove decisive? The *Brown* decision, the crisis in Little Rock, and a series of federal district court rulings caused perceptive women to realize, despite the cavalier reassurances of New Orleans public officials, that genuine school desegregation was inevitably coming. The anti-Long women of New Orleans possessed enlightened outlooks in many ways; certainly they were not among the women who screamed and spat at black elementary students attempting to integrate first-grade classrooms in 1960. Indeed, a coterie of political club women spearheaded community efforts to keep public schools open during the difficult years of 1959–61. However, because these women did not customarily ride public transportation, eat at the Woolworth's lunch counter, or play golf on the city's public courses, and because many had never educated their children in public schools, selecting instead the city's exclusive private or parochial schools, the falling of these racial barriers left them very little affected personally.

Nevertheless, many women felt uncomfortable as barrier after barrier of the southern racial code did fall, breached by blacks' steady assault, which local attorney A. P. Tureaud led. During Martha Gilmore Robinson's campaign for public office in 1954, she had addressed what she called "the Negro question" by asserting that blacks should have justice before the law; the right to serve on juries; equal job opportunity and equal pay for equal work; adequate housing, health care, and education; and fair treatment at the hands of the police.[7] Although her statement sounded reasonably enlightened, nothing she espoused was incompatible with the "separate but equal" doctrine. Bona fide integration in all aspects of life was not her goal in 1954 or in later years. In this attitude, she typified many political club women of New Orleans.

Both the nonpartisan League of Women Voters and the highly partisan Independent Women's Organization took hesitant steps toward considering integration in the 1950s. Although the NOLWV board members did not feel ready to encourage membership for black women, they nonetheless intuited that changes should come. The fact that their organization had no black members weighed on their sense of fairness. In 1953 the leadership cadre appointed a committee to formulate policy on the issue and approached the National League of Women Voters office for guidance on how to educate the rank and file of the local league on the wisdom of accepting black members. Clearly, the general membership of the League of Women Voters in New Orleans was not clamoring for desegregation in the ranks.

The New Orleans league appears to have contemplated beginning with all-black units serving black neighborhoods, with the two races coming together only at infrequent general meetings held in large public spaces. But the response from NLWV quashed this idea, reminding the New Orleans league that all members were full members, free to join any league unit in their city that suited their needs of location, schedule, or programming. With an eye toward southern mores, the national league suggested eliminating serving food at league meetings and convening units in public places rather than in homes.[8] Since such a course would drastically alter the intimate atmosphere of cooperation fostered by convening in small groups in private homes, the NOLWV felt disinclined to follow the advice. Its members understandably valued the intimacy and informality that their meeting arrangements facilitated, but they exhibited at the same time an initial reluctance to work with black women on terms of equality and familiarity. Ultimately, the local League of Women Voters engineered a fairly smooth transition from segregation to desegregation by the mid-1960s. This change, coupled with the significant demographic shifts in league membership begun in the late 1940s, rendered the New Orleans League of Women Voters an association considerably less dominated by the local elite than it had been earlier in its history. Moving into the last one-third of the twentieth century, it continued to exert influence on matters of public policy by following time-tested methods of studying and lobbying, stressing public education and always emphasizing issues over individuals.

The Independent Women's Organization recorded a somewhat different experience. The IWO's reputation as a highly effective, partisan political group rested on its ability to get out the vote for anti-Long candidates, which, in turn, rested on women's energetic unpaid labor. Its policy of giving money to candidates whom it endorsed instead of the usual Louisiana routine of requiring payment from candidates in order to endorse them won the IWO a solid image of quirky integrity and kept the IWO truly independent. The diligent campaign work of legions of members meant that candidates actively sought the meaningful IWO endorsement.[9]

By the mid-1950s, however, the IWO was changing. The group's once formidable exertions to draft candidates, to canvass, to get out the vote, to work at the polls, to monitor sessions of legislature, city council, and school board dwindled markedly. In part these changes were inevitable concomitants of changes in women's lives; women in the paid work force found far less time for the activities that had occupied their mothers and older sisters so fully in the 1940s. But the decline of energetic campaigning traces its roots to other changes as well.

Persuading well-qualified candidates to run for state and local office was not the challenge that it had been in 1939 when the group was founded. The elections of anti-Long candidates Sam Jones and Robert Kennon to the governorship in 1940 and 1952 demonstrated that Longism was not invincible. Particularly effective in making this point were the four consecutive electoral successes of the anti-Long deLesseps Morrison in New Orleans. Once a juggernaut that crushed opposition candidates so thoroughly that few would offer themselves as political human sacrifices, the still viable Long machine no longer inspired awe and fear by the 1950s; it was formidable but not unbeatable. As a consequence, numerous acceptable anti-Long candidates began to offer themselves for state and local offices.

The IWO dilemma lay in reaching consensus on its endorsements; the group faced increasing difficulty in agreeing on which reform candidate to back. The IWO constitution required a two-thirds vote of the membership for endorsement, but often the disgruntled one-third sat on their hands during a campaign or even worked for a candidate whom the IWO did not endorse. Unanimity had been the key to IWO strength, and losing it was costly to IWO effectiveness. It is ironic that in their efforts to boost democracy and free choice in Louisiana politics, the anti-Long women succeeded so well that choice became a problem. Their efforts brought a more robust brand of democratic politics and a plethora of good choices, but what was beneficial for state and local politics was detrimental to the smooth functioning of the IWO.

When the IWO admitted black members in the early 1970s, its cohesiveness declined again. Black women of the middle class held views sometimes at odds with those of their white counterparts in the IWO and on occasion sought IWO support for candidates whom some white members viewed without enthusiasm. Fundamental changes resulted. The IWO became still less unified in support of the candidates whom it endorsed. Even board members, the most committed of the IWO membership, sometimes worked publicly for candidates not endorsed by the IWO. No longer the paragon of solidarity it had once been, merely giving an increasingly irrelevant endorsement to candidates to be duly reported in the newspaper, the IWO by the 1970s met less often than in the glory days of the forties and fifties. At first glance, its members seemed to lack the trademark IWO zeal, but on closer examination it becomes evident that they were women of such disparate life experiences and outlooks that political cohesiveness was frequently impossible.[10]

The entry of black members into the IWO coincided with the rebirth of feminism then sweeping the nation and being felt in New Orleans as well. Many of the younger IWO members held decidedly feminist views and wanted to focus their organization's political activity on improving the status of women. The outlines of a generational rift are discernible. In 1975, founding IWO president July Waters snapped to the group's current president, thirty-two-year-old Gail Gagliano, "You young women are selfish because you are mainly concerned about women." One can only wonder what the octogenarian Waters thought of Gagliano's response, which was to quote Germaine Greer on "enlightened narcissism."[11]

Some longtime members urged disbanding the organization. "How about consigning the aging IWO to graceful retirement and giving the present organization a new name?" suggested Mary Morrison. "Her face-lifting has rendered her almost unrecognizable to her contemporaries and often ridiculous to her enemies."[12] The IWO continued to exist, however, though as Mary Morrison and others had long since realized, its lack of vigorous campaigning for its endorsed candidates made it less and less relevant in city politics. Many original members quietly abandoned it.

Middle- and upper-class white women in New Orleans enjoyed about thirty years that could be called their golden age of unity in politics. Beginning with the 1930s, they became politically active, engaged and excited by political participation. They earned a reputation for effectiveness. Hilda Phelps Hammond's unrelenting anti-Long crusade, Martha Gilmore Robinson's nonpartisan League of Women Voters and its many civic projects, the reliable IWO and its work for Sam Jones, Chep Morrison, and school reform led the roster of women's political organizations.

Many in the next generation of native New Orleanian women of the middle and upper classes pursued professions, eliminating adequate time for a reprise of their mothers' invisible careers in political activism. Furthermore, the dominance of the elite of the city in women's political organizations could not be sustained. The original leaders had enjoyed a social intimacy that came via birth into the city's elite and could be acquired by others only slowly, if at all. Observers have remarked on the clannishness of New Orleans insiders and the difficulty newcomers experience in "breaking in" in the Crescent City; it was this phenomenon to which Angela Gregory referred when she spoke wistfully of her city having once been "a little closed corporation."

But even insular New Orleans could not avoid Sunbelt consequences after World War II; the influx of new business meant new businessmen and their wives, educated, affluent, and "not from here." The "little closed corporation" waned, and with it the ability of the elite to dominate.[13]

In the 1960s, the race issue, which had been muted in state politics as the class-based politics of Long versus anti-Long dominated, resurfaced in New Orleans with a vengeance, brought on by the chaotic gubernatorial race of 1960, followed by the unsettling school crisis of 1960–61. A segregationist frenzy swept city and state. When John Kennedy's death elevated Lyndon Johnson to the presidency, the wave of sentiment for a slain leader, coupled with the parliamentary abilities of the former Senate majority leader, prepared the way for adoption of a sweeping civil rights bill. Intense racial politics shattered the bifactionalism of the Long era; race overshadowed all other considerations. A candidate's stand on the old Long orthodoxies of low taxes, the homestead exemption, and state spending for social welfare, or a candidate's measure by the crucial anti-Long yardsticks of integrity and demeanor, now paled beside the crucial litmus test of his or her attitudes on matters of race.[14]

The tilt toward a majority of African-American voters was well under way in New Orleans by the late 1950s. The percentage of the electorate represented by white males declined every year from 1946 on. In contrast, the white women's electorate increased in steady increments until 1964, when it reached 41.4 percent; thereafter it too declined. The black male electorate grew after 1946, with one drop in 1952 and two periods in which its percentage barely advanced (1956–64 and 1970–72). The black female electorate increased strikingly in every year except 1954, passing registered black males permanently in 1960. Table 6 reveals how fully the Orleans Parish electorate underwent transformation in the postwar decades.

The demise of bifactionalism in Louisiana rendered a coherent anti-Long, antimachine women's movement impossible. Beginning with the gubernatorial race of 1959–60, in which for the first time since 1924 no candidate identified with the Long faction made the runoff, and repeated in 1963, Longism and anti-Longism seemed irrelevant. All candidates backed the generous welfare benefits that had once been the cornerstone of Longism but were now part of the fabric of Louisiana itself. A scramble to define vote-getting positions on the race issue replaced the politics of rich versus poor. With race, long absent or muted in state politics, now the defining issue, politics became a contest between whites and blacks, or more precisely, between whites and blacks and their real or alleged white allies.

When New Orleans women first mobilized for political participation in

TABLE 6. *Voter Registration, Orleans Parish, 1946–1976*

Year	Total	White Men	%	White Women	%	Black Men	%	Black Women	%
1946	183,346	96,231	52.5	82,293	44.9	3,494	1.9	1,328	0.7
1948	208,436	104,768	50.3	89,711	43.0	9,426	4.5	4,531	2.2
1950	212,895	100,450	47.2	86,416	40.6	16,003	7.5	10,026	4.7
1952	232,115	108,287	46.6	95,823	41.3	15,934	6.9	12,071	5.2
1954	197,994	88,146	44.5	84,324	42.6	14,172	7.2	11,352	5.7
1956	212,895	93,888	44.1	86,429	40.6	17,701	8.3	14,877	7.0
1958	194,421	83,766	43.1	79,366	40.8	16,368	8.4	14,927	7.7
1960	213,025	88,944	41.7	87,788	41.2	18,002	8.4	18,291	8.6
1962	198,949	82,020	41.2	82,159	41.3	16,886	8.5	17,884	8.9
1964	197,951	80,314	40.6	81,901	41.4	17,244	8.7	18,492	9.3
1966	210,185	76,529	36.4	80,395	38.2	23,642	11.2	29,619	14.1
1968	224,296	78,329	34.9	82,802	36.9	29,643	13.2	33,522	14.9
1970	215,949	70,296	32.5	78,837	36.5	31,674	14.6	35,142	16.3
1972	263,998	78,738	29.8	97,214	36.8	38,690	14.6	49,356	18.7
1974	220,841	61,465	27.8	75,831	34.3	37,447	16.9	46,098	20.9
1976	216,223	59,539	27.5	70,006	32.4	39,194	18.1	47,484	22.0

Source: Report of the Secretary of State to His Excellency the Governor of Louisiana (Baton Rouge: Ramires-Jones Printing Co., 1947, 1949, 1951, 1953, 1955, 1957, 1959, 1961, 1963, 1965, 1967, 1969, 1971, 1973, 1975, 1977).

the 1930s, they rallied around the standard of "good government." Subsumed under this rubric were desires for many changes: dignity, probity, and morality in public officeholders, efficiency and honesty in government services and in those who delivered them, fairly conducted elections, a firm commitment to the democratic process, an end to government reprisals against dissident citizens, broader participation in politics by the general population, a civil service system to safeguard against arbitrary dismissals of government workers and prevent the politicization of state institutions, restoration of Louisiana's good name outside the borders of the Pelican State. For some thirty years, these were the ingredients of "good government" in Louisiana in the view of middle- and upper-class women.

But what was the "good-government" position on race? Should the candidate promise energetic compliance with federal court orders? Should he agree to comply, but grudgingly and minimally? Or should he pledge to close down the entire school system rather than admit one black pupil to a previously all-white school? Should a candidate defend segregation publicly, privately, or not at all? Should she manifestly seek the votes of black citizens, court them covertly, or blast her opponent for having black support and maintain that she did not want it? Would desegregated schools lead to casual contact between the races, and on to interracial dating and intermarriage? If so, would that be intolerable, merely uncomfortable, inconsequential, or beneficial? In the heat surrounding these prickly questions of race, the women's consensus of what constituted "good government" evaporated like water in a desert.

The departure of Chep Morrison from city hall to accept John Kennedy's offer of an ambassadorship with the Organization of American States created an unstable situation, as the focal point of women's reform politics for nearly two decades turned his attentions to Latin America. His onetime protégé Vic Schiro cynically manipulated the race issue in the 1962 mayoral race, tapping white fears over racial change to narrowly defeat the "reform" candidate, a racial moderate backed by many but not all of Morrison's upper-class supporters in a contest that fractured the carefully crafted Morrison CCDA.[15] In the ensuing years of political disarray, the Independent Women's Organization frequently found difficulty in reaching consensus in the new political order. What exactly constituted a reform candidate? What, indeed?

The New Orleans League of Women Voters at midcentury had transformed itself into a more diverse body via measures aimed at recruiting women who worked outside the home, who lived in all parts of the city, who were newcomers to New Orleans. By the early 1960s, it had welcomed its first black members. Demographic diversity did not preclude homogeneity in other areas; league members were generally well educated, affluent, and progressive. But different points of view were the ingredient on which the League of Women Voters thrived, since its nonpartisan charter shaped it into a discussion society within which facts were gathered, considered, and debated. The league had no need to strive for unanimity in the political preferences of individual members. Although it was constitutionally barred from partisanship as an organization, individual league members freely supported candidates without precipitating conflicts with other members.

The IWO, by contrast, existing for partisan purposes, required a united front. For years it retained a leadership cadre that was highly homogeneous in terms of class, nativity, and race. But as the IWO's reputation grew, so did its membership. With every new member who enrolled, the odds of the elite maintaining dominance over the organization dwindled. Moreover, nonnatives, feminists, African Americans all diluted the unified vision of the original anti-Long IWO. Furthermore, even had the IWO remained as it had begun, a body of white natives, many of them wealthy, the large field of acceptable "good-government" candidates precluded the members' unity. And finally, the increasingly obvious American dilemma of race shrunk their chances of finding unanimity.

Some of the original participants in early women's political organizations learned to work with nonnatives, feminists, and women of color and adopted agendas that embraced economic and social as well as political reforms. Founding IWO member Lindy Boggs became a congresswoman in 1972 and earned a reputation as a dedicated liberal representative who tenaciously supported an agenda of causes popular with blacks and feminists. Even after redistricting left her with a majority of black constituents, she held on to her seat, a feat attributable to her progressive voting record and her inclusive rhetoric on racial issues. Rosa Keller stood firmly for civil rights, deplored race baiting, supported the national Democratic Party, and worked with enthusiasm in black voter registration efforts in her hometown. Carolyn Gay Labouisse, Sarah Sharp, Mary Morrison, and many other early IWO members were enlightened moderates on race. But, chilled by their differences and beset by misgivings about the effects of school desegregation, IWO members gradually abandoned their ambitious and promising campaign to reform the public schools of New Orleans, to oust a venal state superintendent of schools, and to change state law to require that his replacement be appointed rather than elected.[16] July Waters and other founding members turned toward the Republican Party. Indisputably, the early cohesiveness of the IWO evaporated with the passage of years, the addition of members, and the injection of race into politics as the most salient issue.

The year 1963 marks the end of activities encompassed in this study. Barriers to effective political cooperation among elite women of the city had existed well before 1963, as noted here; however, that year represents a watershed of sorts. Prior to 1963, independent women's support had generally coalesced around the chosen antimachine candidates, individuals with clean records and respectable demeanor, though by the 1950s wholehearted support for the endorsees was not always forthcoming. But after matters of race fractured unanimity, such cooperation evaporated. And matters of race, which had simmered for several years, had begun to boil by 1963. When the Congress of Racial Equality (CORE) sponsored demonstrations by young blacks on Canal Street and an African-American march on city hall in the fall of 1963, both events served to underline the increasing insistence of the local civil rights movement, insistence that brought change but also ignited white resentment and disillusionment.

Corresponding with Congressman Hale Boggs, Carolyn Gay Labouisse, a charter member of the IWO, reported on the local civil rights movement and ongoing demonstrations downtown. In November 1963, she posted her observations on the mood of "the Negro organizations" and glumly summed up the white majority's view of the situation. "The whole pitch here nowadays is that the Kennedys are in league with Soviet Russia plus the fact that our basic freedoms are being abolished by the power-mad White House."[17]

On November 22, 1963, Rosa Keller attended a luncheon for "the city's important people" at the Royal Orleans, an elegant hotel in the French Quarter, hosted by producer Otto Preminger, whose film *The Cardinal* was premiering in New Orleans. Because Preminger insisted that African Americans attend the affair, the uncertain mayor's office had turned to Keller, who once again used her familiarity with the black community to prepare a guest list. Because Keller was the only one present who knew the black guests, she stayed near Preminger and the mayor to make introductions and facilitate small talk. But shortly, the dreadful news from Dallas smothered all conversation.

It seems appropriate to end the story here, as the shock of a president's murder settled over the scene, in a hushed room in which sat the first black guests ever to dine at the elegant New Orleans hotel, a mayor unsympathetic to the civil rights movement's goals, an outsider who insisted on racial change, and a racial ambassador whose gentle tactics were increasingly passé. Race matters would assume center stage more and more often in the months and years to come, crowding out other considerations such as class, demagoguery, and demeanor, other considerations that had bound middle- and upper-class white women of New Orleans in camaraderie and cooperation for three decades.

What conclusion should one draw from the patterns of political activity described here? During their golden age of unity, a period of three decades spanning the thirties, forties, and fifties, these New Orleans women worked within the existing patterns, voting, campaigning, participating in organized interest groups. We expect feminists to challenge business as usual in the political arena with their particular beliefs and approaches to politics, but the women of this study carried no feminist banner. One cannot discern that politics became less confrontational or more harmonious as their participation increased. Few sought office and even fewer actually held office. Yet although they cooperated with men in politics, they were notably adamant in their refusals to allow their organizations to become women's auxiliaries or mere adjuncts to more powerful men's groups.

Their impact on politics was real and lasting. These New Orleans women fought Huey Long and all that he represented, labored to bring civil service protection to Louisiana, by their presence made the polls of New Orleans less intimidating to women voters, and enrolled thousands of first-time voters, thereby broadening popular political participation significantly. They struggled to elect candidates whom they saw as progressive and good for their city and state, all the while battling "a traditional public tolerance for political corruption . . . on a scale perhaps grander than anywhere in the United States."[18] They worked to bring improvement to the dismal condition of public education in their community, took on the lonely task of persuading reluctant community leaders to speak out against extremists during the appalling weeks and months of the city's school desegregation crisis, and, by their examples, encouraged other women to become interested and involved in political affairs.

Some applied moral suasion in one-to-one encounters; some pursued traditional pressure-group politics and tried to influence government in the time-honored fashion of women's voluntary groups. But others plunged straight into electoral politics and employed ballots to change Louisiana for themselves and their children. In so doing, they surely gave the lie to Martin Behrman's description of "the silk stocking," whom he characterized dismissively as "a type of citizen who knew all about municipal government because he read magazines and books and the Life of Jefferson and did not know where to file his complaint if the garbage man did not come around early enough to suit him."[19] Learning the nuts and bolts of precinct politics meant that these women certainly knew whom to call if city services failed to live up to expectations; they were far from being the naive and ineffectual "silk stockings" of Behrman's image. Simultaneously "society ladies" who knew the manners of the cotillion and "silk stockings" who knew and practiced the realities of the ballot box, these women lived and worked between the suffragists' generation and the advent of the second-wave feminists. Their story is a part of the history of the important bridge generation of the thirties, forties, and fifties.

We do women of the past an injustice if we make feminism the measure of their activities. Feminist attitudes were not the norm for most of the twentieth century, and it is indeed doubtful that they are even as the century ends. After the breakthrough of the Nineteenth Amendment in 1920, and before the 1960s blossoming of the reborn women's movement, women's progress toward full citizenship in the United States proceeded haltingly, marked by setbacks and inertia. Yet even in the decades when the women's rights movement seemed becalmed in the doldrums, even when women seemingly made little progress toward greater inclusion in political life, and even in regions such as the South, where old attitudes and traditions often opposed expanded political roles for women, when examining the political history of the mid-twentieth century, we would do well to borrow and adapt a pair of questions first posed by historian Alice Kessler-Harris about women and organized labor. We would do well to ask not "Why weren't women active in politics before the 1960s?" but rather "At what were women active?"[20] In the city of New Orleans, we find that the answer to that question requires considerable telling. Indeed, though details will vary with participants and issues, it seems indisputable that in locales far beyond the Crescent City, patterns of intense political activity among prefeminist women will be discerned when historians trouble to seek them.

NOTES

INTRODUCTION

1. Mary M. Morrison, interview by author, New Orleans, September 15, 1988.

2. Nancy Cott and Paula Baker encourage historians of women to take such a broad view of "politics." See Cott, "Across the Great Divide: Women in Politics before and after 1920," in *Women, Politics, and Change,* ed. Louise Tilly and Patricia Gurin (New York: Russell Sage Foundation, 1990), 153-76, and Baker, "The Domestication of Politics: Women and American Political Society, 1789-1920," *American Historical Review* 89 (June 1984): 620-47.

3. Carrie Chapman Catt quoted in Mildred Adams, *The Right to Be People* (Philadelphia: Lippincott, 1967), 170.

4. Eleanor Flexner, *Century of Struggle: The Woman's Rights Movement in the United States* (Cambridge: Harvard University Press, Belknap Press, 1959). Some examples of the pathbreaking contributions of A. Elizabeth Taylor to the understanding of southern women and the suffrage movement are "The Woman Suffrage Movement in Arkansas," *Arkansas Historical Quarterly* 15 (spring 1956): 17-52; "The Woman Suffrage Movement in Florida," *Florida Historical Quarterly* 36 (July 1957): 422-60; and "The Woman Suffrage Movement in North Carolina," *North Carolina Historical Review* 38 (January and April 1961): 45-62, 173-89. Aileen Kraditor, *The Ideas of the Woman Suffrage Movement, 1890-1920* (Garden City, N.Y.: Anchor Books, 1971); Ellen Carol DuBois, *Feminism and Suffrage: The Woman's Rights Movement in the United States* (Ithaca, N.Y.: Cornell University Press, 1978); Andrew M. Scott and Anne Firor Scott, *One Half the People: The Fight for Woman Suffrage* (Philadelphia: Lippincott, 1975); Marjorie Spruill Wheeler, *New Women of the New South* (New York: Oxford University Press, 1993); Elna Green, "Those Opposed: Southern Antisuffragism, 1890-1920" (Ph.D. diss., Tulane University, 1992; forthcoming from University of North Carolina Press).

5. Kristi Andersen, "Women and Citizenship in the 1920s," in Tilly and Gurin, *Women, Politics, and Change,* 180.

6. J. Stanley Lemons, *The Woman Citizen: Social Feminism in the 1920s* (Urbana: University of Illinois Press, 1973), 73-74; Susan M. Hartmann, *The Home Front and Beyond: American Women in the 1940s* (Boston: Twayne, 1982), 136; Linda Kerber, "Women and Jury Service," paper presented at the National Humanities Center, Research Triangle Park, North Carolina, March 1992.

7. Virginia Sapiro, *The Political Integration of Women: Roles, Socialization, and Politics* (Urbana: University of Illinois Press, 1983), 114.

8. Ibid., chap. 6, passim.

9. Suzanne Lebsock, "Women and American Politics, 1880–1920," in Tilly and Gurin, *Women, Politics, and Change*, 35.

10. William Chafe, *The Paradox of Change: American Women in the Twentieth Century* (New York: Oxford University Press, 1991), 21–23.

11. Indeed, "liberalism" is not an unchanging concept, having shown differing faces over the past century; the liberalism of our own time is not the liberalism of the interwar period, which itself differed from Progressivism, for example. Nor is the southern liberal tradition identical to that of the rest of the United States. Gary Gerstle, in a perceptive analysis of the changing ingredients of American liberalism, states that it is "unwise to presume that the criteria for identifying liberals in one period can be applied to another," insisting that each reference to policies or persons as liberal must fix the phenomenon in place and time. See Gary Gerstle, "The Protean Nature of American Liberalism," *American Historical Review* (October 1994): 1043–73.

12. Susan Lynn, *Progressive Women in Conservative Times: Racial Justice, Peace, and Feminism, 1945 to the 1960s* (New Brunswick, N.J.: Rutgers University Press, 1992).

13. Arlene Kaplan Daniels, *Invisible Careers: Women Civic Leaders from the Volunteer World* (Chicago: University of Chicago Press, 1988).

14. Darlene Rebecca Roth, "Matronage: Patterns in Women's Organizations, Atlanta, Georgia, 1890–1940" (Ph.D. diss., George Washington University, 1978), 177.

15. Daniels, *Invisible Careers*, ix. Anne Firor Scott, a pathbreaker in so many ways, anticipated Daniels's concept four years earlier, when she stated that women's associations served two purposes, their announced purpose (temperance, for example) and an unannounced purpose, "providing talented women with an opportunity to exercise their ambitions and develop their abilities." Anne Firor Scott, *Making the Invisible Woman Visible* (Urbana: University of Illinois Press, 1984), 38.

16. Anne Firor Scott, "Historians Construct the Southern Woman," in *Sex, Race, and the Role of Women in the South*, ed. Sheila Skemp and Joanne Hawks (Jackson: University Press of Mississippi, 1983), 131.

17. In "Who Rules New Orleans? A Study of Community Power Structures: Some Preliminary Findings on Social Characteristics and Attitudes of New Orleans Leaders," *Louisiana Business Survey* (October 1971): 2–11, Charles W. Chai made the indictment quite strongly. Similar assessments are offered in James R. Bobo, *The New Orleans Economy: Pro Bono Publico?* (New Orleans: University of New Orleans, 1975), and Arnold R. Hirsch, "New Orleans: Sunbelt in the Swamp," in *Sunbelt Cities: Politics and Growth since World War II*, ed. Richard M. Bernard and Bradley Rice (Austin: University of Texas Press, 1983). One local observer slammed "the damn bigoted fools" in the city who would "put out for Mardi Gras, French Opera, and a lot of tomfoolery, but they bemoan[ed] high taxes [and] the slightest inconveniences." Industrialist Andrew Jackson Higgins, quoted in

Jerry E. Strahan, *Andrew Jackson Higgins and the Boats That Won World War II* (Baton Rouge: Louisiana State University Press, 1994), 235–36.

18. Angela Gregory, interview by author, New Orleans, February 6, 1986.

19. A. J. Liebling, *The Earl of Louisiana* (Baton Rouge: Louisiana State University Press, 1970), 18.

CHAPTER 1: WOMAN SUFFRAGE

1. Regional Planning Commission of Orleans, Jefferson, and St. Bernard Parishes, "History of Regional Growth of Jefferson, Orleans, and St. Bernard Parishes," November 1969, 13.

2. Joe Gray Taylor, *Louisiana: A Bicentennial History* (New York: W. W. Norton & Co., 1976), 17.

3. William Ivy Hair, *Bourbonism and Agrarian Protest: Louisiana Politics, 1877–1900* (Baton Rouge: Louisiana State University Press, 1969), 112.

4. J. Morgan Kousser, *The Shaping of Southern Politics: Suffrage Restriction and the Establishment of One-Party Politics* (New Haven: Yale University Press, 1974), 26, 153.

5. Henry E. Chambers, *A History of Louisiana, Wilderness—Colony—Province—Territory—State—People*, 3 vols. (Chicago: American Historical Society, 1925), 1: 707, quoted in C. Vann Woodward, *Origins of the New South, 1877–1913* (Baton Rouge: Louisiana State University Press, 1951), 14; Hair, *Bourbonism and Agrarian Protest*, 27–29, 141; David Goldfield, *Cotton Fields and Skyscrapers: Southern City and Region, 1607–1980* (Baton Rouge: Louisiana State University Press, 1982), 87–97.

6. V. O. Key Jr., *Southern Politics in State and Nation* (New York: Alfred A. Knopf, 1950), 159; Harold Zink, *City Bosses of the United States* (Durham, N.C.: Duke University Press, 1930), 317, 324–25.

7. George M. Reynolds, *Machine Politics in New Orleans, 1897–1926* (New York: Columbia University Press, 1936), 231, 228, 136; Matthew Schott, "John M. Parker of Louisiana and the Varieties of American Progressivism" (Ph.D. diss., Vanderbilt University, 1969), 103. The conservative *New Orleans Times-Picayune,* usually staunch in support of good-government reformers, added its voice to praise Behrman in his comeback campaign of 1925, noting floridly that he stood "above the average of his faction mates like peaks in a desert." *Times-Picayune,* May 4, 1925, quoted in Zink, *City Bosses,* 327.

8. For the following details of the operation of the Regular Democratic Organization during its heyday, I have relied chiefly on Reynolds, *Machine Politics.* I also found much useful information in audio tapes of the "Jambalaya" series, a forum sponsored by the New Orleans Public Library. A session entitled "The Nuts and Bolts of Ward Politics in New Orleans," held October 4, 1978, featuring Old Regulars John Casserino and Lawrence Comiskey, and another, "Old Regulars and Reformers," a talk by William W. Shaw, were particularly informative.

Tapes of the sessions are housed in the Louisiana Collection, New Orleans Public Library. I am grateful to archivist Wayne Everard for calling these to my attention.

9. Schott, "John M. Parker," 100.

10. Reynolds, *Machine Politics*, 117.

11. Schott, "John M. Parker," 102.

12. T. Harry Williams, *Huey Long* (New York: Alfred A. Knopf, 1970), 188–91; Reynolds, *Machine Politics*, 111–17; W. J. Cash, *The Mind of the South* (New York: Vintage Books, 1941), 293.

13. Hermann B. Deutsch, "New Orleans Politics: The Greatest Free Show on Earth," in *The Past as Prelude: New Orleans, 1718–1968*, ed. Hodding Carter (New Orleans: Tulane University, distributed by Pelican, 1968), 317.

14. Allan P. Sindler, *Huey Long's Louisiana: State Politics, 1920–1952* (Baltimore: Johns Hopkins University Press, 1956), 25–26.

15. William Chafe made this statement concerning the power of voteless women around the turn of the century in *The Paradox of Change: American Women in the Twentieth Century* (New York: Oxford University Press, 1991), 42. Other historians, including Paula Baker, Suzanne Lebsock, Nancy Hewitt, and Anne Firor Scott, agree with this viewpoint.

16. Anne Firor Scott, "Women's Voluntary Associations: From Charity to Reform," in *Lady Bountiful Revisited: Women, Philanthropy, and Power*, ed. Kathleen McCarthy (New Brunswick, N.J.: Rutgers University Press, 1990), 44.

17. L. E. Zimmerman, "Josephine Louise Newcomb," in *Notable American Women, 1607–1950*, 3 vols., ed. Edward T. James (Cambridge: Harvard University Press, Belknap Press, 1971), 2: 618–19; Lynn D. Gordon, *Gender and Higher Education in the Progressive Era* (New Haven: Yale University Press, 1990), 166–69.

18. "The H. Sophie Newcomb Memorial College [Catalog]" ([New Orleans]: Tulane University Press, 1910).

19. Brandt V. B. Dixon, quoted in Gordon, *Gender and Higher Education*, 177.

20. Viola Mary Walker, "Sophie Bell Wright: Her Life and Work" (M.A. thesis, Tulane University, 1939).

21. Katherine Hardesty, "Eleanor McMain: Trail-Blazer for Social Service" (M.S.W. thesis, Tulane School of Social Work, 1939).

22. John Duffy, "Sara Tew Mayo," in *Notable American Women*, 2: 5177.

23. Marcus Christian, "History of Flint-Goodridge," manuscript, 22, Marcus Christian Collection, Earl K. Long Library, University of New Orleans.

24. "Expansion—Building on a Quarter Century of Service: Flint-Goodridge Hospital of Dillard University," brochure, c. 1957, Flint-Goodridge Collection, Dillard University Library.

25. Caroline Merrick, *Old Times in Dixie Land: A Southern Matron's Memories* (New York: Grafton Press, 1901), 125.

26. Merrick, *Old Times*, 22–23.

27. Anne Firor Scott has delineated the path from community outreach efforts to suffrage work followed by most southern suffrage leaders in *The Southern Lady:*

From Pedestal to Politics, 1830-1930 (Chicago: University of Chicago Press, 1970). See particularly chaps. 5-7.

28. Merrick, *Old Times*, 218-20; L. E. Zimmerman, "Kate Gordon," in *Notable American Women*, 2: 66.

29. Kathryn W. Kemp, "Jean and Kate Gordon: New Orleans Social Reformers, 1898-1933," *Louisiana History* 24 (Fall 1983): 389-401.

30. Jean Gordon, "The Forward Step in Louisiana," *Annals of American Academy of Political and Social Science* 23 (1909), quoted in Carmen Lindig, *The Path from the Parlor: Louisiana Women, 1879-1920* (Lafayette: Center for Louisiana Studies, 1986), 119.

31. Kate Gordon to Laura Clay, in 1923, quoted in Marjorie Spruill Wheeler, *New Women of the New South* (New York: Oxford University Press, 1993), 190.

32. First quote from Lindig, *Path from the Parlor*, 118; second quote from *New Orleans Daily Picayune*, July 7, 1901.

33. Merrick, *Old Times*, 224.

34. Kemp, "Jean and Kate Gordon," 391.

35. Quote from ibid., 392.

36. *New Orleans Daily Picayune*, July 7, 1901.

37. Lindig, *Path from the Parlor*, 116-17.

38. Ibid., 118-20; Wheeler, *New Women*, 51-52; L. E. Zimmerman, "Jean Gordon," in *Notable American Women*, 2: 65.

39. Quoted in Wheeler, *New Women*, 69.

40. Zimmerman, "Kate Gordon," 2: 67; Kemp, "Jean and Kate Gordon," 392.

41. Wheeler, *New Women*, 101; Kate Gordon quoted in the *New Orleans Daily Picayune*, July 7, 1901; Dr. Anna Howard Shaw, quoted in Wheeler, *New Women*, 118.

42. Wheeler, *New Women*, 102-10.

43. Wheeler, *New Women*, 134-35, 157.

44. Elna Green, "Those Opposed: Southern Antisuffragism, 1890-1920" (Ph.D. diss., Tulane University, 1992; forthcoming from University of North Carolina Press), 83-84; *New Orleans Item*, November 10, 1913. Ethel Hutson, prominent in the Woman Suffrage Party, was a writer for the *Item;* because of her influence, the *Item* tended to report favorably on the federal suffragists' activities.

45. Era Club minutes, December 10, 1914, April 24, 1915, March 25, 1916, and April 8, 1916, microfilm, Louisiana Collection, New Orleans Public Library; Gordon, *Gender and Higher Education*, 180.

46. Era Club minutes, January 27, 1917, and March 10, 1917.

47. Era Club minutes, August 3, 1916.

48. Kenneth Johnson, "Kate Gordon and the Woman Suffrage Movement in the South," *Journal of Southern History* 38 (August 1972): 386; emphasis mine.

49. Wheeler, *New Women*, 161-62.

50. Gordon quoted in Wheeler, *New Women*, 165, 167.

51. Kate Gordon to Laura Clay, June 6, 1918, in Laura Clay Papers, University

of Kentucky Archives, Lexington. I am indebted to Marjorie Spruill Wheeler for this quotation.

52. Kate Gordon to Laura Clay, July 8, 1918, in Clay Papers.

53. Wheeler, *New Women*, 168; Era Club minutes, November 17, 1918.

54. Era Club minutes, November 17, 1918.

55. Ted Tunnell, *Crucible of Reconstruction: War, Radicalism, and Race in Louisiana, 1862-1877* (Baton Rouge: Louisiana State University, 1984), 202-3.

56. See Hilda Phelps Hammond, *Let Freedom Ring* (New York: Farrar & Rinehart, 1936), 20-21, for an example of a filiopietistic account of White League exploits. Another illustration of the reverential tone reserved for the Liberty Place episode is found in Grace King's *Memories of a Southern Woman of Letters* (New York: Macmillan, 1932), 375-76. See also William Ivy Hair, who writes, "Well into the twentieth century, a man who had fought at Liberty Place could claim special status in Louisiana. Even the children of White Leaguers shone in the reflected light." Hair, *The Kingfish and His Realm: The Life and Times of Huey P. Long* (Baton Rouge: Louisiana State University Press, 1991), 10.

57. Era Club minutes, November 24, 1918. The Era Club had entertained a suggestion to drape the venerated monument with black crepe to signify the women's mourning of the lost chance at suffrage, but fearing that such a gesture might be misinterpreted, found offensive, or seen as mocking the heroes of September 1874, Gordon vetoed the suggestion. No symbolism was worth that risk.

58. Undated newspaper clipping entitled "Federal Law Called Useless by the Era Club," in Era Club Papers, Louisiana Collection, New Orleans Public Library.

59. Carrie Chapman Catt and Nettie Rogers Shuler, *Woman Suffrage and Politics: The Inner Story of the Suffrage Movement* (1929; Seattle: University of Washington Press, 1969), 451-52, quoted in Wheeler, *New Women*, 35.

60. *New Orleans Times-Picayune*, August 19, 1920, quoted in Lindig, *Path from the Parlor*, 169.

61. Schott, "John M. Parker," 201, 250, 393.

62. Green, "Those Opposed," 93-108, 89.

63. *New Orleans Daily Picayune*, July 7, 1901; Sake Meehan to Agnes Rogers, May 24, 1913, quoted in Green, "Those Opposed," 299.

64. Kristi Andersen, "Women and Citizenship in the 1920s," in *Women, Politics, and Change*, ed. Louise Tilly and Patricia Gurin (New York: Russell Sage Foundation, 1990), 190-91.

65. *New Orleans Item*, September 5, 1920.

66. Information concerning female voter registration in locales beyond New Orleans in the 1920s comes from Sophonisba Breckinridge, *Women in the Twentieth Century: A Study of Theory of Political, Social, and Economic Activities* (New York: McGraw Hill, 1933), quoted in Andersen, "Women and Citizenship," 191-93.

67. Charles Edward Merriam and Harold Foote Gosnell, *Non-Voting: Causes and Methods of Control* (Chicago: University of Chicago Press, 1924), 110-11, 255-56.

68. *New Orleans Times-Picayune*, December 11, 1920.

69. Marguerite Wells, quoted in Andersen, "Women and Citizenship," 179.

70. Quote from Nancy Cott, "Across the Great Divide: Women in Politics before and after 1920," in Tilly and Gurin, *Women, Politics, and Change*, 170.

71. Catt quoted in Cott, "Across the Great Divide," 158.

72. Resolution adopted November 1, 1921, by New Orleans League of Women Voters; copy found in National League of Women Voters Papers, Library of Congress (hereafter cited as "NLWV Papers").

73. E. J. Rockenback, Secretary, Organization Department, National League of Women Voters, to Mrs. Philip Werlein, October 13, 1921; NLWV memo "Louisiana League of Women Voters," December 21, 1921; both in NLWV Papers.

CHAPTER 2: CLASS, GENDER, AND THE KINGFISH

1. Edwin M. Yoder Jr., "Louisiana's Kingfish: Misunderstood and Underrated?" *Saturday Review*, November 1, 1969, 32.

2. Walter Adolphe Roberts, *Lake Pontchartrain* (Indianapolis: Bobbs-Merrill, 1946), 331, quoted in Allan P. Sindler, *Huey Long's Louisiana: State Politics, 1920–1952* (Baltimore: Johns Hopkins University Press, 1956), 99.

3. Hilda Phelps Hammond, *Let Freedom Ring* (New York: Farrar & Rinehart, 1936), 12–13.

4. Lynn D. Gordon, *Gender and Higher Education in the Progressive Era*, (New Haven: Yale University Press, 1990), 175–77. Indeed, decades after her years at Newcomb, observers remembered that Hammond "liked to argue." Blanche Hammond (Mrs. Nauman S.) Scott and Nauman S. Scott Jr., interview by author, Alexandria, La., October 24, 1984.

5. Isoline Rodd Kendall, *Brief History of Woman's Committee, Council of National Defense: New Orleans Division* (New Orleans: N.p., [1919]), 5–7.

6. Blanche Hammond Scott, interview by author; Hammond, *Let Freedom Ring*, 27–29; William L. Deacon, *Reference Biography of Louisiana Bench and Bar, 1922* (New Orleans: Cox Printing Co., 1922), 64.

7. Senate, Special Committee on Investigation of Campaign Expenditures, "Hearings before the Special Committee on Investigation of Campaign Expenditures," vol. 1, 72d Cong., 2d sess., Pursuant to S. Res. 174 (Washington, D.C.: U.S. Government Printing Office, 1933), 1212 (hereafter cited as "Overton Hearings"). July B. (Mrs. Arthur) Waters, interview by author, New Orleans, March 6, 1985, and Blanche Hammond Scott, interview by author.

8. T. Harry Williams, *Huey Long* (New York: Alfred A. Knopf, 1970), 441; James Norman Duffy, "Huey Long and the 'Spite School' Controversy" (M.A. thesis, Louisiana State University at New Orleans, 1971), 16. Long particularly resented the *Times-Picayune* for its caustic coverage of his impeachment battle of the year before. Carleton Beals, *The Story of Huey P. Long* (Westport, Conn.: Greenwood Press, 1935), 165.

9. Hammond, *Let Freedom Ring*, 45, 9–10.

10. Blanche Hammond Scott, interview by author.

11. *New Orleans States*, September 13, 1933. Hilda Phelps Hammond had inherited some stock in the *Times-Picayune* upon her father's death in 1919, but the income from it was insufficient to support the family. With the onset of the depression years, the dividends declined drastically. Hammond, *Let Freedom Ring*, 28–29.

12. Blanche Hammond Scott, interview by author.

13. Senatorial Campaign Expenditures Committee Report (Report No. 191), 73d Cong., 2d sess., January 11 (calendar day January 16), 1934, 3 (hereafter cited as "Connally Report").

14. *New Orleans Times-Picayune*, February 4, 1933.

15. Quote is from *New Orleans States*, February 8, 1933. See also *New Orleans Item* for February 3, 1933, and *States*, February 7, 1933.

16. Hammond, *Let Freedom Ring*, 52–74; Overton Hearings, 1: 328–30, 564–609, 628–71.

17. *New Orleans Item*, February 12, 1933; Hammond, *Let Freedom Ring*, 160.

18. Charles Wesley (hereafter cited as "C. W.") Robinson, interview by author, New Orleans, August 5, 1985; Beals, *Huey P. Long*, 173.

19. *New Orleans States*, February 3, 1933, February 7, 1933. See John F. Kasson's comments on laughter in *Rudeness and Civility: Manners in Nineteenth-Century Urban America* (New York: Hill & Wang, 1990), 162–63.

20. Samuel Tilden Ansell (Senate committee legal counsel), quoted in Hammond, *Let Freedom Ring*, 77.

21. Hammond, *Let Freedom Ring*, 22, 79.

22. Ibid., 79.

23. July B. Waters, interview by author, March 6, 1985.

24. Hammond, *Let Freedom Ring*, 29, 47.

25. Ibid., 83.

26. *Congressional Record*, 73d Cong., 1st sess., vol. 77, pt. 2, April 14, 1933, p. 1713; *New York Times*, April 22, 1935. Long's objections served only to swell the flood of petitions; thirty-five more anti-Long petitions arrived between April 14 and May 8, 1933.

27. Martha Gilmore Robinson to Senator Tom Connally, April 15, 1933, in Martha Gilmore Robinson Papers, Howard-Tilton Memorial Library, Tulane University (hereafter cited as "MGR Papers").

28. Maude T. Burson to Senator Royal Copeland, November 12, 1933, in Hilda Phelps Hammond Papers, Howard-Tilton Memorial Library, Tulane University (hereafter cited as "HPH Papers, Tulane").

29. Martha G. Westfeldt to Hilda Phelps Hammond, August 21, [1933], in Hilda Phelps Hammond Papers, Historic New Orleans Collection (hereafter cited as "HPH Papers, HNOC").

30. Hammond, *Let Freedom Ring*, 88.

31. July B. (Mrs. Arthur) Waters, interview by author, New Orleans, August 3, 1984; Hammond, *Let Freedom Ring*, 92–93.

32. Hammond, *Let Freedom Ring*, 94–98, 102.

33. Sindler, *Huey Long's Louisiana*, 80; William Leuchtenberg, *Franklin D. Roosevelt and the New Deal* (New York: Harper & Row, 1963), 96–97 and passim; Arthur Schlesinger Jr., *The Politics of Upheaval* (Boston: Houghton Mifflin Co., 1960), 55.

Allan Sindler also suggests that Senate majority leader Joseph Robinson had a hand in the origination of the committee investigation, noting that Long's 1932 whirlwind speaking tour through Robinson's home state of Arkansas that resulted in Hattie Carraway's election left Robinson livid. He decided to encourage the investigation, which would of course discredit Long, as a form of retaliation.

34. Harnett T. Kane, *Louisiana Hayride: The American Rehearsal for Dictatorship, 1928–1940* (New York: William Morrow & Co., 1941), 118–19.

35. *New Orleans States*, August 30, 1933; *New Orleans Times-Picayune*, August 31, 1933; Sindler, *Huey Long's Louisiana*, 88.

36. Hollinger F. Barnard, ed., *Outside the Magic Circle: The Autobiography of Virginia Foster Durr* (University: University of Alabama Press, 1985), 174.

37. *New Orleans States*, September 2, 1933.

38. Ibid., August 31, 1933, September 13, 1933.

39. Ibid., July 26, 1933, September 2, 1933; *New Orleans Times-Picayune*, June 19, 1934.

40. Richard Hofstadter, *The Age of Reform: From Bryan to F.D.R.* (New York: Vintage Books, 1955), 135.

41. Martha Gasquet Westfeldt, "Alice in Hueyland: Not a Play, Not a Parody, Not a Political Satire, As Seen by the Dodo," undated manuscript, HPH Papers, Tulane.

42. Huey P. Long, *Every Man a King* (New Orleans: National Book Co., 1933), 335.

43. *New York Times*, October 24, 1933.

44. Hammond, *Let Freedom Ring*, 104.

45. Hilda Phelps Hammond to Senator Marvel M. Logan, September 10, 1933, quoted in "Petition to the Senate of the United States of Hilda Phelps Hammond on behalf of the Women's Committee of Louisiana," May 23, 1935, 43–45, HPH Papers, Tulane.

46. Senator Marvel M. Logan to Hilda Phelps Hammond, September 12, 1933, quoted in "Petition to the Senate," 46.

47. Hilda Phelps Hammond to Senator Marvel M. Logan, September 13, 1933, quoted in "Petition to the Senate," 46–47.

48. Lowell Mellett, editorial in *Washington Daily News*, undated, quoted in Hammond, *Let Freedom Ring*, 127–28.

49. Fragment of letter from Senator Marvel M. Logan to unknown recipient (Women's Committee member), undated, HPH Papers, Tulane.

50. *New Orleans States,* November 2, 1933, November 6, 1933, November 9, 1933, November 11, 1933.

51. *New York Times,* November 5, 1933.

52. Tom Connally as told to Alfred Steinberg, *My Name Is Tom Connally* (New York: Thomas Y. Crowell & Son, 1954), 168; *New York Times,* November 23, 1933; *Omaha World Herald,* quoted in *New Orleans Times-Picayune,* November 16, 1933.

53. Angela Gregory, interview by author, New Orleans, February 6, 1986.

54. Overton Hearings, 2: 1233.

55. Ibid., 1909–18.

56. Ibid., 2083.

57. "Huey Long: Is Senate Afraid of the Big, Bad Kingfish?" *Newsweek,* December 9, 1933, 12.

58. *American Progress,* November 16, 1933. Hammond recounted an incident that illuminates the social class issue between herself and Long. Returning from lobbying in Washington, she found herself sharing a coach on the train to New Orleans with the Kingfish himself. For the entire journey she icily ignored him. She thought that he tried to force her to notice him with his whistling and singing, noisily buying food and drink from the roving vendor, flinging himself about on the furniture, barking orders to his bodyguards. Convinced that he hoped to force a complaint or reprimand from her so that he could then have a little fun at her expense, Hammond simply refused to notice him, though she records that she saw him looking at her "with a little leer." The journey ended with each acutely conscious of the other yet never formally acknowledging the other's presence. Hammond, *Let Freedom Ring,* 259–64.

59. Overton Hearings, 2: 1217.

60. Beals, *Huey P. Long,* 178.

61. William Ivy Hair, *The Kingfish and His Realm: The Life and Times of Huey P. Long* (Baton Rouge: Louisiana State University Press, 1991), 244–45.

62. Overton Hearings, 2:1525, 1530.

63. *New York Sun* and *Birmingham Age-Herald,* quoted in *New Orleans Times-Picayune,* November 17, 1933.

64. *New Orleans Times-Picayune,* January 3, 1934.

65. Ibid., January 11, 1934. The women accompanying Hammond were Ethelynn (Mrs. Charles) Dunbar, Catherine Labouisse, Olive (Mrs. Armant) Legendre, and Doris (Mrs. Roger T.) Stone. Ibid., January 8, 1934. All were listed in the Social Register, and all had male relatives affiliated with the Boston Club. The Women's Committee did not pay their expenses for them as they did for Hammond.

66. Connally Report, 17–19.

67. Ibid., 19–22.

68. Ibid., 23; Connally as told to Steinberg, *My Name,* 167–68.

69. *American Progress,* January 18, 1934. Long's newspaper had begun life as the *Louisiana Progress,* but in August 1933, reflecting his growing ambitions outside the Bayou State, it underwent a name change and became the *American Progress.*

70. Hammond, *Let Freedom Ring,* 235.

71. Ibid., 140.

72. Their "budget" consisted solely of contributions that members solicited from the planter-business establishment. "I have to walk the streets to collect this money," wrote Hammond in explaining the committee's tardiness in paying a printing bill, "and it is of course a tiresome and lengthy matter." Hilda Phelps Hammond to Paul Wooton, February 29, 1936, HPH Papers, HNOC.

73. "Petition from Hilda Phelps Hammond for and on behalf of the Women's Committee of Louisiana to the United States Senate," February 14, 1934, 20, in HPH Papers, Tulane; *New Orleans Times-Picayune,* January 26, 1934.

74. Senate Committee on Privileges and Elections, "Hearings before the Committee on Privileges and Elections," 73d Cong., 2d sess., Relative to the Petitions and Memorials Seeking the Expulsion of the Senators from the State of Louisiana, May 2, 3, and 19, 1934, 19 (hereafter cited as "George Hearings").

75. Ibid., 25.

76. "Petition to the Senate of the United States of Hilda Phelps Hammond on behalf of the Women's Committee of Louisiana," 106–7.

77. George Hearings, 95–96.

78. Petition from Hilda Phelps Hammond to members of the U.S. Senate, June 16, 1934, quoted in "Petition to the Senate of the United States of Hilda Phelps Hammond on behalf of the Women's Committee of Louisiana," 110.

79. *New Orleans Times-Picayune,* June 17, 1934.

80. Ibid., June 19, 1934.

81. Ibid., June 17, 1934. Hammond quoted Long's threats accurately. See the full text of his remarks, made on the Senate floor, in the April 5, 1934, *Congressional Record,* 73d Cong., 2d sess., vol. 78, pt. 6, April 5, 1934, p. 6105.

82. Kane, *Louisiana Hayride,* 95–100.

83. Williams, *Huey Long,* 592; Alan Brinkley, *Voices of Protest: Huey Long, Father Coughlin, and the Great Depression* (New York: Vintage Books, 1983), 47–53.

84. Quoted in Brinkley, *Voices of Protest,* 46.

85. July B. Waters, interview by author, August 3, 1984.

86. Hammond, *Let Freedom Ring,* 110–16.

87. Ibid., 203–4.

88. Quoted in "Is the Senate Afraid of Huey Long?" undated pamphlet published by Hilda Phelps Hammond, fall 1934, in William B. Wisdom Collection, Howard-Tilton Memorial Library, Tulane University. *News* quote, p. 15; *Tribune,* p. 19; *Commercial Appeal,* p. 16.

89. *Houston Post* quoted in *New Orleans Times-Picayune,* June 25, 1934.

90. *American Progress*, August 7, 1934.

91. *New York Times*, September 14, 1934; *New Orleans Times-Picayune*, May 17, 1935.

92. Roy E. Larsen to Hilda Phelps Hammond, April 17, 1935. There are numerous letters to journalists seeking coverage and editorial comment in Box 1 of HPH Papers, HNOC.

93. *New York Times*, February 8, 1934.

94. *New York Times*, September 1, 1933, September 5, 1933, September 15, 1933; *New Orleans States*, September 5 and 8, 1933.

95. *New York Times*, January 9, 1934; *New Orleans Times-Picayune*, January 9, 1934.

96. Richard D. Hupman, *Senate Election, Expulsion, and Censure Cases: From 1793 to 1972* (Washington, D.C.: U.S. Government Printing Office, 1972), 101-2, 119-24.

97. "Is the Senate Afraid of Huey Long?" 4 (punctuation and emphasis from Hammond's original).

98. Quoted in ibid., 77-79.

99. Ibid., 18.

100. *American Progress*, November 23, 1933, February 15, 1934, January 4, 1935, February 1, 1935.

101. Williams, *Huey Long*, 441.

102. Hilda Phelps Hammond radio address, undated, c. 1936, in HPH Papers, Tulane; *New Orleans Times-Picayune*, December 17, 1933; Hilda Phelps Hammond to Senator Robert Carey, October 3, 1933, HPH Papers, Tulane.

103. Handbill advertising Women's Committee of Louisiana, undated, in MGR Papers.

104. Hammond, *Let Freedom Ring*, 193-94.

105. July B. Waters, interview by author, August 3, 1984.

106. Quote from *New Orleans States*, November 6, 1933.

107. Hammond, *Let Freedom Ring*, 123.

108. Frances Parkinson Keyes, *Crescent Carnival* (New York: Franklin Watts, 1942), 8-9.

109. Ibid., 610. Hammond's reaction to Keyes's fiction was recognition and rueful amusement. "She got me good, didn't she?" she laughed to a friend. Her friends responded by loyally refusing to read, or to admit to reading, any of Keyes's books.

110. Barnard, *Outside the Magic Circle*, 179.

111. Overton Hearings, 2:1534.

112. Ibid., 1245; Hammond, *Let Freedom Ring*, 100.

113. Hupman, *Senate Election*, 101-2, 120-24. Actually, Hammond did have one senatorial ally, the Nebraska Republican Robert Howell, who had chaired the February 1933 Senate hearings into Overton's election. Long's disrespectful

conduct before the investigating committee clearly offended Howell, who was shocked by the evidence presented during the two-week investigation and enraged that Long's associates came armed into the committee chamber. Deeply disturbed by the political situation he had encountered in Louisiana, he intended to request of the Senate that controversial Senator-elect John Overton be asked to stand aside until the circumstances surrounding his election could be determined. However, upon his return from New Orleans to Washington, he fell ill of pneumonia; he died at Walter Reed Hospital less than a month after the Senate hearings that he had chaired. See Hammond, *Let Freedom Ring*, 244–51; *New Orleans Times-Picayune*, March 12, 1933; Williams, *Huey Long*, 617–18.

114. Hammond, *Let Freedom Ring*, 237.

115. Hammond press release, September 11, 1935, quoted in ibid., 284.

116. Ibid., p. 285.

117. Sindler, *Huey Long's Louisiana*, 129.

118. Ibid., 136.

119. Hilda Phelps Hammond, undated radio address, c. 1936, in HPH Papers, Tulane.

120. Hammond, undated radio speech, c. 1936, in HPH Papers.

121. Raymond Daniell, "After Huey, the Deluge," *New York Times Magazine*, July 16, 1939, 21.

122. Raymond Daniell, "Huey Long's Empire Unshaken," *New York Times Magazine*, February 23, 1936, 7, 22.

123. *New Orleans Item*, January 5, 1936; *New Orleans States*, March 5, 1936.

124. Angela Gregory, interview by author.

125. Jacquelyn Dowd Hall, *Revolt against Chivalry: Jessie Daniel Ames and the Women's Campaign against Lynching* (New York: Columbia University Press, 1978), 251–52.

126. See various passages in Hammond, *Let Freedom Ring*, for examples of her testiness. In particular, note her encounters with Senator Hugo Black (155–56), Senator Carter Glass (240–41), Senator George Norris (270–73), and with an unnamed government employee (185–86).

127. Hammond, *Let Freedom Ring*, 277.

128. Hilda Phelps Hammond to Mrs. Joseph Friend and Executive Board of Women's Committee of Louisiana, quoted in *New Orleans Times-Picayune*, June 20, 1934.

129. Kane, *Louisiana Hayride*; Glen Jeansonne, *Messiah of the Masses: Huey P. Long and the Great Depression* (New York: HarperCollins, 1993); Sindler, *Huey Long's Louisiana*; Henry C. Dethloff, ed., *Huey P. Long: Southern Demagogue or American Democrat?* (Lafayette, La.: University of Southwestern Louisiana, 1976); Hair, *Kingfish*; Williams, *Huey Long*.

130. Williams, *Huey Long*, 646.

131. Ibid., 688.

132. Ibid., 784; *New Orleans Times-Picayune,* January 7, 1935, January 15, 1935, January 16, 1935, January 17, 1935.

133. Sindler, *Huey Long's Louisiana,* 108; Schlesinger, *Politics of Upheaval,* 61; Cecil Morgan, review of *Huey Long* by T. Harry Williams, in *Tulane Law Review* 45 (April 1971): 680.

134. Sindler, *Huey Long's Louisiana,* 108.

135. *New York Times,* July 22, 1934.

136. Hodding Carter, "Huey Long, American Dictator," in *The Aspirin Age,* ed. Isabel Leighton (New York: Simon & Schuster, 1949), 357.

137. Hammond, *Let Freedom Ring,* 29, 222.

138. Erving Goffman, "The Nature of Deference and Demeanor," in *Interaction Ritual: Essays on Face-to-Face Behavior,* ed. Erving Goffman (Garden City, N.Y.: Anchor Books, 1967), 77. See also Warren I. Susman, "'Personality' and the Making of Twentieth-Century Culture," in *New Directions in American Intellectual History,* ed. John Higham and Paul K. Conkin (Baltimore: Johns Hopkins University Press, 1979), 212–26, for an illuminating discussion of the contrasting values represented by "character" and "personality."

139. Edmund Burke quoted in Kasson, *Rudeness and Civility,* 62.

140. Kasson, *Rudeness and Civility,* 3. Many passages in Kasson's book, which describe "rude" behavior according to late-nineteenth-century standards, are almost literally descriptive of Huey Long's actions. The code of behavior, with its definitions of what was "refined" and what was not, is of course the code that Hilda Phelps Hammond, as a well-bred child of the 1890s, would have had imprinted upon her from infancy onward.

141. Hair, *Kingfish,* 278–81, 289–90, 292–94, 301–6, 316–20. Lippmann quote from undated clipping from *New York Times* in MGR Papers.

142. Hilda Phelps Hammond to Martha Westfeldt, July 7, 1935, in HPH Papers, HNOC.

143. Allan Sindler scores "the immorality" of Longism, which he calls "neither deniable nor justifiable," and argues that "no dictatorship would have been required to effectuate an even more coherent and penetrating class program than that which Long did perform. The guidestar of the Kingfish was politics, not service." *Huey Long's Louisiana,* 107–8, 115.

William Ivy Hair is even more blunt. "In Louisiana, anything of political importance that Huey did not dominate, he fought unreservedly. . . . To Huey, only one thing truly mattered: power and more power for himself, by the most expeditious means." *Kingfish,* 232, 226.

144. A longtime New Orleans reporter recalled Hammond as "very vigorous, very intelligent, a little bit intolerant." "She could be unpleasant . . . she could be short with people who disagreed with her. I don't ever remember seeing her smile. She always impressed me as a grim figure, very intent on her objective, somebody who saw nothing funny about it. . . . She could be very tart, very

righteous." James H. Gillis, interview by author, New Orleans, January 24, 1986. A *Washington Star* analysis of Hammond noted, "In ordinary conversation her voice is gentle and she has a charming laugh." A Jekyll and Hyde transformation occurred, however, when she started talking about her cause: "Her eyes harden, her voice sharpens and her enunciation becomes clipped." *Star* article reprinted in *New Orleans Times-Picayune,* January 5, 1934. A New Orleans woman, remembering Hammond's intensity, said simply, "I was always scared of her." Beatrice Field, interview by author, New Orleans, October 31, 1984. Conversely, friends and family members mentioned Hammond's "warmth," "laughter," "style," and "charm." John P. Hammond, interview by author, February 14, 1995; author's interviews with Blanche Hammond Scott, Angela Gregory, and July B. Waters.

CHAPTER 3: "WOMEN OF BRAINS AND STANDING"

1. Wendy Kaminer, *Women Volunteering: The Pleasure, Pain, and Politics of Unpaid Work from 1830 to the Present* (Garden City, N.Y.: Anchor Press, Doubleday & Co., 1984), 46.

2. Ethel Klein, *Gender Politics: From Consciousness to Mass Politics* (Cambridge: Harvard University Press, 1984), 35.

3. *New Orleans Times-Picayune,* November 7, 1930.

4. Mrs. Cleanth Brooks to Martha G. Robinson (hereafter cited as "MGR"), August 27, 1940, in New Orleans League of Women Voters Papers, Howard-Tilton Memorial Library, Tulane University (hereafter cited as "NOLWV Papers, Tulane").

5. *New Orleans Times-Picayune,* March 15, 1952, February 22, 1963. James Comiskey was the "boss" of the Third Ward, a legendary Old Regular and longtime tax assessor with great power in local politics. In addition to the Pilsbury sisters' own strong bonds with old Regulars, their brother Michael Culligan served as assistant city attorney in the 1930s under Old Regular administrations.

6. Alice Owen, NLWV secretary to Florence Stone, NOLWV, September 16, 1930; B. H. Marsh to Miss Rockwood, "confidential" memo, February 29, 1932; both in NLWV Papers. The woman who "made waves" was the wife of Francis Williams, who became leader of the "New Regulars" and subsequently of the "Independent Regulars" as the internecine squabbles of New Orleans politics produced divisions and subdivisions in the mayoral and gubernatorial elections of the 1920s. The partisan tinge of NOLWV officers is evident from a look at their correspondence with the NLWV, some of which is written on letterhead stationery from "Registration Office, Parish of Orleans, City Hall," "City Board of Health," and so on. The posts that these women held were patronage jobs, dependent on the holder's loyalty to the machine in power, in this case, the Old Regulars.

7. Mrs. William G. Hibbard, chairman, Special Committee on Affiliation Standards, to NLWV Board of Directors, "Report of Progress," December 5, 1934, in NLWV Papers.

8. Madeline Hackett to NLWV, May 26, 1936, and Anonymous to NLWV, June 8, 1936, in NLWV Papers.

9. Harriet Eliel to Marguerite Wells, president, NLWV, November 25, 1936, NLWV Papers.

10. Marguerite Wells, president, NLWV, to Mrs. Ed Pilsbury, November 20, 1936, NLWV Papers.

11. Wells to Pilsbury, December 3, 1936, NLWV Papers.

12. Anonymous [in New Orleans] to NLWV headquarters, June 3, 1936, in NLWV Papers.

13. William Chafe, *The Paradox of Change: American Women in the Twentieth Century* (New York: Oxford University Press, 1991), 29–31; J. Stanley Lemons, *The Woman Citizen: Social Feminism in the 1920s* (Urbana: University of Illinois Press, 1973), 233–35. *Report of the Secretary of State to His Excellency the Governor of Louisiana* (Baton Rouge: Ramires-Jones Printing Co., 1923), 306 (hereafter cited as "*Report of the Secretary of State*" and year).

14. *Report of the Secretary of State*, 1937, 41.

15. Indeed, this hesitation on the part of women to become politically aware and active is not a phenomenon that ended in the 1930s. A Louis Harris poll in 1972 found that 71 percent of respondents agreed with the statement "Women should take care of running their homes and leave running the country up to men." Sixty-six percent agreed with this sentence: "Most men are better suited emotionally for politics than are most women." Virginia Sapiro, *The Political Integration of Women: Roles, Socialization, and Politics* (Urbana: University of Illinois Press, 1983), 30, 24.

16. MGR, interview by Dorothy Schlesinger, August 6, 1972, Friends of the Cabildo Collection, Howard-Tilton Memorial Library, Tulane University.

17. *Jambalaya* 1909, Special Collections, Howard-Tilton Memorial Library, Tulane University; speech by Anna Many honoring MGR, October 9, 1953, MGR Papers.

18. Klein, *Gender Politics*, 49–51.

19. Robinson did receive at least some encouragement to develop interests away from the domestic scene. Shortly after the birth of her fourth child, a fond letter from a former professor of hers at Newcomb College cautioned, "Don't let the children take too much of your life, Dear love." Imogene Stone to MGR, January 20, 1923, in MGR Papers.

20. Undated fragment, MGR Papers.

21. MGR radio speech, December 28, 1953, in MGR Papers.

22. Act 130, *Acts Passed by the Legislature of the State of Louisiana* (1916), 290–318.

23. See Chapter 2 for details of the findings of the 1934 Connally Report on Louisiana elections.

24. Quote from "What a Citizen Can Do to Safeguard Elections," Honest Election League handbill, [1934], MGR Papers.

25. Handbill, n.d., MGR Papers.

26. *New Orleans Times-Picayune,* January 18, 1934; Anne Firor Scott, "After Suffrage: Southern Women in the Twenties," *Journal of Southern History* 30 (August 1964): 302.

27. Unidentified press clipping, February 4, 1934, MGR Papers.

28. Jacquelyn Dowd Hall, *Revolt against Chivalry: Jessie Daniel Ames and the Women's Campaign against Lynching* (New York: Columbia University Press, 1978), 181.

29. Burt Henry, HEL president, to C. S. Barnes, Orleans Parish registrar, December 22, 1933, in MGR Papers.

30. *New Orleans Morning Tribune,* January 31, 1934.

31. MGR to Burt Henry, May 19, 1934, in MGR Papers.

32. Woman Citizens' Union minutes, June 1, 1934, in MGR Papers. The women's organizations represented at the initial meeting were the New Orleans Council of Parent-Teachers, Business Girls' Group of the YWCA, Louisiana chapter of the Association of Social Workers, Gulf District of the Association of Medical Social Workers, Child Guidance Center, Council of Jewish Women, Federation of Protestant Churchwomen, American Association of University Women, Newcomb Alumnae Association, New Orleans Business and Professional Women's Club, YWCA, New Orleans Women's Club, New Orleans Federation of Clubs, New Orleans Hadassah, Council of Catholic Women, New Orleans Public School Teachers Association, Women's Auxiliary of the American Legion, Louisiana branch of A.W.V.S., New Orleans Junior League, Women's Engineering Society, and the U.S. Children's Bureau.

33. *New Orleans Times-Picayune,* June 2, 1934.

34. Mrs. V. K. Casserlly, secretary, New Orleans Federation of Women's Clubs, to MGR, January 25, 1935, in NOLWV Papers, Tulane.

The twenty-eight-member board of directors of the New Orleans Federation of Women's Clubs had but one member listed in the city's Social Register, and only one connection with the prestigious Boston Club, that through one woman's father-in-law. Clearly, they were not an elite group.

35. T. Harry Williams, *Huey Long* (New York: Alfred A. Knopf, 1970), 726–27.

36. MGR radio script, August 17, 1934, MGR Papers.

37. MGR radio script, September 6, 1934, MGR Papers.

38. Among the things forbidden by law were open saloons within one mile of the poll, solicitation of votes within the poll barrier, the presence of persons other than commissioners and voters in the room with ballot boxes, placing ballot boxes out of plain sight, and use of previously marked ballots.

39. Eleanor Flexner, *Century of Struggle: The Woman's Rights Movement in the United States* (Cambridge: Harvard University Press, Belknap Press, 1959), 177.

40. MGR, quoted in Rosa Keller, "League of Women Voters in New Orleans History, 1942–1977" (1977; ms. in author's possession), 10.

41. *New Orleans States,* August 18, 1944.

42. July B. (Mrs. Arthur) Waters, interview by author, New Orleans, March 6, 1985; Carolyn Gay (Mrs. F. Monroe) Labouisse, interview by author, New Orleans, September 10, 1985; Blanche Hammond (Mrs. Nauman S.) Scott, interview by author, Alexandria, La., October 24, 1984.

43. Quote from MGR radio script, June 21, 1934, MGR Papers.

44. MGR radio script, undated, MGR Papers.

45. *Report of the Secretary of State,* 1935 and 1937, 397, insert #3.

46. MGR to Mrs. Patrick Anderson, December 24, 1934, in MGR Papers.

47. Talbot quoted in Nancy Woloch, *Women and the American Experience* (New York: Alfred A. Knopf, 1984), 270.

48. MGR radio script, June 21, 1934, MGR Papers.

49. MGR's political science notes, fall semester, 1934, MGR Papers.

50. A. L. Dunn to MGR, September 21, 1940, in WCU portion of NOLWV Papers, Tulane.

51. Undated draft, MGR Papers.

52. Charles Hyneman, "Political and Administrative Reform in the 1940 Legislature," *Louisiana Law Review* 3 (1940–41): 1.

53. *New Orleans Times-Picayune,* October 11, 1941; Edward F. Haas, *DeLesseps S. Morrison and the Image of Reform: New Orleans Politics, 1946–1961* (Baton Rouge: Louisiana State University Press, 1974), 21.

54. Act 46, *Acts Passed by the Legislature of the State of Louisiana* (1940), 171–219.

55. "A Petition," in MGR Papers.

56. MGR to Lem Nolan, June 18, 1940, MGR Papers.

57. Robert Wiebe in *The Search for Order* (New York: Hill & Wang, 1967), 60–61, Geoffrey Blodgett in *The Gentle Reformers* (Cambridge: Harvard University Press, 1966), 44–45, and John G. Sproat in *The Best Men* (New York: Oxford University Press, 1968), 264–65, all discuss the attention devoted to civil service reform by municipal reformers in the late nineteenth and early twentieth centuries.

58. William W. Shaw, *Charles E. Dunbar Jr. and Civil Service Reform in Louisiana* (New Orleans: Tulane University, 1981), 1; Perry H. Howard, *Political Tendencies in Louisiana, 1812–1952* (Baton Rouge: Louisiana State University Press, 1957), 41–42, 46–47, 59–60, 64–65, 69–70.

59. Harold A. Stone, director, New Orleans Bureau of Governmental Research, to Howard P. Jones, March 16, 1936, in MGR Papers.

60. MGR speech, undated, in MGR Papers; L. Vaughn Howard, "Civil Service Development in Louisiana," *Tulane Studies in Political Science* 3 (1954): 1–190.

61. *New Orleans Times-Picayune,* November 2, 1941.

62. Marguerite Wells, NLWV president, to Mrs. Roscoe Anderson, December 9, 1936, in NLWV Papers.

63. Constance Roach to Mrs. Bailey Calvin, December 3, 1941, in NLWV Papers.

64. Emily Blanchard to Marguerite Wells, May 20, 1942, in NLWV Papers.

65. Quotes from Eleanor Parker to "Dear Delphine," at NLWV headquarters, [April 1942], in NLWV Papers; and Constance Roach, NLWV organizing secretary, internal NLWV memo, April 5, 1938, NLWV Papers.

66. Marguerite Wells to Emily Blanchard, May 18, 1942, in NLWV Papers.

67. Emily Blanchard to Mrs. Louise Baldwin, NLWV vice president, September 23, 1942, NLWV Papers.

68. Helen Semmerling "confidential" to Marguerite Wells, October 31, 1942, in NLWV papers.

69. Margaret LeCorgne and Elsie Martinez, *Uptown/Downtown: Growing Up in New Orleans* (Lafayette: Center for Louisiana Studies, 1986), 164; Jerry E. Strahan, *Andrew Jackson Higgins and the Boats That Won World War II* (Baton Rouge: Louisiana State University Press, 1994); John Morton Blum, *V Was for Victory: Politics and American Culture during World War II* (New York: Harcourt, Brace, Jovanovich, 1976), 93.

70. "Robinson Home Journal," January 22, 1944, MGR Papers.

71. MGR to Natalie Scott, September 24, 1944, in Natalie Scott Papers, Howard-Tilton Memorial Library, Tulane University (hereafter cited as Scott Papers); "Robinson Home Journal," May 12, 1945. Her colleagues in LWV work noticed the strain and felt concerned for Robinson's well-being, aware that she had sons in combat, a dying mother living with her, and the responsibilities of the presidency of the state League of Women Voters. Wrote a Baton Rouge member solicitously, "We all think you look tired and that you are burning yourself out. And we all love you dearly. There is a limit to what one person can keep going." Maidie Nason to MGR, July 15, 1945, in NOLWV Papers, Tulane.

72. "Robinson Home Journal," January 22, 1944; MGR speech delivered January 9, 1941, in MGR Papers. See also Silver Thimble Papers in Howard-Tilton Memorial Library, Tulane University.

73. "Robinson Home Journal," February 6, 1944, and June 3, 1944. Robinson was quite unhappy with her daughter for serving thick steaks that she had bought on the black market.

74. Ibid., February 15, 1944, and March 4, 1944.

75. Ibid., Easter Sunday, 1945. There was one exception to Martha Robinson's equanimity about rationing. In 1942, new guidelines appeared to regulate consumption of coffee, a beverage dear to New Orleanians, who consumed nearly twice as much coffee annually as other Americans. Robinson commented tartly that New Orleanians were suffering because "Yankees," who were abysmally ignorant of how to make good coffee, had been allowed to write the coffee regulations.

See J. W. Reily to Governor Sam Houston Jones, November 25, 1942, in Sam Jones Papers, Howard-Tilton Memorial Library, Tulane University.

76. "Robinson Home Journal," August 20, 1944.

77. "Salisbury Entertains," *Time*, August 24, 1942, 11-12; Howard W. Odum, *Race and Rumors of Race* (Chapel Hill: University of North Carolina Press, 1943), chap. 12.

78. Edith R. Stern, "Riddle of the Race Riots" undated typed manuscript, Collection M667, Howard-Tilton Memorial Library, Tulane University. See Howard Odum's extended discussion of the phenomenon of the Eleanor Club rumors in *Race and Rumors,* chaps. 9 and 10.

79. The relationship between Robinson and Leila Melancon, her household servant from 1916 until her death in 1950, was a close one. On Melancon's fifty-seventh birthday, April 20, 1944, which was also Adolf Hitler's birthday, Robinson presented her with a corsage made of one hundred dollars' worth of war savings stamps, accompanied by a fond note. "To my dear friend and companion Leila from her devoted Miss Martha," it read. "Something good happened on this day for you sort of offset Schickelgruber." MGR Papers.

80. "Robinson Home Journal," November 2, 1944.

81. Ibid., September 18, 1944, September 23, 1944.

82. Ibid., February 11, 1945.

83. Ibid., June 23, 1944; MGR to Natalie Scott, February 22, 1947, in Scott Papers.

84. MGR to Robert G. Robinson, September 26, 1939; MGR to "Mousa" [her mother], September 13, 1939; both in MGR Papers. Pamela Robinson Plater, interview by author, Thibodaux, La., March 10, 1985.

85. MGR to Natalie Scott, February 22, 1947, in Scott Papers; "Robinson Home Journal," May 17, 1945.

86. D'Ann Campbell's research reveals that the Red Cross had more volunteer women than it needed but felt obligated to provide "work" for them to do rather than risk offending anyone. "The most spectacular waste of volunteer time," she writes, "was the Production Corps, which attracted 4 or 5 million women. Their job was to hand-knit millions of garments for soldiers and to roll billions of surgical dressings. The Red Cross vehemently denied that machines could do this job." Campbell, *Women at War with America* (Cambridge: Harvard University Press, 1984), 69.

87. Postcard, Scrapbook 2-A, in NOLWV Papers, Tulane; MGR to Maidie Nason, June 17, 1945, NOLWV Papers, Tulane.

88. Keller, "League of Women Voters," 11.

89. Ruth H. Preston to Helen Semmerling, NLWV office, March 9, 1943, NLWV Papers.

90. Jeanne Blythe to Anna Lord Strauss, NLWV president, undated field report, c. 1946, NLWV Papers.

91. *New Orleans States,* February 17, 1945.

92. Lemons, *Woman Citizen*, 245 n. 10.

93. *New Orleans Times-Picayune*, July 15, 1943; *New Orleans Item*, July 18, 1943.

94. Sarah Heath Sharpe, interview by author, New Orleans, May 7, 1985.

95. Louisiana LWV board minutes, December 3, 1943, and January 28, 1944, in NOLWV Papers, Tulane.

96. Ibid., July 19, 1943.

97. *Report of the Secretary of State*, 1943, 27, and 1945, 45.

98. William H. Chafe, *The American Woman: Her Changing Social, Economic, and Political Role, 1920-1970* (London: Oxford University Press, 1972), 33.

99. Lincoln Steffens, *The Shame of the Cities* (1904; New York: Sagamore Press, 1957), quoted in Richard Hofstadter, *The Age of Reform: From Bryan to F.D.R.* (New York: Alfred A. Knopf, 1955), 205, 208.

100. Typescript of MGR speech, undated (approximately one week after Pearl Harbor attack), MGR Papers.

101. *New Orleans Item*, February 18, 1943, February 19, 1943; *New Orleans Times-Picayune*, July 13, 1943, August 17, 1949. A letter to the editor, written in bad dialect and purporting to be from a Cajun, mocked the "high club ladys" who wanted to serve on juries and asserted that the writer's wife could not serve. "She got to bade and dress de chillens for school. She got to cook breakfast for me, pepere, and de chillens. She got housework to do too, and sew for de blessed Red Cross. You see, high club ladys got so much time dey kin go on jury." *New Orleans Item*, March 8, 1943.

102. Some topics of radio scripts presented on local stations by the NOLWV included "Forced Savings" (an exploration of compulsory bond buying as an anti-inflationary measure, with LWV members discussing pros and cons but taking no side), "O.P.A." (defense of rationing and price controls), "The New Isolationism" (criticism of those who felt World War II was being fought only because of the Pearl Harbor attack, had no interest in fascist ideology, and wanted to revert to isolation at war's end), and "Beyond Victory" (a script aimed at building support for the future United Nations after the war).

103. *New Orleans Times-Picayune*, December 15, 1943, and January 19, 1944.

104. *New Orleans Item*, August 16, 1944; *New Orleans Times-Picayune*, August 17, 1944; *New Orleans Item*, September 7, 1944.

105. MGR to Mrs. A. D. Tisdale, September 13, 1948, in NOLWV Papers, Tulane; minutes of Louisiana LWV board, December 3, 1943, and January 28, 1944, in NOLWV Papers, Tulane; *New Orleans Item*, February 21, 1944.

106. *New Orleans States*, May 13, 1944.

107. Ibid., February 17, 1945.

108. Ibid., April 9, 1944.

109. Norita K. Black to MGR, July 21, 1948, in MGR Papers.

110. Louise Meyer to Ruth H. Preston, November 13, 1943, in NOLWV Papers, Tulane.

111. MGR to Ruth H. Preston, November 18, 1943, in MGR Papers.

112. Quote from Keller, "League of Women Voters," 11; *New Orleans Times-Picayune*, July 8, 1952. Black voter registration actually showed a decline from 1950 to 1952 and another decline from 1952 to 1954. However, in the wake of the crucial *Smith v. Allwright* ruling in 1944, wherein the U.S. Supreme Court had outlawed the white primary, a clear trend toward greater black voter registration in Orleans Parish had begun. Black assertiveness and confidence grew steadily during the 1940s; at mid-decade, the New Orleans chapter of the NAACP boasted six thousand members. The overall trend was toward higher numbers of registered African-American voters, but the cause was the *Smith v. Allwright* ruling coupled with a more confident mood among African Americans, not the Louisiana statute concerning permanent registration. See Steven Lawson, *Black Ballots: Voting Rights in the South, 1944-1969* (New York: Columbia University Press, 1976).

113. Hollinger F. Barnard, ed., *Outside the Magic Circle: The Autobiography of Virginia Foster Durr* (University: University of Alabama Press, 1985), 120.

114. Thomas A. Krueger, *And Promises to Keep: The Southern Conference on Human Welfare, 1938-1948* (Nashville: Vanderbilt University Press, 1967), 22-23, 29-38, 124. See also Linda Reed, *Simple Decency and Common Sense: The Southern Conference Movement, 1938-1963* (Bloomington: Indiana University Press, 1991).

115. George B. Tindall, *The Emergence of the New South, 1913-1945* (Baton Rouge: Louisiana State University Press, 1967), 637.

116. Barnard, *Outside the Magic Circle*, 191.

117. Tindall, *New South*, 638.

118. Cleanth Brooks [Emily Blanchard's son-in-law] to Pamela Tyler, June 20, 1988.

119. Emily Blanchard to MGR, April 23, 1947, in NOLWV Papers, Tulane; Emily Blanchard to Rosa Keller, July 24, 1974, in Keller, "League of Women Voters," 3.

120. MGR to Ruth H. Preston, September 2, 1947, in NOLWV Papers, Tulane.

121. MGR to Kay Bates, September 3, 1947, in NOLWV Papers, Tulane.

122. Lemons, *Woman Citizen*, 120-21.

123. Walter Gellhorn, "Report on a Report of the House Committee on Un-American Activities," *Harvard Law Review* 60 (October 1947): 1221, 1233.

124. Ruth H. Preston to MGR, January 28, 1948, in NOLWV Papers, Tulane.

125. Krueger, *Promises*, 184.

126. Jane W. Stubbs, secretary, Louisiana LWV, to Emily Blanchard, April 2, 1948, in NOLWV Papers, Tulane.

127. Emily Blanchard to Rosa Keller, quoted in Keller, "League of Women Voters," 3.

128. Ruth Dreyfous, interviews by author, New Orleans, October 30, 1983, and June 16, 1988; Ruth Hamill (Ms. Stanley) Preston, telephone interview by author, October 15, 1983.

129. Mrs. A. D. Tisdale, "Field Report," May 22, 1948, in NOLWV Papers, Tulane.

130. Annual report for 1948, NOLWV Papers, Tulane; Helen Fox, "Vital Statistics of L.W.V. Board Members," 1951, New Orleans League of Women Voters Records, League of Women Voters office, 534 Loyola Avenue, New Orleans (hereafter cited as "NOLWV HQ Papers").

131. MGR, "A Summary of the Reports to the Membership of the Officers and Directors of the League of Women Voters of Orleans," April 22, 1950, NOLWV HQ Papers; Mathilde (Mrs. George) Dreyfous, interview by author, New Orleans, March 10, 1989.

132. MGR to Ruth H. Preston, January 24, 1944, in NOLWV Papers, Tulane.

133. Ruth H. Preston to Helen Semmerling, March 9, 1943, in NLWV Papers.

134. Arnold R. Hirsch, "New Orleans: Sunbelt in the Swamp," in *Sunbelt Cities: Politics and Growth since World War II*, ed. Richard M. Bernard and Bradley R. Rice (Austin: University of Texas Press, 1983), 118.

135. MGR to Mrs. A. D. Tisdale, July 15, 1948, in NOLWV Papers, Tulane.

136. Rae R. Horner to Anna Lord Strauss, president, NLWV, October 2-16, 1948 (field report from Louisiana), NLWV Papers; MGR, Annual Report, April 22, 1950, NLWV Papers.

137. Susan Ware, "American Women in the 1950s: Nonpartisan Politics and Women's Politicization," in *Women, Politics, and Change*, ed. Louise Tilly and Patricia Gurin (New York: Russell Sage Foundation, 1990), 287-88.

138. William L. O'Neill, *American High: The Years of Confidence, 1945-1960* (New York: Free Press, 1986), 158-66.

139. MGR, Annual Report, 1948, NOLWV Papers, Tulane.

140. Rosa Keller, quoted in Linn Foster, "The League of Women Voters: Political Impact on New Orleans, 1942-1952" (honors' thesis, Tulane University, 1983), 26.

141. Quoted in Hall, *Revolt against Chivalry*, 55.

CHAPTER 4: THE PLEASURES OF PARTISAN POLITICS

1. Henry Luce, ed., *Time Capsule/1939: A History of the Year Condensed from the Pages of Time* (New York: Time-Life Books, 1968).

2. Harnett T. Kane, *Louisiana Hayride: The American Rehearsal for Dictatorship, 1928-1940* (New York: William Morrow & Co., 1941), 337; *New York Times*, July 23, 1939, August 6, 1939; L. Vaughn Howard, "Civil Service Development in Louisiana," *Tulane Studies in Political Science* 3 (1954): 69.

3. V. O. Key, Jr., *Southern Politics in State and Nation* (New York: Alfred A. Knopf, 1950), 156.

4. Joseph B. Parker, *The Morrison Era: Reform Politics in New Orleans* (Gretna, La.: Pelican, 1974), 18.

5. Jerry Purvis Sanson, "Sam Jones, Jimmie Noe, and the Reform Alliance, 1940-1942," *Louisiana History* 27 (Summer 1986): 239-48.

6. Lindy Boggs, with Katherine Hatch, *Washington through a Purple Veil: Memoirs of a Southern Woman* (New York: Harcourt, Brace & Co., 1994), 62–63; Mary M. Morrison, interview by author, New Orleans, September 6, 1986, and July B. (Mrs. Arthur) Waters, interview by author, New Orleans, March 6, 1985; *New Orleans Item,* January 29, 1946.

7. Mary M. Morrison, interviews by author, September 6, 1986, and New Orleans, September 15, 1988.

8. *New Orleans Times-Picayune,* February 4, 1940. They worked without Martha Gilmore Robinson, whose emphasis on nonpartisanship meant that as head of the Woman Citizens' Union, she would not endorse a candidate, though personally she also strongly favored Sam Jones. "Lord preserve me from partisan politics—reform or otherwise," she once wrote. "I'll always work for principles and policies—never for candidates." MGR to Emily Blanchard, undated [1942], in NLWV Papers.

9. Allan P. Sindler, *Huey Long's Louisiana: State Politics, 1920–1952* (Baltimore: Johns Hopkins University Press, 1956), 56–57.

10. Lindy Boggs, interview by author, New Orleans, August 17, 1988.

11. *New Orleans Times-Picayune,* December 24, 1939.

12. Mary M. Morrison, interview by author, September 6, 1986. The mere act of registering to vote often proved almost absurdly complex if the registrar chose to make it so. Mary Morrison recalled going to the registrar's office three times to register herself. "He kept telling me, 'You've made a mistake here.' Well, I asked him, 'What mistake have I made?' He said, 'Well, we can't tell you that. That's for you to find out.'"

This experience is echoed by Virginia Foster Durr, another southern white woman whose efforts to register in Virginia during the same period ran afoul of similar intransigence. Voter registrars served at the pleasure of the incumbent political machine and realized that a small, easily controlled electorate worked to the advantage of the faction in office; they perpetuated the existence of the small electorate by throwing obstacles in the path of would-be voters, particularly if the prospective voters seemed antimachine. Hollinger F. Barnard, ed., *Outside the Magic Circle: The Autobiography of Virginia Foster Durr* (University: University of Alabama Press, 1985), 177–78. See also Edward F. Haas, *DeLesseps S. Morrison and the Image of Reform: New Orleans Politics, 1946–1961* (Baton Rouge: Louisiana State University Press, 1974), 27.

Louisiana maintained its extremely complex system of registration until the passage of the Voting Rights Act of 1965. Before 1965, registering involved completing a two-page questionnaire unassisted (with the registrar forbidden by law to explain where mistakes, if any, were made), answering queries about one's private life (whether one had fathered or given birth to an illegitimate child, for example), reading aloud from the Preamble to the Constitution and writing it as the registrar dictated a passage, and answering correctly four of six far-from-elementary questions about government. A sample question: "The President of the United States can be impeached and removed from office after a trial by A. the U.S. Supreme Court; B. the U.S. Senate; C. a vote of the people." From "League of Women Voters of New Orleans Aids to Registration," January 1965, unpaginated, Louisiana Collection Vertical File, Howard-Tilton Memorial Library, Tulane University.

13. *New Orleans Times-Picayune,* February 4, 1940.

14. Mary M. Morrison, interview by author, September 6, 1986.

15. Boggs with Hatch, *Purple Veil,* 65.

16. *New Orleans Times-Picayune,* February 4, 1940; July B. (Mrs. Arthur) Waters, interview by author, New Orleans, August 3, 1984, and Mary M. Morrison, interview by author, September 6, 1986.

17. Mary M. Morrison, interview by author, September 6, 1986.

18. *New Orleans Times-Picayune,* January 11, 1940, January 15, 1940. Concerning blacks and southern politics in the first half of the twentieth century, V. O. Key's analysis is succinct and to the point. "In its grand outline, the politics of the South revolves around the Negro. It is at times interpreted as a politics of cotton, as a politics of free trade, as a politics of agrarian poverty, or as a politics of planter and plutocrat. Although such interpretations have a superficial validity, in the last analysis the major peculiarities of southern politics go back to the Negro. Whatever phase of the southern political process one seeks to understand, sooner or later the trail of inquiry leads to the Negro." Key, *Southern Politics,* 5.

19. *New Orleans Times-Picayune,* January 30, 1940; MGR to U.S. attorney general Robert H. Jackson, undated (probably January 1940), MGR Papers.

20. Kane, *Louisiana Hayride,* 434.

21. *New Orleans Times-Picayune,* January 16, 1940.

22. Ibid., February 4, 1940.

23. Author's interviews with Mary M. Morrison (September 6, 1986) and July B. Waters (August 3, 1984); Carolyn Gay Labouisse, interview by author, New Orleans, September 10, 1985.

24. Boggs with Hatch, *Purple Veil,* 68. Boggs reports that when she was serving in Congress, she heard Strom Thurmond offer the same advice about the value of orange juice to Ted Kennedy as they planned a filibuster.

25. Mary M. Morrison, interview by author, September 6, 1986.

26. *New Orleans Times-Picayune,* January 17, 1940. Morrison's encounter became the stuff of legend. Decades later, a friend of Morrison's who was herself a participant in the anti-Long political effort told reporters that Mary Morrison had been attacked by "goons" while defending honest elections at the polls. See also Boggs with Hatch, *Purple Veil,* 68, for the former congresswoman's account of the incident.

27. Author's interviews with Mary M. Morrison (September 6, 1986) and July B. Waters (March 6, 1985); William B. Monroe Jr., "Women with a Broom," *Ladies Home Journal* (May 1946): 34; Boggs with Hatch, *Purple Veil,* 67–69.

28. *New Orleans Times-Picayune,* January 17, 1940.

29. Iris Kelso and Rosemary James, "When the Caucus Ruled the World," *New Orleans* (May 1971): 23.

30. *New Orleans Times-Picayune,* January 23, 1940, and February 18, 1940.

31. *New Orleans Times-Picayune,* January 17, 1940; *New Orleans States,* January 17, 1940.

32. Sanson, "Sam Jones," 241. In 1940, the Republican Party had no strength to speak of in the state of Louisiana. The general election counted as merely a pro forma exercise in democracy, since the candidate who won the Democratic Party's nomination would be governor. The factionalism between the Longs and the anti-Longs was the closest thing to a two-party system in Louisiana until the emergence of the real thing in the 1950s. For discussions of Louisiana's bifactionalism as a substitute for a two-party system, see Key, *Southern Politics,* 168–82; Perry H. Howard, *Political Tendencies in Louisiana, 1812–1952* (Baton Rouge: Louisiana State University Press, 1957), 124–56; Allan P. Sindler, "Bifactional Rivalry as an Alternative to Two-Party Competition in Louisiana," *American Political Science Review* 49 (September 1955): 641–62.

33. July B. Waters, interview by author, August 3, 1984.

34. *New Orleans Times-Picayune,* January 21, 1940.

35. Ibid., February 22, 1940.

36. Ibid., February 21, 1940; Kane, *Louisiana Hayride,* 454; author's interviews with July B. Waters (August 3, 1984), Mary M. Morrison (September 6, 1986), and Carolyn Gay Labouisse; Sarah Heath Sharp, interview by author, New Orleans, May 7, 1985; Gerda Weissman Klein, *A Passion for Sharing: The Life of Edith Rosenwald Stern* (Chappaqua, N.Y.: Rossel Books, 1984), 168–69.

37. July B. Waters, interview by author, March 6, 1985.

38. Victory telegrams, Sam Jones Papers, uncataloged, Howard-Tilton Memorial Library, Tulane University.

39. *New Orleans Times-Picayune,* February 4, 1940, and January 10, 1940.

40. *Independent Tenth Warder* 1 (January 1941), in July B. Waters Papers, privately held.

41. *Independent Tenth Warder* 2 (February 1941).

42. See Linda Kerber's important work *Women of the Republic: Intellect and Ideology in Revolutionary America* (Chapel Hill: University of North Carolina Press, 1980).

43. *Independent Tenth Warder* (February 1941).

44. *New Orleans Item,* February 21, 1946. Anne Firor Scott cites "the unwillingness of male politicians to promote women of independent mind and political skill." Scott, "After Suffrage: Southern Women in the Twenties," *Journal of Southern History* 30 (August 1964): 313.

45. A possibly apocryphal story that makes fun of the Old Regulars illustrates their legendary tendency to view everything through partisan lenses with emphasis on delivering goods for interest groups with the heaviest clout. Allegedly,

a group of women approached the mayor, an Old Regular, with a request that the city build the planned Municipal Auditorium in the form of a classic Greek temple, only to be told by His Honor that there were not enough Greeks in New Orleans to make such a venture worthwhile. Kane, *Louisiana Hayride*, 33.

46. T. Harry Williams, *Huey Long* (New York: Alfred A. Knopf, 1970), 848–54; Haas, *DeLesseps S. Morrison*, chap. 1.

47. Lindy Boggs, interview by author.

48. Mary M. Morrison, interview by author, September 6, 1986.

49. Walter Lippmann, *A Preface to Politics* (New York: Henry Holt, 1917), quoted in Henry Steele Commager, *The American Mind: An Interpretation of American Thought and Character since the 1880s* (New Haven: Yale University Press, 1950), 320.

50. Haas, *DeLesseps S. Morrison*, 29–30.

51. July B. (Mrs. Arthur) Waters, interview by author, New Orleans, May 11, 1984; Carolyn Gay Labouisse, interview by author.

52. Haas, *DeLesseps S. Morrison*, 4–5, 30–32.

53. *New Orleans States*, December 8, 1945.

54. Boggs with Hatch, *Purple Veil*, 98–99.

55. Parker, *Morrison Era*, 66; Haas, *DeLesseps S. Morrison*, 35; Jacob Morrison, interview by Edward Haas, September 18, 1970, tape housed in Special Collections, Howard-Tilton Memorial Library, Tulane University.

56. July B. Waters, interviews by author, August 3, 1984, and March 6, 1985.

57. Pamela Robinson Plater, interview by author, Thibodaux, La., March 10, 1985.

58. Kenneth P. O'Donnell and David F. Powers, with Joe McCarthy, *"Johnny We Hardly Knew Ye": Memories of John Fitzgerald Kennedy* (New York: Pocket Books, 1973), 60.

59. *New Orleans Times-Picayune*, December 12, 1945.

60. Author's interviews with July B. Waters (March 6, 1985), Carolyn Gay Labouisse, and Mary M. Morrison (September 6, 1986); Parker, *Morrison Era*, 85–86, 101.

61. Carolyn Gay Labouisse, interview by author; undated cartoon from *New Orleans Times-Picayune*, July B. Waters Papers.

62. *New Orleans States*, December 17, 1945; *Report of the Secretary of State*, 1947, 22, insert B.

63. *New Orleans States*, numerous issues in December 1945.

64. *New Orleans Times-Picayune* and *New Orleans States*, January 20, 1946.

65. Frances Willard quoted in J. Stanley Lemons, *The Woman Citizen: Social Feminism in the 1920s* (Urbana: University of Illinois Press, 1973), 85; "The Editor's Page," *Ladies Home Journal* (March 1920); Klein, *Passion for Sharing*, 162.

66. John Gunther, *Inside U.S.A.* (New York: Harper & Brothers, 1946), 795.

67. Undated clipping in July B. Waters Papers.

68. *New Orleans Times-Picayune*, January 20, 1946.

69. July B. Waters, interview by author, August 3, 1984; Ralph G. Martin, "New Orleans Has Its Face Lifted," *New Republic*, June 2, 1947, 18.

70. Monroe, "Women with a Broom," 34.

71. *New Orleans States*, January 15, 1946; *New Orleans Times-Picayune*, January 23, 1946.

72. James H. Gillis, interview by author, New Orleans, January 24, 1986.

73. *New Orleans Times-Picayune*, January 23, 1946; Haas, *DeLesseps S. Morrison*, 26–27.

74. *New Orleans Times-Picayune*, January 23, 1946; Haas, *DeLesseps S. Morrison*, 26–27.

75. Haas, *DeLesseps S. Morrison*, 27.

76. *New Orleans Times-Picayune*, January 23, 1946; *New Orleans Item*, January 29, 1946.

77. *New Orleans Item*, August 12, 1948, in Scrapbook #5, DeLesseps S. Morrison Papers, Special Collections, Howard-Tilton Memorial Library, Tulane University (hereafter cited as "Morrison Papers, Tulane").

78. *Shreveport Times*, January 24, 1946; *Memphis Press-Scimitar*, February 1, 1946; *Christian Science Monitor*, January 30, 1946; all in July B. Waters Papers.

79. Charles P. Fenner to July B. Waters, January 23, 1946, in July B. Waters Papers.

80. *New Orleans Item*, January 29, 1946.

81. *New Orleans Times-Picayune*, February 20, 1946.

82. *New Orleans States*, February 21, 1946.

83. "Constitution," Independent Women's Organization, unpaginated, in July B. Waters Papers.

84. IWO Board of Governors minutes, June 27, 1946, in July B. Waters Papers. Members of the first board of governors of the IWO were, in addition to IWO president Waters, Mrs. Robert Baker, Bland Cox (Mrs. Logan) Bruns, Frances (Mrs. Francis) Demarest, Ida Weiss (Mrs. Joseph) Friend, Mrs. Lawrence Goodspeed, Catherine Labouisse, Catherine (Mrs. Edward) Moore, Mary Meek (Mrs. Jacob) Morrison, Mrs. Lionel G. Ott, Gladys (Mrs. J. W.) Reily, and Mrs. Gustave Ricau.

85. Carolyn Gay Labouisse, interview by author; appointment books, 1946, 1947, 1948, for Mayor deLesseps Morrison, in Morrison Papers, Tulane.

86. Parker, *Morrison Era*, 80–83, 93–94.

87. July B. Waters, interview by author, August 3, 1984, emphasis mine.

88. Haas, *DeLesseps S. Morrison*, 291 and passim.

89. Quoted in Peirce Lewis, *New Orleans: The Making of an Urban Landscape* (Cambridge: Ballinger, 1976), 14.

90. MGR, interview by Edward Haas, February 27, 1971, tape housed in Special Collections, Howard-Tilton Memorial Library, Tulane University.

91. *New Orleans Times-Picayune*, January 4, 1946; "The South: Creole Flush," *Newsweek*, June 10, 1946, 29; deLesseps S. Morrison quoted in "Covering Huey's Spoor," *Newsweek*, February 4, 1946, 28.

92. At this time, although illegal, gambling played a large role in Louisiana politics. Opposition to legalization of gambling in New Orleans came not only from the religious element but also from parish sheriffs, who feared that if legal gambling succeeded in the city, it might spread to their rural domains and cut off a significant source of their income, namely, their cut of the take at illicit roadhouses that operated in their parishes with their knowledge. Key, *Southern Politics*, 171–72. Quote from July B. Waters, interview by author, August 3, 1984.

93. July B. Waters, interview by author, March 6, 1985.

94. Appointment book for 1946, for Mayor deLesseps Morrison, in Morrison Papers, Tulane.

95. July Waters, IWO president, to Mayor deLesseps Morrison, May 21, 1946, July B. Waters Papers.

96. *New Orleans States*, March 22, 1946.

97. *New Orleans Item*, May 21, 1946; author's interviews with July B. Waters (August 3, 1984) and Carolyn Gay Labouisse.

98. The version of events that follows is agreed upon by two charter members of the IWO, Bland Cox Bruns and July B. Waters.

99. Carolyn Gay Labouisse, interview by Dorothy Schlesinger, January 31, 1983, tape housed at Special Collections, Howard-Tilton Memorial Library, Tulane University.

100. MGR, interview by Haas.

101. *New Orleans Times-Picayune*, April 14, 1947; *New Orleans Times-Picayune, Item, States*, April 16, 1947.

102. *New Orleans Times-Picayune*, August 24, 1948; *New Orleans States*, August 24, 1948, and September 5, 1948.

103. *New Orleans Times-Picayune*, January 20, 1948.

104. "Old Girl's New Boy," *Time*, November 29, 1947, 27. A study of upper-class women found that these women prefer volunteer work to paid work because the former is usually interesting, whereas they view the latter as dull. "Volunteerism is indeed a better arena than paid work for getting the kinds of work they want to do, and for getting into decision-making and leadership positions." Recognizing that her education had not prepared her for a sophisticated career, one woman is quoted as saying, "If I went into paid work, I would have to put up with a job too menial for me." Susan Ostrander, *Women of the Upper Class* (Philadelphia: Temple University Press, 1984), 118.

105. "Report on Schools," prepared by IWO members Mrs. Lucien Lamar, committee chair, Mrs. Charles Keller, Mrs. Robert Kottwitz, Mrs. Roger Sharp, and Mrs. William Wiedorn, May 8, 1946, in July B. Waters Papers.

106. Sarah Heath Sharp, interview by author.

107. IWO board minutes, September 19, 1946; IWO board minutes, October 18, 1946; both in July B. Waters Papers; *New Orleans Item,* November 7, 1946, in Scrapbook #1, Morrison Papers, Tulane.

108. *New Orleans Item,* October 15, 1946, in Scrapbook #1, Morrison Papers, Tulane; author's interviews with Sarah Heath Sharp and Carolyn Gay Labouisse.

109. *New Orleans Times-Picayune,* October 25, 1952.

110. Haas, *DeLesseps S. Morrison,* 170–71; Jacqueline T. Leonhard, "Good Schools Are Worth Fighting For," *American Magazine* (May 1955): 81; *New Orleans Item,* November 3, 1948; Sarah Heath Sharp, interview by author; Orleans Parish School Board minutes, vol. 32, April 21, 1950, 230–39, Archives–Special Collections, Earl K. Long Memorial Library, University of New Orleans. The schools had contracted for "all-meat wieners," but their supplier was delivering a product that was only 15 percent meat, the remainder composed of cereal filler.

111. Morton Inger, *Politics and Reality in an American City: The New Orleans School Crisis of 1960* (New York: Center for Urban Education, 1969), 15.

112. Leonhard, "Good Schools," 82–83; *New Orleans Times-Picayune,* October 27, 28, November 1, 1950.

113. Leonhard, "Good Schools," 82; *New Orleans Times-Picayune,* November 7, 1950.

114. Orleans Parish School Board minutes, vol. 32, December 8, 1950, 499–501, 515–16.

115. Haas, *DeLesseps S. Morrison,* 170–71; *New Orleans Times-Picayune,* October 24, 1952.

116. IWO resolution, July B. Waters Papers; *New Orleans Times-Picayune,* October 24, 1952.

117. *New Orleans Times-Picayune,* October 25, 1952.

118. Ibid., October 24, 25, November 4, 1952; Leonhard, "Good Schools," 83; Inger, *Politics and Reality,* 15–16.

119. *New Orleans Times-Picayune,* March 8, 1955; *New Orleans Item,* April 8, 1955; *New Orleans States,* March 1, 1955.

120. *New Orleans Item,* May 15, 1955; *New Orleans Times-Picayune,* May 15, 1955; *New Orleans States,* May 21, 1955.

121. *New Orleans Item,* November 24, 1955; *New Orleans Times-Picayune,* November 22, 1955; *New Orleans States,* December 19, 1955, and January 6, 1956; *New Orleans Item,* January 23, 1956; all clippings in IWO scrapbook on State Board of Education Controversy, in Special Collections, Howard-Tilton Memorial Library, Tulane University.

122. July B. Waters, interview by author, August 3, 1984.

123. Barnard, *Outside the Magic Circle,* 27, 42.

CHAPTER 5: "THE CITY FATHERS NEED A MOTHER"

1. Classic expressions of the postwar antifeminist attitude include Marynia Farnham and Ferdinand Lundberg, *Modern Woman: The Lost Sex* (New York: Harper, 1947), and Philip Wylie, *Generation of Vipers* (New York: Rinehart, 1942). For analysis of this antifeminist message in popular culture, see Betty Friedan, *The Feminine Mystique* (New York: W. W. Norton & Co., 1963).

General background on this phenomenon can be found in William Chafe, *The Paradox of Change: American Women in the Twentieth Century* (New York: Oxford University Press, 1991), Nancy Woloch, *Women and the American Experience* (New York: Alfred A. Knopf, 1984), and Leila Rupp and Verta Taylor, *Survival in the Doldrums: The American Women's Rights Movement, 1945 to the 1960s* (New York: Oxford University Press, 1987).

2. Susan Ware, "American Women in the 1950s: Nonpartisan Politics and Women's Politicization," in *Women, Politics, and Change*, ed. Louise Tilly and Patricia Gurin (New York: Russell Sage Foundation, 1990), 290. Joanne Meyerowitz offers a brilliant challenge to the idea that fifties women were imprisoned in domesticity. Meyerowitz, "Beyond the Feminine Mystique: A Reassessment of Mass Postwar Culture, 1946–1958," *Journal of American History* 79 (March 1993): 1455–82. See also Eugenia Kaledin, *Mothers and More: American Women in the 1950s* (Boston: Twayne, 1984), and Elaine Tyler May, *Homeward Bound: American Families in the Cold War Era* (New York: Basic Books, 1988).

3. Meyerowitz, "Beyond the Feminine Mystique," 1468 nn. 35 and 36.

4. *New Orleans Times-Picayune*, January 25, 1950, October 11, 1951, December 7, 1951, March 13, 1952; Edward F. Haas, *DeLesseps S. Morrison and the Image of Reform: New Orleans Politics, 1946–1961* (Baton Rouge: Louisiana State University Press, 1974), 108.

5. Joseph B. Parker, *The Morrison Era: Reform Politics in New Orleans* (Gretna, La.: Pelican, 1974), 62–112; Haas, *DeLesseps S. Morrison*, 84–88.

6. James H. Gillis, interview by author, New Orleans, January 24, 1986, and Fred J. Cassibry, interview by author, New Orleans, January 19, 1989.

7. Parker, *Morrison Era*, 80; Haas, *DeLesseps S. Morrison*, 83.

8. Annual Report of the Mayor, 1952–53, copy in author's possession.

9. Haas, *DeLesseps S. Morrison*, 177–217, 290–91; author's interviews with James H. Gillis and Fred J. Cassibry; Ruth Sullivan, interview by Edward Haas, March 6, 1971, and Thomas Brahney, interview by Edward Haas, January 30, 1971, tapes housed in Special Collections, Howard-Tilton Memorial Library, Tulane University. See in particular Haas's account of police corruption in New Orleans and the efforts of Morrison to undercut investigations of the police department in chap. 10, "The Police Scandals," and the papers of the Special Citizens' Investigating Commission, Howard-Tilton Memorial Library, Tulane University.

10. New Orleans municipal affairs had previously been subject to legislative control, with Baton Rouge lawmakers empowered to regulate even the most

minute details of city governance. Whenever a Long occupied the statehouse, the compliant legislature had directed outbursts of punitive populism at the helpless city. The zenith of legislative meddling with New Orleans affairs came during the special session of July 1935, when Huey Long tightened his grip on the nearly prostrate city with the passage of a bill that deprived New Orleans of two-thirds of its annual revenues. In 1948, a second "rape of New Orleans" ensued at the direction of newly elected governor Earl Long, who also engineered the passage of bills that reduced the city's revenue base and increased expenses. T. Harry Williams, *Huey Long* (New York: Alfred A. Knopf, 1970), 850-51; Haas, *DeLesseps S. Morrison*, 124-29.

11. Charter commission members and the organizations that nominated them were state senator Robert Ainsworth Jr., Loyola University; Denis Barry, Young Men's Business Club; Moise Dennery, Louisiana Civil Service League; A. P. Harvey, AFL Central Trades and Labor Council; Lester Lautenschlager, Chamber of Commerce; Harry McCall, New Orleans Bar Association; Dr. Eugene Nabors, Tulane University; Martha Gilmore Robinson, New Orleans League of Women Voters; Edgar B. Stern, Bureau of Governmental Research; Robert W. Stevens, CIO; and Clifton Ganus and Ralph Nolan, New Orleans Commission Council. *New Orleans Times-Picayune*, February 1, 1951.

12. Bureau of Governmental Research, *A Summary of the Bureau's Recommendations for Improved Government in New Orleans. As Submitted to the Mayor and Commission Council March–July 1946* (New Orleans: Bureau of Governmental Research, 1946); James H. Gillis, interview by author.

13. Harry McCall, radio script, December 14, 1953, in MGR Papers.

14. Haas, *DeLesseps S. Morrison*, 166-67; James H. Gillis, interview by author.

15. July B. (Mrs. Arthur) Waters, interview by author, New Orleans, August 3, 1984, and Carolyn Gay Labouisse, interview by author, New Orleans, September 10, 1985. The anecdote about John Kennedy's version of Lyndon Johnson's acceptance of the vice presidential nomination is from Arthur Schlesinger Jr., *A Thousand Days: John F. Kennedy in the White House* (Boston: Houghton-Mifflin, 1965), 48.

16. A little more than a decade ago, Ruth Mandel found League of Women Voters participation a primary path by which women entered politics to seek elective office. "Very frequently, and all over the country, one hears political women echoing the remark, 'I got my training in the League of Women Voters.'" Mandel, *In the Running: Women as Political Candidates* (New Haven: Ticknor & Fields, 1981), 137.

17. *New Orleans Times-Picayune*, October 9, 1953.

18. C. W. Robinson, interview by author, New Orleans, August 5, 1985; Samuel Gilmore Robinson, interview by author, New Orleans, August 5, 1985; Pamela Robinson Plater, interview by author, Thibodaux, La., March 10, 1985. C. W. Robinson recalled his father saying resignedly, "It looks like she's gonna do this thing—and we've gotta support her." Mayor Martin Behrman wrote of Samuel

Gilmore, "He was one of my best friends and wisest advisors and counsellors." Martin Behrman, *Martin Behrman of New Orleans: Memoirs of a City Boss,* edited and with an introduction by John R. Kemp (Baton Rouge: Louisiana State University Press, 1977), 246.

19. Susan J. Carroll and Wendy S. Strimling, *Women's Routes to Elective Office: A Comparison with Men's: Report* (New Brunswick, N.J.: Center for the American Woman and Politics, 1983), cited in R. Darcy, S. Welch, and J. Clark, *Women, Elections, and Representation* (New York: Longman Press, 1987), 44 n. 18.

20. *New Orleans Times-Picayune,* January 24, 1954; Carolyn Gay Labouisse, interview by author.

21. Pamela Robinson Plater, interview by author; Haas, *DeLesseps S. Morrison,* 83; Thomas Brahney, interview by Haas, Fred J. Cassibry, interviews by Edward Haas, October 27, 1970, and July 1, 1971, and Jacob Morrison, interview by Edward Haas, September 18, 1970, all tapes at Howard-Tilton Memorial Library, Tulane University; Natalie Scott to MGR, November 20, 1953, in Natalie Scott Papers, Howard-Tilton Memorial Library, Tulane University.

22. Haas, *DeLesseps S. Morrison,* 166–67; author's interviews with James H. Gillis and Fred J. Cassibry.

23. Thomas Brahney, interview by Haas.

24. Carolyn Gay Labouisse, interview by author; July B. (Mrs. Arthur) Waters, interview by author, New Orleans, March 6, 1985; Mary M. Morrison, interview by author, New Orleans, September 15, 1988; Thomas Brahney, interview by Haas.

25. Author's interviews with Carolyn Gay Labouisse, July B. Waters, and James H. Gillis; Mary M. Morrison, interview by author, New Orleans, September 6, 1986; *Report of the Secretary of State,* 1955, insert #1 after p. 28.

26. MGR radio script, December 7, 1953, in MGR Papers; Cassibry, interview by Haas (October 27, 1970); author's interviews with James H. Gillis and Fred J. Cassibry.

27. Haas, *DeLesseps S. Morrison,* 85; Parker, *Morrison Era,* 78.

28. Among the members of the Cold Water Committee were Gervais Favrot, Darwin S. Fenner, Lester Kabacoff, Harry Kelleher, Charles Keller, Herman Kohlmeyer, John P. Labouisse, and Arthur C. Waters. Women sometimes cited as members of the powerful group were Bland C. Bruns, Gladys W. Reily, and Edith R. Stern, all of whom were members of the Independent Women's Organization. Parker, *Morrison Era,* 92–93, 143–44.

29. Author's interviews with Carolyn Gay Labouisse, July B. Waters (March 6, 1985), and Mary M. Morrison (September 6, 1986); Carolyn Gay Labouisse, interview by Dorothy Schlesinger, January 31, 1983, tape housed at Special Collections, Howard-Tilton Memorial Library, Tulane University; Haas, *DeLesseps S. Morrison,* 175–76; Parker, *Morrison Era,* 93.

30. Haas, *DeLesseps S. Morrison,* 175; author's interviews with James H. Gillis and Fred J. Cassibry.

31. July B. Waters, interview by author, March 6, 1985.

32. Parker, *Morrison Era*, 86.

33. Gregory Roberts, "What Ever Happened to Vic Schiro?" *Dixie Magazine, New Orleans Times-Picayune,* August 5, 1984, 11; Jim Amoss, "Victor H. Schiro: The Once and Always Mayor," *Lagniappe, New Orleans States-Item,* January 15, 1976, 8; Victor Schiro, interview by Edward Haas, September 29, 1970.

34. Ruth Sullivan, interview by Haas.

35. *New Orleans States,* January 5, 1954.

36. Fred J. Cassibry, interview by author.

37. Unidentified election memo, MGR Papers; author's interviews with July B. Waters (March 6, 1985), Carolyn Gay Labouisse, and Mary M. Morrison (September 15, 1988).

38. MGR radio script, December 7, 1953, in MGR Papers.

39. *New Orleans Times-Picayune,* February 9, 1954, in Scrapbook 15, Morrison Papers, Tulane.

40. MGR radio script, January 25, 1954, in MGR Papers.

41. Ibid., n.d. [early February 1954], MGR Papers.

42. *New Orleans Times-Picayune,* March 9, 1954.

43. MGR radio script, March 8, 1954, in MGR Papers.

44. *New Orleans States,* January 16, 1954.

45. Author's interviews with Pamela Robinson Plater, C. W. Robinson, and Samuel Gilmore Robinson; Ruth Hamill (Ms. Stanley) Preston, telephone interview by author, October 15, 1983.

46. Natalie Scott to MGR, September 6, 1953, in Scott Papers.

47. MGR campaign literature with photograph; anonymous special delivery letter to MGR, March 8, 1954; both in MGR papers.

48. Radio script (n.d.); radio script, March 5, 1954; both in MGR Papers. Robinson could have understood the feelings that animated Elizabeth Cady Stanton, who in 1857 wrote these words to Susan B. Anthony when she was forty-two years old: "Courage, Susan—this is my last baby, and she will be two years old in January. Two more years and—time will tell what! You and I have the prospect of a good long life. We shall not be in our prime before fifty, and after that we shall be good for twenty years at least." Quoted in Eleanor Flexner, *Century of Struggle: The Woman's Rights Movement in the United States* (Cambridge: Harvard University Press, Belknap Press, 1959), 89.

49. Unidentified campaign memos, n.d.; Naomi Damonte Marshall memo, n.d.; all in MGR Papers.

50. Joel G. Myers, "A Reputational Study of Women Leaders of New Orleans" (M.A. thesis, Tulane University, 1971), 53.

51. The fact that the IWO's Bland Cox Bruns held a post in the state legislature would seem to indicate that the New Orleans electorate had no problems with accepting a female candidate for office. However, Bruns won her seat by polling fewer than four thousand votes in a small district in which the IWO was entrenched and in which women constituted more than half the registered voters

in one of the two wards that constituted the district. Robinson's more difficult challenge involved drawing a majority of votes citywide, when only five of the seventeen wards had female majorities.

52. MGR radio script, March 5, 1954, MGR Papers.

53. Fred J. Cassibry, interview by author.

54. Margaret Mary ("Sunny"; Mrs. Victor) Schiro, interview by author, New Orleans, August 23, 1985.

55. Author's interviews with James H. Gillis, Margaret Mary Schiro, Fred J. Cassibry, Carolyn Gay Labouisse, and July B. Waters (March 6, 1985). In a dismissive comment that summed up her view of Schiro, Rosa Keller said of him, "Nice little man, but he never had an idea in his life." Rosa Keller, interview by author, New Orleans, November 4, 1983.

56. MGR radio script, March 8, 1954, in MGR Papers.

57. Radio script, January 18, 1954, in MGR Papers.

58. Ibid., December 14, 1953. Laura Clay of Kentucky had confided similar sentiments to the secrecy of her diary in 1864: "I am a woman, but I think I have a mind superior to that of many boys my age, and equal to that of many more. Therefore when we get to heaven we will be equal." Quoted in Anne Firor Scott, *The Southern Lady: From Pedestal to Politics, 1830–1930* (Chicago: University of Chicago Press, 1970), 175.

59. *New Orleans Item,* January 17, 1954; *New Orleans States,* January 24, 1954; *New Orleans Times-Picayune,* January 25, 1954; paid advertisement in *Times-Picayune,* March 7, 1954.

60. Haas, *DeLesseps S. Morrison,* 251.

61. *Louisiana Weekly,* January 2, 1954, and January 23, 1954; Mrs. Thornhill's radio script, January 23, 1954, in MGR Papers; *New Orleans States,* January 8 and 17, 1954.

62. *New Orleans States,* January 17, 1954.

63. Nora Towles Marsh, "The Story of a Good Citizen: Sarah Towles Reed" (n.d.), 11 pp., Earl K. Long Library, University of New Orleans; Orleans Parish School Board minutes, vol. 31, August 26 and 27, 1948, 351–54, Earl K. Long Library, University of New Orleans.

64. A. J. Liebling, *The Earl of Louisiana* (Baton Rouge: Louisiana State University Press, 1970), 160–61.

65. Williams, *Huey Long,* 851–54. Of the Old Regular organization in its heyday, Williams writes appreciatively that it "controlled the registration office and padded the rolls generously, with the names of dead people, imaginary people, and people who had moved elsewhere. It paid the poll taxes of large numbers of indigents and voted them in blocs. It controlled the selection of commissioners, who could often determine the outcome of an election in a close ward. Commissioners policed the polls, challenged the voters who were expected to vote wrong, and made sure that their people voted right" (189).

See also Perry H. Howard, *Political Tendencies in Louisiana, 1812–1952* (Baton

Rouge: Louisiana State University Press, 1957), 107, 154, 164; and George M. Reynolds, *Machine Politics in New Orleans, 1897–1926* (New York: Columbia University Press, 1936).

66. Liebling, *Earl of Louisiana*, 51; Haas interviews with Fred J. Cassibry (October 27, 1970) and Thomas Brahney; Fred J. Cassibry, interview by author.

67. The congressman was F. Edward Hebert, quoted in Arnold R. Hirsch, "New Orleans: Sunbelt in the Swamp," in *Sunbelt Cities: Politics and Growth since World War II*, ed. Richard M. Bernard and Bradley R. Rice (Austin: University of Texas Press, 1983), 122; Haas, *DeLesseps S. Morrison*, 291.

68. Carolyn Gay Labouisse, interview by author.

69. Haas interviews with Sullivan, Brahney, and Cassibry (October 27, 1970); James H. Gillis, interviews by Edward Haas, August 24, 1970, and March 9, 1971, tapes housed at Special Collections, Howard-Tilton Memorial Library, Tulane University.

70. Liebling, *Earl of Louisiana*, 181.

71. *New Orleans Times-Picayune*, January 24, 1954.

72. *New Orleans Item, New Orleans Times-Picayune*, January 26, 1954; *Times-Picayune*, March 6, 1954; author's interviews with James H. Gillis, Carolyn Gay Labouisse, and Mary M. Morrison (September 15, 1988).

73. Scott Wilson to Gervais Favrot, January 30, 1954, in Scott Wilson Papers, Special Collections, Howard-Tilton Memorial Library, Tulane University (hereafter cited as "Wilson Papers"); Carolyn Gay Labouisse, interview by author; MGR, interview by Edward Haas, February 27, 1971, tape housed in Special Collections, Howard-Tilton Memorial Library, Tulane University.

74. *New Orleans Times-Picayune*, January 27, 1954; *New Orleans States*, February 12, 1954. Martha Robinson's husband R. G. Robinson wrote a heated letter to the Louisiana Civil Service League president to protest the situation with the firemen but received a response from him stating that although Morrison's "action was ill-advised," there was "no basis to justify prosecution." R. G. Robinson to Ralph Pons, March 11, 1954, and Ralph Pons to R. G. Robinson, March 15, 1954, in MGR Papers.

75. Bland Bruns to MGR, n.d. [January 1954]; unidentified memo to MGR; both in MGR Papers.

76. Scott Wilson to Gervais Favrot, January 30, 1954, in Wilson Papers; author's interviews with C. W. Robinson and Margaret Mary Schiro.

77. *New Orleans Times-Picayune*, January 24 and 31, 1954; *New Orleans States*, January 27, 1954.

78. *New Orleans Times-Picayune*, January 30, 1954.

79. Dave McGuire to Scott Wilson, "Personal," January 27, 1954, in Wilson Papers.

80. *New Orleans Times-Picayune*, January 30, 1954.

81. *New Orleans Item, New Orleans States*, February 3, 1954; Fred J. Cassibry, interview by author.

82. Fred J. Cassibry, interview by author.

83. Author's interviews with Pamela Robinson Plater and C. W. Robinson.

84. *New Orleans States*, February 18, 1954; *New Orleans Times-Picayune*, February 23, 1954.

85. *New Orleans Times-Picayune*, February 23, 1954.

86. Author's interviews with Fred J. Cassibry, Pamela Robinson Plater, and James H. Gillis; Cassibry, interview by Haas.

87. *New Orleans Times-Picayune*, February 28, 1954.

88. Dave McGuire to Scott Wilson, March 3, 1954, in Morrison Papers, Tulane.

89. MGR letter to voters, March 5, 1954, in MGR Papers.

90. *New Orleans States, New Orleans Times-Picayune*, March 10, 1954.

91. Rosalie Brenner Grad, interview by Edward Haas, n.d., tape housed in Special Collections, Howard-Tilton Memorial Library, Tulane University.

92. Henry May, *The End of American Innocence: A Study of the First Years of Our Own Time, 1912–1917* (Chicago: Quadrangle Books, 1959), 27–28.

93. July B. Waters, interview by author, March 6, 1985.

94. After the first primary, an unidentified adviser had warned Robinson against attacking the mayor. "MR. MORRISON HAS JUST BEEN GIVEN A TREMENDOUS VOTE OF CONFIDENCE BY THE PEOPLE AND MR. MORRISON HAS APPOINTMENTS AND JOBS TO GIVE OUT. IT WOULD BE STRATEGICALLY UNWISE TO ATTACK HIM." Memo in MGR papers.

95. Dave McGuire to deLesseps Morrison, March 15, 1954, in Morrison Papers, Tulane.

CHAPTER 6: IN TWO WORLDS

1. Helen Fuller, "New Orleans Knows Better," *New Republic*, February 16, 1959, 14–17; Joseph Logsdon and Caryn C. Bell, "The Americanization of Black New Orleans, 1850–1900," in *Creole New Orleans: Race and Americanization*, ed. Arnold R. Hirsch and Joseph Logsdon (Baton Rouge: Louisiana State University Press, 1992), 208; Virginia Young Collins, quoted in Kim Lacy Rogers, "Humanity and Desire" (Ph.D. diss., University of Minnesota, 1982), 67; Edward F. Haas, *DeLesseps S. Morrison and the Image of Reform: New Orleans Politics, 1946–1961* (Baton Rouge: Louisiana State University Press, 1974), 252–53.

2. U.S. Department of Commerce, *Census of the Population: 1950*, vol. 2, part 18 (Louisiana) (Washington, D.C.: U.S. Government Printing Office, 1952); Adam Fairclough, *Race and Democracy: The Civil Rights Struggle in Louisiana, 1915–1972* (Athens: University of Georgia Press, 1995), 149–50.

A letter to Mayor Chep Morrison provides a vivid example of the police brutality. The correspondent related an incident in the French Quarter in which "a decrepit, bloat-faced, bleary-eyed policeman" abused a blameless shoeshine boy, calling him "black bastard" and kicking the contents of his shoeshine box down the storm drain and banging the wooden box until it splintered into pieces. "He was never provoked in any way," the writer noted, adding, "I could have cried for shame and fury." An investigation confirmed the incident but earned the offending officer only a transfer to another, less public beat. Mrs. Armand St. Martin to deLesseps Morrison, June 5, 1956, and deLesseps Morrison to Mrs. St. Martin, June 22, 1956, in Morrison Papers, New Orleans Public Library.

In the mid-1950s, the parish school superintendent admitted that 9,214 black children were being platooned and receiving only a half day of school because of overcrowding, whereas no white children experienced platooning. Indeed, some white schools were underpopulated. *Louisiana Weekly,* October 6, 1956.

3. Robert J. Norrell, *Reaping the Whirlwind: The Civil Rights Movement in Tuskegee* (New York: Alfred A. Knopf, 1985), 108.

4. Many observers have noted the tendency of whites of a half century ago to rationalize away the problem of race relations, or even to fail to acknowledge it altogether. See Gunnar Myrdal, *An American Dilemma* (New York: McGraw-Hill, 1964), 30–32 and passim; Benjamin Mays, "Plea for Straight Talk between the Races," *Atlantic* 206 (December 1960): 85; Edith R. Stern, "Riddle of the Race Riots," undated typed manuscript, Collection M667, Howard-Tilton Memorial Library, Tulane University; Joan Bahm to Anita Morrison, November 25, 1946, Morrison Papers, Tulane; Fairclough, *Race and Democracy,* 80–81; Howard W. Odum, *Race and Rumors of Race* (Chapel Hill: University of North Carolina Press, 1943).

5. Morton Sosna, *In Search of the Silent South: Southern Liberals and the Race Issue* (New York: Columbia University Press, 1977), viii. Obviously influenced by Gunnar Myrdal's ideas on creed versus deed, Daniel C. Thompson, an African-American sociologist and a close student of race relations in his native New Orleans, observed that white liberals "maintain that all persons, regardless of race, religion, or national origin, should have equal opportunities to develop to the fullest extent . . . unhampered by laws or traditions. Therefore, no matter how difficult or unpleasant . . . the liberal insists that the basic principle of the American Creed—equality of citizenship—should never be compromised." Thompson, *The Negro Leadership Class* (Englewood Cliffs, N.J.: Prentice-Hall, 1963), 70–71.

6. Glen Jeansonne, *Leander Perez: Boss of the Delta* (Baton Rouge: Louisiana State University Press, 1977), 220; *New Orleans Times-Picayune,* May 18, 1956; Rogers, "Humanity and Desire," 119–20; Rosa Keller, interview by author, New Orleans, November 4, 1983.

Based on the denunciations of the Urban League and specific references to its policies made at the Citizens' Council rally, it was apparent that someone in the Citizens' Council was privy to virtually everything being discussed in Urban League board meetings. Not knowing the source of the leak, Keller and the Urban League decided to cease mailing copies of minutes to board members. Urban League minutes, June 25, 1956, Giles Hubert Papers, Amistad Research Center, Tulane.

7. The concept of an "invisible career" is developed by Arlene Kaplan Daniels in a splendid study of affluent women and their volunteer work. See Daniels, *Invisible Careers: Women Civic Leaders from the Volunteer World* (Chicago: University of Chicago Press, 1988).

8. Cash asserts that in the decades leading up to the Civil War, the South's increasing intolerance of dissent led to a "strait-jacket conformity" in the region, from which "it was but an easy step to interpreting every criticism of the South on whatever score as disloyalty—to making such criticism so dangerous that none but a madman would risk it." This universal smothering of dissent, questioning, and criticism of southern institutions and practices by southerners Cash labels "the savage ideal." During Reconstruction and after, intolerance reigned supreme, accompanied by a demand for conformity of opinion. His description of the epithet commonly employed for a dissenter in the Reconstruction years, "a damned nigger-loving scoundrel in league with the enemy," is an eerie echo of words flung at Keller in the 1950s. W. J. Cash, *The Mind of the South* (New York: Vintage Books, 1941), 91–94, 137–38.

9. Rosa Keller, interview by Kim Lacy Rogers, April 8, 1988, tape housed at Amistad Research Center, Tulane University.

10. Rosa Freeman Keller, untitled autobiographical manuscript, parts 9, 10, 11, ms. in author's (Tyler's) possession.

11. Ibid., parts 12 and 26; Carol Flake, *New Orleans: Behind the Masks of America's Most Exotic City* (New York: Grove Press, 1994), 80–81.

12. Rosa Keller, interview by author, November 4, 1983.

13. Rosa Keller, interview by Dorothy Schlesinger, July 7, 1977, transcript, 4–5, Special Collections, Howard-Tilton Memorial Library, Tulane University. W. E. B. Du Bois had noted the same situation fifty years earlier, when he commented, "It means so much to take a man by the hand and sit beside him, to look frankly into his eyes. . . . A social cigar or cup of tea together means more than legislative halls and magazine articles." Quoted in David Goldfield, *Black, White, and Southern: Race Relations and Southern Culture, 1940 to the Present* (Baton Rouge: Louisiana State University Press, 1991), 5. Lillian Smith echoed this sentiment, observing, "All the movements in the world, all the laws, the drives, the edicts will never do what personal relationships can do—and must do." Quoted in Anne Loveland, *Lillian Smith: A Southerner Confronting the South* (Baton Rouge: Louisiana State University Press, 1986), 43.

14. Numerous memoirs by white southern men and women record early lessons in segregation and discrimination. Lillian Smith wrote, "I do not remember how or when, but by the time I had learned that God is love, that Jesus is His Son and came to give us a more abundant life, that all men are brothers . . . I also knew that I was better than a Negro, that all black folks have their place and . . . that a terrifying disaster would befall the South if I ever treated a Negro as my social equal." Smith, *Killers of the Dream* (New York: W. W. Norton & Co., 1949), 28. Ferrol Sams in *Run with the Horsemen* (Atlanta: Peachtree, 1982) and

Virginia Foster Durr in *Outside the Magic Circle: The Autobiography of Virginia Foster Durr,* ed. Hollinger F. Barnard (University: University of Alabama Press, 1985), express similar epiphanies.

15. YWCA board minutes, September 28, 1948, in New Orleans YWCA Papers, Howard-Tilton Memorial Library, Tulane University.

Lillian Smith, in articles written in 1948 and 1949, commented, "Hundreds, thousands of whites in the past six years have met with, worked with, eaten with Negroes in full friendship and democracy." She noted that often they did so secretly or "so quietly that next-door neighbors [were] not aware that Jim Crow [was] being flouted." Quoted in Loveland, *Lillian Smith,* 96. David Goldfield stresses "the particular connotations" that eating together held in the South's racial code. "To break bread together implied a rough equality," he writes. The integrated lunches that Keller endorsed and ate thus carried great symbolic importance for all who participated. Goldfield, *Black, White, and Southern,* 119.

16. Rosa Keller, interview by Rogers.

17. Arnold R. Hirsch, "Simply a Matter of Black and White: The Transformation of Race and Politics in Twentieth Century New Orleans," in Hirsch and Logsdon, *Creole New Orleans,* 208 and passim.

18. Sosna, *Silent South,* 38.

19. Thompson, *Negro Leadership Class,* 25–27; Fairclough, *Race and Democracy,* xiv.

20. Albert Dent to Miss Elizabeth Edwards, December 23, 1949, New Orleans Public Library correspondence, New Orleans Public Library, Central Branch. Emphasis mine. The prominent citizens who initiated the contact were Isaac Heller, John Minor Wisdom, and Charles Denechaud. Dent had provided them with facts regarding racial practices in public libraries of comparable southern cities. This is another example of white patrons acting in behalf of black clients to gain rights for them.

21. The correspondent's exact words invoking the presence of African Americans in his family burial plot as credentials for understanding race relations were: "Once I was told that perhaps I did not understand the negro and in reply I asked if the commentator had any buried in his graveyard plot, where our old Uncle Billy is buried with us in North Carolina and Mammy is buried next to my aunt, Mrs. Reynolds, in Frankfort, Kentucky, which makes me feel I know as much as the average philanthropist." George Westfeldt to John Hall Jacobs, Librarian, June 27, 1950, in "Librarian's Correspondence," New Orleans Public Library. Westfeldt flatly refused to meet with "these philanthropists" to discuss voluntary integration of the public libraries. Westfeldt to Jacobs, July 7, 1950.

22. Haas, *DeLesseps S. Morrison,* 73, 253; Rosa Keller, interview by author, New Orleans, June 11, 1990; Rogers, "Humanity and Desire," 85–90; Rosa Keller, interview by Schlesinger, 12–15. The mayor had been pressured since 1950 to use his influence with the library board to desegregate the libraries but had ducked the issue. See letters from Monte Lemann to Chep Morrison, September 21, 1950,

and September 28, 1950, in "Librarian's Correspondence," New Orleans Public Library.

23. Rosa Keller, interview by Schlesinger, 13.

24. City attorney's opinion of May 20, 1954, quoted in library board minutes, May 21, 1954, Louisiana Collection, New Orleans Public Library.

25. Library board minutes, March 10, 1954; April 15, 1954; May 24, 1954; Rogers, "Humanity and Desire," 89–90; Keller, interview by Dorothy Schlesinger, 12–16.

26. Keller quoted in Rogers, "Humanity and Desire," 90.

27. Myrdal, *American Dilemma*, 929.

28. June 14, 1959, memo and letters from August 1960, in folder "Segregation," in "Librarian's Correspondence," New Orleans Public Library; Thompson, *Negro Leadership Class*, 106–7. Of the library "victory," liberal white attorney John P. Nelson snorted, "Sure, they let blacks use the libraries—but they took out all the tables and chairs." Nelson quoted in Rogers, "Humanity and Desire," 90. The policy of segregated water fountains continued at least until the early 1960s. A typed memo in the librarian's files, dated June 14, 1959, urgently instructs the first employee who arrives to take down the White and Colored signs at fountains. "Please do this immediately as an NCB [National Consistency Board] inspection team will probably reach there quite early today." The 1960 files contain letters of complaint from visitors from other states who were offended by the segregated arrangements.

29. "Maid of New Orleans," *Missionary Herald* (August 1937): 345, in Flint-Goodridge Hospital Papers, Dillard University Library.

30. Marcus Christian, "History of Flint-Goodridge," manuscript, 5–7, Marcus Christian Collection, University of New Orleans Library; Edwin R. Embree, *Julius Rosenwald Fund Review for the Year* [1929–1930] (Chicago: N.p., 1930), 25.

31. *New Orleans Times-Picayune*, January 31, 1932.

32. Wilma Dykeman and James Stokely, *Seeds of Southern Change: The Life of Will Alexander* (Chicago: University of Chicago Press, 1962), 174–75.

33. Ibid.; Rosa Keller to Dr. Edgar Hull, January 14, 1955, in Proceedings of the Orleans Parish Medical Society Board of Directors, 1955; *Louisiana Weekly*, May 30, 1953.

34. Dykeman and Stokely, *Seeds*, 174; "Expansion—Building on a Quarter Century of Service: Flint-Goodridge Hospital of Dillard University," brochure, c. 1957, Flint-Goodridge Collection, Dillard University Library; Keller, autobiographical ms., vol. 2, pt. 1, 1–2; Rosa Keller, interview by author, New Orleans, July 13, 1993, and Dr. Henry E. Braden III, interview by author, New Orleans, July 24, 1993.

35. Orleans Parish Medical Society Board of Directors Proceedings (1955), February 15, 1955; March 10, 1955; April 12, 1955; June 13, 1955; October 10, 1955; December 12, 1955. Minutes for February 9, 1965, offer a summary of how membership in the AMA could be secured.

36. Keller, autobiographical ms., vol. 2, pt. 7, 16.

37. *New Orleans Times-Picayune,* February 16, 1955.

38. Rosa Keller to Dr. Edgar Hull, January 14, 1955; minutes of meeting of the Hospital Committee of Orleans Parish Medical Society, February 15, 1955, both in *Proceedings,* Orleans Parish Medical Society, 1955; Keller, autobiographical ms., vol. 2, pts. 6 and 7, 12–16.

39. This account of what transpired at the meeting is taken from minutes of the meeting of the Hospital Committee, Orleans Parish Medical Society, February 15, 1955. A full decade passed before the subject of integrating the medical society arose again. In 1965 the receipt of requests for membership application forms from five black physicians sent the local society into a tailspin of discussions, futile hunts for alternatives, and consideration of a transparent scheme to break the society into two segments (one offering membership for scientific programs, the other including social functions.) At last the Orleans Parish Medical Society voted to change its bylaws and strike the word "white." Orleans Parish Medical Society Board of Directors *Proceedings,* pt. 1 (1965), February 9, 1965, April 13, 1965, May 11, 1965, June 8, 1965, October 12, 1965.

40. Keller, autobiographical ms., vol. 2, pt. 7, 16.

41. Rosa Keller, interview by author, July 13, 1993, and Dr. Henry E. Braden III, interview by author; *Louisiana Weekly,* July 16, 1955, August 13, 1955.

42. John Wilds and Ira Harkey, *Alton Ochsner: Surgeon of the South* (Baton Rouge: Louisiana State University Press, 1990), 127, 177–83, 188, 191.

43. Ibid., 146–55.

44. Ibid., 198; David E. Rosenthal, "Managing Conflict: The Rhetoric of the Information Council of the Americas" (M.A. thesis, Tulane University, 1986).

45. Keller, autobiographical ms., vol. 2, pt. 3, 5–7; Rosa Keller, interview by author, July 13, 1993; Rosa Keller, interview by Rogers; Rosa Keller, interview by Forrest LaViolette, July 13, 1959, in Giles Hubert Papers, Amistad Research Center, Tulane University.

46. Keller, autobiographical ms., vol. 2, pt. 3, 7–8. Dr. Henry E. Braden III was an African-American physician on staff at Flint-Goodridge in the 1950s. He recalls that Keller gave generously to the hospital herself. "She was lovely. And what she did for Flint-Goodridge Hospital! If we needed stuff at the hospital, and we told her, she would say 'order it' and she would pay for it. Nobody will ever know how much she gave the hospital." Braden, interview by author; *Louisiana Weekly,* March 24, 1955.

47. The meeting with Earl Long was successful but lengthy. When Keller rejoined Weil, she felt keenly the sting of his exclusion from a conference at which he would have been the best informed participant. Perhaps as an unconscious gesture of atonement, knowing that the state capitol had no facilities for Weil, Keller refrained from visiting the whites-only women's room. She became quite uncomfortable on the trip back but, acutely conscious of the unorthodoxy of a white woman and a black man motoring together during the height of massive resistance, did not suggest stopping at a service station. (Indeed, it was the

provocation of seeing a black man riding with a white woman that prompted Martin Luther King's traffic arrest in Atlanta in 1961, according to Loveland, *Lillian Smith*, 217.)

48. Keller, autobiographical ms., vol. 2, pt. 3, 8-9.

49. Haas, *DeLesseps S. Morrison*, 69, 72-73; *Louisiana Weekly*, April 1, 1953, July 10, 1954; Keller quoted in Rogers, "Humanity and Desire," 40-41.

50. *Louisiana Weekly*, November 12, 1955. Keller's husband told her that they could embark on the Pontchartrain Park project only by investing the money that she had brought to the marriage. This posed an enormous financial risk for the couple. As she recalls the conversation, he said, "We stand to lose everything we've got." Rosa Keller, interview by Schlesinger.

51. Rosa Keller, interview by Schlesinger, 20.

52. Hirsch, "Matter of Black and White," 278-79; Rogers, "Humanity and Desire," 42-44; *Louisiana Weekly*, November 19, 1955; Judge Revius Ortique, telephone interview by author, June 12, 1992. The distinction that sociologist Daniel C. Thompson (*Negro Leadership Class*, 62-75, 119) draws between "race men" and "racial diplomats" is relevant here. Those who found Pontchartrain Park subdivision objectionable were "race men"; its supporters were "racial diplomats."

53. Rosa Keller, interview by Schlesinger; Rosa Keller, interview by author, July 13, 1993; Orleans Parish School Board minutes, vol. 37, September 12, 1955, Earl K. Long Memorial Library, University of New Orleans; December 19, 1955, 96, Earl K. Long Library, University of New Orleans; Julian Feibelman, *The Making of a Rabbi* (New York: Vantage Press, 1980), 449-52. The sterile minutes of the meeting give no indication of high emotions, however, stating without comment only that a petition was received, "offering to assist the school board in any way possible in orderly carrying out of the laws of the United States, dealing particularly with the ending of segregation in the public schools."

54. *New Orleans Times-Picayune*, September 13, 1955; Feibelman, *Making of a Rabbi*, 452; Rosa Keller, interview by author, November 4, 1983.

55. Presenting the petition was Robert G. Robinson, husband of Martha Gilmore Robinson. He was a close friend of Judge Leander Perez's and assumed a prominent role in the local chapter of the Citizens' Council.

56. Orleans Parish School Board minutes, vol. 37, September 26, 1955, 561-62; Rosa Keller, interview by author, November 4, 1983.

57. Urban League minutes, February 18, 1954, May 28, 1954, October 22, 1954, December 17, 1954, January 20, 1955, December 15, 1955, all in Giles Hubert Papers, Amistad Research Center, Tulane University; Rosa Keller, interview by author, November 4, 1983; Keller, autobiographical ms., vol. 2, pt. 8, 19.

58. Thompson, *Negro Leadership Class*, 64, 67-70.

59. Ibid., 68-70; Rogers, "Humanity and Desire," 464-66; *Louisiana Weekly*, 1956-57, various issues; J. Harvey Kerns, interview by John Walton, June 30, 1959, unpaginated typescript, Giles Hubert Papers, Amistad Collection, Tulane University.

60. Mary Keller Zervigon, interview by author, New Orleans, June 2, 1990; Sue Thrasher and Eliot Wigginton, "You Can't Be Neutral: An Interview with Anne Braden," *Southern Exposure* 12 (November–December 1984): 85.

61. Jesse T. Moore Jr., *A Search for Equality: The National Urban League, 1910–1961* (University Park: Pennsylvania State University, 1981), 47, 49; Hirsch, "Matter of Black and White," 303.

62. Moore, *Search for Equality*, 182–84.

63. J. Westbrook McPherson, executive director, New Orleans Urban League, to Lester Granger, president, National Urban League, April 11, 1956, in National Urban League Papers, Library of Congress. "Incidentally," McPherson wrote, "I want to say at this point that Mr. and Mrs. Keller were superb in the meeting."

64. *New Orleans Times-Picayune*, May 18, 1956.

65. The Urban League endured some uneasy times. In 1957, to protect a valuable community resource from a Citizens' Council boycott, the league decided against requesting Community Chest funds and instead had its budget financed by "friends" who contributed twenty-seven thousand dollars. Some had long believed that Keller's standing in the community had insulated the league from the roughest attacks. Once she was no longer shielding the Urban League, the criticism was stepped up and the inevitable happened. The United Fund ousted the Urban League from membership. Later, when tensions subsided, membership was restored.

66. J. Westbrook McPherson, "1953 Yearly Report," Giles Hubert Papers, Amistad Research Center, Tulane University; J. Harvey Kerns, interview with John Walton.

67. Rosa Keller, interview by Rogers.

68. Ibid.

69. Ibid.; Rosa Keller, interview by author, November 4, 1983. *New Orleans Times-Picayune*, September 29, 1991. "I became accustomed to my friends' bewilderment and misunderstanding," Keller said. "That they [African Americans] might share our schools, restaurants, job opportunities, and hospitals was so distasteful to these friends that it was unthinkable." She admitted, "It was hard to find *anybody* you could discuss it with." Keller, autobiographical ms., vol. 2, pt. 9, 21.

70. Elizabeth Mullener, "Mrs. Roosevelt Remembered," *Dixie Magazine, New Orleans Times-Picayune*, November 25, 1984, 8; Keller, autobiographical ms., vol. 1, unpaginated. Sybil Haydel Morial was the wife of Ernest ("Dutch") Morial, who later became New Orleans's first black mayor. Keller had worked with her on voter registration campaigns after the passage of the 1965 Voting Rights Act.

71. Martha Gasquet Westfeldt to Mrs. J. W. Reily, November 25, 1955, in Martha G. Westfeldt Papers, New Orleans Public Library.

72. Rogers, "Humanity and Desire," 169. SOS minutes, February 20, 1960, March 23, 1960, May 27, 1960, in Amistad Research Center, Tulane University. Thompson, *Negro Leadership Class*, 157–62.

The SOS gave prominent roles to three men for reasons of public relations, naming as cochairmen a Protestant minister, a Catholic priest, and a Jewish rabbi, but these roles were titular and honorary rather than functional. Although there were some male members who contributed ideas and time to the group (Jack Nelson, Ted Baptist, Victor Hess, for example), women were always the heart and soul of SOS.

73. Jack Bass, *Unlikely Heroes: The Southern Judges Who Made the Civil Rights Revolution* (New York: Simon & Schuster, 1981), 116.

74. Rosa Keller, interview by Schlesinger, 32; Rogers, "Humanity and Desire," 196; Haas, *DeLesseps S. Morrison,* 267-69; Morton Inger, "The New Orleans School Crisis of 1960," in *Southern Businessmen and Desegregation,* ed. Elizabeth Jacoway and David Colburn (Baton Rouge: Louisiana State University Press, 1982), 88-89. For vivid accounts of the pressures applied to white parents who did not withdraw their children from the affected schools, see Alan Wieder, "One Who Stayed: Margaret Conner and the New Orleans School Crisis," *Louisiana History* 26 (Spring 1985): 194-201, and Isabella Taves, "The Mother Who Stood Alone," *Good Housekeeping* (April 1961): 30, 32, 24, 36, 121.

75. Inger, "New Orleans School Crisis," 94. The crisis is recounted in greater detail in Morton Inger, *Politics and Reality in an American City: The New Orleans School Crisis of 1960* (New York: Center for Urban Education, 1969). John Steinbeck, passing through the city on his "travels with Charley," observed with fascination and horror and offered his comments in *Travels with Charley* (New York: Viking, 1963).

76. See various copies of SOS September 1961 letter to parents that were returned, in SOS Papers, Amistad Research Center, Tulane University. Angry comments included: "I'd rather be dead than a Red rat"; "Don't send this red trash to me again"; "How many of you out-of-town bastards send your kids to public schools? Not one white N.O. native in the bunch—only a lot of trouble-making bastards out to make a fast buck. God help the U.S.A."; "You red bastards aren't as good as niggers."

77. Haas, *DeLesseps S. Morrison,* chap. 12, esp. 255-58; Hirsch, "Matter of Black and White," 279-80; Inger, "New Orleans School Crisis," 86-87, 97; Goldfield, *Black, White, and Southern,* 111-12; Tony Badger, "Segregation and the Southern Business Elite," *Journal of American Studies* 18 (April 1984): 105-9.

78. Badger, "Segregation and the Southern Business Elite," 108.

79. *New Orleans Times-Picayune,* December 16, 1960.

80. "Tabulation of Special Survey," May 9, 1960, in Matthew Sutherland Papers, Earl K. Long Library, University of New Orleans. The exact figures show 2,819 whites voting to keep schools open; 12,017 blacks voting to keep schools open; 12,724 whites voting to close schools; 691 blacks voting to close schools. This was a postcard survey, with whites having a 63.59 percent rate of return and blacks a 49.45 percent rate of return.

81. SOS minutes, November 3, 1960; Inger, *Politics and Reality,* 86-87; Rogers,

"Humanity and Desire," 198-99, 233-34; Inger, "New Orleans School Crisis," 89, 95.

82. *New Orleans Times-Picayune,* December 20, 1960.

83. The *New Orleans States-Item* editorial of September 9, 1961, stated, "Due credit should go to the committee of business and civic leaders, headed by Darwin Fenner, who rallied support for an orderly operation of the public schools and the preservation of law and order."

Most accounts of the easing of the school crisis give credit to male civic leaders, chiefly to Harry Kelleher and Darwin Fenner. However, the evidence strongly indicates that Kelleher and Fenner, though highly influential when they did take a public stand in favor of keeping the public schools open, were coaxed into taking that stand by women. See Charles DuFour, *Darwin Fenner* (New Orleans: Privately printed, 1984), 79-80.

84. "Rewards to simple-mindedness in females" is Lillian Smith's phrase; Smith, *Killers of the Dream,* 141. Rosa Keller, interview by author, November 4, 1983; Rosa Keller, interview by Rogers.

85. SOS minutes, February 12, 1962; Haas, *DeLesseps S. Morrison,* 280-81.

86. Cheryl Cunningham, "The Desegregation of Tulane University" (M.A. thesis, University of New Orleans, 1982), 4-5.

87. Ibid., 14.

88. Keller's title was "Chairman of the Community Hospitality Committee, Division of Student Life." She served three years, from 1959 to 1961. See 1959 *Jambalaya,* the Tulane yearbook. "Native garb" anecdote from Mary Keller Zervigon, interview by author.

89. Tulane *Hullabaloo,* April 12, 1954, May 7, 1954, in "Students: Black," Vertical File, University Archives, Howard-Tilton Memorial Library, Tulane University; Board of Administrators, Tulane Educational Fund, minutes, vol. 37, June 14, 1961, and April 12, 1961; Jackson Ricau, executive director of South Louisiana Citizens' Council, to Tulane University, April 18, 1960, in "Students: Black," Vertical File, University Archives.

90. Tulane Board of Administrators minutes, vol. 37, March 8, 1961, 124-25. Only a month earlier, the Tulane board had discussed the likelihood that the new Kennedy administration would place restrictions on federal appropriations to colleges whose admissions policies barred African Americans. Ibid., February 8, 1961, 106.

91. Keller, autobiographical ms., vol. 2, pt. 18, 377; Cunningham, "Desegregation of Tulane," 19-23.

92. John B. Furey to Dr. Cliff Wing, director of admissions, Tulane University, March 13, 1961, in John P. Nelson Papers, Amistad Research Center, Tulane University; W. L. Kindelsperger, dean of School of Social Work, Tulane University, to Pearlie Hardin Elloie, April 19, 1961; R. M. Lumiansky, dean of Graduate School, Tulane University, to Barbara Guillory, June 23, 1961; both in "Students: Black,"

Vertical File, University Archives; Cunningham, "Desegregation of Tulane," 16–18; Tulane Board of Administrators minutes, vol. 37, April 12, 1961, 132–33.

93. Tulane Board of Administrators minutes, vol. 37, May 10, 1961, 146; Mrs. Katherine B. Wright to John P. Nelson, undated [c. June 29, 1961], and Nelson to Wright, July 11, 1961, both in Nelson Papers, Amistad Research Center, Tulane University; John P. Nelson, interview by Rogers, June 22, 1988, tape housed at Amistad Research Center, Tulane University; John P. Nelson, interview by author, New Orleans, June 12, 1990.

94. Rosa Keller, interview by author, July 13, 1993; Rosa Keller, interview by Rogers; Keller, autobiographical ms., vol. 2, pt. 19, 40–41; Rosa Keller, interview by Schlesinger, 53.

95. Cunningham, "Desegregation of Tulane," 35–44 and chap. 4, passim.

96. Ibid., 69.

97. Rogers, "Humanity and Desire," 285–86. During this trip, a naive Keller approached Skelly Wright, eager to tell of her efforts to bring a lawsuit against Tulane University, only to hear his friendly but firm rebuff, "Rosy, you can't discuss that with me; it might come up in my court!" Rosa Keller, interview by Schlesinger, 577.

98. Cunningham, "Desegregation of Tulane," 71; Rogers, "Humanity and Desire," 290; Fairclough, *Race and Democracy,* chap. 6, "Race and Red-Baiting," esp. 146–47. See also Katherine B. Wright to John P. Nelson, undated [c. June 29, 1961], in which she, a liberal integrationist, expressed her horror at the thought of what a Fourteenth Amendment suit could entail. Obviously envisioning Tulane's being declared a state university and the reactionary state legislature thus having license to tamper with academic freedom at the school, she wrote, "There are so many ramifications to this thing that it isn't funny." She and her husband, a mathematics professor at Tulane, would leave the university if it should be declared a state school. "Please, please make them [the Tulane board] understand that they have more to lose from your suit than if they went on and did it [desegregation] themselves," she implored. Letter in John P. Nelson Papers, Amistad Research Center, Tulane University.

99. Cunningham, "Desegregation of Tulane," 75–100; *New York Times,* December 6, 1962; Tulane *Hullabaloo,* December 12, 1962.

100. Keller, autobiographical ms., pt. 18, 39; Murray Work, chairman, Special Unitarian Fund Committee, to Rosa Keller, August 6, 1961, in Natalie Midlo Papers, Amistad Research Center, Tulane University, and Keller to Work, July 7, 1963, in John P. Nelson Papers, Amistad Research Center, Tulane University. John P. Nelson to Keller, June 28, 1961, in Rosa Keller Papers, Amistad Research Center, Tulane University.

101. Rosa Keller, interview by Schlesinger, 54–55; Keller, autobiographical ms., vol. 2, pt. 20, 41–44. Pearlie Elloie, interview by author, New Orleans, July 23, 1992. Keller's efforts to micromanage events included a request to Jessie Dent,

wife of Dillard University president Albert Dent, that she intervene with one of the plaintiffs and persuade her to adopt a different hairstyle. This exemplifies again her cultural assumptions. Keller made the request of Mrs. Dent, whom she considered a friend, with the best of intentions, and Mrs. Dent received it in the spirit in which it was made. Both women agreed on the wisdom of the change in coiffure.

102. John Furey to Rosa Keller, December 15, 1962; Edith Stern to Keller, undated; Pearlie Elloie to Keller, December 13, 1962; all in Rosa Keller Papers, Amistad Research Center, Tulane University.

103. 1963 *Jambalaya;* Cunningham, "Desegregation of Tulane," 102; John P. Nelson, interview by author; Fairclough, *Race and Democracy,* 262.

104. Rosa F. Keller to President John F. Kennedy, June 12, 1963, copy in Hale Boggs Papers, Howard-Tilton Memorial Library, Tulane University.

105. Dutch Morial quoted in Hirsch, "Matter of Black and White," 287.

106. Rosa Keller, interview by Rogers.

107. John P. Nelson, interview by author.

CONCLUSION

1. Eleanor Roosevelt, *It's Up to the Women* (New York: Frederick A. Stokes Co., 1933). The New Orleans YWCA conducted classes for unemployed women and girls, and its employment service found jobs for 513 of them in 1933. It provided 14,879 nights' lodging for girls and women in 1933, and its food service sold 18,022 more meals in 1933 than in the previous year (average check: seventeen cents). *New Orleans Times-Picayune,* January 31, 1934; Charles L. Dufour and Samuel Wilson Jr., *Women Who Cared: The One Hundred Years of the Christian Woman's Exchange* (New Orleans: Christian Women's Exchange, 1980).

2. Perry H. Howard, *Political Tendencies in Louisiana, 1812–1952* (Baton Rouge: Louisiana State University Press, 1957), 124–56; Allan P. Sindler, "Bifactional Rivalry as an Alternative to Two-Party Competition in Louisiana," *American Political Science Review* 44 (September 1955): 641–62; Paul Grosser, "Political Parties," in *Louisiana Politics: Festival in a Labyrinth,* ed. James Bolner (Baton Rouge: Louisiana State University Press, 1982), 257–69.

There is disagreement over whether bifactionalism really provided a satisfactory equivalent to the two-party system. Kenneth Vines, in a perceptive study of the Republican boomlet in New Orleans at the time of the 1952 presidential election, felt that the upsurge of support for Eisenhower among city voters not registered as Republicans indicated a desire for bona fide two-party competition. Even assuming that every one of the 2,715 New Orleanians registered as Republicans cast their votes for Eisenhower, some 80,000 Democrats also liked him and voted accordingly. Thus, the number of registered Republicans was not an accurate indicator of Republican strength. Moreover, Vines felt a significant number of New Orleanians were willing to vote for Republican candidates at the local and state levels as well as in presidential elections, if such candidates were available.

More than 40 percent of New Orleans whites who registered Republican in the years immediately preceding the Eisenhower-Stevenson contest of 1952 cited ideological motivations, and most mentioned their opposition to the welfare state and excessive government spending, the canonical anti-Long attitudes. Significantly, the five wards showing the greatest Republican support, Wards 12, 13, 14, 16, and 17, all featured a high percentage of home owners with relatively high incomes in the city's Uptown area, were all strongly anti-Long, and ranked as Chep Morrison enclaves. The lowest Republican support came from Old Regular strongholds Wards 1, 2, and 3.

See Kenneth Vines, *The Republican Party in New Orleans*, Tulane Studies in Political Science, vol. 2 (New Orleans: Tulane University, 1955), 93-134.

3. This statement from a *Times-Picayune* editorial typifies much of the economically driven male opposition to Long: "Under our dictatorship the word economy has been deleted, in practical effect, from the lexicon of Louisiana state officialdom. Multiplication of wastes and useless political jobs goes along with multiplication of taxes." *Times-Picayune*, January 7, 1935.

4. Lindy Boggs, with Katherine Hatch, *Washington through a Purple Veil: Memoirs of a Southern Woman* (New York: Harcourt, Brace & Co., 1994), 65-66.

5. *New Orleans Times-Picayune*, March 12, 1954, January 18, 1956, February 23, 1956; Adam Fairclough, *Race and Democracy: The Civil Rights Struggle in Louisiana, 1915-1972* (Athens: University of Georgia Press, 1995), 206. Another factor in Bruns's defeat was her decision to challenge an incumbent for his seat in the state Senate rather than seeking reelection to her House seat.

6. For discussions of the effects of the war on women, see Susan Hartmann, *The Home Front and Beyond: American Women in the 1940s* (Boston: Twayne, 1982); Karen Anderson, *Wartime Women: Sex Roles, Family Relations, and the Status of Women during World War II* (Westport, Conn.: Greenwood, 1981); and D'Ann Campbell, *Women at War with America: Private Lives in a Patriotic Era* (Cambridge, Mass.: Harvard University Press, 1984).

7. MGR to Mrs. P. A. Taylor, February 24, 1954, in MGR Papers.

8. Mrs. Charles Crawford, NOLWV, to Mrs. John G. Lee, NLWV president, February 27, 1953, and Mrs. Robert Leonard, NLWV, to Mrs. Charles Crawford, March 3, 1953, in NLWV Papers.

9. This practice of having candidates offer financial contributions to political organizations in return for their endorsement remains common operating procedure in Louisiana politics. See John Wildgen, "Voting Behavior in Gubernatorial Elections," in Bolner, *Louisiana Politics*, 342-43.

10. These impressions were taken from a roundtable discussion among IWO members held May 11, 1984, at the home of Carolyn Gay Labouisse, recorded by Pamela Tyler.

11. *New Orleans States-Item*, August 26, 1975.

12. Mary M. Morrison to IWO Board of Governors, no date [c. 1960], copy in possession of Mary Morrison.

13. Carol Flake, *New Orleans: Behind the Masks of America's Most Exotic City* (New York: Grove Press, 1994), 56–58, 62–63, 136–38, and passim. Other observations on the insular nature of society in New Orleans are to be found in James R. Bobo, *The New Orleans Economy: Pro Bono Publico?* (New Orleans: University of New Orleans, 1975); Phyllis Raabe, "Status and Its Impact: New Orleans Carnival, the Social Upper Class, and Upper-Class Power" (Ph.D. diss., Pennsylvania State University, 1973); and Arnold R. Hirsch, "New Orleans: Sunbelt in the Swamp," in *Sunbelt Cities: Politics and Growth since World War II*, ed. Richard M. Bernard and Bradley Rice (Austin: University of Texas Press, 1983).

14. Grosser, "Political Parties," 266–68.

15. Edward F. Haas, *DeLesseps S. Morrison and the Image of Reform: New Orleans Politics, 1946–1963* (Baton Rouge: Louisiana State University Press, 1974), 285–88; Arnold R. Hirsch, "Simply a Matter of Black and White: The Transformation of Race and Politics in Twentieth Century New Orleans," in *Creole New Orleans: Race and Americanization*, ed. Arnold R. Hirsch and Joseph Logsdon (Baton Rouge: Louisiana State University Press, 1992), 283–84.

16. Comments from roundtable discussion held May 11, 1984, at the home of Carolyn Gay Labouisse, recorded by Pamela Tyler.

17. Carolyn Gay Labouisse to Congressman Hale Boggs, November 2, 1963, in Hale Boggs Papers, Tulane University.

18. Jack Bass and Walter DeVries, *The Transformation of Southern Politics: Social Change and Political Consequence since 1945* (New York: Basic Books, 1976), quoted in Bolner, *Louisiana Politics*, 87.

19. Martin Behrman, *Martin Behrman of New Orleans: Memoirs of a City Boss*, edited and with an introduction by John R. Kemp (Baton Rouge: Louisiana State University Press, 1977), 108.

20. Alice Kessler-Harris, "Where Are the Organized Women Workers?" *Feminist Studies* 3 (Fall 1975): 92–110.

INDEX

Adams, W. R., 214
Addams, Jane, 15, 29
African-American community of New Orleans: 1950 population of, 204; statistics regarding, 204; police brutality toward, 204, 289 (n. 2); institutions of, 209; Rosa Keller's contacts with, 209, 210, 211; male dominance of leadership in, 210; gender roles in, 210, 211; gains of, made through negotiation, 212–13; hospital service to, 213; heady climate in, following *Brown* decision, 215; and postwar housing shortage, 219, 220; rising determination of, 241
African-American elite, 210; accommodationism of, 221; gentility of, 221; gradualism of, 222
African-American men: as registered voters, 27, 28, 82, 91, 177; college-educated, 204; and death penalty for rape, 204; as professional workers, 204; monopoly of community leadership by, 210; as professionals, 220; as "racial diplomats," 220, 221, 222, 236, 295 (n. 52)
African-American soldiers, in World War II, 208–9
African-American voter registration, 106, 111, 249, 274 (n. 112). *See also* Voter registration
African-American women: civic activities of, 16, 17; thwarted by race and sex, 16, 17; in home v. in community, 17; out of their sphere, 17; political influence of, indirect, 17; as registered voters, 27, 28, 29, 82, 91, 144, 177; exclusion of, from WCU, 88; exclusion of, from NOLWV, 109, 114, 118–19; in OPPVL auxiliary, 188; college-educated, 204; and the YWCA, 208; as community leaders, 210–11; rebuffed by IWO, 225; accepted into NOLWV, 242–43; accepted into IWO, 244–45
Albany (N.Y.) News: salutes "Sacrifice Week," 60
Allen, O. K., 33
American Association of University Women (AAUW), 162, 163
American Federation of Labor (AFL): and the SCHW, 110; and the New Orleans Classroom Teachers Federation, 189
American Medical Association, 215
American Progress, 51; reaction of, to Connally Report, 54; mocks "Sacrifice Week," 60; political cartoons of Hammond in, 62–63
Americans for Democratic Action (ADA), 119
Ames, Jessie Daniel, 70, 86, 120
Ansell, General Samuel Tilden, 38; and findings of Overton hearings, 40; retained by Women's Committee, 54–55
Anthony Amendment, 25, 26. *See also* Woman suffrage
Antifeminism of post–World War II period, 169, 170
Anti-Long movement: supported by urban press, 49, 124; after Huey Long's death, 68; as characterized by historians, 73; ineptness of, 73; as ultraconservative, 73; motivations

Anti-Long movement (*cont'd*)
of, 74, 301 (n. 3); and Long supporters, 83; as associated with urbanism, 126; segregationist attitudes of women in, 225. *See also* Social class in New Orleans; Upper-class women
Anti-Long vote: 1936 and 1940, 134–35; 1940 and 1946, 150–51; 1936–1946, 150–52
Anti-Long women's movement. *See* Upper-class women
Anti-Semitism, 207
Antisuffragist attitudes: persistence of, 27, 90
Antisuffragists: and states' rights suffragists, 25; ties of, to antebellum past, 26
Anti-Tuberculosis League, 16
Association of Southern Women to Prevent Lynching, 70, 86

Ballot box stuffing, 10, 53, 85
Bankhead, John, 111
Baton Rouge League of Women Voters: and civil service law of 1940, 96
Battle of Liberty Place, 24, 25, 258 (n. 56)
Behrman, Martin, 11, 13, 14, 22, 80, 154, 155, 175, 196, 200, 251: popularity of, with all classes, 11; efforts of, against state suffrage amendment, 24; supported by *Times-Picayune*, 255 (n. 7)
Besse, C. P., 163, 164
Bifactionalism: as two-party system in Louisiana, 193, 239, 278 (n. 32), 300–301 (n. 2); shattered by race politics, 246
Bingham, Barry, 61
Bisso, Captain William ("Billy"), 191
Black, Hugo, 110

Blair, Emily Newell (quote), 169
Blanchard, Emily Price (Mrs. Paul), 96; and goal of a Louisiana LWV, 97, 98; and the SCHW, 112, 113, 114, 115; and Martha Robinson, 112–13, 114, 119; advocates black membership in LWV, 113, 114; severs connection with LWV, 114
Boggs, Corinne Claiborne ("Lindy"), 1 (quote), 125, 126, 128, 139, 140, 240, 249
Boggs, Hale, 124, 140, 249
Borah, William, 62
Boston Club, 36, 37, 45, 46, 88, 116, 125, 153, 224, 262 (n. 65), 269 (n. 34). *See also* New Orleans Social Register
Bourgeois, Lionel, 164
Braden, Anne, 222
Brahney, Thomas, 176, 188, 190, 192; endorsed by Martha Robinson, 178
Bratton, Sam G., 43
Breazeale, Phanor, 141
"Broom Brigade," 145
Broussard, Edwin, 36, 37, 38, 50, 54
Brown, Bruce, 214
Brown v. Board of Education, 205; and heady climate in black community, 215; and the Orleans Parish School Board, 220; and militant segregationists, 222; and National Urban League, 222; and segregation measures of state legislature, 241
Bruns, Bland Cox, 125, 136, 170, 176, 195, 240–41, 286 (n. 51), 301 (n. 5)
Burke, Major E. A., 10
Burke, Edmund, 75
Burn, Harry, 25
Burns, Leonard, 220
Byrd, Daniel, 220

Capone, Al: letter to, from Huey Long, 44
Capote, Truman, 6

Cardinal, 250
Carey, Robert D., 43
Carnival. *See* Mardi Gras
Carraway, Hattie, 58, 261 (n. 33)
Carter, Hodding, 61, 74
Cash, W. J., 206, 290 (n. 8)
Cassibry, Fred, 186, 188, 198, 199
Catt, Carrie Chapman, 2, 30; "Winning Plan" of, 23
Caucus, the. *See* Old Regulars
Chapital, A. J., 220
Charity Hospital, 37, 83, 84, 115, 175, 188, 213
Chicago Tribune: salutes "Sacrifice Week," 60; on pamphlet, "Is the Senate Afraid of Huey Long?," 62
Childhood: of Hilda Phelps Hammond, 34; of Martha Gilmore Robinson, 83; of July B. Waters, 141; of Rosa Freeman Keller, 206
Child labor, 17; and act of 1906, 19
Child Welfare Association: case committee of, and Martha Robinson, 84, 174
Choctaws. *See* Old Regulars
Chopin, Kate, 184
Christian Science Monitor: credits women with Morrison win, 150
Citizens for Progress in the Public Schools, 162, 165
"Citizenship school" movement, 85
City charter of 1952, 170, 171
Civil rights movement (in New Orleans), 236, 242; increasing insistence of, 249
Clasen, Glenn, 175, 179, 187, 196
Class. *See* Social class in New Orleans
Clay, Laura, 21, 25, 287 (n. 58)
Cold War: impact of, on liberal organizations, 112, 241–42; and liberal-moderate split in the NOLWV, 112–19; and women's political activities, 241, 242

Cold Water Committee, 154, 177, 193, 194, 201, 285 (n. 28)
Colonial Dames of Louisiana, 146
Comiskey, James A., 80, 196, 197, 267 (n. 5)
Committee for Action on the Peabody Survey (CAPS), 165
Committee of 100, 228
Communism: accusations of, flung at racial moderates, 218, 222, 223, 250, 297 (n. 76)
Community Chest (United Fund): and New Orleans Urban League, 222–23, 296 (n. 65)
Conformity of thought: insistence on, 206, 233, 290 (n. 8)
Congress of Industrial Organizations (CIO), 110; and the SCHW, 111; endorses Martha Robinson, 189
Congress of Racial Equality (CORE), 249
Connally, Thomas, 42, 43, 54
Connally Report, 53, 54, 55, 85. *See also* Overton hearings
Constitutional convention of 1898; rights granted to women at, 18–19; and clauses for illiterate white voters, 21; disfranchisement of black voters at, 21
Council of National Defense. *See* Woman's Committee of the Council of National Defense
Cowley, Malcolm, 61
Crescent Carnival, 65
Crescent City Democratic Association (CCDA), 156; support for, from IWO, 159, 160; women's auxiliary of, 170; as political machine, 171; refuses to endorse Martha Robinson, 177, 178; supports Schiro, 193; uses sample ballots in 1954 election, 193–94, 199, 240–41; 1954 city election rallies of, 195

Dabney, Virginius, 110
Dallas News: on pamphlet, "Is the Senate Afraid of Huey Long?," 62
Daughters of the American Revolution, 67
Davis, Abraham Lincoln ("A. L."), 188, 198
Deano, Guy, 188
Dear, Cleveland, 134
Dent, Albert, 212, 214, 215, 220, 230
Dent, Jessie, 220
Dewey, Thomas E., 102
Dillard, James Hardy, 213
Dillard University, 213, 214
Dinkins, Cecile Airey, 125
Disappointing Clubs. *See* Eleanor Clubs
Dix, Dorothy, 184
Domesticity: of Hilda Phelps Hammond, 64; daily tasks of, 78–79; and link with politics, 144–46; of Martha Gilmore Robinson, 185–86
Domestic servants, 78, 272 (n. 79); dearth of, in World War II, 101; percentage of employed black women as, 204
Donaldson, Fred, 188
Dreyfous, George, 115
Dreyfous, Mathilde, 118
Dreyfous, Ruth, 114, 115
"Dummy candidate" device, 38, 53
Dunbar, Charles E., Jr., 96
Dunbar, Ethelynn, 96, 262 (n. 65)
Durr, Virginia Foster, 65, 276 (n. 12)

Eleanor Clubs, 101
Election fraud, 10, 13, 37, 38–39, 53–54, 62, 66, 85–87, 123, 126–27, 129–33, 147, 287 (n. 65)
Elite women. *See* Upper-class women
Ellender, Allen, 129
Ellis, Frank, 234
Elloie, Pearlie Hardin, 231, 232, 233, 234, 235
Embree, Edwin, 213
Emerson, Ralph Waldo (quote), 238
Equal Rights Association. *See* Era Club
Era Club, 18, 20, 23, 26; as backers of state suffrage amendment, 22; recognition sought for, 22; considers support for federal amendment, 24; evolves into New Orleans League of Women Voters, 79; and Liberty Place Monument, 258 (n. 57)
Ethridge, Mark, 110
Every Man a King, 47, 72

Fat Tuesday. *See* Mardi Gras
Favrot, Charlotte, 125
Favrot, Gervais, 194
Federal suffrage amendment, 23, 25, 26; defeated by state legislature, 27; perceived effect of, on southern blacks, 27. *See also* Woman suffrage
Feibelman, Julian, 220, 221
"Feminine mystique," 169, 170
Feminism, 76, 229, 245, 251
Fenner, Darwin, 232
Fernandez, J. O., 139
Fifteenth Amendment, 65
Flint, John D., 213
Flint-Goodridge Hospital, 16, 213, 214, 215, 217, 218, 219
Folsom, Big Jim, 146
Fourteenth Amendment: and Tulane University, 232, 233, 299 (n. 98)
Freeman, A. B., 206, 207
Freeman, Ella West, 207, 208
Freeman, Richard West, 229, 230, 232
French Quarter, 1, 79, 124, 131, 139; as site of Women's Committee headquarters, 59
Friedan, Betty, 169, 170, 185

306 □ INDEX

Furey, John, 231, 235

Gagliano, Gail, 245
Gambling, 10, 155, 156, 157, 158, 159, 281 (n. 92)
Garden District, 40, 104, 116, 132, 135, 141, 154
Garner, John Nance, 52, 56, 57
Gayle, James, 214
Gender ideology: and women's political behavior, 27, 29, 41, 42, 63–64, 74–75, 82, 84, 86–87, 89, 90–92, 95, 106–7, 128, 136, 144, 145–46, 152, 160, 161, 185, 268 (n. 15); restrictions of, on girls and women, 34, 83, 169, 183, 184, 185, 188, 229, 268 (n. 15), 286 (n. 48), 287 (n. 58); women's transgressive violations of, 39–40, 50–51, 76, 103, 107–8, 132, 163, 164, 176
George, Walter, 55, 56, 57, 62, 72
George Committee, 55; testimony of Anne Pleasant before, 56
Gillis, James H., 175, 198, 199
Gilmore, Samuel, 83, 175
Glass, Carter, 59
Goodridge, Sarah, 213
Gordon, Jean, 18, 31, 185; campaign of, to gather proxy votes, 19; as "Jane Addams of the South," 20; noblesse oblige instincts of, 20; as opponent of Nineteenth Amendment, 25–26
Gordon, Kate, 18, 19, 20, 27, 31, 185; campaign of, to gather proxy votes, 19; as opponent of federal suffrage amendment, 21, 22, 23, 24; as proponent of state suffrage amendment, 21, 22, 23, 25, 26; as opponent of black suffrage, 21, 23, 65; as Negrophobic, 21, 25; as opponent of Nineteenth Amendment, 21, 25, 65
Graham, Frank Porter, 110
Greater New Orleans Citizens' Council (GNOCC): 1956 rally of, 205, 223, 290 (n. 6); petition of, supporting school segregation, 221
Greer, Germaine, 245
Gregory, Angela, 7, 50, 245–46
Griffin, Marvin, 205
Guillory, Barbara, 231, 232, 233, 234, 235

Hammond, Arthur B., 35, 36, 39, 63, 64
Hammond, Hilda Phelps, 32 (quote), 55, 58, 83, 87, 125, 143, 240; compared with Huey Long, 32–33; activities of, at Newcomb College, 34; marriage of, 35; stoic reaction of, to financial reverses, 35–36; as recipe writer for *Times-Picayune*, 36; attendance of, to Overton hearings, 37; expectations of government held by, 40, 75; and home v. politics, 40–41; "Monday messages" of, 41; criticized for traveling alone, 43; Washington trip of, 43; condemns Long for attacks against FDR, 45; first national appeal of, 45; calls for Senate investigation, 47; chastizes Senate committee members, 48; anti-Long tour of the East by, 49; photograph of, in *New York Times*, 49; loses faith in U.S. Senate, 50; addresses Overton committee, 50, 51; chastizes Senate for cowardice, 51, 57–58, 59; epithets of, by Long, 52; and battle with Long as class issue, 52, 262 (n. 58); files Senate petition against Long, 52–53; presses Senate for committee change, 53, 262 (n. 65); caricatured by *American Progress*, 54; vandalism against, 54; continues petition fight in Senate, 56, 57; seeks national publicity for cause, 60, 61; as author of pamphlet, "Is the Senate Afraid

Hammond, Hilda Phelps (cont'd)
of Huey Long?," 62; delivers speech at *Collier's* fundraiser, 62; political cartoons of, 62–63; belief of, in moral superiority of women, 63; as allegedly motivated by revenge, 63, 71–72; and enjoyment of celebrity, 64; as not contented in domestic role, 64; as viewed by contemporaries, 64; as Josephine Cutler (character in *Crescent Carnival*), 65, 264 (n. 109); and issue of states' rights, 66; lack of national support for, 67; continuing opposition to Longism by, 68, 69; denies being motivated by hatred, 68–69; at odds with anti-Long elite, 69; personal motivations of, 70, 71; overidentification of, with the Women's Committee of Louisiana, 70, 116; as self-righteous, 70, 265 (n. 126), 266–67 (n. 144); effect of efforts of, on Louisiana, 71; references to, in histories of Long era, 71, 72, 73; treatment of, by T. Harry Williams, 71–73; and Square Deal Association, 72; as of the "nonpolitical gentility," 74; behavior of, as departure from definition of woman's place, 76; as nonfeminist, 76; chooses not to use "charm," 76, 266–67 (n. 144); legacy of, to New Orleans women, 76–77; ignored by historians of Long era, 77; as inspiration to women, 77; and an increasing female electorate, 82; *Let Freedom Ring*, 117; inheritance of, 260 (n. 11); as fundraiser, 263 (n. 72); and Robert Howell, 264–65 (n. 113)
Harris, Rufus C., 229
Harrison, Pat, 59
Harvard Liberal Club, 61
Hays, Brooks, 110
Henry, Burt, 131

Hill, Lister, 110, 111, 214
Holland, John, 47–48, 55
Hollins College, 206
Honest Election League (HEL), 50, 54, 83, 86. *See also* Women's Division of the HEL
House Un-American Activities Committee (HUAC), 112, 114
Houston Post: salutes "Sacrifice Week," 60; on pamphlet, "Is the Senate Afraid of Huey Long?," 62
Howell, Robert, 264–65 (n. 113)
Hubert, Leon, 199
Hull, Edgar, 215
Hull House, 15

Ickes, Harold, 52
Independent Citizens' Committee, 139, 140
Independent Women's Organization (IWO), 77, 120; as stronghold of New Orleans elite, 121; roots of, 122–34; initial goal of, 141; leadership of, from New Orleans elite, 142; revised expectations of, 142; efforts on behalf of deLesseps Morrison by, 143; first meeting of, 143; voter registration efforts of, 143, 144; editorial cartoon of, 144; March of Brooms of, 145; use of household imagery by, 145; as election commissioners and poll watchers, 146, 147; and effect of voter registration drive on 1946 mayoral election, 147–48; becomes permanent body, 151; as changed by growth in women's confidence, 151, 152; acceptance of gender roles by, 152; credited by press for superior morality, 152; opens membership, 152–53; white membership in, 153; power of board of, 153, 154; and New Orleans elite, 153, 280 (n. 84); political rewards

of, 154; viewed as good-government group, 156, 157; and board's stand against legalized gambling, 156, 157, 158, 159; rejects invitation to become CCDA auxiliary, 156–57; access to deLesseps Morrison by, 159; reputation of, as blindly supportive of Morrison, 159; as backers of the CCDA, 159, 160; support of, for deLesseps Morrison, 159, 191, 192, 200; influence of, in getting out the vote, 160; preference of leaders of, for volunteer over paid work, 160; ties of, to Women's Committee of Louisiana, 160, 161; dissatisfaction with deLesseps Morrison among, 161; and school board elections, 161, 162, 163, 164, 165; and school reform, 161, 162, 163, 164, 165, 166; and the AAUW, 162, 163; and efforts against Shelby Jackson, 165, 166; appeal of, to middle- and upper-class women, 170; asks Martha Robinson to run for city council, 175, 202; and Cold Water Committee, 177, 285 (n. 28); and Martha Robinson campaign, 180, 186, 190, 191, 192, 198; and Old Regular support for Robinson, 191, 192, 200; segregationist attitudes of, 225; and school desegregation crisis of 1960, 228, 229; independence of, 243; admission of black members to, 244; decline in campaign vigor of, 244, 245; loss of unanimity in, 244, 245, 248, 249; emerging feminist views in, 245; gradual abandonment of goals by, 249; as moderates on race, 249

Intolerance. *See* Cold War; Communism; Conformity of thought

"Invisible career," concept of, 6, 205, 209, 225, 236, 291 (n. 7)

Irwin, Emmett, 223

"Is the Senate Afraid of Huey Long?" (pamphlet), 62

Jackson, Shelby, 165, 166, 227, 228
Jacobs, John Hall, 211
Jim Crow, 78, 204, 206, 215
Johnson, Lyndon B., 246
Jones, Joseph M., 230, 232
Jones, Sam Houston, 93, 94, 96, 97, 124, 139, 140, 146, 166, 167, 190, 240, 244; gubernatorial campaign of, 126, 128, 129, 133; characterized as "High Hat Sam," 129; New Orleans press support for, 129; effectiveness of women in gubernatorial campaign of, 143. *See also* Women supporters of Sam Jones
Jury service for women, 2, 3; as project of the NOLWV, 107

Kearney, Belle (quote), 203
Keller, Charles, Jr., 207, 223
Keller, Rosa Freeman: and fledgling NOLWV, 104; and respect for Martha Robinson, 104; as racial liberal, 205; as worker for racial justice, 205, 206; and 1956 GNOCC rally, 205, 223, 290 (n. 6); early life of, 206; as student at Hollins College, 206; as student at Newcomb College, 206; marriage of, 207; and anti-Semitism, 207, 209; and rationing, 207–8, 241; as member of YWCA board of directors, 208; volunteer work of, 208; initial awareness of racial discrimination by, 208, 291 (n. 13); as member of board of Dillard University, 209; as chairwoman of Flint-Goodridge Hospital board, 209, 211, 214, 215, 216, 217, 218, 219, 294 (n. 46); as president of New Orleans Urban League, 209, 211, 222, 223; as investor in Pontchartrain

Keller, Rosa Freeman (cont'd)
Park, 209, 219, 295 (n. 50); and desegregation of public schools, 209, 220, 221, 225; "invisible career" of, 209, 225, 236; integrated lunches of, 209, 292 (n. 15); as conduit between black and white communities, 209–10, 212, 214, 217, 221, 250; as worker for racial justice, 210, 236; and desegregation of public libraries, 211, 212; as member of library board, 211, 212; assimilationist views of, 212; and Alton Ochsner, 218, 221; and housing shortage for blacks, 219, 220; as perpetuator of segregation, 219, 220; meets with Earl Long, 219, 294 (n. 47); supported by "racial diplomats," 220; petition by, urging compliance with *Brown* decision, 220, 221, 295 (n. 53); shot at, 221; charged with being a Communist, 222, 223; as member of National Urban League Board of Trustees, 223; public role of, in race relations, 223; and United Fund controversy, 223; lack of familial support for, 224; as most effective white liberal in New Orleans, 224; social contacts of, with black New Orleanians, 224, 225; quiet consistency of, 224, 236, 237; as walking "in two worlds," 225; and school desegregation crisis, 225, 226; and the SOS, 225, 226; as aware of male sexism, 229; and desegregation of Tulane University, 229, 230, 231, 232; as liaison between Tulane international students and community, 230, 298 (n. 88); and management of Roosevelt Hotel, 230, 298 (n. 88); and financing of Tulane desegregation suit, 231, 232, 233, 234, 235; concern of, for Judge Wright, 233, 299 (n. 97); criticisms of, by black and white friends, 234; and integration of Tulane, 234, 235, 299 (n. 101); letter by, to JFK on civil rights, 235–36

Kennedy, John F.: appeal of, to New Orleans women, 142; letter to, from Rosa Keller, 235–36; and deLesseps Morrison, 248
Kennon, Robert, 160, 244
Keyes, Frances Parkinson, 65
King, Grace, 184–85
Kingfish medal, 61, 62
Kingsley House, 15, 16
Kohn, Aaron, 172

Labouisse, Carolyn Gay: as IWO president, 178, 191; and Martha Robinson campaign, 191, 192; and New Orleans civil rights movement, 249–50
Labouisse, Catherine, 125, 262 (n. 65)
"Ladyhood," 23–24, 76, 104, 132–33, 186, 218, 229
League of Women Voters (LWV), 29, 67; philosophy of, 98–99; as political training ground for women, 284 (n. 16). *See also* Louisiana League of Women Voters; National League of Women Voters (NLWV); New Orleans League of Women Voters (NOLWV)
Leche, Richard, 68, 123, 124, 166, 167
Legal status of women, 17, 19
Legendre, Olive, 262 (n. 65)
Lemann, Monte, 214
Le Petit Salon, 79
Le Petit Theatre du Vieux Carre, 79, 84
Let Freedom Ring, 117
Lewis, John L., 189
Liberalism: concept of, in nineteenth-century usage, 5; as changing concept, 254 (n. 11)
Liberty Place Monument, 24; and the

Era Club, 258 (n. 57). *See also* Battle of Liberty Place
Liebling, A. J., 190, 193
Lippmann, Walter, 61, 76, 139
Little Women, 59
Logan, Marvel, 43, 48–49, 50, 66
Long, Earl K., 123, 124, 126, 129, 133, 157, 166, 167, 188, 219
Long, Huey P., 31, 32 (in quote), 40, 53, 55, 87, 141; compared with Hilda Hammond, 32–33; accomplishments of, as governor, 33; as U.S. senator, 33; control of state by, 33, 53–54; patronage system of, 33, 95; loyalty to, as means of job security, 34; capacity of, for retaliation, 34, 75; fires Arthur Hammond, 35; behavior of, at Overton hearings, 37–38, 39–40, 50, 51, 264–65 (n. 113); and the Roosevelt Hotel, 38, 74, 117; exclusion of, from Mardi Gras balls, 39; clashes with club women, 39–40; and Women's Committee campaign, 41, 260 (n. 26); support of, for national Democratic ticket, 43; breaks with FDR, 44; as most talked-about member of Congress, 44; national press attention to, 44; incident at Sands Point Beach Club involving, 44, 45, 47, 48; reaction of, to Hammond's first national appeal, 45; women supporters of, 45, 82–83; contempt of, for New Orleans elite, 46, 75; *Every Man a King*, 47; weakening of political grip of, on state, 49; class animosity of, 52; sobriquets coined by, 52; cross-examination of Anne Pleasant by, 56; as feared by Senate colleagues, 58–59; assassination of, 67; Share Our Wealth movement of, 67; as more clever than his successors, 69, 123; as threat to upper-class standards, 74, 75; as threat to women's standards, 74–75, 82, 239; personal conduct of, 74–75, 266 (n. 140); blocking of criticism by, 75; conduct of, in office, 75; and 1934 special legislative sessions, 75, 76, 89; imposes martial law on New Orleans, 75, 89–90; imposes martial law on Baton Rouge, 76; New Orleans as enemy of, 89; graft of successors of, 93; and civil service laws, 95; state employees deliver votes for, 95; and forced campaign contributions, 95–96; successors of, imprisoned, 123; "devil image" of, 166, 201; viewed as "common," 167
Long, Russell B., 70, 160
Longism, 33, 51, 63, 67, 69, 70, 77, 83, 93, 117, 124, 126, 142, 168, 190, 239, 244; as viewed by historians, 76, 266 (n. 143)
Long judges, 33, 36
Lorimer, William, 62, 66
Los Angeles Times: on pamphlet, "Is the Senate Afraid of Huey Long?," 62
Louisiana Board of Institutions: and Martha Robinson, 173
Louisiana League of Women Voters: as goal of Robinson and Blanchard, 97; creation of, 98; voter registration efforts of, 106; focus of, on civil service laws, 113; focus of, on electoral reform, 113; support of, for progressive issues, 113; and the SCHW, 114. *See also* New Orleans League of Women Voters (NOLWV)
Louisiana Legislative Council, 165
Louisiana State Lottery, 10, 156
Louisiana Weekly (African-American newspaper), 222
Louisiana Woman Suffrage Association, 18, 20

Luce, Clare Booth, 6, 184

Maestri, Robert S., 68, 94, 126, 133, 138, 139, 144–45, 147, 148, 161, 162, 171, 190, 191, 201; as Damon Runyon character, 138, 166; lackluster campaign of, 140–41, 150; defeated by deLesseps Morrison, 147; view of, as "common," 167
Mahoney, R. E., 163
Many, Anna, 175
March of Brooms, 145, 146
Mardi Gras, 9, 33, 39, 131, 133, 206, 207
Marriage: of Hilda Phelps Hammond, 34–36, 64, 70–71; of Martha Gilmore Robinson, 84, 100–103; of July B. Waters, 141; of Rosa Freeman Keller, 207, 209, 224
Mason, Henry, 231
Mayo, Sara Tew, 16
McCall, Harry, 173
McCullough, Jacqueline T., 162, 163, 164
McGill, Ralph, 110, 112
McGuire, Dave, 194, 197, 199, 201–2
McIlhenny, Margaret Polk, 165
McLean, Franklin, 215, 216
McMain, Eleanor, 15, 16
McPherson, J. Westbrook, 220, 221
Mellett, Lowell, 48
Memphis Commercial Appeal: salutes "Sacrifice Week," 60
Memphis Press-Scimitar: credits women with Morrison win, 150
Merrick, Caroline Thomas, 17, 18
Metropolitan Crime Commission, 172
Meyer, Eugene, 61, 114, 115
Miller, Arthur, 33
Miller, T. L., 214
Milne Home for Girls, 31
Monroe, Bill, 235
Moore, A. Brown, 177, 188, 199
Moore, Catherine, 125

Morality, as women's issue in politics. *See* Women voters
Morial, Ernest N. ("Dutch"), 236
Morial, Sybil Haydel, 225, 296 (n. 70)
Morris, Mrs. James Craik, 45
Morrison, deLesseps Story ("Chep"), 139, 140, 166, 167, 170, 171; mayoral campaign of, 140, 141; importance of women in mayoral campaign of, 141, 143, 148; and New Orleans elite, 142; appeal of, to New Orleans women, 142–43; veterans' support for, 144, 150; defeats Robert Maestri, 147; IWO access to, 154, 159; and illusion of reform, 154–55, 175–76, 190, 191, 192; legalized gambling plan of, 155, 156, 157, 158, 159; asks IWO to become CCDA women's auxiliary, 156, 157; cools toward IWO, 159; IWO dissatisfaction with, 161; and school board politics, 164, 165; as big city "boss," 171, 172, 190, 191; investigations of police department under, 172, 283 (n. 9); as opponent of new city charter, 173, 174; and Martha Robinson's candidacy, 175, 176, 177–78, 180; supports Schiro, 180, 181, 193, 195, 198, 199; black voter support for, 188; opposed by Old Regulars, 190; and meeting at Central Fire Hall, 194, 195, 288 (n. 74); reelected in 1954, 196; as moderate segregationist, 211, 212; and desegregation of the libraries, 211, 212, 292 (n. 22); desire of, to be governor, 212; and school desegregation crisis of 1960, 227; becomes U.S. ambassador, 248. *See also* Women supporters of deLesseps Morrison
Morrison, Jacob H. ("Jake"), 124, 126, 131, 140

Morrison, Mary Meek, 124, 125, 131, 133, 245, 249, 276 (n. 12), 277 (n. 26)
Motherhood: of Hilda Phelps Hammond, 41, 43; and morality, 69, 74, 82, 89, 91, 95, 135–36, 144; and childrearing practices, 82, 84, 286 (n. 48); of Martha Gilmore Robinson, 99–100, 102, 103, 183, 268 (n. 19); of Rosa Freeman Keller, 104, 224; of July B. Waters, 137
Mudge, Caroline Goodridge, 213
Municipal charter, 172, 173, 174, 283–84 (n. 10)
"Municipal housekeeping," 29, 92, 106, 144–45, 185
Murray, Peter M., 215, 216, 217
Myrdal, Gunnar, 212

National American Woman Suffrage Association (NAWSA): 1903 convention of, in New Orleans, 20; support of, for federal suffrage amendment, 21, 22; strategy of, in the South, 23; worldly facade of New Orleans faction of, 23–24; evolves into League of Women Voters, 29
National Association for the Advancement of Colored People (NAACP), 112, 220, 222
National Citizens' Protective Association, 222
National Committee to Abolish the Poll Tax, 65
National Council of Jewish Women, 45
National League of Women Voters (NLWV), 79, 80, 93; assessment by, of New Orleans League, 80; revokes charter of New Orleans chapter, 81; doubts viability of reaffiliated NOLWV chapter, 96, 97, 98, 99, 104; terms of, for reaffiliation of NOLWV chapter, 96–97; reaffiliates NOLWV, 98; postwar planning by, 108; support of, for United Nations, 108; support of, for permanent registration law, 109; and conservative climate of state leagues, 113; desire of, for broadened NOLWV membership, 118; and partisanship problem in Louisiana, 120; guidance by, on desegregation of NOLWV, 243
National Urban League, 222. *See also* New Orleans Urban League
Nelson, John P. 231, 232, 233, 235, 236, 237
Newcomb, Josephine Louise, 14, 15, 184
New Dealers: and anti-Long movement, 74
New Orleans: as an area of historical research, 7; as a "closed corporation," 7, 245–46; and elements of Crescent City culture, 8; and Mardi Gras, 8, 9, 39; and jazz, 8, 9, 155; reputation of, for sexual tolerance, 8, 155; reputation of, for casual race relations, 8, 203; as "the city that care forgot," 9; lack of municipal services in, 10–11, 17; levee system for, 11; port of, 11; voting strength of, 13; public baths in, 15; public playgrounds in, 15; first hospital for women and children in, 16; anti-Long sentiment in, 38, 117, 124; Carnival season in, 39; life in, during World War II, 99; view of nonnatives in, 118; high consumption of alcohol in, 155; local mores of, 155; toleration of vice in, 155; racial segregation in, 204
New Orleans Bureau of Governmental Research, 173

New Orleans Classroom Teachers Federation, 189
New Orleans Council of Church Women, 155, 156
New Orleans Dock Board, 35, 37
New Orleans Educational Society: sex discrimination in, 17
New Orleans Federation of Clubs: response of, to WCU membership invitation, 88; non-elite status of, 269 (n. 34)
New Orleans Item: credits women with Morrison win, 148–49; on IWO opposition to legalized gambling, 157
New Orleans League of Women Voters (NOLWV), 29, 30, 79, 80, 174; and strained relationship with national League, 30–31, 80; as identified with Old Regulars, 79–80, 87–88; initial charter of, revoked, 81; and "women of brains and standing," 81; efforts of, to reestablish chapter, 96–98; membership of, from "silk stocking" district, 104; as suspected of partisanship, 104, 105; voter registration efforts of, 105, 106, 108, 111, 113; bypassing of black neighborhoods by, 106; attainment of stature by, 107; and jury service for women, 107; precinct patrols of, 107; press coverage of, 107, 108; educational programs of, 107, 273 (n. 102); plans of, to picket polls, 107–108; and postwar issues, 108; proposed "Colored Chapter" of, 109; and permanent registration law, 109, 110; and racial issues, 109, 110, 115; as racially segregated, 109, 118, 119; and the SCHW, 111, 112, 113, 114; liberal-moderate split of, 114, 115, 116, 118, 119, 242; overidentification of, with Martha Robinson, 115, 116; unit groups of, 116; as more inclusive group, 116, 118, 119, 121, 189, 243, 248; social class composition of, 116, 118, 121; nonpartisanship of, 119, 120; opposes Shelby Jackson, 166; and school desegregation crisis of 1960, 228, 229; admission of black members to, 242, 243, 248
New Orleans Levee Board, 35, 37
New Orleans Playground Committee, 16
New Orleans Recreation Department (NORD), 172
New Orleans school desegregation crisis of 1960, 225, 226, 227, 229; lack of white leadership in, 227; women's role in, 227, 228, 229, 298 (n. 83)
New Orleans Social Register, 37, 45–46, 88, 116, 125, 141, 153, 262 (n. 65), 269 (n. 34). See also Boston Club
New Orleans States: on Overton hearings, 38
New Orleans States-Item: on school desegregation crisis of 1960, 228, 298 (n. 83)
New Orleans Times-Picayune. See Times-Picayune
New Orleans University, 16
New Orleans Urban League: and 1956 GNOCC rally, 205, 223, 290 (n. 6); function of, 222; Community Chest support for, 222, 223, 296 (n. 65); white membership of, 224
New Orleans White League, 24, 258 (n. 56)
New York Times: and Women's Committee of Louisiana, 49; on Overton hearings, 50; on diminution of opposition to Long, 69; on problems plaguing anti-Longs, 73
Nineteenth Amendment, 25, 82, 84, 251; and full citizenship for women, 2, 251; opposition to, by prominent

Louisianians, 26; and black voting, 65; tenth anniversary of, 105. *See also* Woman suffrage
Noe, James A., 124, 133
Nolan, Martha, 83

Ochsner, Alton, 217, 218
O'Keefe, Arthur, 80
Old Regulars, 11, 13, 137, 191, 192, 197; as deliverers of city services, 11; determining of political candidates by, 11; thwarting of reform element by, 11, 190; as opponents of civil service laws, 12; and ballot box stuffing, 13; and "disabled" voters, 13; and governors elected between 1900 and 1924, 13; and padding of voter rolls, 13; and the police, 13; paying of poll taxes by, 13, 287 (n. 65); control of Orleans legislative delegation by, 14; Caucus of, 14, 24; and business elite, 14, 154; and anti-Long movement, 74; and NOLWV, 79–80, 81, 267 (n. 6); legislative opposition to Huey Long by, 89; desire of, for a small electorate, 106, 148; rally of, to anti-Long cause, 124; political favoritism of, 138, 278–79 (n. 45); as decimated by defections to CCDA, 171, 190; as eclipsed by Longism, 190; as organized opposition to deLesseps Morrison, 190; support of, for Martha Robinson, 190; in "Jambalaya" series, 255–56 (n. 8); organization of, 287 (n. 65)
Order of the British Empire (OBE), 100
Orleans Club, 79
Orleans Parish Medical Society: and women, 16; and black physicians, 214, 215, 216, 223, 294 (n. 39)
Orleans Parish Progressive Voters League (OPPVL): support of, for Martha Robinson, 188; withdraws support of Robinson, 197, 198
Orleans Parish School Board: and *Brown* decision, 220; and school desegregation crisis of 1960, 226, 227, 297 (n. 80)
Ortique, Revius, 220
Ott, Lionel, 187, 188, 197, 199
Overton, John, 36, 38, 39, 40, 41, 47, 50, 53, 55, 56, 60, 66, 72, 83, 87, 160, 264-65 (n. 113); and charges of election fraud, 37; reactions of, to Connally Report, 54; death of, 70
Overton hearings: behavior of Huey Long at, 37–38, 50, 51, 264–65 (n. 113); and "dummy candidate" device, 38; testimony on voting irregularities at, 38, 39, 40, 47; coverage of, by daily newspapers, 39; resumption of, 43, 44, 47, 49; lack of confidence in, 50; national editorial opinion of, 52; formal report of, 53–54

Parent-Teacher Association (PTA), 79, 112, 161
Park, Maud Wood, 83
Parker, John M., 11, 124, 125; backs away from woman suffrage, 26; charges made against Long by, 53
Peabody Survey, 165
People's League, 124
Pepper, Claude, 110, 111
Perez, Leander, 205, 223, 225, 227
Perkins, Frances, 184
Permanent registration law. *See* Voter registration
Phelps, Esmond, 35, 36, 52, 103
Philadelphia Inquirer: on pamphlet, "Is the Senate Afraid of Huey Long?," 62
Phillis Wheatley Club, 16
Phillis Wheatley Sanitarium, 16
Pilsbury, Edna Culligan, 80, 81, 88

Pilsbury, May Culligan, 80, 88
Planter-business elite, 5, 14, 68, 263 (n. 72)
Pleasant, Anne: as states' rights suffragist, 25; as opponent of Nineteenth Amendment, 26; as an anti-Long, 56; testimony of, before George Committee, 56; references to, in *Huey Long* (Williams), 72
Pleasant, Ruffin G.: and state suffrage amendment, 23; as opponent of Nineteenth Amendment, 26
Police action at polling places, 131, 132
Police corruption: at turn of century, 10; investigations of, under deLesseps Morrison, 172, 283 (n. 9)
Polling places: police activity at, 13, 93, 131, 132; legal requirements of, 90, 94-95, 130, 132, 193, 269 (n. 38); threatening atmosphere at, challenged by women's presence, 132, 147; voting machines used in, 146, 147
Poll tax, 12, 13, 85; as race issue, 65; southern opposition to reform of, 65; abolition of, 91, 111
Pontchartrain Park, 209, 219, 220; as issue between "racial diplomats" and "race men," 295 (n. 52)
Portia Club, 18
Post, Emily, 182
Preminger, Otto, 250
Prentiss, Una and Jennie, 34
Preston, Ruth Hamill, 98, 114, 117, 118
Prison Reform Association, 15
Progressive Era: women of, 3, 15, 17, 29, 35
Progressive Party: endorses woman suffrage, 26
Prohibition, 44
Prostitution, 17, 155
Public Belt Railroad, 11
Public playgrounds, 15

Race relations: in New Orleans, 203-5; white rationalizations of, 204-5, 211, 292 (n. 21); and white southern liberals, 205, 290 (n. 5); and paternalism, 210
Racial segregation: support for, in South, 119; in New Orleans, 204; in public schools, 204, 226; and creation of a "small world" for blacks, 208, 209, 291 (n. 13); in public libraries, 211, 212, 213, 292 (n. 20), 293 (n. 28); in medical care, 213, 214, 215, 218; and black physicians, 214, 215, 216; at Ochsner Hospital, 218
Railly, Mary, 45
Rainach, Willie, 227
Rationing (in World War II), 99, 100, 207-8, 241, 271 (n. 73, n. 75)
RDO. *See* Old Regulars
Red Cross service (in World War II), 103, 272 (n. 86)
Reed, Sarah T., 189
Registered voters (Orleans Parish): white women as, 27, 28, 29, 82, 91, 92, 144, 177; black women as, 27, 28, 29, 82, 91, 144, 177; black men as, 27, 28, 82, 91, 177; white men as, 27, 28, 82, 91, 177; women as, 81, 106, 144, 148, 149, 177, 196
Regular Democratic Organization (RDO). *See* Old Regulars
Reily, Gladys, 125, 162
"Republican motherhood," 137
Reuther, Walter, 119
Ring, the. *See* Old Regulars
Robinson, Joseph, 58, 261 (n. 33)
Robinson, Martha Gilmore, 42, 45, 86, 88, 98, 127, 129, 142, 168; activities of, at Newcomb College, 83; childhood of, 83; as president of Women's Division of the HEL, 83, 84, 85; marriage of, 84; outside activities of, before 1930s, 84, 85;

child care years of, 84, 183, 268 (n. 19); and independence of Women's Division of HEL, 87; as WCU president, 88; and morality as standard for public life, 89; belief of, in moral superiority of women, 89, 90, 91; radio addresses of, 89, 90, 106, 180, 181–82, 187, 188, 198; as "the Senator," 89, 117; hope of, for a women's voting bloc, 91; efforts of, to get women to vote, 92, 106–7; belief of, in "municipal housekeeping," 92, 185; enrolls at Tulane, 93; efforts of, to broaden electorate, 94; and voting machine law, 94; and passage of Act 46, 95; efforts of, to get reaffiliated NOLWV chapter, 96, 97; and goal of a Louisiana LWV, 97, 98; as president of reaffiliated NOLWV chapter, 98, 116; "Robinson Home Journal" of, 99, 103; support of, for war effort, 99–100; awarded Order of the British Empire, 100; and rationing, 100, 271 (n. 75); rejection of class prejudice by, 101, 102; marital disharmony of, 101, 102, 103; as supporter of FDR and the New Deal, 101, 119; transformation of, into public figure, 102–3; and Leila Melancon (servant), 103, 272 (n. 79); recruits "right sort" of members for NOLWV, 104; view of LWV as war work held by, 104, 105; press coverage of, 107, 108, 174; argues for international cooperation, 108; as president of Louisiana LWV, 108, 115, 116, 117, 182; and black voter registration, 109; and permanent registration law, 109, 110; and the SCHW, 112, 113; breaks with Emily Blanchard, 112–13, 114, 119; on race and communism, 115; dominant role of, in NOLWV, 115–16; LWV recruitment efforts of, 116; as supporter of United Nations, 119; as critic of deLesseps Morrison, 155, 175–76, 178, 191, 192, 200, 201; views IWO as "Chep's Women's Organization," 159; as member of city charter commission, 172, 173, 174, 176; as board member of New Orleans Bureau of Governmental Research, 173; as member of Louisiana Board of Institutions, 173; support of, for "little Hatch Act," 173; ambition of, 174; work of, on Child Welfare Association, 174; work of, on Council of National Defense, 174; as leader of causes, 174–75, 200; announces candidacy, 175, 284 (n. 18); on police corruption, 176; city council campaign of, 176, 177, 180, 184, 186, 187, 188, 193, 200, 202, 242, 286 (n. 51); and Cold Water Committee, 177; as the women's candidate, 177, 180, 184, 185, 186, 202; ego of, 177, 188; principled stubbornness of, 178; refuses to endorse Morrison, 178, 191; independent label of, 180, 181, 184, 187, 188, 201; and historical preservation, 180, 182–83; as "No Deals" Robinson, 180–81, 184, 193; obstructionist label of, 181, 182, 186, 187, 195; age of, as campaign issue, 182, 183, 184, 186, 200, 286 (n. 48); as leader of Louisiana Landmarks Society, 183; sex of, as campaign issue, 184, 186, 200, 286 (n. 51); class of, as campaign issue, 185, 186, 200; endorsements of, 188; support for, from black voters, 188, 189; support for, from labor, 189; change in provincial attitudes of, 189–90, 117, 118, 119; Old Regular support of, 190, 191, 192, 193, 196, 200, 202; support for, from women voters, 196; faces runoff, 196, 197;

Robinson, Martha Gilmore (cont'd)
loses support of black voters, 197, 198; loses Old Regular support, 197, 198, 199; loses runoff, 199; conviction of, regarding right and wrong, 201; overlooking of good politics by, 202, 240; addressing of "the Negro question" by, 242; strain on, caused by war years, 271 (n. 71); emphasis of, on nonpartisanship, 276 (n. 8)
Robinson, Robert Gibson, 84, 101, 102, 295 (n. 55)
Robinson, Samuel Gilmore, 183
Rogge, O. J., 123, 128, 129
Roosevelt, Eleanor, 119, 122 (quote), 184, 224, 239; as champion of Negro cause, 101; and the SCHW, 110, 111
Roosevelt, Franklin, 40, 52, 64, 101, 102, 110, 145, 184, 239; reevaluation of Huey Long by, 43–44; role of, in resumption of Overton hearings, 44; Louisiana support for, 67, 68
Roosevelt Hotel: as unofficial Long headquarters in New Orleans, 38, 117; as Long's second home, 74; boycott of, by anti-Long women, 117; and young July Waters, 141; as site of 1961 testimonial dinner, 228; management of, rebuffs Rosa Keller, 230
Rosenwald, Julius, 101

"Sacrifice Week," 59, 60, 73
Sample ballots: in 1954 election, 193, 194, 195–96, 199, 241
Sand, Mary, 227
Sanger, Margaret, 30
"Savage ideal." See Conformity of thought
Save Our Schools (SOS), 225–26; and the Brown decision, 226; and desegregation crisis of 1960, 226, 227, 228,
297 (n. 76); role of women in, 228, 229, 296 (n. 72)
Scheps, Clarence, 163, 164
Schiro, Victor Hugo, 175, 178, 179, 193, 201; as politically unaware, 179; as "cooperator," 181, 194; campaign strategy of, 182, 187, 189, 194, 195, 200; political advantages of, 186; faces runoff, 196; wins runoff, 199; elected mayor, 248
Schlesinger, Arthur, Jr.: and negative characterizations of anti-Longs, 73
School desegregation crisis of 1960. See New Orleans school desegregation crisis of 1960
Scott, Natalie, 99, 102, 176, 183
Semmerling, Helen, 98
Senatorial Campaign Expenditures Committee: members of, 43. See also Connally Report; Overton hearings
"Separate spheres" tradition, 4, 17, 79, 92
Sewerage and Water Board, 19, 22
Shame of the Cities, 106
Share Our Wealth movement, 67. See also Long, Huey P.
Sharp, Sarah Heath, 161, 162, 249
Shepard, Theodore, 165
Shreveport Times: credits women with Morrison win, 150
"Silk stocking" district, 104, 127. See also Garden District
"Silk stockings," 1 (quote); Behrman description of, 251
Silver Thimble League, 100
Smith, Frank L., 62, 66
Smith, Gerald L. K., 222
Smith, Margaret Chase, 184
Smith v. Allwright (1944), 274 (n. 112)
Social class in New Orleans: barriers between women created by, 5, 82–83, 88, 116–17, 128, 134–35; as factor

in Hilda Phelps Hammond's life, 36, 51–52, 62–63; as factor in Long/anti-Long division in Louisiana, 39, 44–45, 51–52, 62–63, 74–75, 239–40, 246; as factor in Martha Gilmore Robinson's life, 83–84, 179, 182, 185–86; and 1944 presidential election in Louisiana, 101–2; as factor in July B. Waters's life, 141; as factor in Rosa Freeman Keller's life, 206–8, 224, 232; in African-American community in New Orleans, 208, 221–22, 225; as factor in New Orleans school desegregation crisis, 226–27
"Society ladies": as stereotype, 6; patronizing of, 236; and "silk stockings," 251
Sophie Newcomb College: founding of, 14; influence of alumnae of, 15; percentage of women faculty at, 15; curriculum of, 15, 92; scholarships for, 22; Hilda Phelps Hammond's experiences at, 34; sororities at, 79, 206; Martha Gilmore Robinson's experiences at, 83; as site of 1908 suffrage speech, 83; July B. Waters's experiences at, 141; Rosa Freeman Keller's experiences at, 206
Southern Conference for Human Welfare (SCHW), 110; first convention of, 111; membership in, 111; New Orleans convention of, 111; and southern progressives, 111, 112; and the NOLWV, 111, 112, 113, 115, 118–19; alleged to be Communist front, 112; New Orleans press reports of, 112
Southern lady: image of, 18, 82, 86; traditional role of, 24. *See also* "Society ladies"
Southern Manifesto, 22
Southern Patriot, 112, 113
Southern progressives: and the SCHW, 110, 111, 112

Southern States Woman Suffrage Convention (SSWSC), 22
Southern suffragists: on black suffrage, 20, 21; as Negrophobic, 21; as backers of federal suffrage amendment, 21, 22, 24; NAWSA dictum to, regarding state suffrage amendments, 23; as backers of state suffrage amendment, 24. *See also* Gordon, Kate
Square Deal Association, 72
St. Anna's Asylum, 16, 17
States' rights suffragists, 25, 26. *See also* Gordon, Kate
State suffrage amendment, 23; failure of, at the polls, 24; passage of, by legislature, 24. *See also* Woman suffrage
Steffens, Lincoln, 106
Stern, Edgar B., 214, 215, 216, 219
Stern, Edith Rosenwald, 101, 156, 219, 235
Stone, Doris Zemurray, 262 (n. 65)
Stringer, Alice, 166
Sutherland, Matthew, 227, 228

Talbot, Marion, 92
Tessier, George, 180
Thomas, Elbert, 51
Times-Democrat, 34
Times-Picayune: and passage of Nineteenth Amendment, 25–26; and anti-Long efforts of Esmond Phelps, 35; prints voting instructions, 129; and Sam Jones win, 134; credits women with Morrison win, 148; and school desegregation crisis of 1960, 227, 228; coverage of, integration of Tulane, 235
Times-Picayune Loving Cup award, 16, 217
Townsend, John G., 43
"Transients" (newcomers), 117, 118

Truman, Harry S., 111
Tulane, Paul, 229, 230, 232, 235
Tulane Medical School, 16; pressured to admit women, 18, 22
Tulane University; as "Harvard of the South," 229; segregated admissions policy of, 229–30, 231, 233, 298 (n. 90); and Fourteenth Amendment, 232, 233; as state, not private university, 232, 233, 234, 299 (n. 98); opened to black students, 234; integration of, 234–35
Tureaud, A. P., 220, 231, 242
Two-party system in Louisiana: as CCDA v. RDO, 193; as Long v. anti-Long 239, 278 (n. 32), 300–301 (n. 2). *See also* Bifactionalism

Unamerican Activities Committee (Louisiana), 233
Union support: negative view of, 189
United Daughters of the Confederacy, 15
United Fund (Community Chest). *See* Community Chest (United Fund)
Unmarried state: as choice for educated women, 35
Upper-class women: viewed as conservative, 1–2, 5; in the political arena, 2; in Progressive Era, 3; reluctance of, to repudiate patriarchal ethos, 4; negative images associated with, 6, 236; alleged disdain of, for outsiders, 7, 245; response of, to Old Regular grip on city, 14; early civic activities of, 17; and anti-Long movement, 37, 39, 40, 45–47, 59, 74–75, 124–25, 134–35, 166–67, 244; summer habits of, 43; domestic duties of, 78–79; early club affiliations of, 79; perceived as impartial, 86–87; dominance of, in WCU, 88; end of control of, in NOLWV, 116–18, 243; attitudes of, toward nonnatives, 118; participation of, in Sam Jones campaign (1940), 124–26, 134–35; as disliking machine politics, 128; dominance of, in IWO, 142, 152–53; influence of, with deLesseps Morrison, 154, 159; preference of, for volunteer over paid work, 160, 281 (n. 104); view of "common" persons held by, 167; appeal of the IWO for, 170; behind-the-scenes effectiveness of, 184, 185; political splintering of, 201; political participation of, 241; golden age of unity in politics among, 245; consensus view of, regarding good government, 247, 248. *See also* Social class in New Orleans

Vare, William S., 62, 66
Volunteer work: as undervalued, 187
Voter registration, 91, 92, 148, 247; as daring venture for women, 27; and woman suffrage, 27; statistics for, in Orleans Parish, 27–28, 246, 247; as issue of municipal reformers, 94; and efforts of the NOLWV, 105, 106, 109; and efforts of Louisiana LWV, 106; as a race issue, 106, 109; and drive by black New Orleanians, 109; and permanent registration law, 109, 110; and effect on number of registered blacks, 110; and efforts by women supporters of Sam Jones, 126, 127, 276 (n. 12); in Louisiana, before Voting Rights Act of 1965, 276 (n. 12)
Voting machines: required use of, 94; law regarding, 140; first used in New Orleans, 146, 147

Wagner, Emile, 165
Wallace, Henry, 114, 119
Walmsley, T. Semmes, 69, 80, 138

Waters, Arthur C., 139–40, 141, 176
Waters, July Breazeale, 45, 125, 131–32, 139, 140, 143, 154, 176, 192, 198, 201, 249; and theme of "republican motherhood," 136–37; political upbringing of, 141; as IWO president, 141, 142, 170, 174; as participant in anti-Long crusade, 142; rejection of nonpartisan focus of NOLWV by, 142; as leader of March of Brooms, 145; credited with Morrison win, 150; credits women with Morrison win, 151; and deLesseps Morrison, 157, 158, 159; views politics as Right v. Wrong, 166, 167, 201; on stubbornness of Martha Robinson, 178; on younger IWO members, 245
Weil, Clif, 215, 219
Weiss, Seymour, 38, 66
Wells, Marguerite, 29, 81, 97
Werlein, Elizabeth Thomas, 24, 29; as president of NOLWV, 30
Werlein, Philip, 29
Westfeldt, Kitty Monroe, 37, 125, 143; home of, as "cradle of democracy," 40
Westfeldt, Martha Gasquet, 46–47
Wharton, Edith, 45
White, Sue Shelton (quote), 78
White Citizens' Council: anti-Urban League crusade of, 222–23. *See also* Greater New Orleans Citizens' Council (GNOCC)
Willard, Frances, 145
Williams, Fannie C., 214
Williams, T. Harry: treatment of Hilda Hammond by, 51, 71–73; dismissive attitude of, toward club women, 73
Willy Loman, 33, 45
Wilson, Scott, 194
Wilson, Woodrow: support of, for federal suffrage amendment, 23
Wisdom, Betty, 227

Wogan, Victor, 158
Woman Citizens' Union (WCU): founding of, 87, 269 (n. 32); bias of, toward the elite in leadership positions, 88; nonelitism of, 88; noninclusion of African-American women in, 88; objective of, 88; nonpartisanship policy of, 88, 276 (n. 8); offers to escort women to the polls, 90; voter registration efforts of, 91; and belief in "municipal housekeeping," 92; community reputation of, 93; progressive issues of, 93; urges repeal of poll tax, 93; and election reform, 93, 94, 95; and civil service laws, 93, 95, 96; efforts of, to broaden electorate, 94; and implementation of voting machine law, 94; and passage of Act 46, 94–95; works with Baton Rouge LWV, 96; reconstituted as the NOLWV, 98
Woman's Committee of the Council of National Defense, 34, 174
Woman suffrage: as chronicled by historians, 2; effect of, on women in politics, 2, 3, 4; and women on juries, 2–3; opposition to, 15; as direct political influence, 17–18; embraced by Progressive women reformers, 17–18; and the Portia Club, 18; as bulwark of white supremacy, 20–21; as states' rights issue, 21, 22, 25; federal effort toward, seen as threat to white supremacy, 23; endorsed by Progressive Party, 26; viewed as attack on planter class, 26; and women in the political arena, 30; utopian expectations of, 105; history of, in Louisiana, 239
Woman Suffrage Party (WSP) of Louisiana, 22, 23, 26; evolves into New Orleans League of Women Voters, 29

Women candidates: Sarah Heath Sharp, 161–62; Jacqueline T. McCullough, 162–63; Bland Cox Bruns, 170, 240–41, 286 (n. 51), 301 (n. 5). *See also* Robinson, Martha Gilmore

Women on juries, 2–3, 107, 273 (n. 101)

Women property owners: granted right to vote on tax issues, 19; reluctance of, to vote, 19

"Women's bloc": fear of, 2; as postsuffrage alternative, 4; belief in, 29, 136; failure of, to materialize, 238

Women's Christian Temperance Union, 15

Women's clubs, 4, 17, 79; as vehicles for collective action, 4; dismissive attitudes toward, 6; as Progressive Era reform, 15; effect of, on getting women to vote, 29

Women's Committee of Louisiana: beginnings of, 40, 41; faith in government held by, 41; letter writing campaigns of, 41, 47, 60, 67; self-effacing tone of letters by, 41–42; disclaiming of political involvement by, 42; moral tone of, 42, 57, 75; class orientation of, 45–46, 59; shift of, to anti-Long efforts, 47; demands resignations of Senate committee members, 49; attendance of, at Overton hearings, 50; petition fight in Senate by, 52–53, 54, 55–56, 57; reaction to Connally Report by, 54; stands ground against attacks, 54; anonymous contributions to, 59; and "Sacrifice Week," 59, 60; neglects Louisiana electorate, 60; and Kingfish medal, 61, 62; *Collier's* fundraiser for, 62; and pamphlet, "Is the Senate Afraid of Huey Long?," 62; atrophying of, 69, 70; overidentification of, with Hilda Hammond, 70, 116; effect of, on Louisiana, 71; references to, in histories of Long era, 71; national press response to, 72, 73; as of the "nonpolitical gentility," 74; as beginning of New Orleans women's movement, 77; effect of, on women's interest in politics, 82; influence of, on the WCU, 87

Women's Division of the HEL, 84, 85, 94; and "citizenship school" movement, 85; as election commissioners, 85, 86; press reporting of, 86; respectability of, 86, 87; becomes independent group, 87

Women's League for Sewerage and Drainage, 19

Women's political influence. *See* Women's political participation

Women's political participation: definition of, 2; indirect, 3, 4, 14–18, 19, 20, 228–29, 236–37, 238, 251. *See also* Women voters

Women's Regular Democratic Organization, 80

Women's roles, enlargement of, 4–5

Women's Trade Union League, 110

Women supporters of deLesseps Morrison, 141; credited with win, 148, 149, 150, 151, 159, 161

Women supporters of Huey Long, 45, 82–83

Women supporters of Sam Jones, 126, 127, 128, 133, 134; upper-class status of, 125, 142; voter registration efforts of, 126, 127, 276 (n. 12); harassment of, 127, 129; political naivete of, 128; as poll watchers, 129, 130, 131; developing pragmatism of, 133, 134; high ideals of, 135, 136; from New Orleans elite, 142

Women's voluntary associations: as political activity, 2, 4, 14, 239, 251; as Progressive Era tradition, 3

Women's vote: and election of Sam Jones, 136; and election of deLesseps Morrison, 147–48, 149; and Martha Robinson campaign, 196

Women voters: role of, in 1899 tax increase, 18–19; reluctance of, to participate in politics, 19, 27–29, 31, 92, 105–7, 144, 239; registration statistics on, 27–28, 81–82, 91, 105, 106, 144–47, 149, 177, 246–47; and morality in politics, 40, 42, 45, 54, 57, 61, 63–64, 68, 74–76, 82, 86, 89, 128, 136–37, 155–59, 166–67, 247; efforts to discourage, 82, 90; as poll workers, 85–86, 129–32, 146–47, 149–50, 195; efforts of, against fraudulent registration, 86–87, 94, 126–28; specific appeals to, 89–90, 91, 124, 126, 137, 143, 144, 146, 157–58, 177, 180, 185; as unpaid campaign workers, 160, 163, 180, 191, 192, 243. *See also* Women supporters of deLesseps Morrison; Women supporters of Sam Jones

Wood, Trist, 54

Working-class women: and club membership, 88

World War II: and hiring of women workers, 99; rationing during, 99; effects of, on Martha G. Robinson, 99–104; and increased job opportunities for blacks, 101; black troops in, 208–9; effect of, on women, 241

Wright, Helen, 233

Wright, J. Skelly, 226, 227, 232, 233, 234

Wright, Katherine, 227

Wright, Sophie Bell, 15, 16, 184

CPSIA information can be obtained
at www.ICGtesting.com
Printed in the USA
LVHW041718311018
595495LV00002B/147/P